FROM
EXEGESIS
TO
EXPOSITION

Also by Robert B. Chisholm Jr.
Interpreting the Minor Prophets

Robert B. Chisholm Jr. is professor of Old Testament studies at Dallas Theological Seminary. In addition to his several scholarly articles, he has written *Interpreting the Minor Prophets*.

FROM
EXEGESIS
TO
EXPOSITION

A Practical Guide to Using Biblical Hebrew

Robert B. Chisholm Jr.

Baker Books

A Division of Baker Book House Co
Grand Rapids, Michigan 49516

Published by Baker Books
a division of Baker Book House Company
P.O. Box 6287, Grand Rapids, MI 49516-6287

Third printing, January 2002

Printed in the United States of America

Library of Congress Cataloging-in-Publication Data

Chisholm, Robert B.
    From exegesis to exposition : a practical guide to using biblical Hebrew /
Robert B. Chisholm, Jr.
      p. cm.
    Includes bibliographical references and indexes.
    ISBN 0-8010-2171-5 (paper)
     1. Bible. O.T.—Language, style. 2. Bible. O.T.—Criticism, interpretations, etc.
3. Hebrew language—Grammar. 4. Bible. O.T.—Homiletical use. I. Title.
BS1171.2.C55   1999
221.4′4—dc21   98-43458

For information about academic books, resources for Christian leaders, and all new releases available from Baker Book House, visit our web site:
http://www.bakerbooks.com

Contents

1 Credibility, Competence, and Confidence

The Necessity of Using Your Hebrew Bible

Mention the subject of Hebrew to a group of seminary-trained pastors and you'll get a variety of responses, mostly negative. Many will tell you in no uncertain terms, "Hebrew was a waste of time and money. I never use it in the ministry. The seminaries could spare their ministerial students a lot of grief and frustration by making it optional." Some acknowledge the value of Hebrew, but are quick to add, "Hebrew is fine for those who have a gift for learning languages, but it's a luxury, not an essential. I suppose it's great if you have the ability to work with it, but you can do just fine without it." Others sound more regretful: "I wish I could use Hebrew, because there's no substitute for studying in the original, but no one really showed me how to use it in sermon preparation. Besides I don't have the time to do that kind of in-depth study for my sermons."

Understandably testimonies like these create a great deal of skepticism about the value of studying Hebrew. As they wander through a maze of Hebrew paradigms, seminary students in first-year Hebrew classes hear these testimonies and begin to doubt if all the blood, sweat, and tears will be worth it. Administrators and faculties, when receiving this kind of feedback on alumni questionnaires and surveys, wonder whether they should continue to require ministerial candidates to study Hebrew. Some drop Hebrew requirements, while many others opt for a "Hebrew Lite" program that requires only a bare minimum of linguistic study and naively stresses the use of "tools," as if they can somehow mysteriously make one a competent interpreter.

Is the study of Hebrew a luxury or an essential for a busy pastor? Can one reasonably expect a pastor to work in the Hebrew text when preparing sermons? In my opinion a working knowledge of Hebrew is essential, not optional, for those who desire to preach and teach from the Old Testament. You may think I'm being unrealistic, but I believe that if one grasps the essentials of the language, develops skill in exegesis, and learns how to transform that exegetical research into a theologically accurate exposition, there is no reason why even the busiest pastor cannot

7

preach accurate, informative, and even exciting sermons that are solidly rooted in the Hebrew text and do not require an inordinate amount of time to prepare. As more pastors preach these kinds of messages, their pulpit ministries will be revived, people will gain renewed excitement about the Old Testament as they hear it "come alive" from the pulpit, and the church will become more deeply rooted in its understanding of God and his purposes.

Of course, pastors do not just preach sermons; they also teach Sunday school lessons, lead Bible studies and seminars, counsel parishioners, answer a variety of interpretive and practical questions, refine their theology, and, hopefully, cultivate their spiritual life. Study in the original text will impact all of these areas as well, for such study provides exegetical accuracy and theological depth, which in turn should give substance to the various facets of ministry and stimulate spiritual growth.

Why Pastors Often Don't Use Their Hebrew Training

Why do pastors often fail to "use" the Hebrew they once studied? In some cases the reasons are philosophical. Despite Paul's clear endorsement of the Old Testament (2 Tim. 3:16), some persist in demeaning it as theologically obsolete or second-rate. Others decide that text-based, expositional preaching is irrelevant or not conducive to church growth and prefer to moralize or trivialize the text in the interests of so-called application and contemporary relevance. For proponents of this preaching theory, looking at the original text is a waste of time. Unfortunately this approach, which reflects a popular trend toward reader-centered interpretation, substitutes eisegesis for exegesis and is devoid of biblical authority.

Most pastors trained in evangelical seminaries would probably reject the philosophical position just outlined. They give at least lip-service to the relevance of the Old Testament and are convinced that expositional preaching is still the preferable method. Yet many do not utilize their Hebrew training in any significant way. Why is that? Let's be honest—some never learned the language well enough to find it useful in study. Burdened by a pile of outside responsibilities while they were in seminary and forced to be part-time students, they made it through their required Hebrew courses by the skin of their teeth, breathed a sigh of relief when the ordeal ended, and are content to rely on a couple commentaries when preparing sermons from the Old Testament.

However, many did fairly well in Hebrew, had good intentions of keeping up with it, but let it slip away. This is due in part to the incessant and urgent demands of ministry, but this is usually not the fundamental reason why pastors "lose" their Hebrew skills. In many cases the shortsightedness of Hebrew professors, combined with the shortcomings of the typical seminary curriculum, are the culprits.

Idealistic Hebrew professors sometimes forget why their students are studying the language and fail to integrate what they are teaching with the student's ministerial goals. The professor forces the student to master by rote the morphology and basic vocabulary of the language in the first year, and then focuses on "translating" Hebrew during the second year. What passes for translation, however, is often a wooden, slavishly word-for-word rendering that is stylistically abominable and reflects few real interpretive decisions. Only the most basic exegetical skills are developed and the student is rarely, if ever, shown how exegesis impacts interpretation, let alone sermon preparation.

Many students come away from this process weary, but still eager and hopeful of a payoff. Then they experience a rude awakening. They want to use Hebrew in their study of the Old Testament, but suddenly realize their professor never really showed them how to do that. They can parse verbs and "translate" (at least relatively easy, nonpoetic passages), but how does that kind of analysis contribute to one's ministry? They sense there is a great gulf between language study and sermon preparation, and that a bridge is needed to connect the two worlds. That bridge involves learning how to do exegesis and then transforming one's exegetical conclusions and observations into a relevant theological exposition of the text that is the backbone of a biblical, text-based sermon or lesson. But usually no one has built this bridge for the student. Perhaps the Hebrew professor thought the homiletics professor would build the bridge, but the homiletics professor may have never learned how to use the language himself and, besides, he has enough to do teaching the would-be preacher how to organize material, gesture properly, choose good illustrations, and eliminate nasty communication flaws. The seminary has failed him by not forcing its professors to work more closely together and/or by not allowing room in the curriculum for professors to build the exegetical bridge linking language study with preaching.

If the experience just described is yours, then this book is for you. Take heart, it's not too late to renew your belief in the relevance of Hebrew, regain a knowledge of the essentials of the language, and, more important, learn how to use your Hebrew Bible effectively and profitably in sermon preparation, other facets of ministry, and personal study.

Perhaps you are a seminary student who has just completed an introductory Hebrew grammar course. You've labored hard and are wondering, "What next? I still don't see how learning this language is going to contribute to my Bible study and ministry." Well, this book is for you too. In fact, it's designed to be a textbook for a second-year seminary Hebrew course. I believe if you study the principles laid out in the following pages and develop your exegetical skills through practice, you will find that study in the Hebrew Bible can be both profitable and enjoyable. You're in the middle of the journey right now. It may seem dark, but there is a light at the end of the tunnel. Hopefully this book will guide you toward it. When you arrive, I believe you'll discover a big, wide, exciting world where God's word comes alive for you in ways it never did before.

Why You Need to Buck the Trend

It's easy to "go with the flow," assume that Hebrew is a luxury, not an essential, and rely on the opinions of others when preaching and teaching the Old Testament. However, I challenge you to reevaluate the current trend. After all, we who preach and teach the Bible have an awesome responsibility (James 3:1). God's people look to us for insight and direction, often assuming that our education and experience give us the credibility and competence needed for the task. But if we do not really possess that credibility and competence, are we not living a lie? Without credibility and competence, do we have the right to stand before God's people and proclaim his word in an authoritative tone? We set high standards in our society for occupations that involve the physical well-being of people (physicians, pharmacists, airline pilots, etc.). Should we not set even higher standards for those responsible for the spiritual well-being of God's people? There is no board, bar, or federal commission that screens and approves teachers of the Bible; we must set our own standards and then, to the best of our ability and with God's blessing, strive to meet them.

One cannot preach credibly and competently from the Old Testament without a working knowledge of Hebrew and basic exegetical skills. Granted, there are numerous translations, language tools, and commentaries available to the would-be preacher. The appearance of new, up-to-date study helps, especially computer aids, is exciting, for some of these tools, in the right hands, have the potential to revolutionize our study of the text. However, these tools are not substitutes for language study, nor do they magically elevate one to the level of credibility and competence. To use these tools effectively one must have a working knowledge of the language and some basic skill in doing exegesis. Otherwise one will end up trying to decode the language, rather than understanding and appreciating its nuances, and be forced into arbitrarily picking interpretive options without any sound basis for a decision. Translations and commentaries differ frequently and sometimes significantly in their interpretation of the text. If one cannot critically evaluate them, does one just flip a coin or choose the one that "sounds best" or agrees with one's preconceptions? Tools are designed to be used by competent laborers and craftsmen. Superficial use of tools makes one more dangerous than competent when interpreting the Old Testament. In the hands of the wrong person—one without adequate knowledge of how the tool operates, what it is designed to accomplish, and how the information it contains contributes to interpretation—a "chainsaw massacre" of the text becomes a distinct and very real possibility!

How This Book Can Help You Become a Credible, Competent, and Confident Interpreter of the Old Testament

My strategic purpose is to (re)kindle your interest in using the Hebrew Bible in your preaching and teaching ministry. My primary tactical goal is to show you how to use your Hebrew training to produce more accurate and relevant sermons and lessons. This book is not a thorough review of Hebrew grammar per se. It does include a concise survey of the essentials of Hebrew syntax, but it does very little with morphology. In fact, if it's been a while since you took first-year Hebrew, you may find it helpful to consult an introductory Hebrew grammar in conjunction with the chapter on syntax. This book focuses instead on the principles and methods of Hebrew exegesis. Along the way I will:

(1) introduce you to the best language tools (including computer aids),
(2) offer guidance on how to make text-critical decisions,
(3) discuss how to determine the precise meaning of Hebrew words and phrases and avoid some of the common mistakes that are made in word studies,
(4) survey Hebrew syntax and demonstrate how basic grammatical observations can impact exegesis,
(5) discuss the structure of Hebrew narrative and poetry and how it contributes to interpretation,
(6) show how a text's literary form and features impact interpretation, and
(7) outline and illustrate an interpretive method.

Since "a picture is better than a thousand words," I have included numerous illustrations, worked examples, and exercises that guide you through the exegetical process and give you an opportunity to develop your skill. Exegesis is an acquired skill, like riding a bike or shooting free throws. It requires constant practice and may seem awkward, tedious, and mechanical before it becomes "second nature." However, the more you do, the more competent and confident you become.

After discussing and illustrating the exegetical process, I discuss how to develop an exposition from one's exegetical work and include several sample expositions. Exegesis answers the question, "What did the text mean to its original audience?" With that question answered, it is a very short step to exposition, which addresses the questions, "What does the text mean to us?" and, "What should we believe and/or do in light of what the text means?"

A Word to You Nonpastors in the Audience

Perhaps you are seminary-trained but are neither a pastor nor the "son of" a pastor (to adapt an Old Testament idiom!). Maybe you have never preached a sermon, never want to preach a sermon, or never will preach a sermon. Your ministry takes a different form. Perhaps you translate the Bible, or teach Bible studies, or write Christian ed curriculum, or have some other type of teaching ministry. No problem! This book is not just for pastors or would-be pastors. It is designed as a guide for all who attempt to explain to people what the Bible means and how it is relevant to their lives. As noted above, all it presupposes is that you have had a course in the basics of Hebrew grammar and are ready to move on to the next step.

2 Finding Help in the Right Places

Tools and Power Tools

Before embarking down the path of biblical interpretation, one must be properly equipped for the journey. It is essential to have the right tools, and, even more important, to know how to use these tools intelligently. This chapter introduces the would-be interpreter to the best basic tools for Old Testament exegesis.

Translation Aids

After several years of intense study in the Hebrew language, Old Testament specialists can usually "sight read" most passages, recognize most words without the aid of a dictionary, and parse most verbs without consulting a grammar. But most busy pastors and teachers need help in analyzing the many difficult forms and constructions one encounters in the Hebrew Old Testament. Fortunately many translation and morphological aids have appeared in recent years, including among others:

(1) Armstrong, Terry A., Douglas L. Busby, and Cyril F. Carr. *A Reader's Hebrew-English Lexicon of the Old Testament.* 4 vols. Grand Rapids: Zondervan, 1982–88.
(2) Beall, Todd S., and William S. Banks. *Old Testament Parsing Guide.* 2 vols. Chicago: Moody, 1986–90.
(3) Kohlenberger, John, ed. *The NIV Interlinear Hebrew-English Old Testament.* Grand Rapids: Zondervan, 1987.
(4) Owens, John Joseph. *Analytical Key to the Old Testament.* 4 vols. Grand Rapids: Baker, 1989.

Owens's *Analytical Key* is the most helpful of the tools in this category. Utilizing a verse-by-verse format, Owens gives a morphological analysis of every word in the Hebrew text, as well as a translation of the word or phrase. He also includes the page number in BDB (see p. 14) where each word (with the exception of particles) is found.

Lexical Tools

Major Hebrew lexical tools include the following:

(1) Botterweck, G. Johannes, Helmer Ringgren, and Heinz-Josef Fabry. *Theological Dictionary of the Old Testament.* 8 vols. Grand Rapids: Eerdmans, 1977–. (TDOT)

(2) Brown, Francis, S. R. Driver, and Charles A. Briggs. *The New Hebrew and English Lexicon.* Reprinted. Peabody, Mass.: Hendrickson, 1979. (BDB)

(3) Clines, David J. A., ed. *The Dictionary of Classical Hebrew.* 8 vols. Sheffield: Sheffield Academic Press, 1993–. (DCH)

(4) Even-Shoshan, Abraham, ed. *A New Concordance of the Old Testament.* 2nd ed. Grand Rapids: Baker, 1989. (E–S)

(5) Koehler, Ludwig, and Walter Baumgartner. *Lexicon in Veteris Testamenti Libros.* Leiden: E. J. Brill, 1958. (KBL)

(6) Koehler, Ludwig, and Walter Baumgartner. *The Hebrew and Aramaic Lexicon of the Old Testament.* Revised Walter Baumgartner and Johann J. Stamm, trans. and ed. under the supervision of M. E. J. Richardson. 4 vols. Leiden: E. J. Brill, 1994– . (K–B)

(7) VanGemeren, Willem A., ed. *New International Dictionary of Old Testament Theology and Exegesis.* 5 vols. Grand Rapids: Zondervan, 1997. (NIDOTTE)

The classic dictionary of Brown, Driver, and Briggs (BDB) remains a standard tool for Old Testament exegesis because of its breadth of coverage, thorough categorization of usage, and reasonable cost. The Hendrickson reprint edition keys the dictionary entries into *Strong's Concordance* and has placed the entries from the list of additions and corrections on the appropriate pages in the dictionary.

BDB has many commendable features, but the interpreter must also be aware of its limitations and weaknesses, due primarily to its age (BDB was published in 1907): (1) BDB's treatment of Semitic cognates is woefully outdated and unreliable in many places. This is of particular concern in the study of rare words, where data from the cognate languages are of special importance. (2) The English glosses given in BDB are sometimes archaic and outdated, and, if utilized uncritically, can be misleading and inaccurate. (3) BDB often fails to recognize the existence of homonymic roots, many of which have been isolated by more recent linguistic research. (4) The bibliographical data included in BDB's discussions are frequently outdated and, practically speaking, inaccessible. (5) BDB's arrangement of all words according to their root derivation is helpful in one respect (all words derived from a root appear together, facilitating semantic analysis of derivatives), but problematic in another (one must be informed about such morphological phenomena as nun assimilation, etc. to be able to find some words). Fortunately this problem has been alleviated by the appearance of morphological aids keyed into BDB (e.g., Owens's *Analytical Key*).

Another useful dictionary is the second edition of Ludwig Koehler and Walter Baumgartner's Hebrew-German/English *Lexicon in Veteris Testamenti Libros* (KBL), which includes a supplemental volume containing numerous additions and corrections. KBL contains more up-to-date etymological data than BDB and lists words in alphabetical order (rather than under their root). The interpreter can use KBL as a helpful and affordable supplement (and in some cases corrective) to BDB.

The field of Hebrew lexicography is constantly expanding and changing due to new discoveries and linguistic research, making it important for any dictionary to be periodically updated. In 1967 a third edition of KBL (sometimes abbreviated HALAT, HAL, or KBL[3]) began to appear in fascicles, but only in a Hebrew-German format. A Hebrew-English version (K–B) is now appearing. Though it would be advantageous for every interpreter to have access to this new dictionary, unfortunately the exorbitant price will be prohibitive for most pastors and students.

K–B is of special value in the area of etymological research on rare words and homonymic roots. For example, K–B correctly defines the meaning of the hapax legomenon חַשְׁרָה in 2 Samuel 22:12 as "sieve" and relates it to the verbal root חשׁר attested in Ugaritic as well as postbiblical Hebrew and Aramaic (p. 363). Earlier dictionaries erroneously harmonized the text to Psalm 18:12 or attempted to relate the word to an unlikely Akkadian or Arabic cognate. K–B (p. 836) also correctly proposes homonymic roots for עָלַס, which they define as "taste" (see Job 20:18 and Prov. 7:18) and "become agitated" (see Job 39:13), respectively.[1]

For the most part, the categories of usage offered in K–B reflect sound semantic and interpretive decisions and an awareness of recent research. For example, the entry for אוֹת, "sign," distinguishes the various referents of the term in a very helpful manner and correctly shows that the word need not refer to some miraculous display (p. 26). The entry for אֶרֶץ correctly includes a category "underworld" (p. 91), the entry for אֱמוּנָה correctly distinguishes the meanings "trustworthiness, faithfulness," and "honesty" (pp. 62–63), the discussion of בָּשָׂר recognizes that the phrase "all flesh" includes both humankind and animals in Genesis 6:12–17 (p. 164), and the N stem use of the verbal root ברך in Genesis 12:3, 18:18, and 28:14 is accurately glossed as reflexive, "to wish on oneself a blessing," and then explained in light of the formula employed in Genesis 48:20 (p. 160).

On the other hand, one can detect an occasional deficiency in K–B's definitions and handling of semantic categories. For example, the entry

---

1. BDB (p. 763) assumes there is only one verbal root, which they incorrectly relate to עלץ/עלז and define as "rejoice."

on אוֹב II, "spirit of the dead" (p. 20), fails to recognize that the term can have three distinct senses or that it refers to a ritual pit in 1 Samuel 28:7 (see TDOT, 1:133). The glosses "rebuke, threat" are not strong enough for the noun גְּעָרָה in theophanic contexts where it refers to Yahweh's loud shout or battle cry (see TDOT, 3:49–53). The entries for אָב, "father," and אָהַב, "love," do not adequately reflect the covenantal nuances these terms often possess. (Isa. 9:5, placed by K–B under category 7, should appear under category 3 or 4. See pp. 1–2.) The discussion of חֶסֶד (pp. 336–37) needs to be revised in light of K. Sakenfeld's and Gordon Clark's research of the term.[2] Also K–B's categorization based on human and divine use is not helpful from a semantic standpoint, for the term's basic nuances of meaning are attested in both the secular and theological spheres.

Another excellent new dictionary, *The Dictionary of Classical Hebrew* (DCH), is currently in the process of publication. At the present time, only two of the projected eight volumes have appeared. Unfortunately, like K–B, the price of this lexicon will probably be prohibitive for most pastors and students.

With the exception of a few common words, DCH lists every occurrence of every Hebrew word. The arrangement and discussion of words is linguistically sound and especially helpful. Nouns are categorized according to syntactical function. For example, the entry on אֳנִיָּה, "ship" (1:341), groups together passages where the noun appears as the subject of a verb and then lists each of those verbs and the texts where the particular noun–verb construction occurs. Other categories list passages where the noun appears in a nominal clause, as object of a verb, in construct with a following genitive, in combination with various prepositions, and in combination with various adjectives. For verbs the entries list the various subjects and objects that appear with the verb, as well as collocations with various prepositions. This type of categorization greatly facilitates semantic and syntactical analysis.

So-called theological dictionaries can also be useful tools when doing Old Testament word studies and interpretation. These dictionaries are concerned with the theological implications of Hebrew words in their various contexts, not simply semantic categorization. Perhaps the most well-known tool in this category is the multivolume TDOT, eight volumes of which have been now been translated into English from the original German work. NIDOTTE is a similar work, but written from a broadly evangelical perspective.

Interpreters of the Old Testament should also have a good concordance at their disposal. Even-Shoshan's is the best available. Like other

---

2. See Katharine Doob Sakenfeld, *The Meaning of Hesed in the Hebrew Bible: A New Inquiry* (Missoula, Mont.: Scholars, 1978); and Gordon R. Clark, *The Word* Hesed *in the Hebrew Bible* (Sheffield: JSOT, 1993).

Hebrew concordances, E–S lists words according to their attested grammatical forms. An added and immensely useful feature of E–S is its lists of phrases and syntactical constructions prior to the list of attested passages. The lists of phrases and constructions are keyed into the list of passages, allowing the interpreter to find quickly the texts where a particular collocation occurs.

Grammatical and Syntactical Tools

Major Hebrew grammatical and syntactical tools include the following:

(1) Jouön, Paul. *A Grammar of Biblical Hebrew*. Trans. and rev. T. Muraoka. 2 vols. Rome: Pontifical Biblical Institute, 1993. (J–M)
(2) Kautzsch, E., ed. *Gesenius' Hebrew Grammar*. Trans. A. E. Cowley. 2nd English ed. Oxford: Clarendon, 1910. (GKC)
(3) Waltke, Bruce K., and M. O'Connor. *An Introduction to Biblical Hebrew Syntax*. Winona Lake, Ind.: Eisenbrauns, 1990. (W–O)

Many still consider GKC the "cadillac" of Hebrew grammars. Though it contains a wealth of valuable information, it is outdated in some respects and uses technical Latin terminology that will be an obstacle for those without training in the classical languages. For matters of syntax the interpreter will find the more up-to-date works listed above more user-friendly and readable.

Power Tools: Computer Search Programs

Biblical exegetes now have at their disposal computerized research tools that can speed up the interpretive process and have the potential to revolutionize biblical studies, especially in the areas of semantics and syntactical research. One can now acquire at a fairly reasonable price computer programs that give a morphological analysis of every word in the Hebrew text, provide a translation of the word or phrase, and include for each word a condensed lexical entry based on BDB. These same programs also allow one to find quickly all of the passages in which a given word or precise grammatical form of a word occurs. In other words, these programs fulfill the same function as Owens's *Analytical Key* and Even-Shoshan's concordance.

But that's not all! With these same programs one can now find all the passages in which any given syntactical combination occurs. These searches can be lexically specific. For example, if I want to find all the passages where the phrase "good and evil" (טוֹב וָרָע) follows the verb יָדַע, "to know," I can set up a Hebrew syntactical construct in the acCordance program (see below) that looks something like this:

עֵר (within one word of) וְ- (within one word of) טוֹב (within five words of [just to be safe!]) the verb יָדַע, "know"

When I hit the "OK," in a matter of seconds the program tells me that this construction occurs in three passages: Genesis 3:5, 22, and Deuteronomy 1:39. If I change the formula and substitute the verbal noun derivative דַּעַת, "knowledge," for the verb יָדַע, the search lists Genesis 2:9, 17 as the only passages where the collocation occurs.

These syntactical searches can also be general. For example, let's suppose I want to study the functions of various verbal forms when they occur with a prefixed waw after the imperative in the Book of Genesis. Let's start with the imperative joined to another imperative. I set up a Hebrew syntactical construct with the acCordance program that looks something like this:

> verb: imperative (within one word of) וְ- (within five words of) verb: imperative

The search yields fifty-eight examples of such a sequence in Genesis distributed in thirty-eight different passages. When I change the second form to an imperfect, the search yields thirty-four examples in thirty texts. When the second form is changed to a perfect, the search yields eight examples in four texts. Of course, all these passages would need to be studied carefully to make sure that each example is valid. One might even want to broaden the range between the initial imperative and the following verb to ten words just to make sure no examples were missed.

Programs with this kind of search capability include:

(1) acCordance (for Mac users), produced by the Gramcord Institute, 2218 N.E. Brookview Drive, Vancouver, WA 98686 (360-576-3000)
(2) Bible Windows (for IBM-PC users), produced by Silver Mountain Software, 1029 Tanglewood, Cedar Hill, TX 75104 (800-214-2144)
(3) BibleWorks for Windows (for IBM-PC users), produced by Hermeneutika Computer Research Bible Research Software, P.O. Box 2200, Big Fork, MT 59911-2200 (800-742-4253)

3 The Most Basic Question of All

What Is the Text?

Text criticism is basic to all interpretation. Before one can ask, "What does the text mean?" the interpreter must first answer the question, "What is the text?" While this is a basic question and the discipline of text criticism is foundational to the interpretive task, students and nonspecialists often shy away from this aspect of exegesis because they perceive it as being too technical and beyond their level of training.

Text criticism, as done by specialists, does demand a great deal of training and expertise. Ideally the text critic must be aware of the history of the text, be able to read the various witnesses to the text (which requires facility in Hebrew, Greek, Aramaic, Syriac, Latin, and other languages), and be familiar with ancient scribal practices and tendencies. The text critic must also have access to tools and texts that are often expensive and sometimes out of print.

The task seems daunting, but one need not ascend to the rarefied atmosphere of the world-class text critic in order to develop a working knowledge of text-critical method and attain an adequate level of competence in this area. Fortunately, many good introductions to text criticism are available (see the bibliography at the end of this chapter). With the help of such tools and an awareness of proper text-critical method, one should be able to discern the textual base of any given translation, interact with the best critical commentaries, and make intelligent text-critical choices. This chapter will not repeat all or even most of what the text-critical introductions have to say. Instead it will focus on the basic principles of text-critical decision making and illustrate those principles from a variety of passages. (If it has been some time since you read an introduction to text criticism, you might find it helpful to do so prior to launching into this chapter.)

If the topic seems just too frightening at this point and you're tempted to dismiss this entire book as too technical, stop! Go on to the next chapters and return to this chapter later. Granted, text criticism is the logical starting point in exegesis because, as noted above, it addresses the most basic question of all, "What is the text?" But in actual practice one needs to become familiar with the text at the semantic, syntactical, and literary levels before attempting to solve text-critical problems. Text-critical decisions are usually made in conjunction with other exegetical steps (see the interpretive method outlined in chapter 8), so it won't hurt you to postpone your reading of this chapter until later.

Some Basic Operating Principles

(1) One should not make text-critical decisions solely or even primarily on the basis of external evidence.[1] In other words, one should not automatically choose a reading from a given textual witness (e.g., the MT, Septuagint, a Qumran scroll, etc.), no matter how ancient, relatively superior, or generally reliable that witness may be. Nor should one automatically choose a reading that has the weight of the external evidence on its side. Text-critical problems must be evaluated in light of internal factors (see principle 2 below). If such an analysis reveals that two readings are equally probable, then one may choose the reading from the better tradition. When determining the "better tradition," it is helpful to know the tendencies of the witnesses being considered. A good critical commentary will usually discuss in its introduction the character of the textual witnesses to a given book.

(2) One should base text-critical decisions primarily on internal factors, such as graphic, lexical, syntactical, and contextual considerations.[2] The preferred reading is the one that best explains the existence of others. For example, assuming that reading A is original, the critic attempts to explain how reading B arose. One then reverses the process, assuming reading B is original and attempting to explain how reading A arose. At this point one of the explanations should be more plausible than the other and a choice can be made. (This process is illustrated below in the discussion of sample problems.)

There are no hard and fast rules or so-called canons. When internal considerations suggest an intentional change, the more difficult reading is preferable because the tendency in textual transmission and especially translation (which is inherently interpretive) is to clarify meaning and smooth out difficulties. However, where one suspects an unintentional error (e.g., confusion of similar-looking letters, dittography, haplography, homoioteleuton, etc.), this principle is not applicable, for the more difficult reading is too difficult and in some cases lexically or grammatically impossible. Likewise, the shorter reading is often preferable, at least where one suspects expansion and clarification. However, one must

---

1. P. Kyle McCarter Jr., *Textual Criticism* (Philadelphia: Fortress, 1986), 71–72.
2. Ibid., 72–74.

remember that an unintentional scribal error (such as haplography or homoioteleuton) might have produced a shorter reading.

(3) Conjectural emendation or textual reconstruction is sometimes necessary, especially in difficult poetic texts.[3] It is possible that some textual errors appeared at a relatively early stage in the process of transmission and contaminated the extant witnesses, all of which date to a relatively late period in transmissional history. Occasionally one will encounter a reading that is non-sensical or contextually incompatible and clearly corrupt. When faced with such circumstances, the text critic must try to reconstruct an original reading, keeping in mind the graphic environment of the non-sensical reading and the types of scribal errors that may have produced such a reading. In other words, a valid reconstruction must be able to explain plausibly how the non-sensical or incompatible corruption developed from the proposed original.

In such situations one will sometimes encounter a textual witness that provides a clear reading. However, if it is difficult or impossible to explain how the non-sensical or incompatible reading could have derived from the clear reading, then the easier reading should be rejected as an attempt to smooth out the difficulty and clarify or guess at the meaning of the text.

Some Examples of Text Criticism

The following examples are designed to illustrate how to reason through a text-critical problem. As the discussion of each problem illustrates, one must be aware of possible causes of textual corruption, be sensitive to contextual factors, and be prepared to do some lexical and grammatical spadework.

(1) Hosea 7:14

The Lord accuses his people of rejecting him:

> "They do not cry out to me with their hearts,
> for they wail on their beds,
> for grain and wine they ??? (Heb. יִתְגּוֹרָרוּ),
> they turn away from me."

The verb form יִתְגּוֹרָרוּ is a hithpolel imperfect third masculine plural from the root גּוּר or גָּרַר. K–B (184–85) lists three homonymic verbal roots גּוּר, meaning "live as a resident alien," "attack," and "be afraid," respectively. The first occurs in the hithpolel stem only once (1 Kings 17:20), with the meaning "stay as a resident alien." The other two occur

3. Ibid., 74–75.

only in the qal stem. None of the three provides a lexical nuance that fits the cultic context of Hosea 7:14 (note the reference to ritual lamentation in the first half of the verse). K–B (204) lists one verbal root גָּרַר, which means "drag away" or "ruminate" in the qal and "saw" in the poal. Neither of these lexical nuances fits Hosea 7:14. So the verbal form יִתְגּוֹרָרוּ in Hosea 7:14 is morphologically and semantically problematic.

The letter "c" after the form יִתְגּוֹרָרוּ in BHS indicates that the apparatus contains a text-critical note pertaining to the word. The note says: "Read ("l") with ("c") some ("nonn") medieval Hebrew manuscripts ("Mss"), supported by the Septuagint (G) (which contains the Greek verb form listed) יִתְגּוֹדְדוּ as ("ut") in 1 Kings ("1 R") 18:28."[4] The Greek form listed in the apparatus should be translated, "they cut, mutilate themselves." The Hebrew form in the apparatus is unvocalized because it would have the same vowel pattern as the form in the text: יִתְגּוֹדְדוּ. This form is a hithpolel imperfect third masculine plural from the verb גָּדַד.

The verb גָּדַד occurs six times (Deut. 14:1; 1 Kings 18:28; Jer. 16:6; 41:5; 47:5; Mic. 4:14), always in the hithpolel stem with the meaning "cut oneself" (K–B,177). The verb describes a pagan mourning rite in which a worshiper would mutilate his body. In 1 Kings 18:28, the passage cited in the BHS apparatus, the prophets of Baal mourn their deceased god, who was viewed as being imprisoned in the underworld during times of drought. So Hosea 7:14 alludes to the fact that God's people, rather than trusting him for a good harvest, were engaging in pagan mourning rites (note the reference to "wailing" in the first half of the verse) in an effort to gain Baal's favor and ensure a good crop.

To summarize, יִתְגּוֹדְדוּ is the original reading. It is morphologically preferable (גָּדַד occurs exclusively in the hithpolel stem) and makes excellent sense in this context. The reading יִתְגּוֹרָרוּ is too difficult morphologically and contextually. It arose due to the confusion of the similar letters daleth (ד) and resh (ר).

(2) Judges 20:13

The consonantal Hebrew text (the Kethib, i.e., "what is written") states literally: "and they were not willing, Benjamin, to listen to their brothers." There is incongruity between the plural verb (אָבוּ) and the following singular subject "Benjamin."

---

4. To interpret the symbols for the various textual witnesses listed in the BHS textual apparatus, one should consult pp. xliv–xl of the BHS Prolegomena or Ernst Würthwein, *The Text of the Old Testament*, trans. Erroll F. Rhodes, 2nd ed. (Grand Rapids: Eerdmans, 1995), 232–37. To translate the Latin terms and abbreviations in the BHS textual apparatus, one should consult Hans Peter Rüger, *An English Key to the Latin Words and Abbreviations and the Symbols of Biblia Hebraica Stuttgartensia* (Stuttgart: German Bible Society, 1985) or Ellis R. Brotzman, *Old Testament Textual Criticism* (Grand Rapids: Baker, 1994), 171–92.

Note that BHS has vowel points without consonants between בִּנְיָמִן and אֲבֹו, followed by the letter "b." This indicates that the BHS apparatus contains a textual note. The note says: "Many ("mlt") medieval Hebrew manuscripts ("Mss"), supported by the Septuagint (G), the Syriac (S), and the Targums (T) as well as ("ut") the Qere (Q) (have the reading suggested by the vowel points), insert (the correct consonants)." The correct consonants (בני) can be found in the right-hand margin on the same line as the text. In other words the Qere ("what is to be read") and these other witnesses are reading בְּנֵי בִנְיָמִן, "the sons of Benjamin." In this case the plural subject agrees with the plural verb.

Which reading is preferable, the Kethib ("Benjamin") or the Qere ("sons of Benjamin")? One could argue that the Kethib is a case of a plural verb being employed with a collective proper noun (for statement of the general principle, see GKC, 462), but a closer look at the literary style of Judges 20–21 militates against this. The proper name "Benjamin" appears as the subject of a preceding verb three times; each time the verb is singular (20:25, 40; 21:14). In 20:39 the subject "Benjamin" precedes its verb; the verb is singular. In 20:41 the phrase אִישׁ בִּנְיָמִן, "men (collective singular) of Benjamin," is the subject of a preceding singular verb. Eight times the phrase "sons of Benjamin" appears as the subject of a preceding verb; each time the verb is plural (20:3, 14–15, 21, 31, 32, 36; 21:23). The evidence strongly suggests that the Kethib's lack of agreement is incongruous and the Qere reading consistent with the author's style. However, before we choose the easier reading over the more difficult reading, we must explain how the Kethib arose if the Qere is original. If one looks closely at the sequence of consonants in the Qere reading, one observes that the sequence בני is repeated: בְּנֵי בְנֵימִן. Apparently a scribe committed the error of haplography, writing the sequence only once instead of twice.

(3) Judges 16:13–14

The MT reads: "Delilah said to Samson: 'Up to now you have tricked me and told me lies. Tell me how you can be subdued!' He said to her: 'If you weave the seven braids of my head into the fabric.' And she secured (it) with the pin and said to him, 'The Philistines are here, Samson.' He woke up and tore away the pin of the loom and the fabric."

Note that the BHS text has the letter "b" at the end of verse 13. The text-critical note in the apparatus says: "Several ("nonn") words ("vb") have dropped out ("exc"), the Septuagint (G) adds ("+"). . . ." The note then lists the Greek reading, followed by a retroversion of the Greek text into Hebrew. This "plus" reads: "and you secure (it) with the pin to the wall, then I will become weak and will be like any other man."

The BHS text has the letter "a" after the first word (וַתִּתְקַע) in verse 14. The note says: "Before ("ante") וַתִּתְקַע several ("nonn") words ("vb") have

23

dropped out ("exc"), the Septuagint (G) puts before ("pr") this. . . ." The note then lists the Greek reading, followed by a retroversion of the Greek text into Hebrew. This "plus" reads: "And she made him go to sleep, and wove the seven braids of his hair into the fabric." Another letter ("b") appears after the next word in the BHS text (בַּיָּתֵד); the note observes that the Septuagint adds the phrase "to the wall," which is then retroverted into Hebrew.

One can see from all three notes that the Septuagint contains a much longer version of the account. The following translation of this longer version has in bold print those words that occur only in the Septuagint:

> "Delilah said to Samson: 'Up to now you have tricked me and told me lies. Tell me how you can be subdued!' He said to her: 'If you weave the seven braids of my head *into the fabric* **and you secure (it) with the pin to the wall, then I will become weak and will be like any other man.' And she made him go to sleep, wove the seven braids of his hair into** *the fabric,* and she secured (it) with the pin **to the wall** and said to him, 'The Philistines are here, Samson.' He woke up and tore away the pin of the loom and the fabric."

Is the longer or shorter version original? One could argue that the Septuagint translator decided to expand the text, but this is unlikely here. Note that the last word before the "plus" is "the fabric" (הַמַּסָּכֶת). This same word appears at the end of the "plus," suggesting that a scribe's eye jumped from the first instance of the word to the second and accidentally left the intervening material out.

Contextual factors also support the longer version. In the shorter version Samson's explanation seems truncated and incomplete, especially when compared to the explanations he gives Delilah both before (vv. 7, 11) and after this (v. 17). Furthermore in the shorter version Delilah's response does not correspond to Samson's directions, contrary to the pattern we see before (vv. 8, 12) and after (v. 19) this. In a paneled narrative like this (vv. 6–9, 10–12, 13–14, 15–22), one expects structural symmetry in the panels leading up to the climax, where structural deviation is then common. The longer version provides the symmetry one expects and is contextually more compatible.

(4) Joshua 2:15

In the MT's version of the story, the narrator describes the spies' escape from Jericho as follows: "And she (Rahab) let them down by a rope through the window, for her house was on the surface of the wall; she lived on the wall."

Note, however, that the BHS text has a letter "a" after בַּחֶבֶל, "by a rope," and brackets the entire second half of the verse with the letter "b."

The first note indicates that the phrase "by a rope" is not present in the Greek witnesses that best represent the Old Greek version (G*). The second note indicates that the Old Greek does not contain the material that is within the brackets. In other words, the Old Greek version of the verse is much shorter, reading: "And she let them down through the window."

Is the shorter or longer version of the story original? It is possible that the phrase בַּחֶבֶל, "by a rope," has been accidentally omitted by homoioarchton. Note that the following word בְּעַד, "through," also begins with the letter "beth." Having written the letter "beth" at the beginning of בַּחֶבֶל, a scribe's eye could have jumped from this beth to the one at the beginning of בְּעַד. Thinking he had just written this beth, he would have continued his transcription with ayin, leaving out the preceding sequence חבל.ב in the process. On the other hand, a scribe may have added the phrase as an explanation for how Rahab was able to let the spies down through the window. Originally this explanatory gloss may have been placed in the margin above the line and then later copied into the text. At this point, either explanation (accidental omission by homoioarchton or interpretive expansion) seems possible, but an examination of the rest of the verse suggests the phrase is due to expansion.

The material bracketed by the letter "b" in BHS explains (note the introductory כִּי, "for") why letting the spies down through the window was an effective strategy. The statement looks like a strong candidate for a scribal expansion, for it is the kind of interpretive comment one might expect a scribe to add. However, before labeling it as such, we must first look at the graphic environment of the statement to see if the explanation, if original, could have been accidentally omitted, perhaps by homoioarchton or homoioteleuton. However, the possibility of an accidental omission appears highly unlikely in this case. The first consonant in the bracketed section is a kaph, the first one after it a waw. The last consonant in the bracketed section is a taw, the last one before it a nun. Since the possibility of an accidental omission seems unlikely, we can safely assume that the bracketed section is a scribal explanatory gloss. This suggests that the phrase "by a rope" may also originate with a scribe.

(5) Numbers 13:33

The MT version reads: "'And there we saw the Nephilim' (the sons of Anak come from the Nephilim) 'and we viewed ourselves as being like grasshoppers, and so we looked to them.'" It is highly unlikely that the spies would have stopped in the middle of their impassioned speech to include a genealogical note. Consequently the statement "the sons of Anak come from the Nephilim," if part of the original text, must be a parenthetical note added by the narrator.

Note that the BHS text has this statement bracketed by the letter "a." The text-critical note says: "Delete ("dl"), compare Old Greek." The editor is suggesting, with support from the Old Greek, that the statement be deleted. It may well be a scribal addition that is not part of the original text. (Indeed, if original it presents a very difficult interpretive problem. The Nephilim lived before the Flood [see Gen. 6:4]. If all human life, with the exception of Noah and his family, was destroyed by the deluge, how could the postdiluvian sons of Anak be descended from the antediluvian Nephilim?) However, before we reject the statement too quickly, we must consider the possibility of an accidental omission. Note that "Nephilim" is repeated; in fact it is the last word before and within the bracketed section. It is possible that a scribe's eye jumped from the first instance of "Nephilim" to the second and accidentally left the intervening words out. Apart from further research, it is difficult to make a choice here. One might want to study the Book of Numbers to see how often explanatory material appears and whether or not it is ever inserted within quotations. One would also need to study the Old Greek of Numbers to see if there is evidence elsewhere of textual corruption due to homoioteleuton/homoioarchton.

(6) Deuteronomy 32:8

The MT reads:

> "When the Most High allotted land to the nations,
> when he divided up humankind;
> he set the boundaries of the nations
> according to the number of the sons of Israel (בְּנֵי יִשְׂרָאֵל)."

This reading suggests that when God divided the nations and assigned their boundaries, he did so with the people of Israel in mind, assuring that they would have adequate territory in which to live.

Note, however, that the phrase "sons of Israel" is bracketed in BHS with the letter "d." Note "d" says: "A Qumran witness (Q), supported by the Septuagint (G) (which has the reading listed), Symmachus's Greek version (Σ), the Old Latin (L), and the Syrohexapla (Syh) (the symbol is mistakenly placed above the baseline in BHS note "d–d" on Deut. 32:8), (reads), probably ("prb") correctly ("recte") בני אל or ("vel") בְּנֵי אֱלִים:" In other words, the Qumran witness has "sons of God," or "sons of gods," instead of MT's "sons of Israel." (The precise reading of the Qumran manuscript is debated.)

Which reading is original? First, let's assume that "sons of Israel" was original. Is there any plausible explanation for the existence of the Qumran reading, which omits the consonantal sequence ישׂר? One could account for the absence of the yod by haplography (the letter right before this is also a yod), but there is no apparent reason for the omission of שׂר. On the other hand, if בְּנֵי אֵל (or בְּנֵי אֱלִים) is original, one can easily explain the MT reading as interpretive. A scribe might have assumed that the phrase "sons of God" was a reference to the Israelites on the basis of Hosea 1:10 (Eng., Heb. 2:1), which calls the Israelites "the sons of the living God" (בְּנֵי אֵל־חָי). The evidence suggests that the text originally read "sons of God/gods," not "sons of Israel."

Of course, the next question pertains to the meaning of the phrase, but this is not a text-critical issue per se. The MT understands the referent of "sons of God/gods" as the Israelites, but it is more likely that the phrase refers to the angels, which is the way the Septuagint (which reads "angels of God") takes the phrase. With the exception of Hosea 1:10 (where the divine name is modified by "living"), the phrase בְּנֵי אֵל is unattested elsewhere in the Old Testament, but בְּנֵי אֵלִים clearly refers to the angels in Psalm 89:6 (Eng., Heb. v. 7) and probably in Psalm 29:1 as well. The phrase is also attested in Ugaritic, where it refers to the high god El's divine assembly. (In both Hebrew and Ugaritic it is likely that the final mem on אֵל is enclitic, rather than a plural marker.) If the phrase does indeed refer to the angels in Deuteronomy 32:8, then the text is saying that God gave the angelic host jurisdiction over the nations, while reserving Israel for himself (v. 9). In other words, he rules over the nations indirectly, while he has a direct theocratic arrangement with Israel.

In the two examples that follow, I reconstruct the text:

(7) Isaiah 5:26

The prophet warns:

"He (the Lord) will lift a signal flag for the nations from afar (Heb. לַגּוֹיִם מֵרָחוֹק), and will whistle for it from the horizon of the earth."

BHS brackets the phrase לַגּוֹיִם מֵרָחוֹק with the letter "a," indicating that the apparatus contains a textual note. The note in the apparatus says: "(The following reading) has been proposed ("prp"): לְגוֹי מִמֶּרְחָק, compare ("cf") Jeremiah 5:15." In this case the BHS apparatus refers to a proposed emendation for which there is no external support from existing Hebrew manuscripts or ancient translations.

Why would a text critic make a proposal for which no external evidence exists? A quick look at the context reveals the reason. The first line says that God lifts a signal for the "nations" (plural), but the following context indicates only one nation is in view (note, e.g., לוֹ, "for it," in the parallel line). For the sake of consistency with the context, some critics propose an emendation to לְגוֹי מִמֶּרְחָק, "for a nation from a distant place," a phrase that also appears in Jeremiah 5:15. In this case an error of misdivision has occurred in MT (the mem of the prepositional prefix being accidentally taken as a plural ending on the preceding word). A second possibility, not mentioned in BHS, is to read לְגוֹי מֵרָחוֹק, "for a nation from afar" (see Deut. 28:49; Joel 3:8 [Eng., Heb. 4:8], where the same construction occurs). In this case the final mem on לְגוֹיִם is dittographic. A third option would be to retain the mem on לְגוֹיִם and take it as enclitic rather than a plural ending.[5] The text would read the same as in the previous proposal: לְגוֹי[ם] מֵרָחוֹק, "for a nation from afar."

(8) Habakkuk 2:3a

The text has traditionally been translated something like this: "For the vision is still for the appointed time, and it hastens (lit. "pants") toward the end, and does not lie." This reading assumes that יָפֵחַ is a hiphil prefixed verbal form from the root פּוּחַ, "breathe, blow" (BDB, 806), but this interpretation of the form is incorrect. יָפֵחַ is actually a noun, meaning "witness." It appears in Ugaritic, where the most clearly attested readings use the word to introduce the names of witnesses to legal contracts.[6] It occurs in several passages in Proverbs, where it stands parallel to the noun עֵד, "witness" (6:19; 12:17; 14:5, 25; 19:5, 9). (In these passages the Masoretic tradition apparently understands the form as a verb, for it is pointed with a hireq-yod theme vowel.) K–B (424) finds this word in Psalm 27:12b, where it appears in combination with "violence," and the phrase stands parallel to "lying witnesses." The noun fits very well in Habakkuk 2:3a, where it would refer to the vision functioning as a witness. (See the translation offered below.) If יָפֵחַ is indeed a noun meaning "witness," then it is possible that עוֹד, "still," in the parallel line is a later misinterpretation of an original consonantal עד. Rather than pointing the form as an adverb, it makes better sense to read עֵד, "witness," which forms a word pair with יָפֵחַ in the Proverbs passages cited above. Making this emendation, one can translate Habakkuk 2:3a as follows: "For the vision is a witness at the appointed time, indeed a witness at the end that does not lie." Habakkuk's prophetic vision stood as a reassuring testimony to the faithful remnant that God would eventually vindicate them. At the time of fulfillment it would also be an incriminating witness against those who rejected it.[7]

For Further Reading and Reference

Brotzman, Ellis R. *Old Testament Textual Criticism*. Grand Rapids: Baker, 1994.

5. On enclitic mem, see W–O, 158–60.
6. Dennis Pardee, "*YPH>* 'Witness' in Hebrew and Ugaritic," *Vetus Testamentum* 28 (1978): 204–6.
7. See R. Haak, *Habakkuk* (Leiden: Brill, 1992), 55–57; and J. J. M. Roberts, *Nahum, Habakkuk, and Zephaniah* (Louisville: Westminster, 1991), 105–6.

Klein, Ralph W. *Textual Criticism of the Old Testament*. Philadelphia: Fortress, 1974.

McCarter, P. Kyle, Jr. *Textual Criticism*. Philadelphia: Fortress, 1986.

Rüger, Hans Peter. *An English Key to the Latin Words and Abbreviations and the Symbols of Biblia Hebraica Stuttgartensia*. Stuttgart: German Bible Society, 1985.

Tov, Emanuel. *Textual Criticism of the Hebrew Bible*. Minneapolis: Fortress, 1992.

Würthwein, Ernst. *The Text of the Old Testament*. Trans. Erroll F. Rhodes. 2nd ed. Grand Rapids: Eerdmans, 1995.

4 Who Was Right? Alice or Humpty Dumpty?

How Words Work and Play

In her journey through the land on the other side of the looking glass, Alice encountered a talking egg-shaped creature named Humpty Dumpty. At one point in their conversation, the following interchange took place:

Humpty: "There's glory for you!"

Alice: "I don't know what you mean by 'glory.'"

Humpty: Of course you don't—till I tell you. I meant 'there's a nice knock-down argument for you!'"

Alice: "But 'glory' doesn't mean 'a nice knock-down argument.'"

Humpty: "When *I* use a word, it means just what I choose it to mean—nothing more nor less."

Alice: "The question is whether you *can* make words mean so many different things."

Humpty: "The question is which is to be master—that's all. They've a temper, some of them—particularly verbs: they're the proudest—adjectives you can do anything with, but not verbs—however, *I* can manage the whole lot of them! Impenetrability! That's what *I* say!"

Alice: "Would you please tell me what that means?"

Humpty: "Now you talk like a reasonable child. I meant by 'impenetrability' that we've had enough of that subject, and it would be just as well if you'd mention what you mean to do next, as I suppose you don't mean to stop here all the rest of your life."

Alice: "That's a great deal to make one word mean."

Humpty. "When I make a word do a lot of work like that, I always pay it extra."

Alice: "Oh!"[1]

1. Lewis Carroll, *Through the Looking Glass* (reprint, New York: Random House, 1946), 93–95.

This silly dialogue raises the question of how words work. If Humpty Dumpty were right, sustained communication would be impossible, or at best highly cumbersome. We intuitively sense that Alice is correct. One cannot arbitrarily assign a meaning to a word or load it with assorted ideas.

Usage and Meaning

But how does one determine the meaning of a word? The answer seems simple enough. The meaning of a word is established by usage among a community of speakers in a given time period. But this is where the matter becomes more complicated. When used by a community of speakers, words can develop a wide range of semantic nuances and/or become specialized and achieve idiomatic status. When trying to determine the meaning of a word in a specific context, one cannot view the term in isolation, but must be alert to various contextual and linguistic factors.

The importance of observing context can be illustrated by the use of the English term "Yankee." In former times the term often referred to an inhabitant of New England, but in contemporary usage it is not so limited. On the lips of a Georgian, it probably refers to anyone living in the northern states. If a Brazilian is speaking, the word likely refers to an American in general, no matter which state he or she calls home. If a baseball announcer uses the word, it probably has a very specialized sense and refers to a member of New York's American League team, even if the player happens to be from Alabama or Venezuela! In other words, when we hear someone use the term "Yankee," we have to ask, "'Yankee' in what sense?" Contextual factors provide the answer to that question.

When determining meaning, it is also essential to consider linguistic factors within the framework of context. For example, the verb "run" has the basic, literal meaning, "to move swiftly on foot." However, this definition does not adequately cover the wide range of nuances that this verb carries in contemporary usage, for it shows up in a variety of contexts and syntactical combinations. For example, if we place the phrase "for office" after the verb, it has the nuance "compete against an opponent in an election." If we "run a newspaper article," the verb means "to publish." If I'm standing in a pool room and hear someone put "the table" after the verb, I assume the individual is referring to knocking all the balls on the table into a pocket on consecutive shots. If we put "the store" after the verb, it means "to manage or supervise." If we "run to the store," we go to it and shop in it hurriedly. The phrase "run into" followed by a proper name can mean "to meet, encounter." If "water" is the subject of the verb, it means "to flow." If "the car engine" is the subject, the verb means "to function or operate." In other words the verb "run" is polysemantic (it has more than one nuance of meaning) and, in some contexts, is specialized and/or idiomatic. Despite its wide range of usage, this verb cannot be used, a la Humpty Dumpty, in an arbitrary fashion or utilized in any context that one chooses. Contextual and linguistic factors (such as its combination with certain prepositions) limit its meaning and potential.

In this regard biblical Hebrew words operate like English words. But when dealing with Hebrew words, we are at a disadvantage because we are not part of the original author's community of speakers. We are not always sensitive to how context affects meaning, nor do we pick up intuitively on Hebrew linguistic conventions or recognize subconsciously a specialized or idiomatic use. At the same time, the task of biblical interpretation demands that we do our best to overcome the temporal, linguistic, and cultural obstacles that face us. To do so we must examine the biblical usage of words, noting carefully various contextual and linguistic factors that signal precise nuances of meaning in a given context.

Basic Meaning, Multiple Referents, and Polysemism

The first task in determining the meaning of a Hebrew word is to survey the term's usage in an effort to establish a basic definition. To illustrate the process, let's consider the Hebrew noun שַׁחַת, defined by BDB (1001) as "pit." A survey of usage shows a שַׁחַת can be made (Pss. 7:15, Eng.; 9:15, Eng.) by digging a hole (Ps. 94:13; Prov. 26:27). One can descend, plunge, fall, or sink into a שַׁחַת (Job 9:31; 33:24; Pss. 7:15, Eng.; 9:15, Eng.; 30:9, Eng.; Prov. 26:27; Ezek. 28:8); conversely one can be brought up from one (Jon. 2:6 Eng.). A שַׁחַת can also be used to catch a lion (Ezek. 19:4, 8). The evidence suggests that the noun does indeed mean "pit, hole."

Though the noun שַׁחַת always carries this basic meaning, merely assigning the term the definition of "pit, hole" does not adequately reflect the metaphorical use of this term. The word appears exclusively in poetic texts and is always employed metaphorically. In other words, when a biblical poet uses this word, he never has in mind simply a literal pit dug into the surface of the ground. Instead he is using the word "pit" and the mental image it creates to refer to and characterize an underlying reality. Like many nouns that are utilized metaphorically, שַׁחַת has multiple referents in its full range of usage. For example, in Proverbs 26:27 it represents trouble or calamity, which can ensnare one like a pit. In Ezekiel 19:4, 8 it is part of an extended metaphor and symbolizes Israel's place of exile, where God's people were trapped as if in a pit. Similarly in Isaiah 51:14 it stands metonymically for a dungeon or prison, which in turn symbolizes exile. In contexts where death and dying are in view, the word has become specialized and is used as an epithet for the grave and/or the place of the dead beneath the earth's surface (e.g., Job 17:14; 33:18, 22, 28, 30; Pss. 16:10; 49:9, Eng.; 55:23, Eng.; 103:4; Isa. 38:17; Ezek. 28:8; Jon. 2:6). One wonders if the word, when used as a name for death, has become purely referential and has "lost its punch" as an image. This often happens when a word or phrase achieves idiomatic status.

The word אָב, "father," is another example of a noun with multiple referents. It often refers to a literal progenitor, whether it be a father, grandfather, or more remote ancestor. But usage of the word is not limited to this literal sense. The noun can also refer to the originator of a class of people (Gen. 4:20–21). It is also used as a term of respect (1 Sam. 24:11, Eng.) and can refer metaphorically to a father-like protector (Job 29:16; Isa. 9:6; 22:21). In developing a word study of such nouns, one can make categorical distinctions on the basis of literal (or concrete) and metaphorical (or abstract) use.

The same can be said of many adjectives. For example, the English word "bad" can be defined in a very general way as "failing to measure up to a norm or proper standard." However, the word is used to modify a variety of nouns and this variety of application yields a wide range of specific nuances. For example, if we refer to "bad food," the adjective probably has the nuance "poor-tasting." (But if the food "has gone bad," it is rotten.) If we refer to a "bad back," the adjective now means "sore" or "injured." If we use the phrase "bad boy" or "bad dog," we are probably referring to a "naughty" child or "disobedient" pet. If we refer to a "bad man," the adjective takes on the moral/ethical nuance "evil" and may carry the connotation "dangerous."

The Hebrew adjective רַע, "bad, evil," functions much like its English equivalent and displays nuances of meaning ranging from the concrete (when focusing on a purely physical characteristic) to the abstract (when focusing on an immaterial characteristic). For example, the adjective sometimes focuses on the physical nature of something. It is used to describe "impure" water (2 Kings 2:19), "inedible" figs (Jer. 24:2), and "scrawny" cattle (Gen. 41:3). But it can also focus on immaterial characteristics. It is used of "unpleasant" or "difficult" times (Gen. 47:9) "fierce" or "dangerous" wild animals (Gen. 37:20), and a "saddened" heart (Prov. 25:20). It frequently describes "evil" people (Prov. 11:21), as well as "morally wrong" thoughts (Gen. 6:5) and actions (Deut. 17:5).

Verbs also can be used in both concrete and abstract senses. For example, the verb לָחַץ, which has a basic sense "to exert pressure," can be used of squeezing a foot against a wall (Num. 22:25) or holding a door shut (2 Kings 6:32). However, the verb is not always employed in such a concrete or literal manner. It also describes how the Amorites used their military power to restrict the Danites territorially (Judg. 1:34) and characterizes the Egyptians' socioeconomic oppression of the enslaved Israelites (Exod. 3:9).

As one can see from these examples, many words are polysemantic; they display several distinct nuances of meaning, often under the umbrella of a general semantic sense. Developing categories of meaning for such a word is actually a process of analyzing its polysemantic range. In addition to distinguishing between concrete (or literal) and abstract (or metaphorical) uses, one must also be attentive to the development of specialized meanings in particular contexts, the presence of metonymy, and precise syntactical combinations.

Words often develop specialized meanings in certain contexts. For example, the Hebrew verb יָדַע has the basic sense "to know, be aware, experience." But in its roughly 943 occurrences it displays a wide range of nuances and sometimes carries very specialized meanings. For example, in contexts where sexual intimacy or desire is in view, the verb is euphemistic and has the nuance, "to copulate, have sexual intercourse with" (see, e.g., Gen. 4:1; 19:5, 8). In contexts where an expression of allegiance is in view, the verb means "to recognize the authority of, submit to." For example, when the narrator informs us that Eli's sons "did not know the LORD" (1 Sam. 2:12), this does not mean they were "unaware" of who he was. Rather it means they "did not recognize his authority" over them, as evidenced by their sinful practices. In Jeremiah 22:16 "to know the LORD" does not mean "to be theologically astute" or "acquainted with," but, as exemplified by King Josiah, "to submit to the divine will by obedience to the divine command." (See also Exod. 5:2; Jer. 2:8; 4:22; 1 Chron. 28:9).

Recognizing the presence of metonymy is often the key to understanding a word's polysemantic range. Metonymy is a figure of speech where one word or phrase is substituted for another that is closely associated with it. For example, in the statement, "The White House said today," the phrase "the White House" stands by metonymy for "the President" or "the President's office speaking with his authority." Contextual factors must determine if "the White House" refers to the literal structure in which the president resides (e.g., "The First Lady hosted a party today on the White House lawn") or stands metonymically for its most important resident, the President himself. Often metonymic associations are based on cause-effect relationships. For example, if someone warns a youth, "Don't smoke; smoking can kill you," the speaker is using the word "smoking" in a metonymical sense. Technically speaking, the diseases caused by smoking, such as lung cancer, are what kills, not the literal act of smoking. But it is far more effective rhetorically and practically to bypass the immediate cause and attribute death directly to the ultimate cause.

Hebrew words are often used metonymically. For example, the noun עָוֹן, "sin, iniquity," often refers to a sinful act (e.g., 1 Sam. 20:1; note the question, "What have I done?"). But by metonymy it frequently refers to the immediate effect of sin, "guilt" (e.g., Job 33:9), or to its ultimate consequence, "punishment" (Ezek. 35:5). Contextual factors help one determine which nuance is primary in any given context. For example, when Cain objects to the Lord, "My עָוֹן is too great to bear," what does he mean?

He is not saying his "sin" is too heavy for him, for the idea is non-sensical. Perhaps he means he is overwhelmed by a sense of "guilt" as a result of his sin. In this case, Cain would be on the threshold of repentance. But is this really the case? Right before this the Lord outlines the nature of his punishment (vv. 11–12). Right after this Cain complains about his punishment (v. 14). Therefore, it is apparent that עָוֺן has its metonymic sense "punishment" in verse 13. Rather than expressing a sense of guilt, Cain, the hardened sinner, protests that God's penalty is too severe.

Paying attention to precise syntactical combinations can also be important in determining a word's semantic nuances and range. In fact, as illustrated above with the English word "run," sometimes a word only carries a particular meaning in relation to other words with which it is combined in idiomatic expressions.

For example, the Hebrew verb כָּרַת often means "cut off" or "cut down," but when בְּרִית, "covenant," appears as the object, the idiomatic phrase "cut a covenant" means "transact an agreement." (The origin of the idiom remains uncertain and is irrelevant to interpretation.)

The verb חָזָה means "see, look," but when followed by the preposition -בְּ (as in Job 36:25; Ps. 27:4; Song of Sol. 6:13, Eng.; Isa. 47:13; Mic. 4:11) it carries the nuance "gaze with awe, delight, or special interest" (unless the preposition is followed by the phrase "the days of," in which case it is simply temporal). When used with the object "vision" or a term characterizing a vision (such as "lie"), the verb has a specialized nuance, "see a prophetic vision, receive a prophetic oracle."

Though the noun עוֹלָם may approximate our idea of "eternity" in some contexts, it does not have this nuance when it follows the phrase "days of" (יְמֵי/יְמוֹת), for this idiomatic phrase means "antiquity" and refers to earlier periods in Israel's history (Deut. 32:7; Isa. 63:9, 11; Amos 9:11; Mic. 7:14; Mal. 3:14). In Micah 5:2 (Eng.) the phrase is sometimes understood as referring to the messianic king's eternal preexistence, but this seems unlikely in light of its usage. It is more probable that the prophet envisions this king as the second coming of David (see also Hos. 3:5; Jer. 30:9; Ezek. 34:23–24; 37:24–25), whose origins were in antiquity. (This is not to say that the prophets expected a literal return of the ancient king. For rhetorical effect, they depict the ideal Davidic king of the future as a second "David.")

Paying attention to such syntactical combinations sometimes proves to be the key to resolving exegetical problems. For example, in Ruth 1:21 Naomi laments: "the Lord has testified against me." The phrase עָנָה + -בְּ (qal), "testify against," is a well attested idiom deriving from a legal setting. The Septuagint version reads "humbled me" here, apparently understanding the verb as a piel (עִנָּה) from a homonymic root meaning "afflict." However, עִנָּה, "afflict," never introduces its object with -בְּ; when the preposition -בְּ is used with this verb, it is always adverbial ("in, with, through"). Therefore, to defend the Septuagint reading one would have to eliminate the preposition from the text.

Isaiah 52:13 provides another example of the importance of carefully observing precise linguistic form. Traditionally the verb יַזֶּה (hiphil) has been understood as a causative of נָזָה, "spurt, spatter," and translated, "sprinkle." In this case the passage pictures the Lord's servant in a priestly role as "sprinkling" (or spiritually cleansing) the nations. Though the verb נָזָה does occur in the hiphil with the meaning "sprinkle," there is one serious problem with the usual interpretation. In all other instances where the object or person sprinkled is indicated, the verb is combined with a preposition. This is not the case in Isaiah 52:13, unless one takes the following עָלָיו, "on him," with the preceding line. But then one would have to emend the verb to a plural, make the nations the subject of the verb "sprinkle," and take the Lord's servant as the object. Consequently some interpreters doubt the cultic idea of "sprinkling" is present here. Some emend the text; others propose a homonymic root meaning "spring, leap," which in the hiphil could mean "cause to leap, startle" and would fit the parallelism of the verse nicely. (Arguing for the cultic idiom here would be comparable to eliminating the preposition "to" from the English idiom "run to the store" and then trying to affirm that the resulting expression "run the store" means "go and shop quickly," when the phrase obviously has a different meaning.)

In 1 Chronicles 21:1 the noun שָׂטָן (without the article) is often understood as a proper name, "Satan." However, elsewhere in the Old Testament when this noun appears without the article it refers to a personal or national "adversary" in the human sphere. (In Num. 22:22, 32 the angel of the Lord assumes the role of Balaam's adversary.) Conversely when the noun refers to the spiritual entity known as "Satan," it has the article and is actually a title, "the Adversary" (see Job 1:6–9, 12; 2:1–4, 6–7; Zech. 3:1–2). In light of usage elsewhere, the adversary in 1 Chronicles 21:1 is more likely a nearby nation whose hostility against Israel incited or persuaded David to number the people so he could assess his military strength.[2] (We discover from the parallel passage in 2 Sam. 24:1 that the Lord was actually behind this.)

Some "Semantic Sins" to Avoid

Interpreters often do things with Hebrew words they would never dream of doing with words in their native language. Here are three of the most common "semantic sins" to avoid.

(1) Don't read more than one semantic nuance of a word into a specific usage. When determining the meaning of a word in a specific con-

---

2. For a more detailed defense of this view, see Sarah Japhet, *I & II Chronicles, A Commentary* (Philadelphia: Westminster, 1993), 374–75.

text, one attempts to identify which attested category of usage fits best. If contextual factors demand it, one might propose a unique category. (The latter often happens when usage of a word is relatively limited.) Granted, an author will sometimes employ double entendre, a rhetorical device in which two semantic nuances of a word operate simultaneously. (See our discussion of this literary technique below.) But this rhetorical technique is relatively rare. When determining the meaning of a word in a specific context, the interpreter should choose one, and only one, of the available nuances.

We intuitively recognize this principle when using our native tongue, but unfortunately interpreters often fail to observe it when dealing with Hebrew terms. To illustrate the absurdity of the semantic sin in question, let's use the word "Yankee" again. Suppose a Georgian hears the news that a native Alabaman playing for the Atlanta Braves has been traded to the New York Yankees. A baseball announcer then states that this player is "delighted to be a Yankee." It would be absurd for the Georgian to say: "That no good Alabaman! Not only is he happy to be playing for the Yankees, but he's also betrayed his southern roots and wants to be thought of as a northerner!" The Georgian would be guilty of reading two distinct nuances into a single usage. The Alabaman is not abandoning his southern heritage, but simply saying he is happy to be a member of the New York Yankees, probably because of a salary increase!

To illustrate this error with a Hebrew word, let's use again עָוֹן, "sin." In our earlier discussion we argued that contextual factors indicate that the word means "punishment" in Genesis 4:13. It would be inaccurate for an interpreter to read both "guilt" and "punishment" into Cain's statement and claim that Cain was both repentant and unhappy about his sentence.

(2) Don't assume there is a concrete word picture behind every abstract use of a word or phrase. Making such an assumption can produce some juicy preaching, but it can also lead to fanciful interpretation. Words and phrases often become idiomatic in a language. For example, to most English speakers the idiomatic expression "right from the horse's mouth" simply means "direct from the source." Few stop to think or even realize that the statement derives from a bygone era when horse traders examined a horse's teeth to determine or verify its age. Furthermore, no one envisions the source in question as looking like a horse! Even when an idiom's literal meaning is rather obvious, speakers and listeners rarely form a word picture when they use or hear it. For example, the expression "hold your horses" simply means "be patient" and rarely if ever conjures up an image of a wagon driver pulling back on the reins to keep his team of horses from bolting forward! While these expressions must have produced word pictures in the minds of those who first cre-

ated and used them, those mental images are long gone now that the expressions have achieved idiomatic status.

The same is true with many Hebrew words and phrases. For example, the expression תֹּאכַל הַחֶרֶב, "the sword devours" (see 2 Sam. 11:25), whatever its origin may have been, is purely idiomatic in biblical usage, meaning, "the sword violently kills." The verb אָכַל, "to eat," is often used of literally eating food, but when it appears with "the sword" as subject it should not conjure up an image of a sword with a mouth and teeth eating its victim!

The Hebrew verb חָטָא, "to sin," is sometimes defined as "to miss the mark," which may indeed reflect its original sense. Though the verb is used in Judges 20:16 of the Benjaminite slingers who could hit the smallest target without "missing the mark," it is very unlikely that the word picture of a projectile missing the target of God's moral standard flashed through the minds of an audience when a speaker used the word in a moral/ethical sense. In a moral/ethical context the word probably became idiomatic and, like our English verb "to sin" (the derivation of which most of us are totally unaware because it is irrelevant to meaning), simply conveyed the idea of disobedience.

Of course, this is not to say that biblical authors did not sometimes use words in artful ways to produce word pictures. Biblical poets, like their modern counterparts, often crafted expressions that utilize words in unique, metaphorical ways, creating a vivid and rhetorically effective word picture in the minds of the audience. For example, the author of Psalm 23 confidently declares, "Goodness and faithfulness will pursue me all the days of my life" (v. 6). This is the only place in the Old Testament where either טוֹב, "goodness," or חֶסֶד, "faithfulness," appears as the subject of the verb רָדַף, "pursue," so the word combination does not appear to be an idiom. This verb often describes the hostile actions of enemies, and it is noteworthy that the psalmist, in the preceding verse, tells how his adversaries are forced to stand by helplessly as the Lord wines and dines him as a sign of his favor. One might expect enemies to chase the psalmist, but ironically God's "goodness and faithfulness" (which are personified and stand by metonymy for God himself) pursue him instead. The word "pursue" is used outside its normal context in an ironic manner and creates a unique, but pleasant word picture of God's favor and faithfulness (or a favorably disposed and faithful God) "chasing down" the one whom he loves.

(3) Don't overextend or misapply a specialized meaning. As noted above, words often have specialized meanings in particular contexts. One must not apply a specialized meaning to a word when it is used outside such a context. For example, if a baseball announcer says, "The centerfielder ran into the rightfielder and dropped the ball," we know a literal collision occurred. However, if I say, "I was walking down the street

and ran into my best friend," we know that "ran into" simply means "met" (probably without prior arrangement). It would be absurd to assume that the centerfielder stopped and said hello to the rightfielder, or that I body checked my friend to the sidewalk. The expression "ran into" has distinct meanings in particular contexts and those contextual factors must be observed when determining meaning.

The same is often true of Hebrew words. For example, 1 Samuel 18:1 (see also vv. 3 and 20:17) states that Jonathan "loved" (אָהֵב) David. The verb אָהַב here has the specialized nuance "be loyal, devoted to," as it often does in contexts where a covenantal agreement is in view (see 18:3–4 and 20:16–17).[3] The word probably carries this same nuance in verse 16, which states that "all Israel and Judah loved David." In verse 22, where Saul's servants "love" David, the verb probably means "be attracted to, like." But in verses 20 and 28, where Saul's daughter Michal "loves" David, the word carries a romantic sense. One must be careful not to confuse these nuances. To suggest that Jonathan had some type of homosexual attraction to David would be contextually unwarranted. Granted, in 2 Samuel 1:26 David, in his ode to Jonathan, states: "Your love (אַהֲבָה, a nominal derivative of the verb אָהַב) for me surpassed the love (אַהֲבָה again) of women." But the larger context of the story, especially 1 Samuel 18–20 (where Jonathan's "love" is depicted as "allegiance"), does not justify understanding Jonathan's "love" in 2 Samuel 1:26 as sexual in nature. David's point is that Jonathan's allegiance to him was stronger and more enduring than the mere romantic love that a man receives from a woman. The juxtaposition of אַהֲבָה in two distinct senses produces a powerfully ironic statement that captures the lamenting poet's emotion over the loss of his devoted friend.

When a word develops a new, specialized use, one must be careful not to read this later specialized meaning into chronologically earlier occurrences of the word. For example, the English word "gay" was once used in a wide variety of contexts to mean "happy, jolly." I recall reading a picture book to my children when they were very young in which one of the pictures was captioned "a gay clown." The book was published in the 1950s and was obviously using the term "gay" in its older, general sense. However, the term "gay" has experienced a semantic shift in recent decades and has acquired a highly specialized, euphemistic sense that has crowded out the older meaning. Interpreting the caption to the clown's picture in light of this recent development would lead to an inaccurate anachronistic interpretation of the caption.

While modern mass media facilitates rapid and widespread linguistic change of this type, similar shifts also occurred with biblical Hebrew words. For the most part, lexical usage in the Bible reflects a later period

---

3. In this regard, see J. A. Thompson, "The Significance of the Verb *Love* in the David-Jonathan Narratives in 1 Samuel," *Vetus Testamentum* 24 (1974): 334–38.

of time, so we do not have access to enough truly early Hebrew to be able to trace a lot of chronological shifts of this nature in biblical Hebrew. Nevertheless one can detect some instances of the phenomenon.

For example, the Hebrew word סָרִיס is usually defined as "eunuch" on the basis of etymological data, usage (see Isa. 56:3), and awareness of the ancient practice of utilizing castrated men in royal courts. However, in Genesis 39:1 this word is used of Potiphar, who had a wife. Coarse humor might be involved (if Potiphar were a eunuch, that might explain his wife's actions!), but this seems highly questionable. It is more likely that the term originally referred to a high court official in general and then in the course of time was applied to a more specialized type of official.

Sometimes Hebrew words acquire a specialized meaning or sense after the biblical period. For example, the noun בְּלִיַּעַל, "uselessness, wickedness, good for nothing" (see K–B, 133–34), becomes a name or title for the devil in intertestamental literature and in the New Testament (2 Cor. 6:15; see BAG, 138). However, it should not be understood as a proper name for Satan in the Old Testament, where it is consistently used as a common noun.[4]

Semantic Fields and Synonyms

Examining a word in its larger semantic context is another aspect of lexical study. This involves comparing and contrasting the usage of synonyms, a group of words that share the same general semantic notion. Words are rarely completely synonymous in their total range of usage. An examination of usage usually reveals areas where terms overlap and can be used interchangeably, as well as distinct nuances. For example, consider the English synonyms "hard" and "rough." Both can mean "difficult to endure" (e.g., "it was a rough/hard experience to go through") but each has its own distinct nuances. "Rough" has other nuances of meaning, including "coarse" (as in "rough surface") or "imperfect" (as in "rough draft"). "Hard" has many nuances, including "solid" (as in "hard surface"), "intense" (as in "a hard rain"), "intoxicating" (as in "hard liquor"), and "addictive" (as in "hard drugs"). Sometimes one word in a semantic field may have a broad range of usage which encompasses the semantic nuances of a word that is more restricted in meaning. For example, consider the synonyms "hard" and "difficult." As illustrated above, "hard" has a broad range of usage, which includes the ideas expressed by "difficult": "hard to do," "hard to endure," "hard to comprehend," "hard to please," "hard to manage," and "hard to persuade."

Hebrew synonyms operate the same way. For example, the synonyms נָסָה and בָּחַן are defined as "test." Their usage overlaps at points. Both

---

4. A possible exception is 2 Sam. 22:5/Ps. 18:4 (Eng.), where the noun may be an epithet for Sheol/Death.

often mean "put to the test, examine." נָסָה is used quite often of people trying God's patience, a sense that בָּחַן only rarely has. Each word is also distinct from the other in certain cases. נָסָה can mean "attempt to do" and "train," while בָּחַן can mean "refine (metal)."

If one examines the semantic field for verbs meaning "to kill," one discovers that הָרַג is used in a broad range of contexts and can mean "murder," "strike down in battle," and "execute (in a judicial sense)." רָצַח, the verb used in the sixth commandment of the Decalogue, is used of murder as well, but only rarely does it mean "execute (in a judicial sense)." It can refer to taking someone's life unintentionally or accidentally, but it is never used of killing in the context of war.[5]

One should not be too quick to blur semantic distinctions between synonyms. For example, let's consider the use of the synonyms אָמָה and שִׁפְחָה, both of which refer to a female servant. Based on a statement made by Abigail in 1 Samuel 25:41, some propose that a שִׁפְחָה was a lowly female servant who did the most menial tasks and that an אָמָה was a higher class of servant who might expect some special recognition from her superior. In this passage Abigail says to David: "Look, your אָמָה has become a שִׁפְחָה, washing the feet of my master's servants." There seems to be a distinction here, but does usage outside this single verse support this proposal?

Let's start with Abigail's use of the terms in 1 Samuel 25. In her conversation with David she describes herself with אָמָה six times (vv. 24–25, 28, 31, 41) and with שִׁפְחָה twice (vv. 27, 41). With the exception of verse 41, her usage of the terms seems to be interchangeable. But a closer examination of the passage from a rhetorical angle reveals that she has carefully chosen her terms. When she is requesting an audience (v. 24), pledging her loyalty (v. 25), and asking for mercy (vv. 28, 31) she uses אָמָה, which reflects her subordinate position but may also hint at some obligation on David's part. But when she mentions her gift (v. 27) and expresses her willingness to serve (v. 41), she switches to שִׁפְחָה, which suggests a more abject form of servitude. In doing so, she emphasizes her humble attitude.

The terms are also used in a rhetorically distinct manner in two other passages in the Books of Samuel where they occur together. When conversing with Eli, Hannah uses both אָמָה (1 Sam. 1:16) and שִׁפְחָה (v. 18) to describe herself and acknowledge her subordinate position before the priest. At first, the terms appear to be interchangeable, but a closer look reveals a rhetorical purpose to the word choice and supports a semantic

---

5. The sixth commandment of the Decalogue has murder in mind. Capital punishment cannot be in view, for the Old Testament law frequently authorizes it for certain offenses. Accidental killing is probably not included, because of the imperatival tone of the statement. After all, it would be absurd to command someone, "Don't accidentally kill anybody!" Killing in warfare is not included for the Old Testament authorizes war in many cases, and רָצַח is never used elsewhere in the context of war.

distinction. In verse 16 Hannah uses אָמָה when contrasting herself with "a wicked woman." Using the more elevated term strengthens the contrast. But in verse 18, where she requests Eli's continued favor, she switches to שִׁפְחָה because she now wants to emphasize her humility and absolute dependence.

The woman of Tekoa also uses the terms in a rhetorically distinct manner in her conversation with David, recorded in 2 Samuel 14. She describes herself with שִׁפְחָה six times (vv. 6–7, 12, 15a, 17, 19) and with אָמָה twice (vv. 15b–16). In this case the woman, who has been sent by Joab, uses שִׁפְחָה predominantly because she wants to emphasize her humility before the king. However, in the quote within the quote in verses 15b–16, where she claims to tell the king what she thought prior to this, she switches to אָמָה. Why? Because her request at this point implies some obligation to do justice on the king's part, and the more elevated term, while still expressing due respect for the king's authority, suggests he has some responsibility to her.

Usage of the terms in the Book of Ruth also supports the proposed distinction. In Ruth 2, where Ruth has just arrived from Moab and is very much aware of her position as a foreigner (v. 10), she acknowledges Boaz's kindness and emphasizes her own humility by using the term שִׁפְחָה (v. 13), though she admits that she does not even occupy that lowly position on the social scale. However, in chapter 3, where Naomi sends her to Boaz to seek marriage, she uses the more elevated term אָמָה (v. 9) to describe herself because she is now aware of Boaz's responsibility as a near-kinsman of her deceased husband and she wants to challenge him to fulfill his obligation. In her new social context she is dependent on Boaz (hence the use of אָמָה), but she is no mere שִׁפְחָה.

When one moves to the Book of Genesis, the semantic distinction proposed above seems operative as well, though not necessarily in every instance. For example, in Genesis 29–35 שִׁפְחָה is used of Zilpah and Bilhah, the female servants given by Laban to his daughters Leah and Rachel, respectively (29:24, 29; 30:4, 7, 9–10, 12, 18; 32:22; 33:1–2, 6; 35:25–26). אָמָה is used only twice of Zilpah and Bilhah in this context (30:3; 31:33). In 30:3–4 the narrator refers to Bilhah as Rachel's שִׁפְחָה (v. 4), while Rachel, in requesting that Jacob sleep with Bilhah, employs אָמָה. The terms look purely interchangeable, though it is possible that Rachel uses the more elevated term to try to make Bilhah look better in Jacob's eyes and to encourage him to comply with her request. However, no such explanation presents itself for the narrator's use of אָמָה in 31:33, reminding us that terms, while sometimes distinct in one context, may be interchangeable in another.

Both terms are used of Hagar earlier in Genesis. In chapter 16 she is consistently called a שִׁפְחָה (vv. 1–3, 5–6, 8), but in chapter 21 she is exclusively called an אָמָה (vv. 10, 12–13). Usage seems interchangeable and source critics have pointed to the variation in terminology as evidence for editorial activity, but there may be a better explanation for the use of the terms. In chapter 16 the term שִׁפְחָה is used consistently of Hagar's relationship to Sarai (note "She had an Egyptian servant," v. 1; "my servant," vv. 2, 5; "her servant," v. 3; "your servant," v. 6; "Sarai's servant," v. 8, see also 25:12). However, in chapter 21 Hagar is called an אָמָה in relationship to Abraham (v. 12) and as a mother of Abraham's child (vv. 10, 13). Though Hagar may have been a mere שִׁפְחָה in relation to Sarai, once she became Abram's wife (cf. 16:3) and mothered his child, she gained a more elevated status, becoming the patriarch's אָמָה.

In poetic parallelism, close synonyms are often used in a purely interchangeable manner for stylistic variety. For example, Proverbs 2:11 states: "Discretion will guard you; understanding will protect you." The verbs שָׁמַר, "guard," and נָצַר, "protect," are synonymous and interchangeable here, as are the nouns מְזִמָּה, "discretion," and תְּבוּנָה, "understanding." In Psalm 51:2 (Eng.) the psalmist pleads: "Wash away my iniquity (עָוֹן), and cleanse me from my sin (חַטָּאת)." It is doubtful that he is trying to make any subtle distinction between aspects of sin (the distinction sometimes proposed between these terms is based on etymology, not usage). It is more likely that he is utilizing synonymous terms for "sin" for the sake of stylistic variety. Perhaps he also wants to emphasize the degree of his sin by heaping up terms to describe it. The point would be: Whatever you want to call it, I've done it and need forgiveness.

When terms are only loosely associated, one should preserve semantic distinctions. Sometimes one word will specifically define or illustrate its more general counterpart in the parallel line. For example, in Psalm 2:10 the psalmist exhorts the pagan kings: "Now, you kings, act wisely! Submit to instruction, you rulers of the earth!" The two imperatives are semantically distinct. הַשְׂכִּילוּ is an exhibitive hiphil from שָׂכַל, "be wise," while הִוָּסְרוּ is a tolerative niphal from יָסַר, "instruct." The first verb is a general exhortation to act wisely; the second indicates more specifically how they should do this (by being teachable).

Developing a Usage Survey: A Sample Study of the Verb כָּבַשׁ

If one wanted to research what the Bible has to say about the current environmentalist debate, it would be important to probe the meaning of Genesis 1:28, where God says to the first man and woman: "Be fruitful and increase in number; fill the earth and subdue it." What exactly does the command "subdue it" mean? One of the steps in answering that question would be to survey the usage of the verb "subdue" (כָּבַשׁ) in order to formulate the word's basic definition and determine its range of meaning. To illustrate the process we include an inductive survey of the term followed by a summary of observations and a proposal as to its meaning in Genesis 1:28.

Usage Survey of כָּבַשׁ

This verb appears fourteen times in the Old Testament, eight times in the qal stem, five times in the niphal, and once in the piel.

Qal usage

Genesis 1:28: God commands humankind (the male and female) to subdue the earth (the obvious antecedent of the feminine singular suffix on the verb). This is our target passage and is discussed further below.

Nehemiah 5:5: Some members of the postexilic community lament the fact that they are about to be forced to give their children up as slaves to pay off their debts.

Esther 7:8: The king, seeing Haman sprawled on the bed with Esther, accuses him of attempted rape. The verb could be translated, "rape, sexually assault."

2 Chronicles 28:10: The prophet Oded denounces King Ahaz because of his plan to enslave some of his countrymen.

Jeremiah 34:11, 16: The rich of Jerusalem have "enslaved" many of their countrymen. In verse 11 the consonantal text (kethib) assumes a hiphil form, but the qere (marginal reading) understands the verb as a qal form.

Micah 7:19: The verb describes what the Lord will do to Israel's sin. The precise nuance is uncertain, but the action is the result of divine compassion and depicts the removal of sin. Assigning the verb a more precise nuance must await the completion of the survey.

Zechariah 9:13: The verb is used in a militaristic context and describes the victory of Israelite forces over their enemies. The verb seems to mean "subdue" or "defeat."

Niphal usage

Numbers 32:22, 29: Moses makes reference to the promised land "being conquered" or "subdued."

Joshua 18:1: The narrator observes that Joshua's military success has left the promised land "conquered" or "subdued" before Israel.

1 Chronicles 22:18: David points out to the nation's leaders that the earth (i.e., the people of the surrounding territory) lies "conquered" or "subdued" before Israel.

Nehemiah 5:5: The people lament that some of their daughters have been "enslaved" as payment for their debts.

Piel usage

2 Samuel 8:11: The narrator refers to David's conquest of the surrounding nations. The piel is probably pluralative, referring to David's various campaigns. Note the plural object "nations."

One can assign this verb the following basic definition: "to bring under control for one's advantage." One can detect this general "umbrella" meaning behind the specific semantic nuances, which, with the exception of Genesis 1:28, can be categorized as follows:

(1) to enslave (Jer. 34:11, 16; 2 Chron. 28:10; Neh. 5:5)
(2) to conquer, subdue (Num. 32:22, 29; Josh. 18:1; 2 Sam. 8:11; 1 Chron. 22:18; Zech. 9:13). This is probably the nuance in Micah 7:19, where "sin" is likened to an enemy that needs to be defeated.
(3) to molest, sexually assault (Esther 7:8)

The Meaning of the Verb in Genesis 1:28

Before one can consider the nuance of the verb in Genesis 1:28, the object of the verb (the earth) must be defined contextually. According to Genesis 1, the "earth" is the sphere of humankind's physical existence which the human race is to populate. It is composed of dry land, is distinct from the sky and the sea (vv. 6–10), and includes vegetation (vv. 11–12, 30) and land animals (vv. 24–26, 29).

Now the attested meanings of the verb must be considered. The nuances "enslave" and "rape" are foreign to the context of Genesis 1:28, where humankind's rulership over the earth on behalf of God is a central theme. Because humankind is depicted as God's vice-regent in verse 26, one could understand the verb in the sense of "conquer" or "subdue," but the earth is not cast in the role of an enemy or opponent of humankind.

Since none of the attested nuances adequately meets the contextual demands of Genesis 1:28, we must propose a distinct nuance of meaning that comes under the umbrella of the basic definition we have assigned the word. Taking into account the nature of the object (which includes the physical earth as well as the vegetation and land animals) and the general sense of the word, we propose adding this category of meaning to our list of uses:

(4) to harness the potential of, use for one's benefit (Gen. 1:28).

We offer the following paraphrase of verse 28: "Have a lot of children and populate the earth! Harness its potential and use its resources for your benefit." As one can see, the verb does not mean "ruin" or "destroy," nor does it suggest anything approaching "worship, treat like fragile china, be at one with." The context of rulership militates against abuse of the earth being in view, but it also prohibits putting the earth on a par with humankind, God's designated king over the created order. The point seems to be that the earth is at humankind's disposal. In the ancient Near Eastern context of the passage, harnessing the earth's potential would include, among other things, mining its riches, cultivating its fields, using its trees for lumber, and domesticating its animals so they might be used in the service of humankind. As modern science has developed, we have discovered new ways to carry out this mandate as God's vice-regents over the created order. In short, the earth exists as humankind's dominion and for his benefit.

Determining the Meaning of Rare Words

As we have seen, examining a word's usage is important when trying to determine meaning. However, sometimes, especially in Hebrew poetry, one will encounter a word that is only rarely used in the Old Testament. In fact the Old Testament contains several hapax legomena (words that occur only once). To determine the meaning of rare words and hapax legomena, one must examine derivatives (related words derived from the same root) within biblical Hebrew, evidence from cognate languages, and the context of the passage where the term is used. To illustrate this process we include sample studies of four such words.

(1) The noun מַצּוּת in Isaiah 41:12

In this passage the Lord promises his people:

"You will look for them, but not find them—the men of your ???;
they will completely disappear—the men of your warfare."

The word מַצּוּת, which appears at the end of the first line of the poetic couplet, appears only here in the Old Testament. Both BDB (663) and K–B (623) define the word as "strife." On what basis do they make this proposal?

The structure of the word (note the dagesh forte in the middle letter, indicating an assimilated nun) suggests that it is derived from the root נצה. This root is attested in a verb נָצָה, which occurs several times in the Old Testament and means "struggle" (BDB, 663) or "fight" (K–B, 715). There is also a nominal derivative מַצָּה, which occurs three times and means "strife" (BDB, 623; K–B, 622). These derivatives suggest a meaning "strife" for the related noun מַצּוּת in Isaiah 41:12. Under the verbal root נָצָה K–B (715) also lists several cognate Semitic languages in which the root is attested with the same or similar lexical idea. Of course, all of this information is irrelevant if the context of the passage does not admit the proposed idea. However, in this case the context not only allows the idea, it supports it. The passage refers to the conflict between Israel and its enemies, and our word is part of a phrase that describes these enemies. The phrase in the next line, אַנְשֵׁי מִלְחַמְתֶּךָ, "men of your warfare," corresponds to אַנְשֵׁי מַצֻּתֶךָ. Thus we can safely assume that our word מַצּוּת is associated, at least loosely, with מִלְחָמָה, "warfare." Furthermore, the preceding verse describes this same group as "those who rage against you" and as אַנְשֵׁי רִיבֶךָ, "men of your opposition." The contextual evidence is consistent with what the derivatives and cognates suggest. The noun מַצּוּת means "strife." (The second-person suffix used in these three phrases is an objective genitive. The phrases in vv. 11b–12 may be translated, "the men who oppose you," "the men who strive with you," and "the men who war with you," respectively.)

(2) The verb נָעַר in Jeremiah 51:38

In this passage the prophet describes the Babylonians:

"In unison they roar like young lions,
they ??? like lion cubs."

The verb נָעַר, which appears at the beginning of the second line of the poetic couplet, occurs only here in the Old Testament. Furthermore, there are no derivatives of the verb in biblical Hebrew. Nevertheless, both BDB (654) and K–B (706–7) define the word as "growl." On what basis? K–B indicates that the verb shows up in later Hebrew (where it is used of the braying of a donkey) and in cognate Semitic languages, where it is used of the sounds emitted by donkeys, lions, and oxen. Since lions are in view in Jeremiah 51:38, one can safely assume that the verb refers to a lion's roar or growl. The poetic structure of the verse supports this proposal, for נָעַר corresponds to the well-attested verb שָׁאַג, "roar."

(3) The verb שָׁתַע in Isaiah 41:10a

In this passage the Lord encourages his people:

"Don't be afraid, for I am with you,
don't ???, for I am your God."

According to BDB (1043), the verb תִּשְׁתָּע in the second line of the poetic couplet is a hithpael form from the verb שָׁעָה, "gaze" (with metathesis of the stem prefix and the first root letter). Taking the hithpael as iterative, one may then translate, "do not anxiously look about" (cf. NAS). However, the alleged hithpael form of שָׁעָה occurs only here and in verse 23.

The supplement to the second edition of the Koehler-Baumgartner lexicon (192) proposes that the verb is instead a qal form from the verb שָׁתַע, "fear," the existence of which is not even acknowledged by BDB. What support is there for this newer proposal? Evidence from the cognate Semitic languages, including Ugaritic (discovered after the publication of BDB), suggests the existence of this root. The poetic structure of verse 10 also supports the proposal, for the form in question is parallel to יָרֵא, "fear."[6] (In the Kethib of verse 23, the cohortative form [נִשְׁתָּעָה] of

---

6. See Harold R. (Chaim) Cohen, *Biblical Hapax Legomena in the Light of Akkadian and Ugaritic* (Missoula, Mont.: Scholars, 1978), 44.

the verb שָׁתַע is combined with the prefixed form of יְרָא. The Qere suggests the verb רָאָה, "see," which might favor the older derivation of נִשְׁתָּעָה, but certainly wouldn't necessitate it.)

(4) The noun חַשְׁרָה in 2 Samuel 22:12

In this verse the poet describes the Lord as follows:

"He made darkness his covering around him,
a ??? of water, the clouds of the sky."

According to BDB (366), the hapax legomenon חַשְׁרָה, which appears in a construct form at the beginning of the second line of the poetic couplet, means "collection, mass" (cf. NAS). This proposal is based on supposed evidence (now considered invalid) from the cognate Semitic language Akkadian listed under the root חשׁר. According to the second edition of the Koehler-Baumgartner lexicon (342), the lexical form is not legitimate; they suggest it is a textual corruption of חֶשְׁכָה, "darkness," which appears in the parallel version of the poem (see Ps. 18:11, Eng.).

However, K–B (363) lists the noun חַשְׁרָה with the meaning "(heavenly) sieve." This proposal is based on evidence from later Hebrew and the cognate Semitic languages. In later Hebrew and Aramaic a verb חשׁר, "sift, spread," is attested, while Ugaritic contains a cognate noun meaning "sieve." But does the meaning "sieve" fit the context of 2 Samuel 22:12? One may understand the phrase "sieve of waters" as a reference to the clouds, which are mentioned in the following phrase. The clouds are compared to a sieve that allows water to pour through to the earth below.[7]

Words at Play

The Old Testament sometimes uses words in a highly rhetorical manner. Through repetition and soundplay a speaker or author will sometimes draw attention to a statement or theme. Double entendre may be used in the service of irony, and literary allusion can be used to correlate a statement with an earlier tradition and/or to lend rhetorical punch to a statement.

Word Repetition

Sometimes a speaker or author will emphasize a theme by repeating a "key word." For example, in 1 Samuel 18 the narrator uses the Hebrew verb אָהַב, "to love," six times (vv. 1, 3, 16, 20, 22, 28) to emphasize how

7. See Frank Moore Cross Jr. and David Noel Freedman, *Studies in Ancient Yahwistic Poetry* (Missoula, Mont.: Scholars, 1975), 146.

David won the hearts of all who came in contact with him. Various individuals and groups are said to "love" David, including Saul's son Jonathan (vv. 1, 3), all Israel and Judah (vv. 16, 28), Saul's daughter Michal (v. 20), and all Saul's servants (v. 22). Though the word is used with different semantic nuances in these verses (see our earlier discussion), its repetition highlights the popularity of David. (This verb is only used in three other passages in 1 Samuel [1:5; 16:21; 20:17]. In two of these David, as in chapter 18, appears as the object. According to 16:21, Saul loved David greatly, and 20:17 once more mentions Jonathan's love for David.)

Repetition of a key word can sometimes correlate themes and highlight contrasts. For example, in 2 Kings 1 a royal official twice demands that Elijah "come down" (an imperatival form of יָרַד is used) from his perch on a hilltop and report to the king (vv. 9, 11). In both cases the prophet responds by calling fire down upon the messenger and his troops (Elijah uses a jussive form of יָרַד in both cases, vv. 10, 12). Twice the narrator reports that fire did indeed come down (a preterite form of יָרַד is used) and destroy the captain and his men (vv. 10, 12). The repetition of the word highlights the fact that the messengers' disrespect (epitomized by their command "come down") was the reason for their destruction (described by the report "fire came down"). In the story's third panel, in which the king's third messenger shows the prophet due respect, the Lord gives the command "go down" (v. 15, imperatival form of יָרַד), reminding us that God's prophets march only to the beat of his drum, not that of a mere human ruler. This time Elijah, rather than destructive fire, "goes down" (v. 15, preterite form), emphasizing that respect for a prophet will get positive results, while disrespect will have only negative repercussions.

In 2 Samuel 11 the narrator uses the verb שָׁלַח, "send," seven times with David as subject. David is seemingly all-powerful. He sends people where he wills (vv. 1, 3–4, 12, 27), and by merely sending a message he can accomplish his desires (vv. 6, 14). The repetition of the verb highlights David's sovereignty. But David uses his power to exploit and murder, and God will not sit by idly. He "sends" (שָׁלַח) his prophet Nathan to denounce David's actions (2 Sam. 12:1); God, not David, is the one who is truly sovereign. He announces that David's children will suffer because of their father's sins. From this point on David is a mere pawn in the hands of the divine Judge. He unwittingly "sends" (שָׁלַח) his daughter Tamar to be raped (2 Sam. 13:7) and his son Amnon to his death (2 Sam. 13:27). The appearance of the verb in these chapters highlights the correlation between David's sin and punishment.

In Jonah 1 the Lord commands the prophet: "Get up (קוּם)! Go to Nineveh, the great city, and cry out (קְרָא) against it!" (v. 2). Jonah instead heads the opposite way, toward distant Tarshish. But God prevents his escape by sending a powerful storm. Everybody and everything responds to God's intervention, except Jonah, who falls into a deep sleep in the hold of the ship. But the captain, eager to enlist prayer support from everyone aboard, comes and awakens him with these words, "Get up! Cry out!" (קוּם קְרָא, v. 6). One can just imagine bleary-eyed, half-asleep Jonah waking up to the sound of these strangely familiar words, wondering if God had become incarnate in the person of the captain![8] The repetition highlights the fact that God, through powerful direct intervention in nature and providential control over the lips of a pagan sailor, is not going to allow Jonah to run from his commission.

Soundplay

Quite frequently biblical poets will employ words that sound similar to highlight a statement. For example, Amos warns the people not to engage in religious rituals at Gilgal, "because Gilgal will surely go into exile" (הַגִּלְגָּל גָּלֹה יִגְלֶה, Amos 5:5). The Hebrew text consists of the proper name "Gilgal" followed by the infinitive absolute and a finite form of the verb גָּלָה, "go into exile." The repetition of "g" and "l" sounds (the "g/l" sequence occurs four times in a space of ten letters) draws attention to this highly ironic statement. Gilgal was Israel's first campsite when they crossed the Jordan and invaded the promised land. As such, it symbolized possession of the land and fulfillment of God's promise. Certainly Gilgal, of all places, would be spared the judgment of exile. Not so, Amos declares with rhetorical flair!

In Isaiah 24:17–18a the prophet warns: "Terror, pit, and a snare are ready to overtake you inhabitants of the earth. The one who runs away from the sound of the terror will fall into a pit; the one who climbs out of the pit will be caught in a snare." The names of the three instruments (פַּחַד וָפַחַת וָפָח) of judgment all begin with the letters פ; the first two also end in dental consonants (ד/ת). The repetition of sound draws attention to the statement and contributes to the theme of the inescapability of judgment. As their similar-sounding names suggest, terror, pit, and snare are allies in destroying the objects of divine wrath.

Double Entendre

Occasionally a speaker or narrator will employ double entendre, where a single word has more than one semantic nuance in the same context. For example, in Jonah 4:6a the narrator observes: "The Lord God prepared a plant and caused it to grow up over Jonah to provide shade over his head, to deliver him from his distress." An initial reading of the statement suggests that רָעָה, "distress," refers to Jonah's physical discomfort,

---

8. See Leslie C. Allen, *The Books of Joel, Obadiah, Jonah and Micah* (Grand Rapids: Eerdmans, 1976), 207–8.

caused by the hot sun beating down on his head. Jonah is happy about the plant, but God quickly destroys it, prompting one more complaint from Jonah and the book's final dialogue, which is designed to show Jonah why God has been merciful to Nineveh. At this point the statement in verse 6a takes on deeper meaning. If God were just concerned about Jonah's physical comfort, he would not have destroyed the plant he made. Through the object lesson of the plant, he really wants to purge Jonah of his morally wrong attitude. One can now detect a double meaning in the word רָעָה. On the surface it means "physical discomfort," but it also has deeper meaning. God made the plant grow to give Jonah some temporary relief from his physical discomfort, but his larger purpose in making the plant was to use it as an object lesson in ridding Jonah of his moral "evil," another attested nuance of this noun.[9]

Verbal Allusion

Sometimes a speaker or author will use a key word or phrase to allude to an earlier text of Scripture as part of his or her rhetorical strategy. One must be careful here, for it is easy to misinterpret the use of an idiom as allusion. There is room for creativity, but at the same time caution must be employed. The verbal connection between the passages must be precise, the word or phrase involved must not be used so frequently that it qualifies as an idiom, there should be a thematic link between the two texts, and, ideally at least, there should be other contextual linguistic links between the passages. Consider the following examples:

(1) The use of the phrase תֹהוּ וָבֹהוּ, "unformed and unfilled," in Jeremiah 4:23 looks like a verbal allusion to Genesis 1:2. This precise phrase occurs in only these two texts, and the references to the "earth" (אֶרֶץ) and the "light" (אוֹר) of the "heavens" (שָׁמַיִם) in the immediate context of both passages supports a thematic link. Closer examination shows that Jeremiah is depicting judgment as an undoing or reversal of creation in which the earth will return to its primordial, unformed, and unfilled condition. (By the way, allusion only works one way. It would be unwarranted to assume that Jeremiah's use of the phrase in a context of judgment implies some sort of judgment in the context of Gen. 1:2. Jeremiah is applying the language of Gen. 1:2 to the judgment he foresees; he is not interpreting the meaning of Gen. 1:2. The allusion simply suggests that the coming judgment will disrupt the order that God originally established when he made a world out of the unformed and unfilled condition described in Gen. 1:2.)

In summary, there is a precise verbal connection between the two texts, the phrase in question is limited to these passages, there is a close

9. See Jonathan Magonet, *Form and Meaning: Studies in Literary Techniques in the Book of Jonah,* 2nd ed. (Sheffield: Almond, 1983), 24–25.

thematic connection (description of primordial, uncreated state of earth // description of postjudgment state of earth, which constitutes a return to a primordial, uncreated state), and contextual verbal links are present. It is almost certain that Jeremiah 4:23 alludes to Genesis 1:2.

(2) In Hosea 10:8 the prophet announces that Israel will be judged for its idolatry. He warns that "thorns and thistles" (קוֹץ וְדַרְדַּר) will grow up over the ruined altars. The precise phrase קוֹץ וְדַרְדַּר, "thorns and this- ✓ tles," occurs only here and in Genesis 3:18, where the growth of "thorns and thistles" is announced as one of the consequences of humankind's sin. Since the precise wording is limited to these two contexts, which both deal with the theme of divine judgment, it is possible that Hosea is alluding to the Genesis passage. If so, he would be suggesting that one of the effects of Israel's coming judgment will be similar to one of the consequences experienced by Adam when he rebelled.

However, this proposed allusion would be on more solid ground if one could find other links between the two contexts. Perhaps Hosea 10:13 contains such a link, when it states, "you have eaten the fruit of decep- tion." Both "eat" (אָכַל) and "fruit" (פְּרִי) are prominent words in Genesis 3 (vv. 1–3, 5–6, 11–13, 17), but "fruit" frequently appears as the object of "eat" in the Old Testament. The theme of deception is also present in Genesis 3, but the term used in Hosea 10:13 (כָּחַשׁ) is not the same word used by the woman to describe how the serpent tricked her (Gen. 3:13; she uses the hiphil of נָשָׁא). The phrase פְּרִי כָחַשׁ, "fruit of deception," oc- curs nowhere but Hosea 10:13 in the Old Testament.

In summary, there is a precise verbal connection between the two texts and the phrase in question is limited to these passages. There is a general thematic connection (divine judgment) and contextual verbal links are present. It is probable that Hosea 10:8 alludes to Genesis 3:18, but there is reason to question the validity of the proposal.

(3) In Amos 5:17 the Lord warns sinful Israel: "In all your vineyards there will be wailing, for I will pass through your midst" (אֶעֱבֹר בְּקִרְבֶּךָ). Some have suggested that these words allude to Exodus 12:12, where the Lord announces, "I will pass through the land of Egypt (וְעָבַרְתִּי בְאֶרֶץ־מִצְרַיִם) and strike dead all the firstborn." In both texts the Lord announces divine judgment, using the construction עָבַר (in the qal stem) + -בְּ + noun. If there ✓ is an allusion, the Lord would be making the highly ironic point that he was about to judge his own people the same way he had judged their enemies in the days of Moses.

But is the linguistic evidence restricted enough to support the pro- posed allusion? The construction עָבַר (in the qal stem) + -בְּ + noun is very common in the Old Testament. However, if we restrict our search to in- stances where the verb is first-person singular (whether in the perfect, imperfect, or preterite), the construction occurs just ten times, with God as the speaker only in Exodus 12:12 and Amos 5:17.

Are there any contextual links that would strengthen the proposal? The references to weeping and wailing in Amos 5:16–17 suggest a thematic connection to Exodus 11:6 and 12:30, but a closer examination indicates that one should not put too much weight on this link, for none of the terms used in Amos 5:16–17 (מִסְפֵּד, אֵבֶל, נְהִי) appears in Exodus 11:6 or 12:30, where the phrase צְעָקָה גְדֹלָה refers to the "great wailing" of the Egyptians.

In summary, the phrases similar but not exact, instances of God stating he will "pass through" are limited to these two texts, and a general thematic connection exists (God's passing through brings death and mourning in its wake). It is possible that Amos 5:17 alludes to Exodus 12:12, but there is also reason to challenge the validity of the proposal.

(4) In Isaiah 47:1 the Lord taunts personified Babylon. Picturing the city as a queen who will be humiliated, he says: "You will no longer be called 'delicate' and 'pampered' (רַכָּה וַעֲנֻגָּה)." This collocation of adjectives occurs elsewhere only in Deuteronomy 28:54, 56, where it is used of a "delicate and pampered" man and woman who, acting totally out of character, eat their own children during a time of siege and famine. However, apart from this linguistic connection, there is no basis for proposing a literary allusion in Isaiah 47:1. There is no thematic connection between the passages. Both deal with the general theme of judgment, but Deuteronomy 28 contains a list of "curses" to be implemented against Israel if she disobeys God's law, while Isaiah 47 is a taunt song against Babylon. The phrase "delicate and pampered," though limited to these texts, is probably an idiom, comparable to the English expression "molly-coddled."

For Further Reading and Reference

Barr, James. *The Semantics of Biblical Language.* London: Oxford University Press, 1961.

Caird, G. B. *The Language and Imagery of the Bible.* Philadelphia: Westminster, 1980.

Chisholm, Robert B., Jr. "Wordplay in the Eighth-Century Prophets." *Bibliotheca Sacra* 144 (1987): 44–52.

Cohen, Harold R. (Chaim). *Biblical Hapax Legomena in the Light of Akkadian and Ugaritic.* Missoula, Mont.: Scholars, 1978.

Cotterell, Peter, and Max Turner. *Linguistics and Biblical Interpretation.* Downers Grove, Ill.: InterVarsity, 1989.

Fishbane, Michael. *Biblical Interpretation in Ancient Israel.* Oxford: Clarendon, 1985.

Silva, Moisés. *Biblical Words and Their Meaning: An Introduction to Lexical Semantics.* Grand Rapids: Zondervan, 1983.

Ullmann, Stephen. *Semantics: An Introduction to the Science of Meaning.* Oxford: Blackwell, 1972.

Appendix: How about Some Practice in Lexical Analysis?

If you'd like some practice in doing lexical analysis, give the following questions, taken from Genesis 6:5–13, a try.

(1) What is the precise meaning of יֵצֶר in verse 5? Validate your proposal from the immediate literary context and from usage of the word elsewhere in the Old Testament.

(2) How should לִבּוֹ be translated in verse 5? Support your answer from the immediate literary context and usage of the word elsewhere in the Old Testament. In discussing this issue, evaluate the NIV's translation, "his heart."

(3) How should the verb וַיִּנָּחֶם be translated in verse 6? You will need to survey the use of the niphal stem of נָחַם in the Old Testament and choose the category of meaning that best fits verse 6. Validate your choice from the immediate context and usage elsewhere in the Old Testament.

(4) Do a complete usage survey of the verb עָצַב (v. 6) in all of its stems. Develop categories of meaning that transcend the stem distribution; make sure every passage is accounted for and appears under the appropriate category. Now discuss more fully the precise meaning of the verb in verse 6.

(5) How should לִבּוֹ be translated in verse 6? Support your answer from the immediate literary context (note especially the use of the verb עָצַב) and from usage of the word elsewhere in the Old Testament.

(6) What exactly does the phrase מָצָא חֵן (v. 8) mean? Does this suggest that Noah was the recipient of spontaneous divine favor, or that he attracted divine attention and favor? You will need to study use of the phrase elsewhere in the Old Testament, especially passages where the phrase "in the eyes of" follows.

(7) What is the precise meaning of תָּמִים in verse 9? Support your answer from the immediate literary context and from usage of the word elsewhere in the Old Testament.

(8) How should the phrase בְּדֹרֹתָיו, literally, "in his generations," be translated in verse 9? Evaluate the NIV's translation, "among the people of his time."

(9) What does the statement "Noah walked about with God" mean? You will need to study all other texts where the hithpael form of the verb הָלַךְ is used with the preposition אֶת/אֵת.

(10) What is the precise meaning of וַתִּשָּׁחֵת in verse 11? Support your answer from the immediate literary context and from usage of the verb elsewhere in the Old Testament (especially in the niphal stem).

(11) To what type of behavior might the noun חָמָס, "violence" (v. 11) refer? You will need to survey usage of the term elsewhere in the Old Testament.

(12) What is the referent of the phrase כָּל־בָּשָׂר, literally, "all flesh," in verse 12? Support your answer from the immediate literary context and from usage of the phrase elsewhere in the Old Testament (especially in Gen. 6–9).

(13) What does the statement הִשְׁחִית . . . אֶת־דַּרְכּוֹ (v. 12) mean? Support your answer from the immediate literary context and from usage of the terms elsewhere in the Old Testament.

(14) What does the statement קֵץ כָּל־בָּשָׂר בָּא לְפָנַי, literally, "the end of all flesh has come before me" (v. 13) mean? Among other things, you will need to determine what the expression "come before" means.

(15) What is the precise meaning of מַשְׁחִיתָם in verse 13? Support your answer from the immediate literary context and usage of the verb elsewhere in the Old Testament (especially in the hiphil stem).

5 Getting Down to the Nuts and Bolts

Basics of Hebrew Syntax

Hebrew grammarians ordinarily divide the field of study into three sections: phonology (the study of the sounds of the language), morphology (the study of the forms of the language), and syntax (the study of how forms function, interrelate with other forms, and combine to produce sentences). Introductory Hebrew courses generally focus on phonology and morphology, leaving syntax for more advanced courses. While knowledge of phonology and morphology is essential to understand the Hebrew language and to do Hebrew exegesis, the most challenging and significant exegetical issues are often syntactical in nature. Fortunately many new tools make the task of identifying Hebrew forms much easier and quicker, freeing up the exegete to give more attention to syntactical matters.

The following discussion assumes that the reader has a basic working knowledge of phonology and morphology and is armed with tools that will give morphological assistance when necessary. In this chapter we survey the basics of Hebrew syntax and attempt to illustrate the importance of syntactical analysis to exegesis. Morphological details are only included when they facilitate the discussion or seem especially pertinent.

Grammatical phenomena can be categorized as standard, nonstandard, and rare. In this and the following chapter we discuss and illustrate standard and nonstandard constructions and uses. If we seem to devote more space, relatively speaking, to the nonstandard phenomena, it is because they are usually more problematic to the student of Hebrew grammar and often more rhetorically and exegetically significant than the routine, standard uses and constructions. However, one needs to know the standard uses and constructions to be able to identify and appreciate what is nonstandard. We do not discuss, for the most part, rare phenomena. They are best examined inductively, as one encounters them in the context of exegesis.

The survey is streamlined by design and avoids theoretical debates. The text is not encumbered by extensive footnotes and bibliographical references. If readers wish to study rare uses and constructions, desire more examples of categories, want to read about the issues at a more abstract level, or need extensive bibliography, they should consult the standard grammars, especially GKC and W–O. To facilitate matters, I have cross-referenced the following survey to these tools (page numbers are given).

Nouns (GKC, 389–437; W–O, 83–186)

Hebrew nouns can be classified according to gender (masculine or feminine), number (singular, dual, or plural), state (absolute or construct), and case (nominative, genitive, or accusative).

Gender and Number (GKC, 389–401; W–O, 95–124)

All Hebrew nouns are either grammatically masculine or feminine. Masculine nouns, when grammatically singular, have no special gender/number marker. When plural, masculine nouns typically have the ending םי suffixed. For example, the plural of סוס, "horse" (a masculine singular noun) is םיסוס, "horses."

Feminine singular nouns typically have an ending ה, or ת. When pluralized, feminine nouns usually have the ending תו suffixed. For example the feminine noun הסוס, "mare" (note the addition of ה, to סוס to indicate a female horse) would be pluralized תוסוס, "mares."

Dual forms are used primarily for items that come in natural pairs, such as some bodily parts. The typical dual ending for both masculine and feminine nouns is םי. For example, די, "hand," is written םידי, "hands," when dual.

The *singular* form may indicate:

(1) a single person or item
(2) a group (a number of persons or items considered as one group or a whole). Examples of this collective use include the grammatically singular forms םע, "people, nation," and ערז, "seed, offspring." (BDB will usually indicate when a noun is to be understood in a collective sense.)
(3) a representative of a group. This use is common in the Psalms and in proverbial literature, which often speaks of the typical wise man or fool.

The *dual* form may indicate:

(1) items that occur in natural pairs
(2) two of a kind (usually with numerals or units of measure)

The *plural* form may indicate:

(1) numerical plurality (e.g., סוּסִים, "horses")
(2) abstract ideas (e.g., בְּתוּלִים, "virginity," חַיִּים, "life")
(3) respect or honor (e.g., אֱלֹהִים, "[the one true] God," אֲדֹנִים, "absolute lord, master")

It is sometimes important for an interpreter to determine the precise function of the singular or plural, or at least to recognize the variety of available options.

(1) For example, the grammatically plural name אֱלֹהִים, when it refers to the God of Israel, is a plural of respect. (The plural of respect is sometimes used idiomatically for individual pagan deities as well.) When the form is used as a numerical plural, it refers to the pagan gods or, in some cases, to lesser members of God's heavenly assembly (beings known to us as "angels"). When the plural is one of respect, then it is improper to argue, as many have done, that the form hints at a plurality of persons within the Godhead and thus foreshadows in some cryptic way the doctrine of the Trinity.

The linguistic absurdity of such a view can be illustrated by an example involving another plural of respect. In Judges 19:26–27 the concubine's master is referred to by the plural אֲדֹנִים, "lord." It is clear from the context, where the referent of the plural noun is an individual, that the plural is one of respect; it emphasizes the Levite's absolute authority over the woman.[1] If one were to argue that the plural hints at the man having multiple personalities, such an interpretation would be rightly discarded as farfetched.

(2) Some interpreters of Genesis 3:15 argue that the "seed of the woman" is a somewhat veiled reference to the Messiah, who will crush the serpent, often taken by advocates of this position as a reference to Satan. Space does not allow an evaluation of the strengths and weaknesses of this interpretation, but one observation is relevant to the grammatical point under discussion. Proponents of this messianic interpretation should not argue their case from the presence of the singular noun זֶרַע, "seed, offspring," because this noun, while sometimes referring to an individual descendant, frequently refers to one's offspring or descendants in a collective sense. It is possible that the phrase "seed of the woman" refers collectively to the human race that originated in the first woman. In this case the passage envisions the ongoing struggle between humans and deadly snakes, a conflict that was a grim reality in the ancient world.

The use of the third-person singular pronoun ("he"/"his") to refer to the "seed of the woman" in the second half of the verse does not militate

---

1. This example shows that the plural does not necessarily suggest that the referent is actually honorable or worthy of respect; in this case it simply reflects the cultural reality of his authority over the woman and has probably achieved idiomatic status.

against this collective interpretation, for modifiers of collective nouns and pronouns referring to collectives are often singular. For example, in Genesis 22:17 the Lord promises Abraham, "I will indeed bless you and make your offspring (singular זֶרַע) as numerous as the stars in the sky and the sand on the seashore. Your offspring (singular noun again) will conquer (the verb form is singular) the fortified cities (lit., "gate") of their (the Hebrew has the singular pronominal suffix) enemies." The references to the offspring being numerous make it clear that the noun is used collectively, but the verbal modifiers and pronouns are nevertheless singular.[2] To summarize, the mere presence of the singular noun and pronouns in Genesis 3:15 does not necessitate seeing the referent of זֶרַע as an individual.

(3) Observing the gender of a noun or substantive is often important. For example, Proverbs 5:17 is often translated something like this: "Let them (the springs/streams of water mentioned in the previous verse) be yours alone, never to be shared with strangers." Some interpret the springs/streams of water as symbolic of the husband's sexual virility and understand the statement as an exhortation to marital faithfulness. In this view the "strangers" are sometimes understood as women other than his wife, such as adulteresses and prostitutes (see v. 20). However, the word translated "strangers" (a verbal adjective functioning here as a noun equivalent) is a masculine (not feminine) plural form (זָרִים—note the characteristic masculine plural ending), making this interpretation highly suspect. (Note that in v. 20, where an adulteress is in view, the feminine singular form זָרָה appears.) A more likely interpretation is that the springs/streams of water represent the sexual potential of the wife (who is compared to a cistern/well in v. 15 and a fountain in v. 18). Verse 17 may be reminding the husband that his wife belongs to him alone and that she is fully capable of satisfying his sexual desires. In this case the verse might be translated as a simple statement of fact: "They are yours alone, not intended to be shared with strangers (i.e., other men)."

State and Case (GKC, 410–27; W–O, 125–86)

The basic form of the noun (whether singular or plural) is the absolute state. (BDB lists nouns according to their absolute form.) When two nouns are placed in a syntactical relationship where the second modifies the first (e.g., סוּס הַמֶּלֶךְ, "the horse of the king"), the first is said to be in the construct state and the second is understood as a genitive.

Often nouns in the construct state appear in a different form. Masculine plural nouns (ending in יֵם in the absolute state) have a different ending in the construct (יֵ). (Contrast סוּסִים, "horses," with סוּסֵי, "horses of.") Feminine singular nouns ending in ה, also have a different ending in the

---

2. See Gen. 16:10; 22:17; 24:60 for other examples of singular modifiers being used with collective זֶרַע.

construct (usually ת ָ). (Contrast סוּסָה, "mare," with סוּסַת, "mare of.") Some nouns also exhibit spelling changes in the construct. (Contrast בֵּן, "son," with בֶּן, "son of.")

As in English (but unlike Greek), nouns do not have case endings in biblical Hebrew. Yet all Hebrew nouns do have case function. There are three case functions in Hebrew: nominative, genitive, and accusative. Basically stated, the subject of an action or state is considered to be in the nominative case. A noun following and modifying a construct noun or construct adjective is in the genitive case. Nouns functioning as direct objects or adverbial modifiers are in the accusative case. The particle אֵת (or אֶת־) often appears before accusatives, especially in prose.

A survey of the major uses of the Hebrew noun cases follows:

Nominative (W–O, 128–30)

A noun in the nominative case may be categorized as:

(1) the subject of an action or state
(2) a predicate nominative (a noun equated with the subject by a "to be" verb, whether stated or implied)
(3) a vocative (a noun juxtaposed with a second-person pronoun, whether stated or implied)
(4) a nominative absolute

When used as a nominative absolute, the noun is isolated from the following sentence, often by an intervening subordinate clause or series of appositional terms (cf. Judg. 4:4), and then resumed by a pronoun serving as the subject in the sentence. (The noun and the pronoun are technically in apposition.) For example, Adam's statement in Genesis 3:12 reads:

הָאִשָּׁה אֲשֶׁר נָתַתָּה עִמָּדִי הִוא נָתְנָה־לִּי

"The *woman*, whom you gave to me, *she* gave me (some fruit from the tree and I ate)." The noun אִשָּׁה, "woman," is the nominative absolute in this example; the pronoun הִוא, "she," is resumptive after the subordinate relative clause ("whom you gave to me"). Sometimes, as here, one can detect emphasis in the construction. In this case Adam is making it crystal clear that the woman is responsible for his eating the fruit.[3]

---

3. Sometimes a noun is resumed by a suffixed pronoun that is in the genitive or accusative case. Though a noun so used is often labeled a nominative absolute, it is technically more accurate to label it as a genitive or accusative absolute. See, e.g., Isa. 1:7: אַדְמַתְכֶם לְנֶגְדְּכֶם זָרִים אֹכְלִים אֹתָהּ, "as for your land, right before you foreigners are devouring it." The third feminine singular suffix on the accusative sign at the end of the statement refers back to the feminine singular noun "land." Since the suffixed pronoun is accusative here, its antecedent אֲדָמָה might be labeled an accusative absolute.

Genitive (GKC, 410–23; W–O, 143–54)

Nouns following a construct form are classified as genitival. Genitives can modify the preceding noun or adjective in a variety of ways. Some of the more common categories are listed and illustrated below. Genitives may indicate:[4]

(1) possessor

בֵּית יְהוָה, "the temple *of the* LORD" (2 Kings 25:13)

Genitives indicating the possessor may be translated with the English possessive, for example, "the LORD's temple."

(2) person or item possessed

אֲדֹנֵי הָאָרֶץ, "the master *of the land*" (Gen. 42:30)

(3) subject (authorship, source, or origin)

אַנְקַת־אֶבְיוֹנִים, "the outcry *of the poor*" (Ps. 12:5, Eng.)

There is an action or verbal idea implicit in the first noun. In this case the poor are the subjects of the implied action; they are the ones crying out to God for relief from their oppressors.

(4) object or recipient

שֹׁד עֲנִיִּים, "the violence done *to the oppressed*" (Ps. 12:5, Eng.)

As in category number 3, there is an action or verbal idea implicit in the first noun. In this case the oppressed are the object of the implied action; they are the ones victimized by the violent, oppressive acts of the powerful.

מְטַר־אַרְצֶךָ, "rain *of your land*" (Deut. 28:12), i.e., "rain *for your land*"

In this case the genitive identifies the recipient of the rain.

(5) action

When used in this manner the genitive is a verbal noun that indicates the action which is directed toward the referent of the preceding noun. This genitival construction is the flipside of the objective genitive, where the implied action is indicated by the first noun and the object of the action by the second noun.

עַם עֶבְרָתִי, "the people *of my anger*" (Isa. 10:6), i.e., "the people *who are the objects of my anger*," or, "the people *toward whom I direct my anger*"

---

4. In each instance the genitive is underlined in Hebrew and translated in italics. The same procedure is used throughout this chapter.

(6) means or instrument

מֻכֵּי־חָרֶב, "struck down *by the sword*" (Jer. 18:21)

(7) cause or reason

חוֹלַת אַהֲבָה, "sick *of love*" (Song of Sol. 2:5), i.e., "sick *because of love*" (or "lovesick")

(8) purpose or result

When used in this manner the genitive indicates the intended or actual result of an action implied in the first noun, or the intended use of the referent of the first noun.

מוּסַר שְׁלוֹמֵנוּ, "the punishment *of our peace*" (Isa. 53:5), i.e., "the punishment *that brought us/resulted in our peace*"

In this case the genitive indicates the actual result of the punishment.

צֹאן טִבְחָה, "sheep of *slaughter*" (Ps. 44:22, Eng.), i.e., "sheep *intended for slaughter*"

In this case the genitive indicates the intended use of the sheep.

(9) attribute or characteristic

A genitival noun can sometimes be equivalent to an attributive adjective in that it indicates a quality or attribute of the referent of the preceding noun.

שִׂמְחַת עוֹלָם, "joy of *permanence*" (Isa. 35:10), i.e., "*permanent* joy"

(10) material

Sometimes a genitive indicates the material of which an item consists or out of which an item is made.

כְּלִי־חֶרֶשׂ, "jar of *clay*" (Num. 5:17), i.e., "*clay* jar"

(11) specification

After an adjective in the construct form, genitives often specify who or what is characterized by the quality indicated by the adjective.

טְמֵא־שְׂפָתַיִם, "unclean of *lips*" (Isa. 6:5), i.e., "unclean *with respect to lips*"

Sometimes the genitive is appositional, indicating a specific referent after a noun indicating a general category.

בַּת־צִיּוֹן, "the daughter *of Zion*" (Isa. 1:8), i.e., "daughter Zion"

In this case Zion's daughter is not the referent, but rather, Zion is pictured as a daughter.

(12) larger group or class

A genitive can sometimes designate the whole group or larger class of which the referent of the preceding word is a part.

אֶבְיוֹנֵי אָדָם, "the poor *of humankind*" (Isa. 29:19), i.e., "the poor *among humankind*"

(13) degree or emphasis

To emphasize the quality of an item or the degree of an emotion, a plural form or synonym of the preceding word sometimes appears as a genitive.

מֶלֶךְ מְלָכִים, "king *of kings*" (Ezek. 26:7), i.e., "king *among kings*," or "the greatest king of all"

חֲרוֹן־אַפּוֹ, "the fury *of his anger*" (1 Sam. 28:18), i.e., "his great anger"

One might interpret this as a rhetorical (emphatic) use of an attributive genitive, that is, "his angry fury."

Accusative (GKC, 362–76; W–O, 161–86)

Nouns in the accusative case complete or modify a verb. As such, accusatives can indicate the direct object of a verb (category 1 below) or function as adverbial modifiers (categories 2–8). When accusatives function adverbially, a preposition must sometimes be supplied in the translation. Some verbs (e.g., verbs indicating causation or production) can have two accusatives. Accusatives usually fall into one of the following categories:

(1) direct object

(2) place

אִשָּׁה שֹׁכֶבֶת מַרְגְּלֹתָיו, "a woman was lying *at his feet*" (Ruth 3:8).

The accusative indicates where the action took place.

(3) direction (with verbs of motion)

וַיָּקָם יוֹנָה לִבְרֹחַ תַּרְשִׁישָׁה, "Jonah arose to flee *to Tarshish*" (Jon. 1:3)

As illustrated by this example, the accusative, when indicating direction, can sometimes have the directive ending ָה.

(4) time

When used temporally, an accusative can specify when an action occurred and/or indicate its duration.

יוֹם־צָעַקְתִּי, "*During the day* I cry out" (Ps. 88:1, Eng.)

(5) manner

הוֹלֵךְ בְּתֹם יֵלֶךְ בֶּטַח, "the one who walks in integrity will walk in security" (Prov. 10:9)

When used this way, the accusative can be translated with an adverb, for example, "the one who walks in integrity walks *securely*."

(6) product

וַיִּבְנֶה אֶת־הָאֲבָנִים מִזְבֵּחַ, "he built the stones *into an altar*" (1 Kings 18:32)

"Stones" is the direct object of the verb, while "altar" is an adverbial accusative, indicating what the action produced.

(7) material or instrument

וַיִּיצֶר . . . אֶת־הָאָדָם עָפָר, "The Lord God formed the man *out of dust*" (Gen. 2:7)

"Man" is the direct object of the verb, while "dust" is an adverbial accusative, indicating the material that was used in the action.

(8) state

Sometimes an accusative gives specific details about the condition or state of the subject or object at the time the action took place.

וַיִּשְׁמַע מֹשֶׁה אֶת־הָעָם בֹּכֶה, "Moses heard the people *weeping*" (Num. 11:10)

"People" is the direct object of the verb, while "weeping" is an adverbial accusative of state, indicating the depressed condition of the people at the time Moses heard them.

Interpretation sometimes involves correctly identifying the precise case function of a noun. In such situations grammar alone usually cannot resolve the issue, but awareness of the options can aid one in arriving at a conclusion.

(1) For example, Hosea 13:2b states literally: "Sacrificers of men kiss the calf-idols." The Hebrew phrase זֹבְחֵי אָדָם, "sacrificers of men," consists of the construct plural form of an active participle functioning substantivally (i.e., as a noun equivalent, "sacrificers of") followed by the collective singular noun אָדָם, "men," which must be classified as a genitive following the construct form. What is the precise relationship between the participle and its genitive? One could take "men" as a genitive

indicating the larger class from which the sacrificers come (see genitival category 12 above). In this case one might translate, "the men who sacrifice kiss the calves" (cf. NAS). The author would be emphasizing the absurdity of men worshiping the images of an animal. But another option is to take the genitive "men" as objective (see genitival category 4 above), in which case the phrase refers to those who offer human sacrifices. One might translate, "Those who sacrifice men kiss the calf-idols."[5] Both options are theoretically possible, given the attested uses of genitives. Since the problem cannot be solved by grammar alone, one must examine the immediate literary context and usage of the terms elsewhere to determine which option is more probable here.

(2) Isaiah 11:13a provides another example of an interpretive problem involving the correct classification of a genitive. The passage states, "The jealousy of Ephraim will end, the hostile ones of Judah will be cut off." What is the relationship of the genitive "Judah" to the preceding plural construct participle, "hostile ones"? The genitive could be objective, "the ones who are hostile toward Judah." Usage elsewhere favors this interpretation, for in every instance where the substantival participle of צָרַר, "be hostile," takes a pronominal suffix or is followed by a genitival noun, the suffix or genitive indicates the object of the hostility. In this case both poetic lines are stating that Judah's enemies will disappear. Ephraim will no longer fight with Judah, and the nation's other enemies will be eliminated. However, the solution is not so simple. The second half of verse 13 states, "Ephraim will no longer be jealous of Judah, and Judah will no longer be hostile toward Ephraim." Here the point is that the cessation of conflict will be reciprocal; Ephraim and Judah will no longer be at odds with each other. Greater thematic symmetry is achieved in the poetic parallelism if one interprets "hostile ones of Judah" in the first half of the verse as meaning, "hostile ones from Judah" (a genitive indicating the larger group or a subjective genitive of source).

Adjectives and Participles
(GKC, 355–62, 427–32; W–O, 255–71, 612–31)

Like nouns, Hebrew adjectives also exhibit gender and number. Adjectives consistently utilize the endings mentioned above, except that adjectives have no dual form. (The plural form of the adjective is used when the adjective modifies a dual noun form.)

Adjectives can function:

(1) attributively (the adjective ascribes a quality to a noun)

Attributive adjectives follow the noun they modify and agree with the noun in gender, number, and definiteness/indefiniteness. For example:

5. See Hans Walter Wolff, *Hosea* (Philadelphia: Fortress, 1974), 219.

הַמֶּלֶךְ הַטּוֹב, "the good king" (lit., "the king, the good one"); מֶלֶךְ טוֹב, "a good king" (lit., "a king, a good one").

(2) predicatively (the adjective makes an assertion about a noun and requires a "to be" verb, whether stated or implied)

Predicate adjectives usually precede the noun, though they can follow. Predicate adjectives are almost always indefinite. For example: טוֹב הַמֶּלֶךְ, "the king is good"; טוֹב מֶלֶךְ, "a king is good."

The time frame of such statements must be determined from the context. Consider, for example, the predicative use of the feminine singular adjective הָרָה, "pregnant." In 1 Samuel 4:19 it is translated past ("His daughter-in-law . . . was pregnant"), in Genesis 38:24 it refers to a present reality from the speaker's standpoint ("she is now pregnant"), and in Judges 13:5, 7 it appears in the angel's prophecy of Samson's birth ("you will conceive").

(3) substantivally (the adjective functions as a noun and frequently has an article prefixed)

For example: הַטּוֹב, "the good one/man"

Participles are verbal adjectives (there is an action implicit in the meaning; e.g., "*watching* eyes"). Consequently they can function attributively (e.g., "the king who sits," which would literally be expressed "the king, the sitting one" in Hebrew), predicatively (e.g., "the king is sitting"), and substantivally ("the sitting one").

When participles function in a predicative or verbal manner, the time frame must be determined from the context. Active participles can indicate:

(1) continuous or repeated action in the past

ולוט יֹשֵׁב בשער־סדם, "Lot *was sitting* in the gate of Sodom" (Gen. 19:1)

(2) continuous or repeated action in the present

את־אחי אנכי מבקשׁ, "I *am seeking* my brothers" (Gen. 37:16)

(3) action that is future, in some cases imminent or about to happen

את־הגוי . . . . דָּן אנכי, "I *will judge* the nation" (Gen. 15:14)

אני . . . . מביא את־המבול, "I . . . *am about to bring* the flood" (Gen. 6:17)

Determining the time frame of a predicate adjective or participle can sometimes be important to the interpretation of a passage. For example, the predicate feminine adjective הָרָה and the participle יֹלֶדֶת are often translated with the future tense in Isaiah 7:14 ("The virgin/young woman will be with child and will give birth to a son"). However, theoretically one could just as easily translate the adjective with the present tense (cf. Gen. 16:11; 38:24; 2 Sam. 11:5, where it appears in announcements of pregnancy) and understand the participle in the imminent future sense

("Look, the young woman is pregnant and about to give birth"). In this case, Isaiah may have pointed to a pregnant young woman standing nearby and picked her out to function as part of the sign. (This would explain why he uses the article, "the young woman.") Grammar alone cannot solve the problem, but awareness of the grammatical options is important. In the final analysis the immediate literary context must be determinative.[6]

Sometimes deciding whether an adjective/participle is attributive or predicative is pertinent. For example, it is unclear how the plural participle יֹדְעֵי is functioning in Genesis 3:5b: וֹהְיִיתֶם כֵּאלֹהִים יֹדְעֵי טוֹב ורע. On the one hand, the form could be taken as an attributive adjective modifying אֱלֹהִים. However, in this case אֱלֹהִים would have to be taken as a numerical plural referring to "godlike beings/angels," for if the one true God were the intended referent, a singular form of the participle would almost certainly appear as a modifier. Following this line of interpretation, one might translate, "You will be like godlike beings, who know good and evil." On the other hand, יֹדְעֵי could be taken as a substantival participle functioning as a predicative adjective in the sentence. In this case one might translate: "You will be, like God himself, knowers of good and evil."

With these grammatical options in mind, one must examine the immediate literary context and parallel constructions elsewhere to determine a solution. The literary context certainly allows and may even favor the translation "godlike beings who know good and evil," for in 3:22 God says to an unidentified group, "Look, the man has become like one of *us*, knowing good and evil." An examination of parallel constructions (found by using the acCordance program) shows that a predicative understanding ("you will be, like God, knowers of good and evil") is possible (see Gen. 27:23), but very rare. The statistical evidence strongly suggests that the participle is attributive, modifying "godlike beings." Consider the following examples where the verb הָיָה is followed by a comparative phrase (introduced by the preposition -כְּ) and an adjective/participle:

(1) Genesis 27:23

הָיוּ יָדָיו כִּידֵי עֵשָׂו אָחִיו שְׂעִרֹת "his hands were, like the hands of Esau his brother, hairy"

שְׂעִרֹת, "hairy," is a predicate adjective, complementing "his hands were." To be attributive, it would need the article because the preceding phrase "hands of Esau his brother" is definite.[7]

---

6. Some consider the Hebrew word עַלְמָה to be determinative, for they define this noun as "virgin." However, the noun carries the basic meaning "young woman," not "virgin." Though the woman to whom it refers is sometimes actually a virgin, the word itself focuses on age, not sexual experience. See K–B, 835–36.

7. See, e.g., Gen. 27:15 (note הַחֲמֻדֹת); Deut. 7:15; 1 Sam. 17:13; 2 Sam. 23:1; 2 Kings 10:1; Jer. 48:24; Lam. 4:2.

(2) Isaiah 1:30

תהיו כאלה נבלת "you will be like a faded oak"

The feminine singular participle נֹבֶלֶת is attributive, for it agrees in gender and number with the preceding feminine singular noun (אֵלָה), but not the masculine plural subject of the verb תִהְיוּ.

(3) Jeremiah 20:9

והיה בלבי כאש בערת "and it (the "word of the LORD," cf. v. 8) is in my heart like a burning fire"

The feminine participle בֹּעֶרֶת is attributive, for it agrees in gender with the preceding feminine noun (אֵשׁ), but not the masculine verb הָיָה.

(4) Jeremiah 31:12

והיתה נפשם כגן רוה "and their life (or "they") will be like a watered garden"

The masculine adjective רָוֶה is attributive, for it agrees in gender with the preceding masculine noun (גַּן), but not the feminine verb הָיְתָה.

(5) Jeremiah 48:41 (cf. also 49:22)

והיה לב גבורי מואב ביום ההוא כלב אשה מצרה "and the hearts of the warriors of Moab in that day will be like the heart of a distressed woman"

The feminine participle מְצֵרָה is attributive, for it agrees in gender with the preceding feminine noun (אִשָּׁה), but not the masculine verb הָיָה.

(6) Hosea 7:11

ויהי אפרים כיונה פותה "and Ephraim is like a deceived dove"

The feminine participle פוֹתָה is attributive, for it agrees in gender with the preceding feminine noun (יוֹנָה), but not the masculine verb יְהִי.

(7) Amos 4:11

ותהיו כאוד מצל "you were like a stick grabbed (from the fire)"

The singular participle מֻצָּל is attributive, for it agrees in number with the preceding singular noun (אוּד), but not the plural verb תִהְיוּ.

In several other cases there is grammatical ambiguity, but the sense of the statement favors an attributive understanding of the adjective/participle that follows the comparative phrase. For example, in Jeremiah 23:9 (הָיִיתִי כְּאִישׁ שִׁכּוֹר) the adjective שִׁכּוֹר, "inebriated," must modify the preceding noun (אִישׁ), "I am like an inebriated man." If the adjective were taken as predicative ("I am, like a man, inebriated"), it would imply men are characteristically inebriated. In Psalm 31:12 (Eng.) (הָיִיתִי כִּכְלִי אֹבֵד)

the participle אָבֵד, "ruined," must modify the preceding noun (כְּלִי, "jar"), "I am like a ruined jar." If the adjective were taken as predicative ("I am, like a jar, ruined"), it would imply all jars are ruined.[8]

Pronouns (GKC, 437–49; W–O, 290–340)

Personal pronouns can be independent or suffixed. Independent personal pronouns usually function as subjects of verbs, participles, or implied "to be" verbs. Suffixed personal pronouns can be attached to nouns (including infinitives and substantival participles), prepositions, verbs, and the sign of the accusative (אֵת). When suffixed to nouns, they usually indicate possession. When attached to infinitives, verbal nouns, or substantival participles, they are subjective (e.g., "in the day of your eating," Gen. 3:5 = "when you eat") or objective (e.g., "the violence done to me," Gen. 16:5). When suffixed to a finite verb or the accusative sign, they are objective.

Personal pronouns have person (first, second, third), gender (masculine, feminine), and number (singular, plural). Like modern English, Hebrew distinguishes gender in the third-person singular, but not in the first-person singular or plural. Hebrew is more precise than modern English in its use of third-person plural and second-person pronouns. Unlike English, Hebrew distinguishes gender in the third plural (Hebrew has two distinct forms of "they"—one masculine and the other feminine) and gender and number in the second person (Hebrew possesses four different forms of "you"—masculine singular, feminine singular, masculine plural, and feminine plural).

The following chart compares modern English with Hebrew in this regard. The Hebrew personal independent pronouns are used for illustrative purposes:

English		Hebrew
3 masc. sing.	he	הוּא, "he"
3 fem. sing.	she	הִיא, "she"
3 masc. pl.	they	הֵמָּה/הֵם, "they"
3 fem. pl.	they	הֵנָּה, "they"
2 masc. sing.	you	אַתָּה, "you"
2 fem. sing.	you	אַתְּ, "you"
2 masc. pl.	you	אַתֶּם, "you"
2 fem. pl.	you	אַתֵּנָה/אַתֵּן, "you"
1 sing.	I	אֲנִי/אָנֹכִי, "I"
1 pl.	we	אֲנַחְנוּ, "we"

8. See as well Isa. 13:14; 16:2; 29:5; 58:11; Jer. 14:9.

Because Hebrew is more precise than modern English, especially in direct address, the interpreter cannot afford to trust an English translation when trying to determine the referent or antecedent of many pronouns. For example, in Nahum 1:11–15 several second-person pronouns appear.

(11) "One who plots evil against the LORD, one who makes wicked plans, marches out from you (fem sg). (12) This is what the LORD says, 'Though they have allies and numerous warriors, they will be cut off and will pass away. Though I humiliated you (fem. sing.), I will humiliate you (fem. sing.) no more. (13) Now I will break his yoke from upon you (fem. sing.), and break off your (fem. sing.) chains.' (14) The LORD has decreed concerning you (masc. sing.), 'There will be no more descendents to carry on your (masc. sing.) name. I will cut off the idols and images from the house of your (masc. sing.) gods. I will prepare your (masc. sing.) grave, for you are of no account (masc sg verb)." (15 = 2:1 in Heb.) Look, coming over the hills are the feet of the messenger, the one announcing peace. O Judah, celebrate (fem. sing. verb) your (fem. sing.) festivals, fulfill (fem. sing. verb) your (fem. sing.) vows; for the wicked one will never again pass your (fem. sing.) way, he will be completely destroyed.'"

In verse 11 a second feminine singular suffixed pronoun is used on the preposition מִן (note "from you"). Nineveh (cf. v. 1) is the likely referent, for the Lord's enemy emerges from the place addressed and cities are often personified as women in the Old Testament. In verses 12–13, where the Lord promises his people deliverance, the second feminine singular suffixed pronoun appears four times. Because the message has shifted to one of comfort, it is likely that the Lord is now addressing personified Judah. The Lord specifically addresses Judah a few verses later (v. 15), and uses five feminine singular forms (two verbs and three pronominal suffixes) in doing so. In the judgment announcement in verse 14 the Lord uses five second masculine singular forms in addressing his enemy, including four pronominal suffixes and a verb. The switch in gender indicates that personified Nineveh (cf. v. 11) is no longer the addressee, but rather the one who emerges from Nineveh, the king of Assyria. Confirmation of this occurs in 3:18–19, where the king is specifically addressed and eight second masculine singular suffixed pronouns are used. This shift in addressee, while quite apparent in the Hebrew text, is not discernible from the English translation.

Psalm 12 provides another example of the importance of observing distinctions in gender and number when interpreting Hebrew texts. Verse 7a (Eng., Heb. v. 8a) states, "You, O LORD, will keep them." If confined to a translation, one might think that the antecedent of the pronoun "them" is "words" (v. 6, Heb. v. 7). In this case verse 7a (Heb. v. 8a) would be directly affirming God's faithfulness to his promises. However, "words" (אֲמָרוֹת/אִמְרוֹת) is feminine in both instances, while the suffixed pronoun "them" is masculine, making this interpretation highly improbable. The antecedents of the pronoun are probably the masculine plural forms "afflicted/needy" (עֲנִיִּים/אֶבְיוֹנִים) (v. 5, Heb. v. 6). Thus verse 7a (Heb. v. 8a) is affirming that God protects the helpless. This interpretation is consistent with verse 7b (Heb. v. 8b), where a third masculine singular (or perhaps first plural) pronoun is suffixed to the verb "guard" and refers to each member of the oppressed group (or, if first plural, to the whole group, with which the author identifies).

Hebrew also has *demonstrative, interrogative,* and *relative* pronouns. Demonstrative pronouns exhibit gender and number, while interrogative and relative pronouns do not.

Determining the antecedent of a relative pronoun is important, but not always as easy as it might seem. For example, interpreters have debated the meaning of Naomi's blessing in Ruth 2:20:

בָּרוּךְ הוּא לַיהוה אֲשֶׁר לֹא־עָזַב חַסְדּוֹ אֶת־הַחַיִּים וְאֶת־הַמֵּתִים. Some translate this statement, "May he (Boaz) be blessed by the LORD, who has not abandoned his kindness to the living and dead." In this case the antecedent of אֲשֶׁר would be the immediately preceding "the LORD." However, this understanding of the construction is not accurate. The antecedent of אֲשֶׁר is Boaz, not the Lord. Elsewhere when אֲשֶׁר follows the blessing formula בָּרוּךְ (qal passive participle) + proper name/pronoun, it always introduces the reason the recipient of the blessing deserves a reward. (For this reason one could analyze אֲשֶׁר as a causal conjunction in this construction.) If אֲשֶׁר refers to the Lord here, then this verse, unlike others using the construction, gives no such reason for the recipient being blessed. Second Samuel 2:5, which provides the closest structural parallel to Ruth 2:20, supports this interpretation:

בְּרֻכִים אַתֶּם לַיהוה אֲשֶׁר עֲשִׂיתֶם הַחֶסֶד הַזֶּה עִם־אֲדֹנֵיכֶם עִם־שָׁאוּל, "May you (plural) be blessed by the LORD, you who (plural)/because you (plural) have extended such kindness to your master Saul." Here אֲשֶׁר refers back to the second plural pronoun אַתֶּם, "you," in the formula, as the second plural verb עֲשִׂיתֶם after אֲשֶׁר indicates. Though יהוה is in closer proximity to אֲשֶׁר, it is not the antecedent. The evidence suggests that Ruth 2:20 should be translated and interpreted as follows: "May he (Boaz) be blessed by the LORD, he who (i.e., Boaz)/because he (i.e., Boaz) has not abandoned his kindness to the living and dead."[9]

Article (GKC, 404–10; W–O, 235–52)

Hebrew has a definite article ("the"), but no indefinite article ("a/an"). The usual form of the article is a prefixed הַ (with doubling of the fol-

---

9. For a fuller defense of this view, see Basil A. Rebera, "Yahweh or Boaz? Ruth 2.20 Reconsidered," *Bible Translator* 36 (1985): 317–27.

lowing consonant), though the precise vowel pointing can change if the following letter is a guttural. The form is sometimes הָ (with no doubling of the following consonant), הָ, or הֶ. In poetic style the article is often omitted where one might expect it. When nouns are in a genitival relationship, the article usually does not appear on the word in construct. If the article appears with the genitive, it makes the entire expression definite (e.g., סוּס־הַמֶּלֶךְ, "the horse of the king," or "the king's horse").

The article may indicate:

(1) a definite or unique person or thing

לֶךְ... אֶל־הָאָרֶץ אֲשֶׁר אַרְאֶךָ, "Go . . . to *the land* that I will show you" (Gen. 12:1)

This general heading includes the "dramatic" use of the article, where it refers to something or someone previously unmentioned, but definite in the mind of the narrator. Sometimes it points to something or someone that would typically appear in a scene. For example, in Genesis 22:6 the narrator tells us that Abraham, on his way to sacrifice his son, took in his hand "the fire and the knife," two items previously unmentioned, but which would typically be part of such a scene.[10]

Sometimes the article is used as a vocative to designate a definite addressee. See, for example, הַמֶּלֶךְ, "O, king!" (2 Kings 6:16).

(2) an especially well-known person or thing

שְׁנָתַיִם לִפְנֵי הָרָעַשׁ, "two years before *the earthquake*" (Amos 1:1)

(3) a person or thing previously mentioned in the context

וַיֵּלֶךְ אִישׁ . . . . וְשֵׁם הָאִישׁ אֱלִימֶלֶךְ, "a man went . . . and the name of *the/that man* was Elimelech" (Ruth 1:1–2)

(4) a genre or class

כֹּל אֲשֶׁר־יָלֹק . . . כַּאֲשֶׁר יָלֹק הַכֶּלֶב, "all who lap . . . like *a* (lit., the) *dog* laps" (Judg. 7:5)

The article can be so used with collectives.

אֶת־הַצַּדִּיק וְאֶת־הָרָשָׁע, "*the righteous* and *the wicked*" (Eccles. 3:17).

Determining the precise use of the article can sometimes be important in interpretation. For example, Genesis 1:27 states, "God created humankind (הָאָדָם) in his image." Some might interpret the article on אָדָם as pointing to the man (in contrast to the woman) whom God created. A

10. For discussion and examples of the dramatic sense of the article, see BDB, 207, 1. d; GKC, 407, par. 126q-s; and W–O, 243, par. 13.5.1e.

closer analysis shows this is incorrect. In the preceding verse God declares, "Let us make humankind (אָדָם) in our image." The following context makes it clear that אָדָם is a collective singular here, referring to the male and female. The verb "rule" is plural (v. 26b) and verse 27b explains that male and female comprise אָדָם. Genesis 5:2 clinches the issue, for it states, "Male and female he created them; he blessed them and called their name, 'Humankind' (אָדָם)." Therefore, the contextual evidence demonstrates that the article on the form הָאָדָם in verse 27a is pointing back to the earlier collective use of the term (cf. v. 26), not indicating the male of the species.

Sometimes it is not so easy to pin down the precise significance of the article. In Micaiah's vision of the deliberations of the heavenly assembly, recorded in 1 Kings 22:19–22, a "spirit" volunteers to carry out the Lord's plan to deceive and destroy wicked King Ahab. As this spirit steps to the center of the stage, the text simply calls him הָרוּחַ, "the spirit" (v. 21). What significance does the article have here?

Elsewhere in the Old Testament the article with the singular noun רוּחַ can indicate something that is universally known, such as the spirit of life possessed by all men (Eccles. 12:7) and the wind which all men experience (Eccles. 1:16; 8:8; 11:5). The article can also refer to something specifically defined in the context, such as the spirit of prophecy (Num. 11:17, 25a; note the following relative clause). At other times the article indicates previous reference (see Num. 11:25b–26; 1 Kings 19:11; Ezek. 1:12, 20; 37:9–10). In Hosea 9:7 the article appears to be generic in the phrase אִישׁ הָרוּחַ, "the man of the spirit," which parallels הַנָּבִיא, "the prophet," a reference here to the stereotypical prophet.

In 1 Kings 22:19 the article could be used in a generic or dramatic sense, in which case one could translate "a spirit." In the latter case it would show that this spirit was vivid and definite in the mind of Micaiah the storyteller.

However, the article may indicate a well-known spirit, as the following context suggests. Verse 24 tells how Zedekiah slapped Micaiah in the face and then asked sarcastically, "Which way did the spirit from the Lord (רוּחַ־יהוה, lit., "the spirit of the Lord") go when he went from me to speak to you?" Elsewhere when the phrase "the spirit of the Lord" refers to the divine spirit (rather than the divine breath or mind, see e.g., Isa. 40:7, 13), the spirit energizes an individual or group for special tasks or moves one to prophesy.[11] This raises the possibility that the deceiving spirit of verses 20–23 is the same as the divine spirit mentioned by Zede-

---

11. See Judg. 3:10; 6:34; 11:29; 13:25; 14:6, 19; 15:14; 1 Sam. 16:13–14; 1 Kings 18:12; 2 Kings 2:16; Isa. 11:2; 61:1; 63:14; Ezek. 37:1. In 1 Sam. 19:9 the phrase is followed by the attributive adjective רָעָה, "evil," without the article. This odd construction should probably be translated "an evil spirit from the Lord." This view is suggested in BDB, 925, 9. a.

kiah in verse 24. This would explain why the article is used on רוּחַ; he can be called "the spirit" because he is the well-known spirit who energizes the prophets.[12]

Particles

Prepositions (GKC, 377–84; W–O, 187–225)

Hebrew has several prepositions, most of which display great flexibility in their usage.[13] However, rather than treating prepositions in isolation, one should study particular verb + preposition combinations. In such cases one can consult BDB's discussion of the verb in question.[14]

Adverbs (GKC, 294–97; W–O, 655–73)

Hebrew has relatively few pure adverbs. To express adverbial ideas it more commonly employs prepositional phrases or nouns (used as adverbial accusatives).

Negatives (GKC, 478–83)

Hebrew has a variety of negative particles, the major one being לֹא.

Conjunctions (GKC, 305–7; W–O, 647–55)

Hebrew has relatively few conjunctions, the major ones being וְ, אִם, and כִּי.

Interrogative indicators (GKC, 473–76; W–O, 315–29)

Hebrew has an interrogative particle, which takes the form of הֲ (sometimes הַ or הֶ) prefixed to the first word in the sentence (BDB, 209–10). Not all questions will be indicated by this particle. Sometimes a question is introduced with an interrogative pronoun or adverb; at other times questions were apparently expressed simply by intonation. In this case the interpreter must rely solely on context.

---

12. If so, the irony of the passage is profound. God sent his spirit to deceive Ahab by being a lying spirit in the mouths of the king's prophets. Zedekiah correctly argued that he was an instrument of the divine spirit; what he failed to realize was that the spirit was using him to deceive, not convey the truth.

13. BDB classifies the usage of the prepositions, though its detailed discussions, replete with examples, can sometimes be quite tedious to read. W–O presents more user-friendly outlines of the major uses of the prepositions.

14. For example, see BDB's discussion of the verb בָּטַח, "trust" (p. 105), where, under category I, it outlines the usage of the verb according to the various constructions in which it appears, including those in which a preposition follows.

Existence/Presence

The particle יֵשׁ, "there is," expresses existence or presence (see BDB, 441–42).

Accusative (GKC, 362–66)

The accusative particle אֵת (or ־אֶת), which has no translation value, typically appears before definite accusatives. Proper nouns, nouns with the article, and nouns with a pronominal suffix are considered definite. This particle is relatively rare in poetry.[15]

Infinitives (GKC, 339–55; W–O, 580–611)

Infinitives are verbal nouns. Consequently they can function nominally or verbally in a sentence. Hebrew has two different infinitival forms:

Infinitive Absolute (GKC, 339–47; W–O, 580–97)

The infinitive absolute can function as:

(1) a noun serving as a subject, genitival modifier, or object

הַכֵּר־פָּנִים לֹא־טוֹב, "*Showing partiality* (lit., recognizing a face) is not good" (Prov. 28:21)

The infinitive absolute functions as the subject of the sentence. As a verbal noun, it also has an accusative ("face") following it.

מִדֶּרֶךְ הַשְׂכֵּל, "from the way of *understanding*" (Prov. 21:16)

The infinitive absolute is a genitive after the construct noun "way of."

לִמְדוּ הֵיטֵב, "Learn to *do well*" (Isa. 1:17)

The infinitive absolute is the object of the imperative "learn."

(2) an adverbial accusative indicating manner or an accompanying action

רָדְפוּ מַהֵר אַחֲרֵיהֶם, "Chase after them *quickly*" (Josh. 2:5)

וָאֶכֹּת אֹתוֹ טָחוֹן הֵיטֵב, "I crushed it, grinding (it) *thoroughly*" (Deut. 9:21)

The infinitive absolute טָחוֹן, "grinding," refers to an action that accompanied the crushing. The infinitive absolute הֵיטֵב, "thoroughly" (lit., "well"), is an adverbial accusative of manner in relation to the preceding infinitive ("grinding"), describing how the grinding was done.

15. See BDB, 84–85.

(3) an adverb of emphasis (the most common use)

Here the infinitive typically precedes (though it can sometimes follow) a finite verbal form of the same verbal root. When the main verb is indicative in mood (a simple statement of fact), English adverbs indicating certainty are often adequate translation equivalents (e.g., "certainly, surely, indeed, definitely"). However, sometimes other English adverbs are preferable for stylistic reasons and convey the sense more clearly. When the infinitive follows the finite verb, it usually indicates continuation or repetition of the action.

מוֹת תָּמוּת, "You will *certainly* die" (Gen. 2:17)

The infinitive emphasizes the certainty of the following verbal idea. Some have translated the construction literally, "dying you will die," and then proposed that two types of death are in view (spiritual and physical). This interpretation of the construction is invalid. The infinitive highlights the following concept. The point is that death (however one defines it in this context) is certain.

אָכֹל תֹּאכֵל, "You may *freely* eat" (Gen. 2:17)

The sense of the main verb is not indicative, but subjunctive. The Lord is giving the man permission to eat, not matter-of-factly announcing what he will do. "Certainly" or "indeed" would convey the emphasis carried by the preceding infinitive, but not as well as the English adverb "freely."

הָלְכוּ הָלֹךְ וְגָעוֹ, "they went *along*, mooing (as they went)" (1 Sam. 6:12)

The infinitive absolute follows the finite verb of the same root (the text reads literally, "they went, going") and emphasizes that the main action was continuous. The following form וְגָעוֹ is also an infinitive absolute (with conjunction prefixed), indicating an accompanying action. (See category 2 above.)

(4) a verb

Here the infinitive fills the main verb slot in the sentence. The subject and tense must be determined from the context.

רָגוֹם אֹתוֹ . . . כָּל־הָעֵדָה, "all the congregation *will stone* him" (Num. 15:35)

Infinitive Construct (GKC, 347–55; W–O, 598–611)

The infinitive construct can function as or indicate:

(1) a noun serving as a subject, genitival modifier, or object

לֹא־טוֹב הֱיוֹת הָאָדָם לְבַדּוֹ, "It is not good for the man *to be* alone" (lit. "the *being* of the man alone is not good") (Gen. 2:18)

The infinitive functions as the subject of the sentence. As a verbal noun it is followed by a genitive ("the man").

עֵת סְפוֹד, "a time of *mourning*" (Eccles. 3:4)

The infinitive follows a construct noun and functions as a genitive.

וְשִׁבְתְּךָ וְצֵאתְךָ וּבֹאֲךָ יָדָעְתִּי, "I know *your sitting down, your going out, and coming in*" (2 Kings 19:27)

The three infinitives construct function as objects of the main verb ("I know").

(2) Purpose/result (often with the preposition -לְ prefixed)

וַיָּקָם יוֹנָה לִבְרֹחַ, "Jonah arose *to flee*" (Jon. 1:2)

(3) Manner (often with the preposition -לְ prefixed)

הָעָם חֹטְאִים לַיהוה לֶאֱכֹל עַל־הַדָּם, "The people are sinning against the LORD *by eating* the blood" (1 Sam. 14:33)

(4) Time (often with the preposition -בְּ or -כְּ prefixed)

בְּהִבָּרְאָם, "*when they were created*" (Gen. 2:4)

Verbs (GKC, 114–54, 309–39; W–O, 343–579)

Hebrew finite verbs display person (first, second, third), gender (masculine, feminine), and number (singular, plural). Verbs are also classified according to stem (or theme) and aspect.

Person, Gender, and Number

The person, gender, and number of finite verbs are indicated by pronominal elements prefixed and/or suffixed to the basic verbal root. One should recall from the earlier discussion of pronouns that Hebrew is more precise than modern English in its expression of pronominal elements. The Hebrew prefixed verbal conjugation distinguishes masculine and feminine in the third person plural. Both verbal conjugations distinguish gender and number in the second person. Observing distinctions in gender and number can be especially important in direct address, where second-person forms are used.

Stem (GKC, 114–54; W–O, 351–452)

The Hebrew system of verbal stems indicates voice, causation, and transitivity.[16] The following survey lists and illustrates the basic functions of the seven major stems.

Qal (G)

(1) Stative

The qal stem can be used to express a state or condition of the subject. See, for example, כָּבֵד, "be heavy."

(2) Fientive

The qal is often used to express an action. See, for example, שָׁבַר, "break."

Niphal (N)

(1) Passive

The niphal stem can be used to indicate the passive voice. For example, קָבַר means "bury (an object)" in the qal; in the niphal the verb means, "be buried."

(2) Middle

The niphal can be used in relation to a transitive qal to express an intransitive verbal idea with no agent being expressed. For example, פָּקַח means "open (an object)" in the qal, but in the niphal it can mean simply "open." See, for example, וְנִפְקְחוּ עֵינֵיכֶם, "your eyes will open" (Gen. 3:5).

(3) Reflexive

The niphal sometimes indicates that the subject of a verb is also its implied object. See, for example, וָאֵחָבֵא, "so I hid myself" (Gen. 3:10). (The verbal root is חבא and is unattested in qal.)

(4) Reciprocal

The niphal can indicate mutual action. See, for example, Malachi 3:16a: נִדְבְּרוּ יִרְאֵי יהוה אִישׁ אֶת־רֵעֵהוּ, "those who fear the LORD spoke with one another." (The verbal root is דבר, which is unattested in a finite form in qal, but frequently occurs in the piel with the meaning "speak.")

(5) Tolerative

Occasionally the niphal indicates that the subject permits or submits to an action. For example, דָּרַשׁ means "consult (an object)" in the qal, but in the niphal the verb has the nuance, "allow oneself to be consulted." See, for example, אִדָּרֵשׁ, "I will allow myself to be consulted" (Ezek. 36:37).

Piel (D)

(1) Factitive

The piel stem can be used in relation to an intransitive qal or niphal to indicate the production of a condition or state. For example, גָּדַל means "be great" in the qal, but in the piel the verb means "make great, magnify" (cf. BDB, 152). The so-called delocutive or declarative use of the piel is actually a subcategory of the factitive use. For example, the verbal root נקה means "be innocent" in the niphal; in the piel the verb has the nuance "treat as innocent, acquit" (i.e., "make innocent [in a legal sense]").

(2) Resultative

The piel stem can be used in relation to a transitive qal to indicate the production of the condition that would be the outcome of the action described in the qal. The distinction may be subtle in English, but the qal simply describes the action, while the piel focuses on the result. For example, in Ezekiel 5:2 the Lord instructs Ezekiel: וְהַשְּׁלִשִׁית תִּזְרֶה לָרוּחַ, "and a third (of the hair) you must scatter (qal) to the wind." In Ezekiel 5:12 the Lord, in his explanation of the symbolism behind the action, says: וְהַשְּׁלִשִׁית לְכָל־רוּחַ אֱזָרֶה, "and I will scatter (piel, i.e., "make scattered") a third (of the people) to the wind." Perhaps the piel, by focusing on the outcome of the action, is more emphatic.

(3) Denominative

Sometimes the piel is used in relation to a noun or substantive to indicate a derived verbal idea. For example, the piel verb כִּהֵן means "to act as a priest," and is obviously related to the noun כֹּהֵן, "priest."[17]

(4) Pluralative

Sometimes the piel is used in relation to the qal to indicate, or perhaps emphasize, that an action is repeated and/or directed toward multiple objects. (This would not necessarily imply that the corresponding qal is only used with single or individual objects.) Several examples follow:

(a) In its three qal uses (Gen. 3:7; Job 16:15; Eccles. 3:7) the verb תָּפַר, "sew," refers to a single event or act of sewing. In Ezekiel 13:18, which describes how Israelite women made a practice of sewing amulets, the piel is used.

---

17. See W–O, 410–14, for numerous other examples.

(b) In its numerous qal uses the verb שָׁאַל means "ask, inquire." The piel is used in Psalm 109:10 in a curse requesting that an evil man's offspring become beggars (i.e., those who are forced to make a practice of asking for handouts).[18]

(c) The verb נָשַׁק, "kiss," normally appears in the qal, but in five instances it occurs in the piel. In three cases (Gen. 31:28, 55 [Eng.]; 45:15) multiple objects appear. However, this is not the case in Genesis 29:13 and the problematic Psalm 2:11, where the piel probably envisions repeated kissing of the same object.

(d) רָדַף means "chase, pursue," in the qal, but in Hosea 2:13 (Eng.), where Israel's pursuit of false gods is described, the piel appears. The plural object might account for the piel use (see also Nah. 1:8; Prov. 12:11; 13:21; 19:7; 28:19), but the piel might also indicate repeated or relentless pursuit, as it does in some cases (cf. Prov. 11:19; 15:9, where the object is singular). One can see why many understand the piel as indicating "intensification" of action, for the repetition of certain actions involves an intensification of resolve or effort.

(e) The verb שָׁבַר, meaning "break" in the qal, appears thirty-six times in the piel, always with multiple objects (the object is either a collective singular or grammatically plural or dual form). Many grammarians have pointed to this verb as an example of the intensifying use of the piel stem and translated the piel form "shatter." It is possible that the piel indicates repeated action comprising a whole, perhaps with the nuance "break again and again, break in pieces." If so, the piel would suggest an intensification of effort. (In this regard, note especially Ps. 29:5, where the second line shifts from a qal form of שָׁבַר to the piel as the object shifts from generic "cedars" to "cedars of Lebanon."). However, the consistent use of the piel form with multiple objects may explain its appearance. Another option is to understand the form as a resultative, "make broken" (cf. W–O, 405).

Pual (Dp)

The pual stem is the passive of the piel. For example, the verb קָדַשׁ means "be holy, set apart," in the qal. The piel is factitive, meaning "make holy, consecrate." The pual means "made holy, consecrated." The qal simply describes the state, the pual indicates causation and entry into the condition. The verb זָרָה means "scatter" in the qal. The piel is resultative ("make scattered") and the pual passive ("made scattered"). As with the piel, the pual focuses on causation and the outcome of the action.

18. A pluralative nuance is not readily apparent in 2 Sam. 20:18, the only other passage where the piel of this verb appears. But the verb form should perhaps be emended here to a qal; note the qal infinitive absolute that immediately precedes.

Hithpael (HtD)

(1) Reflexive

The hithpael stem sometimes indicates that the subject of a verb is also its implied object. When used in this manner the hithpael is often employed in relation to the piel. For example, the hithpael of קָדַשׁ, "be holy, set apart," means "make holy, consecrate" in the piel, and "make oneself holy, consecrate oneself" in the hithpael.

A subcategory of the reflexive function is the estimative or exhibitive use, where the subject regards itself as being in a certain state or acts as if it is in a particular condition. See, for example, 2 Samuel 13:6: וַיִּשְׁכַּב אַמְנוֹן וַיִּתְחָל, "and Amnon got in bed and acted as if he were sick." The verb חָלָה means "be sick" in the qal, "make sick" in the piel, and "make oneself appear to be sick" in the hithpael.

Another subcategory of the reflexive function includes instances where the hithpael indicates that the subject acts for its own benefit or advantage. For example, the hithpael of חָנַן, "show favor," has the meaning "seek favor for oneself."

(2) Reciprocal

Sometimes the hithpael indicates mutual action. For example, the five occurrences of the hithpael of רָאָה, "see," all appear in the plural form and mean "look at one another."

(3) Passive

Occasionally the hithpael indicates the passive. For example, the hithpael of הָלַל, "praise" (piel), normally means "make one's boast." But in Proverbs 31:30 it has a passive nuance, "is to be praised." The only hithpael occurrence of the verb שָׁכַח, "forget," is passive, "is forgotten" (Eccles. 8:10). Elsewhere the niphal is used to express the passive of this verb.[19]

(4) Iterative

Occasionally the hithpael indicates repeated action. For example, the hithpael of הָלַךְ, "walk," means "walk about." The verb הָפַךְ, "turn," has the nuances "turn over, tumble" (Gen. 3:24; Judg. 7:13) and "swirl" (Job 37:12).

Hiphil (H)

(1) Causative

The hiphil is most often used in relation to a qal or niphal to indicate causation. For example, the verb יָצָא, "go out," means "cause to go out,

19. It is possible that the verb form in Eccles. 8:10 should be emended to וישׁתבחו, from the root שׁבח, "praise," and translated, "be praised."

bring out" in the hiphil. When the corresponding qal is transitive, the hiphil can take a double accusative. See, for example, Genesis 48:11:

הֶרְאָה אֹתִי אֱלֹהִים גַּם אֶת־זַרְעֶךָ, "God even showed me (in a vision) your offspring."

The so-called delocutive or declarative use of the hiphil is actually a subcategory of the causative use. For example, צָדַק means "be innocent" in the qal; in the hiphil the verb has the nuance "pronounce, treat as innocent" (i.e., "make innocent [in a legal sense]").

(2) Ingressive

An intransitive hiphil can sometimes indicate entry into a state. For example, the hiphil of יָבֵשׁ, "be dry," is transitive and causative ("make dry") in some contexts, but intransitive and ingressive ("become dry") in others (see, e.g., Joel 1:10, 12).

(3) Exhibitive

An intransitive hiphil sometimes indicates that the subject is exhibiting outwardly a particular state or characteristic. For example, the hiphil of רָשַׁע, "be wicked," is transitive and causative/declarative ("pronounce guilty") in some contexts, but intransitive and exhibitive ("act wickedly") in others (see, e.g., Neh. 9:33).

(4) Denominative

Sometimes the hiphil is used in relation to a noun or substantive to indicate a derived verbal idea. For example, the hiphil verb הִמְטִיר means "to send rain," and is obviously related to the noun מָטָר, "rain."[20]

Hophal (Hp)

The hophal stem is the passive of the hiphil. For example, the verb כּוּן means "be established, firm," in the niphal. The hiphil is causative, meaning "establish, make firm." The hophal means "established, made firm." The niphal simply describes the state, the hophal indicates causation and entry into the condition.

The discussion of verbal stem is as much a lexical issue as it is a syntactical one. The dictionaries categorize verbs by their attested stems and reflect the particular nuances of the stems with respect to voice, causation, and transitivity. This is not to say that the use of the verbal stems is always cut-and-dried and beyond debate. Sometimes exegetical debates center around the precise function of a verbal stem in a given context. In such cases the interpreter should do a general survey of the verb's usage in the stem and give attention to immediate contextual factors.

20. See W–O, 443–45, for other examples.

For example, interpreters disagree over the function of the hithpael of בָּרַךְ in Genesis 22:18 and 26:4. Should one understand the verb form as passive and translate, "all the nations of the earth will be blessed through your offspring"? Or should one take the hithpael as reflexive or reciprocal and translate, "all the nations of the earth will pronounce blessings (on themselves or one another) by your offspring"? In the first instance Abraham's/Isaac's offspring are viewed as a channel of divine blessing. In the second instance they are viewed as a prime example of blessing that will appear as part of the nations' blessing formulas, but not necessarily as a channel of blessing to the nations. (For examples of blessing formulas, see Gen. 48:20 and Ruth 4:11.)

The first step in attempting to solve the problem is to survey usage of the hithpael of בָּרַךְ, which occurs in four other passages. (1) In Deuteronomy 29:18 one reads: "When one hears the words of this covenant (or "oath") and invokes a blessing on himself (hithpael of בָּרַךְ) in his heart, saying: 'I will have peace, even though I walk with a rebellious heart.'" In this case the hithpael is clearly reflexive, as the phrases "in his heart" and "I will have peace" indicate. (2) In Psalm 72:17 the psalmist prays on behalf of the ideal king: "May nations pronounce blessings by him, may they regard him as fortunate." Here the hithpael of בָּרַךְ is followed by the prepositional phrase בוֹ, "by him." The verb could theoretically be taken as passive, "may all the nations be blessed through him," for the preceding context describes the positive effects of this king's rule on the inhabitants of the earth. But the parallel line, which employs the piel of אשׁר in a factitive/declarative sense, "regard as happy, fortunate," suggests a reflexive or reciprocal nuance for the hithpael of בָּרַךְ. If the nations regard the ideal king as a prime example of one who is fortunate or blessed, it is understandable that they would use his name in their pronouncements of blessing. (3) The hithpael of בָּרַךְ appears twice in Isaiah 65:16: "The one who invokes a blessing on himself (cf. Deut. 29:18) in the land will invoke that blessing by the God of truth; and the one who makes an oath in the land will make that oath by the God of truth." A passive nuance does not fit here. The parallel line, which mentions making an oath, suggests that the hithpael of בָּרַךְ refers here to invoking a blessing. Both pronouncements of blessing and oaths will appeal to God as the one who rewards and judges, respectively. (4) Jeremiah 4:2 states: "If you swear, 'As surely as the LORD lives,' with truth, integrity, and honesty, then the nations will pronounce blessings by him and boast in him." A passive nuance might work ("the nations will be blessed"), but the context refers to verbal pronouncements (swearing an oath, boasting), suggesting that the hithpael of בָּרַךְ refers here to invoking a blessing. The logic of the verse seems to be as follows: If Israel conducts its affairs with integrity, the nation will be favored by the Lord, which will in turn attract the surrounding nations to Israel's God. To summarize, while the evidence might leave the door open for a passive interpretation, there is no clear-cut passive use. Usage favors a reflexive or reciprocal understanding of the hithpael of בָּרַךְ.

However, the matter is further complicated by the usage of the niphal of בָּרַךְ in three other passages which record God's promise to Abraham and his descendants (Gen. 12:3; 18:18; 28:14). The niphal and hithpael appear to be interchangeable/equivalent in these promises. As with the hithpael, scholars have debated whether the niphal in these texts is passive (in which case Abraham and his offspring are viewed as channels of divine blessing) or reflexive/reciprocal (in which case Abraham and his offspring are viewed as paradigms of blessing whose names will appear in the nations' blessing formulas).

Unfortunately the niphal of בָּרַךְ occurs only in these three texts, making a survey of usage impossible. But there may be a contextual clue in Genesis 12:2–3: "I will make you into a great nation, and bless you, and make your name famous, with the result that you will be a blessing. I will bless those who bless you, and whoever curses you I will curse. All the families of the earth will pronounce blessings by you (reflexive or reciprocal)/will be blessed through you (passive)." The statement "you will be a blessing" at the end of verse 2 may hold the key to understanding the function of the niphal in verse 3. Does "you will be a blessing" mean "you will be a channel/source of blessing" or "your name will be used in blessing formulas"?

A similar statement occurs in Zechariah 8:13, where God assures his people, "You will be a blessing," in contrast to the past when they "were a curse." Certainly "curse" here does not refer to Israel being a source of a curse, but rather to the fact that they became a curse-word or byword among the nations, who regarded them as the epitome of an accursed people (cf. 2 Kings 22:19; Jer. 42:18; 44:8, 12, 22). Therefore the statement "be a blessing" seems to refer to Israel being transformed into a prime example of a blessed people, whose name will be used in blessing formulas, not curses.[21]

If the statement "you will be a blessing" is understood in the same way in Genesis 12:2, its presence lends support to the reflexive or reciprocal interpretation of the niphal in verse 3. God's promise to Abraham, in its original context, included the provision that God would so bless him that other nations would hear of his fame and hold him up as a paradigm of divine blessing in their blessing formulas.

Aspect and Mood (GKC, 309–39; W–O, 455–579)

Traditional Hebrew grammar recognizes two basic verbal conjugations, the so-called perfect and imperfect. Since these function-oriented labels

---

21. In Isa. 19:24 ברכה, "blessing" stands in apposition to שלישיה, "a third," which is a predicate nominative after the verb היה, "to be." Here Israel, along with Egypt and Assyria, becomes a recipient [see v. 25] and paradigm of divine blessing.

are considered by some to be inaccurate or inadequate, the conjugations are often designated by their form: the suffixed conjugation/qatal pattern (= so-called perfect), and the prefixed conjugation/yiqtol pattern (= so-called imperfect). The conjugations do not indicate tense; time frame must be determined contextually. Instead the conjugations indicate aspect, that is, the relation of an action to the passage of time, especially in reference to completion, duration, or repetition.

The Suffixed Conjugation/Qatal Pattern (Perfect) (GKC, 309–13; W–O, 479–95)

The so-called perfect views a situation from the outside, as a whole. As such it expresses a simple fact, whether it be an action or state (including state of being or of mind). When used of actions, it often views the action as complete from the rhetorical standpoint of the speaker or narrator (whether it is or is not complete in fact or reality is not the point). The perfect can pertain to an action/state in the past, present, or future. As noted above, time frame, which influences how one translates the perfect into a tense-oriented language like English, must be determined from the context. To facilitate English translation, the following categories of the perfect are arranged according to the three basic time frames that can be contextually derived.

Usage in a past time frame

(1) simple past

A narrator or speaker may use the perfect to express factually that an action occurred or a state existed in the past.

בְּרֵאשִׁית בָּרָא אֱלֹהִים, "In the beginning God *created*" (Gen. 1:1)

While the perfect in the past time frame usually indicates an action is complete from the speaker's narrational standpoint, this does not necessarily imply that the action was completed at a point in time, as opposed to an extended period of time. For example, Genesis 14:4 states, "For twelve years they served Chedorlaomer" (the verb עָבְדוּ, "they served," is perfect).

With verbs that indicate a state, the perfect can sometimes have an ingressive sense, indicating entry into the state. For example, 2 Kings 8:25 states, "In Joram's twelfth year, Ahaziah *became king*" (i.e., "began to be king"). Genesis 26:13 describes Isaac as follows: "and he kept getting richer, until he *became* very *rich*" (וַיֵּלֶךְ הָלוֹךְ וְגָדֵל עַד כִּי־גָדַל מְאֹד).

References to recent past actions/states (1 Sam. 4:16) and indefinite past actions/states (Ps. 37:35) come under the general heading "simple past."

וַאֲנִי מִן־הַמַּעֲרָכָה נַסְתִּי הַיּוֹם, "I *fled* from the battle lines today" (1 Sam. 4:16)

רָאִיתִי רָשָׁע עָרִיץ, "I *have seen* a ruthless oppressor" (Ps. 37:35)

The speaker describes his experience without indicating when this took place or if the experience was confined to one occasion.

(2) past perfect

A narrator or speaker may use the perfect to indicate an action/state that preceded another action/state in the past. Such uses of the perfect typically appear in subordinate clauses.

לֹא־יָדַע יַעֲקֹב כִּי רָחֵל גְּנָבָתַם, "Jacob did not realize that Rachel *had stolen* them" (Gen. 31:32)

The main verb in the sentence, the perfect יָדַע, "did (not) realize," functions as a simple past. The perfect in the subordinate noun clause ("had stolen") refers to a prior action in the chronology of events.

(3) hypothetical past

A narrator or speaker may use the perfect to refer to a hypothetical action/state that, though contrary to fact, is viewed from the narrator's or speaker's rhetorical standpoint as a past reality with certain consequences.

לוּלֵא חֲרַשְׁתֶּם בְּעֶגְלָתִי לֹא מְצָאתֶם חִידָתִי, "If you *had* not *plowed* with my heifer (but you did), you *would* not *have solved* my riddle (but you did)" (Judg. 14:18)

Usage in a present time frame

(4) simple present

A speaker can use the perfect to describe an action that is occurring, or a state that exists at the time of the statement. In such cases the perfect views the action/state as a whole and simply indicates the factuality of the action/state without drawing attention to its continuation or repetition (as the imperfect does).

הֲרִמֹתִי יָדִי אֶל־יְהוָה, "I *raise* my hand to the Lord" (Gen. 14:22)

זָקַנְתִּי מִהְיוֹת לְאִישׁ, "I *am* too *old* to be married" (Ruth 1:12)

שָׂנֵאתִי מָאַסְתִּי חַגֵּיכֶם, "I *detest*, I *despise* your festivals" (Amos 5:21)

(5) characteristic present

The perfect can be used to state factually universal or well-known truths or a particular subject's characteristic actions or attitudes.

יָדַע שׁוֹר קֹנֵהוּ, "an ox *recognizes* its owner" (Isa. 1:3)

לָמָּה רָגְשׁוּ גוֹיִם, "Why do the nations *rebel?*" (Ps. 2:1)

(6) present perfect

The perfect can be used to describe the present effect(s) of a past action.

כִּי נִחַמְתָּנִי, "for you *comfort* me" (or, "you *have comforted* me") (Ruth 2:13)

Usage in a future time frame

(7) rhetorical or dramatic future

A speaker can use the perfect to describe a future action or state. In this case the action/state, though not yet factual or complete in reality, is viewed as such from the speaker's rhetorical perspective.

הָעָם . . . רָאוּ אוֹר גָּדוֹל, "the people . . . *see* a great light" (Isa. 9:1, Heb. v. 2)

The subject matter (the future appearance of a great light, symbolic of divine glory) begs to be described dramatically, as if both speaker and audience were present. The perfect accomplishes this rhetorical function, whereas the imperfect in such a context would simply anticipate or announce the event.

גָּוַעְנוּ אָבַדְנוּ, "we *are dead,* we *have perished*" (Num. 17:12, Heb. v. 27)

In this case the Israelites, having recognized the error of their ways, are so certain that God's judgment will fall on them that they describe the judgment as if they have already experienced it.[22] Because this rhetorical technique is most often seen in prophetic literature, some have labeled this use the "prophetic perfect." However, it is not confined to visionary contexts or the prophetic genre, so "perfect of certitude," or the "rhetorical/dramatic future" is a better label.

(8) future perfect

A speaker can use the perfect to describe an action/state which the speaker anticipates will precede another future action/state. Though the action/state described by the perfect is in fact future, the perfect can be used because the action/state is viewed as complete or as already existing in relation to the chronologically subsequent future action/state.

---

22. In this context this rhetorical use is emphatic, comparable to the English present tense in the expression, "we're dead meat," which is much more rhetorically arresting than saying "we'll be dead meat (when he gets through with us)." The English past tense is sometimes used rhetorically to describe an event that, though still future, is regarded as certain to occur. Consider the diary entry of a Union soldier killed on June 3, 1864, at the battle of Cold Harbor. Certain that he would die later in the day during the onslaught of the heavily fortified Confederate position, he made this final, tragic entry: "June 3, Cold Harbor, I was killed today."

אֶעֱזָבְךָ עַד אֲשֶׁר אִם־עָשִׂיתִי אֵת אֲשֶׁר־דִּבַּרְתִּי לָךְ, "I will not leave you until I *have done* what I promised" (Gen. 28:15)

In this case two future actions are envisioned. The first (which must be completed before the second can take place) is described with the perfect; the second with the imperfect.

(9) hypothetical future

A speaker occasionally uses the perfect to refer to a hypothetical action/state that is viewed from the speaker's rhetorical standpoint as a future reality with certain consequences.

אִם־גֻּלַּחְתִּי וְסָר מִמֶּנִּי כֹחִי, "if I (i.e., my hair) *were shaved,* then my strength would leave me" (Judg. 16:17)

The Prefixed Conjugation/Yiqtol (Imperfect) (GKC, 313–19; W–O, 498–518)

It is difficult to reduce the essence of the imperfect to a single concept, for it encompasses both aspect and mood. Sometimes the imperfect is used in an indicative manner and makes an objective statement. At other times it views an action more subjectively, as hypothetical, contingent, possible, and so on. To facilitate English translation, the following survey utilizes the broad headings "objective" and "subjective." Distinguishing between objective and subjective uses must be made on a contextual basis.

Objective use of the imperfect

When used objectively, or in an indicative manner, the imperfect sometimes views a situation as underway or incomplete from the rhetorical standpoint of the speaker or narrator (whether it is or is not incomplete in fact or reality is not the point). Very often it anticipates or announces an action that is unrealized in reality. As with the perfect, time frame must be determined from the context, for the imperfect occurs in all three time frames. To facilitate English translation, the following categories of the indicative use of the imperfect are arranged according to the three basic time frames that can be contextually derived.

Usage in a past time frame

(1) customary past

Sometimes a speaker/narrator uses the imperfect to depict an action as occurring regularly or customarily in the past.

וְכֵן יַעֲשֶׂה שָׁנָה בְשָׁנָה, "and so he (Elkanah) *would do* year after year" (1 Sam. 1:7)

Unlike the perfect, which would have simply stated the factuality of the action, the imperfect draws attention to the repeated nature of the action in past time.

וְאֵד יַעֲלֶה מִן־הָאָרֶץ, "now a spring *would bubble up* out of the earth" (Gen. 2:6)

(2) past progressive (or historical present)

Sometimes a speaker/narrator uses the imperfect to depict the progressive nature of an action that occurred in the past. Rather than simply stating the fact (as the perfect would do), the imperfect transports the audience back into the event and allows them to actually see the action as it unfolds. From the narrator's rhetorical stance in past time, the action is in progress. To offer a contemporary analogy, one might say that the perfect, when describing a past action, is comparable to a snapshot—it records a fact visually. The imperfect, when describing a past action, is comparable to a videotape, which allows one to see the action in progress and experience it more readily with one's senses.

וַתִּתְפַּלֵּל עַל־יְהוָה וּבָכֹה תִבְכֶּה, "and she (Hannah) prayed to the Lord, *weeping bitterly*" (1 Sam. 1:10)

This verse illustrates nicely the difference between the progressive past use of the imperfect and the ordinary narrative verbal forms. The first verb (a so-called imperfect with waw-consecutive) is the ordinary narrative verbal form. Like the perfect, it simply states factually that Hannah "prayed to the Lord." In the following clause the verb תִבְכֶּה ("she was weeping") is in the imperfect form. Here the author turns on the video camera, as it were, and allows us to see and hear Hannah weeping.[23]

The use of the imperfect in a past time frame is an effective storytelling device, comparable to the use of the past progressive and historical present in English. While Hebrew narrative does not use the progressive past imperfect in such a sustained way as English storytellers often use the progressive past and historical present, it does occasionally employ the technique for rhetorical effect. When preaching and teaching from the narratives, one should be alert for this dramatic technique and incorporate it into one's own retelling of the event.

(3) historical future

Occasionally the imperfect is used of an event that has already occurred in the past, but was future or incomplete in relation to another action described in the immediate context. In other words, the imperfect indicates an event that followed another event in the past. Such uses of the imperfect typically appear in subordinate clauses.

וֶאֱלִישָׁע חָלָה אֶת־חָלְיוֹ אֲשֶׁר יָמוּת בּוֹ, "and Elisha contracted the disease by which he *would die*" (2 Kings 13:14)

---

23. To emphasize the degree of her grief, he even uses the infinitive absolute before the imperfect. The adverb "bitterly" reflects this form in the translation.

In this case two events are referred to—Elisha's getting ill and his death. The perfect is used to state factually that he became ill; the imperfect is used in the subordinate relative clause to describe his death, which was as yet unrealized in relation to the illness.

Usage in a present time frame

(4) characteristic or habitual present

Like the perfect, the imperfect can express universal or well-known truths or a particular subject's characteristic actions or attitudes. This use of the imperfect is very common in proverbial statements. The perfect focuses on the factual nature of the phenomenon, while the imperfect stresses its repetitive or ongoing nature. In English the statements "rocks sink" and "rocks always sink" convey the same essential idea. The former is simply factual, while the latter is more emphatic because of the addition of the adverb "always." The imperfect seems to provide this same kind of emphasis in Hebrew. For example, the synonymously parallel couplet in Amos 5:10 describes the characteristic attitude that the unjust rulers of the prophet's day displayed toward advocates of the oppressed. The perfect in the first line (שָׂנְאוּ, "they hate") states the fact; the imperfect in the second line (יְתָעֵבוּ, "they abhor") states the fact more emphatically by calling attention to its ongoing or repeated nature.

וַיִּרְדְּפוּ אֶתְכֶם כַּאֲשֶׁר תַּעֲשֶׂינָה הַדְּבֹרִים, "and they chased you just like bees *do*" (Deut. 1:44)

עַל־כֵּן יַעֲזָב־אִישׁ אֶת־אָבִיו וְאֶת־אִמּוֹ, "This is why a man *leaves* his father and his mother" (Gen. 2:24)

The narrator observes that a young man's primary affections typically transfer from his parents to his wife.[24]

(5) present progressive

A speaker sometimes uses the imperfect to depict an action as underway or to indicate that a condition is continuing as he or she speaks.

לָמָּה תַעֲמֹד בַּחוּץ, "Why are *you standing* outside?" (Gen. 24:31)

Usage in a future time frame

(6) simple future

Very often a speaker uses the imperfect to refer to an action that he or she anticipates or announces.

---

24. For other examples of this use of the imperfect after עַל־כֵּן, "therefore, this is why," see Gen. 10:9; 32:32 (Eng.; Heb. v. 33); 1 Sam. 5:5; 19:24; 2 Sam. 5:8. The popular view that takes the imperfect as obligatory ("therefore a man should leave his father and his mother") has no exegetical basis and is unwarranted.

מוֹת תָּמוּת, "you will surely die" (Gen. 2:17)

Of course, the imperfect can be negated, in which case the speaker anticipates or announces that an action will not take place.

לֹא אֲמִיתֶךָ, "I *will* not *kill* you" (1 Kings 2:26)

(7) anterior future

Occasionally a speaker uses the imperfect to refer to a future action that he or she expects will precede another future action. As we have already seen, the perfect can be used in this case as well, since the prior of the two actions is completed in relation to the latter. But since this prior action is unrealized in reality, the imperfect can also be employed.

וְהַעֲלִיתָ עוֹלָה בַּעֲצֵי הָאֲשֵׁרָה אֲשֶׁר תִּכְרֹת, "then offer a burnt sacrifice on the wood of the Asherah pole which *you will have cut down*" (Judg. 6:26)

Two future actions are envisioned, offering the sacrifice and cutting down the Asherah pole. The imperfect is used for the chronologically prior of the two (cutting down the pole). (The perfect with so-called waw-consecutive is used for the subsequent action. This form is discussed below.)

Subjective (hypothetical or contingent) use of the imperfect

As noted above, the imperfect sometimes views an action more subjectively, as hypothetical, contingent, possible, and so on. Precise translational nuances or categories of the subjective use of the imperfect must be derived from the context.

(8) hypothetical future

Sometimes the imperfect appears in the protasis (introductory or "if" section) of a conditional sentence and describes a hypothetical development.

לֹא אֶעֱשֶׂה אִם־אֶמְצָא שָׁם שְׁלֹשִׁים, "I will not do (it), if *I find* 30 people there" (Gen. 18:30)

(9) contingent future

Sometimes the imperfect appears in the apodosis (concluding or "then" section) of a conditional sentence and indicates that an action will occur if the conditions laid out in the protasis (introductory or "if" section) are met.

אִם־תֹּאבוּ וּשְׁמַעְתֶּם טוֹב הָאָרֶץ תֹּאכֵלוּ, "if you are willing and obedient, (then) *you will eat* the good produce of the land" (Isa. 1:19)

Sometimes an imperfect appears in a final (purpose/result) clause, indicating a contingent future.

לְמַעַן יִיטַב־לִי בַעֲבוּרֵךְ וְחָיְתָה נַפְשִׁי בִּגְלָלֵךְ, "so that *it might go well* for me because of you, and my life might be preserved on account of you" (Gen. 12:13)

פֶּן־יִרְאֶה בְעֵינָיו וּבְאָזְנָיו יִשְׁמַע וּלְבָבוֹ יָבִין וָשָׁב וְרָפָא לוֹ, "so that *they might not see* with their eyes, *hear* with their ears, *perceive* with their minds, and turn and be healed" (Isa. 6:10)

(10) possibility

Sometimes a speaker uses the imperfect to indicate that a situation might materialize.

מִי יוֹדֵעַ יְחָנֵּנִי יהוה, "Who knows? The Lord *might show me mercy*" (2 Sam. 12:22)

(11) capability

Sometimes a speaker uses the imperfect to indicate a subject's inherent potential or capability.

קַח־לְךָ מִכָּל־מַאֲכָל אֲשֶׁר יֵאָכֵל, "take any type of food that *can be eaten*" (Gen. 6:21)

הַאֱנוֹשׁ מֵאֱלוֹהַ יִצְדָּק, "*Can* a man *be* more *righteous* than God?" (Job 4:17)

When negated this type of imperfect indicates the lack of inherent potential or capability.

לֹא אֶשְׁמָע, "I *cannot hear*" (Ps. 38:13; Heb. v. 14)

(12) permission

Sometimes the imperfect is used to indicate that the subject is permitted to do something.

מִכֹּל עֵץ־הַגָּן אָכֹל תֹּאכֵל, "from every tree of the garden you *may* freely *eat*" (Gen. 2:16)

The Lord gives the man permission to eat from the designated trees.

(13) obligation or propriety

Sometimes a speaker uses the imperfect to indicate that something should (or should not) be done (or have been done). Occasionally the imperfect is used in this way in rhetorical questions.

מַעֲשִׂים אֲשֶׁר לֹא־יֵעָשׂוּ עָשִׂיתָ, "you have done things which *should* not *be done*" (Gen. 20:9)

An imperfect passive form is negated, indicating that the deeds in question should not have occurred.

הכזונה יעשׂה את־אחותנו, "*Should he have treated* our sister like a harlot?" (Gen. 34:31)

(14) command or prohibition

Sometimes the imperfect is used to express the imposition of an authoritative party's will on a subordinate.

ואליך תשׁוקתו ואתה תמשׁל־בו, "it (sin) desires to overpower you, but you must subdue it" (Gen. 4:7)

The Lord informs Cain that he must suppress the temptation that threatens to overpower him and cause him to sin.

לא תרצח, "you *must* not *murder*" (Exod. 20:13)

(15) desire

Sometimes a speaker uses the imperfect to indicate desire or intention on the part of the subject.

התלכי עם־האישׁ הזה, "Do *you want to go* with this man?" (Gen. 24:58)

(16) request or wish

Sometimes one party, often in a subordinate position, uses the imperfect to express what they would like another party, often in an authoritative position, to do.

תחטאני באזוב, "Please *cleanse* me with hyssop" (Ps. 51:9, Eng. v. 7)

The Short Prefixed Conjugation and Waw-Consecutive (GKC, 326–30; W–O, 496–501, 543–63)

Morphological analysis of some Hebrew prefixed verbal patterns (namely, the shortened forms of third he verbs, hollow verbs, and hiphil forms), studies in comparative Semitic grammar, and contextual considerations indicate that a third verbal conjugation exists in biblical Hebrew, sometimes called the preterite. Though this conjugation is usually indistinguishable from the so-called imperfect, it can be detected in prose by a special form of the prefixed conjunction waw (the so-called waw-consecutive). It also appears after certain temporal adverbs. Recognizing the preterite in poetic texts can be more challenging, for here it often appears without waw-consecutive.

This conjugation is often labeled the "preterite" because of its original function and its frequent use in narrative and archaic poetic texts to indicate past actions. However, this label, which suggests by definition a past tense, is inadequate. A study of usage in the Hebrew Bible indicates that for the most part this conjugation (with or without prefixed waw consecutive) corresponds in function to the suffixed conjugation (or perfect), which cannot be reduced to a simple past tense. When used with a waw-consecutive in a sequence led off by a perfect, the so-called preterite usually carries the same aspectual function as the preceding perfect. Sometimes the so-called preterite with waw-consecutive follows an imperfect or participle and carries a characteristic or even durative sense. Since the label "preterite" is inadequate and inaccurate in some cases, our discussion only uses this label when the form is truly functioning as a past tense. Otherwise the label "short prefixed form" is employed, even though the original morphological distinction between this form and the imperfect is, with a few exceptions, no longer apparent. To sum up, we can say that the preterite/short prefixed form usually looks exactly like the imperfect in form, but usually functions like the perfect. When used with waw-consecutive, it continues the aspectual nuance of the lead verb, whether it be a perfect, participle, or imperfect.

The following categories of the preterite/short prefixed form are arranged according to the three basic time frames that can be contextually derived. Only the best attested categories are listed here.

Usage in a past time frame

(1) simple past

This use of the preterite/short prefixed form is especially common in narrative, where it usually appears with waw-consecutive and states factually that an action occurred or is complete:

וַיִּיצֶר יהוה אלהים את־האדם עפר מן־האדמה וַיִּפַּח באפיו נשמת חיים, "*and* the Lord God *formed* the man out of soil from the ground, *and he breathed* into his nostrils the life-giving breath" (Gen. 2:7)

The preterite/short prefixed form can also function as a simple past tense when used after certain temporal adverbs:

אז יַעֲלֶה חזאל מלך ארם וילחם על־גת וילכדה, "then Hazael king of Syria *went up* and fought against Gath and captured it" (2 Kings 12:18)

In poetic texts the preterite/short prefixed form, used of a past, completed action, often appears without a formal indicator of a past time frame (i.e., without waw-consecutive or a temporal adverb). In such cases, other morphological and/or contextual factors sometimes allow one to recognize the form as being distinct from the imperfect.

נטית ימינך תִּבְלָעֵמוֹ ארץ, "you stretched out your right hand, the earth *swallowed them up*" (Exod. 15:12)

Note how the prefixed form תבלעמו, "swallowed them up," stands parallel to the perfect נָטִיתָ, "you stretched out," in this poetic narrative about God's victory over the Egyptians at the Red Sea.

In Deuteronomy 32:8–13, part of a poetic narrative about God's care for Israel during the nation's formative period, preterites/short prefixed forms and imperfects are mixed together. The author uses fourteen prefixed verbal forms; in twelve of the fourteen instances one can distinguish between the imperfect and preterite on a formal basis. As the following discussion illustrates, distinguishing the two forms is important if one wants to understand the author's emphases.[25] (We include the Hebrew only for lines where a prefixed verb is used.)

> (8) When the Most High gave the nations their inheritance,
> when he divided up humankind,
> *he determined* the boundaries of the peoples,   יַצֵּב גְּבֻלֹת עַמִּים
> according to the number of the sons of God (= Qumran).

יַצֵּב is a hiphil preterite, as indicated by the tone long tsere theme vowel (the imperfect would be יַצִּיב, see Josh. 6:26; note the historically long hireq-yod theme vowel).

> (9) For the LORD's portion is his people,
> Jacob is the portion of his inheritance.

> (10) *He found* him in a desert region,   יִמְצָאֵהוּ בְּאֶרֶץ מִדְבָּר
> in a howling desert wasteland;
> *he was protecting* him, *he taught* him,   יְסֹבְבֶנְהוּ יְבוֹנְנֵהוּ
> *he was guarding* him like the pupil of his eye.   יִצְּרֶנְהוּ כְּאִישׁוֹן עֵינוֹ

According to Rainey, the imperfect uses the nun-form (נֶהוּ) of the accusative suffix; the preterite uses the non-nun form (הוּ). Applying this distinction to this verse, we discover that the first and third verbs are preterites; the second and fourth are imperfects, used in a customary or past progressive sense in this narrative context.

> (11) As an eagle *stirs up* its nest,   כְּנֶשֶׁר יָעִיר קִנּוֹ
> (and) *flutters* over its young,   עַל־גּוֹזָלָיו יְרַחֵף
> *he spread* his wings (and) *took* him,   יִפְרֹשׂ כְּנָפָיו יִקָּחֵהוּ
> *he lifted* him *up* on his wings.   יִשָּׂאֵהוּ עַל־אֶבְרָתוֹ

The first verb is an imperfect, as the theme vowel hireq-yod indicates (the preterite would have a tsere theme vowel, יָעֵר). The imperfect has a characteristic present sense, for it is describing a habit of the eagle. The verb in the parallel line is formally ambiguous, but since it corresponds

---

25. The following analysis draws heavily on Anson F. Rainey's study of these verses in his article, "The Ancient Hebrew Prefix Conjugation in the Light of Amarnah Canaanite," *Hebrew Studies* 27 (1986): 15–16.

with יָעִיר in the structure of the verse, it is undoubtedly an imperfect as well. The fourth and fifth verbs are preterites, for they have the non-nun form of the accusative suffix. They refer to God's historical acts in meta-phorical terms. The formally ambiguous יִפְרֹשׂ, "he spread," is probably a preterite, for it goes with the second half of the verse and refers to God's historical activity.

> (12) The Lord alone *was leading him,*   יהוה בדד יַנְחֶנּוּ
> there was no foreign god with him.

The verb form is an imperfect, for it uses the nun-form of the accusative suffix. Once again the imperfect functions in a customary or past progressive sense.

> (13) *He made him ride* on the earth's heights,   יַרְכִּבֵהוּ עַל־בָּמֳתֵי אָרֶץ
> *and he ate* the crops of the field;   וַיֹּאכַל תְּנוּבֹת שָׂדָי
> he gave him honey from the cliff *to taste*   וַיֵּנִקֵהוּ דְבַשׁ מִסֶּלַע ,
> oil from the rocky crag.

The three verbs in this verse are preterites. The first has the non-nun form of the accusative suffix, the second and third have the prefixed waw-consecutive so typical of narrative (the third verb also has the non-nun form of the accusative suffix).

In this poetic narrative the author uses the preterite form nine times to state historical facts. (In this archaic poetic text the label "preterite" is appropriate, for the form is being used as a narrative past tense.) Twice he employs the imperfect to describe the typical behavior of an eagle. Three times he uses the imperfect to emphasize the continuing or pro-gressive nature of God's activity in the past, namely, his ongoing protec-tive care and guidance of his people.

(2) past perfect

וְרָחֵל לָקְחָה אֶת־הַתְּרָפִים וַתְּשִׂמֵם בְּכַר הַגָּמָל וַתֵּשֶׁב עֲלֵיהֶם, "Now Rachel had stolen the idols, *and had placed them* in the saddlebag of the camel *and had sat* on them" (Gen. 31:34)

The lead verb in the parenthetical clause is a perfect with a past per-fect force. The following short prefixed forms with waw-consecutive carry this same sense. All three verbs refer to past actions that were car-ried out prior to the main actions (Laban's entering Rachel's tent and searching for the idols).

Usage in a present time frame

(3) simple present

עַל־כֵּן שַׂמְתִּי פָנַי כַּחַלָּמִישׁ וָאֵדַע כִּי־לֹא אֵבוֹשׁ, "So I get a determined look on my face *and I know* that I will not be embarrassed" (Isa. 50:7)

The preceding perfect describes the speaker's present attitude and the following short prefixed form with waw-consecutive likewise expresses his state of mind.

הנה המלך בכה וַיִּתְאַבֵּל עַל־אַבְשָׁלֹם, "Look, the king weeps and mourns for Absalom" (2 Sam. 19:2)

Here the short prefixed form with waw-consecutive follows a present durative use of the active participle and carries this same progressive nuance.

(4) characteristic present

אָהַבְתָּ צֶּדֶק וַתִּשְׂנָא רֶשַׁע, "you love justice, *and hate* evil" (Ps. 45:7, Heb. v. 8)

Both verbs, the preceding perfect and the short prefixed form with waw-consecutive, describe characteristic attitudes of the ideal king addressed in the psalm.

לָמָּה תִבְעֲטוּ בְּזִבְחִי וּבְמִנְחָתִי . . . וַתְּכַבֵּד אֶת־בָּנֶיךָ מִמֶּנִּי, "Why do you despise my sacrifice and my offering . . . *and respect* your sons more than me?" (1 Sam. 2:29)

In this rhetorical question the preceding imperfect and the short prefixed form with waw-consecutive allude to Eli's continual failure to discipline his sons.

אֹהֲבַי וְרֵעַי מִנֶּגֶד נִגְעִי יַעֲמֹדוּ וּקְרוֹבַי מֵרָחֹק עָמָדוּ
וַיְנַקְשׁוּ מְבַקְשֵׁי נַפְשִׁי וְדֹרְשֵׁי רָעָתִי דִּבְּרוּ הַוּוֹת וּמִרְמוֹת כָּל־הַיּוֹם יֶהְגּוּ

"My friends and companions stand apart from me because of my illness,
my neighbors keep their distance,
and those who seek my life *set traps*,
those who desire my harm utter threats,
they formulate deceptive plots all day long" (Ps. 38:11–12, Heb. vv. 12–13)

The psalmist describes how others (friends and foes) characteristically treat him now that he has fallen on hard times. He employs an imperfect in line 1, a perfect in line 2, a short prefixed form with waw-consecutive in line 3, another perfect in line 4, and another imperfect in line 5.

(5) present perfect

תָּמַכְתָּ בִּי וַתַּצִּיבֵנִי לְפָנֶיךָ לְעוֹלָם, "you have taken hold of me and *have given me* a permanent place in your presence" (Ps. 41:12, Heb. v. 13)

Usage in a future time frame
(6) rhetorical or dramatic future

וַיִּשַּׁח אָדָם וַיִּשְׁפַּל־אִישׁ וְעֵינֵי גְבֹהִים תִּשְׁפַּלְנָה, "and men *will be humiliated*, men *will be brought low*, and arrogant eyes will be lowered" (Isa. 5:15)

In this judgment announcement (vv. 14–17) the prophet looks forward to the humiliation of proud men. For rhetorical effect he uses the short prefixed form with waw-consecutive to describe as factual or complete that which is yet future. Note the appearance of the imperfect (תשפלנה, "will be lowered") in the second half of the verse.

Psalm 64:7–9 (Eng., Heb. vv. 8–10) appears to provide another example of this use of the short prefixed form with waw-consecutive. In this prayer the psalmist asks for God's intervention and laments the way in which his enemies seek to destroy him (vv. 1–6, Eng.). In verses 7–9 he appears to express his confidence that God will deliver him. These verses use four *wayyiqtol* forms, two perfects, and one prefixed form (probably a short prefixed/preterite) without waw to describe God's intervention and its effects on those who observe it. The psalmist may be using these forms in a rhetorical manner to emphasize his sense of expectancy and certainty. However, another option is that the psalm mixes genres, combining the original lament that prompted divine intervention with a narrative about God's deliverance, written after the fact. In the latter case the verb forms in verses 7–9 simply describe that intervention as factual and completed.

The Suffixed Conjugation/Perfect with Waw-Consecutive (GKC, 330–39; W–O, 519–42)

The suffixed conjugation/perfect is often used with a prefixed waw (also called consecutive) as an apparent functional equivalent of the imperfect. It often appears in a sequence led off by an imperfect and carries the same aspectual function as the preceding imperfect. This phenomenon has puzzled linguists, who have offered various explanations for its existence. Perhaps it originates in an early use of the perfect with waw in conditional sentences. At any rate, usage of the construction reveals that it exhibits most of the same categories as the imperfect. Only the best attested categories are listed here.

Objective (indicative) uses

(1) customary past

ואד יעלה מן־הארץ והשקה את־כל־פני־האדמה, "Now a spring would bubble up out of the earth *and it would irrigate* the entire surface of the ground" (Gen. 2:6)

The perfect with waw-consecutive follows an imperfect with customary force and describes an action that occurred regularly in past time.

(2) characteristic or habitual present

על־כן יעזב־איש את־אביו ואת־אמו ודבק באשתו והיו לבשר אחד, "This is why a man leaves his father and his mother, *clings* to his wife, *and they become* one flesh" (Gen. 2:24)

99

The perfects with waw-consecutive follow an imperfect used in a characteristic sense. All three verbs describe what typically happens when a young man gets married.

(3) simple future

This is probably the most common use of the perfect with waw-consecutive. Here the form is used of an action that is unrealized in fact but which the speaker anticipates or announces will take place.

וּמִפָּנֶיךָ אֶסָּתֵר וְהָיִיתִי נָע וָנָד בָּאָרֶץ, "I will be hidden from you, *and I will be* a wandering vagabond in the earth" (Gen. 4:14)

Subjective (hypothetical or contingent) uses

(4) hypothetical future

Sometimes the perfect with waw-consecutive appears in the protasis (the introductory or "if" section) of a conditional sentence.

וְעָזַב אֶת־אָבִיו וָמֵת, "if *he* (the child) *leaves* his father, then he (the father) will die" (Gen. 44:22)

אִם־שָׁמוֹעַ תִּשְׁמְעוּ בְּקֹלִי וּשְׁמַרְתֶּם אֶת־בְּרִיתִי וִהְיִיתֶם לִי סְגֻלָּה, "If you carefully obey me *and keep* my covenant, then you will become my treasured possession" (Exod. 19:5)

(5) contingent future

Sometimes the perfect with waw-consecutive appears in the apodosis (concluding or "then" section) of a conditional sentence. In this case the speaker assumes that the action will occur if the conditions laid out are met.

וְעָזַב אֶת־אָבִיו וָמֵת, "if he (the child) leaves his father, *then he* (the father) *will die*" (Gen. 44:22)

אִם־שָׁמוֹעַ תִּשְׁמְעוּ בְּקֹלִי וּשְׁמַרְתֶּם אֶת־בְּרִיתִי וִהְיִיתֶם לִי סְגֻלָּה, "If you carefully obey me and keep my covenant, *then you will become* my treasured possession" (Exod. 19:5)

Sometimes the perfect with waw-consecutive appears in a final (purpose/result) clause, indicating a contingent future.

לְמַעַן יִיטַב־לִי בַעֲבוּרֵךְ וְחָיְתָה נַפְשִׁי בִּגְלָלֵךְ, "so that it might go well for me because of you, *and* my life *might be preserved* on account of you" (Gen. 12:13)

פֶּן־יִרְאֶה בְעֵינָיו וּבְאָזְנָיו יִשְׁמַע וּלְבָבוֹ יָבִין וָשָׁב וְרָפָא לוֹ, "so that they might not see with their eyes, hear with their ears, perceive with their minds, *and turn and be healed*" (Isa. 6:10)

(6) possibility

מִי־יוֹדֵעַ יָשׁוּב וְנִחַם הָאֱלֹהִים וְשָׁב מֵחֲרוֹן אַפּוֹ, "Who knows? God might turn *and relent and turn* from his raging anger" (Jon. 3:9)

(7) obligation

דֶּרֶךְ שְׁלֹשֶׁת יָמִים נֵלֵךְ בַּמִּדְבָּר וְזָבַחְנוּ לַיהוה אֱלֹהֵינוּ, "We must make a three day journey into the wilderness *and offer sacrifices* to the Lᴏʀᴅ our God" (Exod. 8:23)

(8) command

קִנִּים תַּעֲשֶׂה אֶת־הַתֵּבָה וְכָפַרְתָּ אֹתָהּ מִבַּיִת וּמִחוּץ בַּכֹּפֶר, "Make rooms in the ark, *and coat it over* with pitch inside and out" (Gen. 6:14)

The perfect with waw-consecutive is often used with an imperatival force after an imperatival form.

וַעֲלוּ אֶל־אָבִי וַאֲמַרְתֶּם אֵלָיו, "Go up to my father *and say* to him" (Gen. 45:9)

Interpretation often involves classifying the aspectual use of verb forms. This is not purely a grammatical decision, for, as illustrated in the preceding discussion, contextual factors are determinative. However, awareness of the options is important to the task.

For example, Ezekiel 14 describes how some Israelite leaders came to Ezekiel seeking an oracle from the Lord (v. 1). The Lord revealed to Ezekiel that these men were not pure worshipers of the one true God. They were actually syncretists, who attempted to hold on to Yahwism while at the same time worshiping idol-gods (vv. 2–3). The Lord refused to tolerate such compromise (vv. 4–6). These idolaters would not receive the oracle they requested, but rather an "answer" from the Lord in the form of severe judgment (vv. 7–8). Verse 9 then envisions a situation where a prophet is persuaded, or "enticed" (pual imperfect of פָּתָה) into cooperating with the idolaters and delivering an oracle. The Lord states, "As for the prophet who is deceived and speaks a word, I the Lᴏʀᴅ have deceived/will deceive (פִּתֵּיתִי, piel perfect of פָּתָה) that prophet."

How should one interpret and classify the perfect פִּתֵּיתִי? This could mean that prior to the prophet's delivering the oracle, the Lord "will have deceived" (future perfect) him, causing him to cooperate with the idolaters. In this case the deception referred to before this ("As for the prophet who is deceived") turns out to be instigated by God. But this is not the only interpretive option. God's statement could mean that a prophet who allows himself to be enticed by idolaters and then cooperates with them, will be the object of subsequent divine deception as a form of judgment. In this case the perfect would be rhetorical and the divine deception is in response to the deception mentioned earlier.

101

How does one resolve the problem? A careful study of the context suggests that the second of these options is preferable. In verse 4 the Lord announces that he will punish idolaters. He says, "I the Lord will answer him." In this future time frame the niphal perfect נַעֲנֵיתִי is rhetorical, "I will answer." In verse 7 the Lord repeats his warning to idolaters, announcing once more, "I the Lord will answer him." (A niphal participle of עָנָה is employed this time.) The structure of verse 9 is very similar to these verses, especially verses 7–8, as the following chart shows:

אֲנִי יהוה נַעֲנָה־לוֹ בִי וְנָתַתִּי פָנַי בָּאִישׁ הַהוּא וַהֲשִׁמֹּתִיהוּ לְאוֹת וְלִמְשָׁלִים וְהִכְרַתִּיו מִתּוֹךְ עַמִּי
(vv. 7b–8a) "I the Lord *will answer* him myself, and I *will set* my face against that man, and I *will make him* a sign and an object lesson, and I *will cut him off* from among my people."

אֲנִי יהוה פִּתֵּיתִי אֵת הַנָּבִיא הַהוּא וְנָטִיתִי אֶת־יָדִי עָלָיו וְהִשְׁמַדְתִּיו מִתּוֹךְ עַמִּי (v. 9a)

"I the Lord *will deceive* that prophet, and I *will stretch out* my hand against him, and I *will destroy him* from among my people."

Verses 4, 7, and 9 all have the declaration "I the Lord," followed by the Lord's announcement of what he will do to the offender. As in verse 8, where the Lord expands the announcement with three perfects prefixed with waw ("I will set . . . I will make him . . . I will cut him off"), so verse 9 adds two perfects with prefixed waw ("I will stretch out . . . I will destroy him"). These structural parallels strongly suggest that the perfect form פִּתֵּיתִי be taken as a rhetorical future. The point is not that the Lord deceived the prophet initially, but that he will use deception as a form of appropriate judgment against a prophet who allows himself to be deceived by idolaters.

Genesis 3:16 provides another prime example of the importance of determining verbal aspect. In this verse the Lord pronounces a sentence of judgment on the woman for her disobedience to God's command. But how should the final statement (וְהוּא יִמְשָׁל־בָּךְ) of the verse be interpreted and translated? One option would be to understand the imperfect as a simple future and translate, "he *will rule* over you." In this case God would be announcing the certainty of the woman's subordination to the man. This would be an appropriate punishment, given the fact that the immediately preceding statement refers to her desire to overpower and control the man.[26]

However, this is not the only option available. Because of the similarity of verse 16b to Genesis 4:7b, some propose that the imperfect is sub-

---

26. The woman's "desire" is an urge to control the man. Apart from this text, the noun occurs only in Gen. 4:7, where it describes sin's "desire" to overpower Cain, and in Song of Sol. 7:10 (Eng., Heb. v. 11), where it refers to a man's urge to have his way sexually with his lover.

junctive here, indicating obligation ("he should rule over you") or command ("he must rule over you"). The imperfect "rule" is used in this way in 4:7, but the genre there is hortatory. God exhorts Cain to prevent him from sinning. The situation is different in 3:16b. The sin has been committed and the sentence of judgment is being pronounced. None of the accompanying sentences have any obligatory or injunctive statements.

A third possibility is to understand the imperfect as indicating desire, "he desires to rule over you." This would make excellent sense contextually, for the Lord has just observed that the woman desires to overpower the man. In this case, the Lord is not necessarily or directly predicting the outcome of the conflict, only announcing that a conflict will take place. Such an announcement is appropriate in a judgment speech, for living in a perpetual war zone is a form of living hell. In support of this one might also point to the surrounding judgment oracles, both of which announce perpetual conflict as part of the judgment on the offending party. Verse 15b announces that the serpent and its offspring will be in perpetual deadly conflict with the woman's offspring, and verses 18–19 announce that the man will be in perpetual conflict with the ground.

Paying attention to shifts in verbal aspect can also be significant. For example, in Genesis 12:7 the Lord uses the imperfect of נָתַן, "to give," to state his intention to someday give Abram and his descendents the promised land. The imperfect carries a simple future or desiderative nuance.[27] In chapter 15, after conducting a covenantal ceremony, the Lord begins to fulfill this promise, as he hands over to Abram, on behalf of his offspring, the title deed to the land. In verse 18 the Lord uses the perfect of נָתַן, "to give." The perfect is probably used in a simple present sense; the Lord states factually that he is formally deeding the land to Abram's offspring ("I give this land to your offpsring"). Another option is that the perfect is used as a rhetorical future. The fulfillment of the promise is no longer conditional; it has been secured, so God can talk about giving Abram's offspring the land as if it has already taken place. In either case the shift from the imperfect (in 12:7) to the perfect (in 15:18) marks formally the ratification of the earlier promise.

Volitional Forms (GKC, 319–26; W–O, 564–79)

The Hebrew verbal system also includes a group of volitional forms used to express a speaker's will—the jussive, imperative, and cohortative.

Jussive

The jussive is the volitional form of the third person and sometimes the second person. In most cases it overlaps with the imperfect and/or the

---

27. At this point God's covenant promise to Abram is not yet ratified; its ultimate fulfillment depends on Abram's response. So one might translate, "I intend/desire to give."

short prefixed conjugation (without the waw-consecutive). However, like the short prefixed conjugation, the jussive is distinct from the imperfect in some verbal patterns (for example, the hiphil stem, third he verbs, and hollow verbs). Sometimes jussives can also be spotted by the presence of the particle נָא and, when negated, by the use of the particle אַל. The precise force of the jussive can vary, depending on contextual factors such as the speaker's position relative to the one(s) being indirectly addressed.

(1) command or prohibition

Sometimes a party in a superior position uses the jussive to issue a command or prohibition.

תּוֹצֵא הָאָרֶץ נֶפֶשׁ חַיָּה, "*Let* the earth *produce* living creatures!" (Gen. 1:24)

This hiphil jussive form with theme vowel tsere (תּוֹצֵא) is distinct from the hiphil imperfect form with theme hireq yod (תּוֹצִיא, see Isa. 61:11).

אַל־תֹּאכַל לֶחֶם, "*Don't eat* food!" (1 Kings 13:22)

The Lord commands the prophet not to stop and dine with anyone in Israel. The jussive is marked by the preceding negative particle אַל.

(2) advice

יֵרֶא פַּרְעֹה אִישׁ נָבוֹן וְחָכָם, "Pharaoh *should find* (lit. "see") a wise and discerning man" (Gen. 41:33)

Joseph, who is subordinate to Pharaoh, uses the jussive to give the king advice or counsel. The short jussive form of רָאָה, "to see," with apocopated final he (יֵרֶא) is distinct from the longer imperfect form of the verb יִרְאֶה (see Gen. 22:8).

אַל־יֹאמַר הַמֶּלֶךְ כֵּן, "The king *should not say* such a thing" (1 Kings 22:8)

King Jehoshaphat of Judah advises King Ahab of Israel that he should not criticize a prophet of the Lord. The jussive is marked by the preceding negative particle אַל.

(3) request or prayer

יֵשֶׁב־נָא עַבְדְּךָ תַּחַת הַנַּעַר, "*Please* let your servant *stay* in the young man's place" (Gen. 44:33)

Judah, who is subordinate to Joseph (note "your servant"), requests that he be allowed to stay as Joseph's servant instead of Benjamin. The jussive is marked by the particle נָא.

אַל־נָא יִחַר לַאדֹנָי, "*May* the Lord *not be angry*" (Gen. 18:30)

Abraham requests that the Lord not get angry over his persistence in interceding for Sodom. The jussive is marked by the preceding אַל־נָא. The short jussive form of חָרָה, "to be angry," with apocopated final he (יִחַר) is distinct from the longer imperfect form of the verb יֶחֱרֶה (see Exod. 32:11).

The jussive can be used in formal blessings and curses, where a petitioner asks God to reward or punish someone.

יָאֵר יהוה פָּנָיו אֵלֶיךָ, "*May* the LORD *make* his face *shine* on you" (Num. 6:24)

This hiphil jussive form with theme vowel tsere (יָאֵר) is distinct from the hiphil imperfect form with theme hireq yod (יָאִיר, see Job 41:24).

פַּחֲמֵי אֵשׁ (MT has פַּחִים) יַמְטֵר עַל־רְשָׁעִים, "*Let* him (God) *rain down* coals of fire (MT, "snares") on the wicked" (Ps. 11:6)

This hiphil jussive form with theme vowel tsere (יַמְטֵר) is distinct from the hiphil imperfect form with theme hireq yod (תַּמְטִיר, see Amos 4:7). This jussive form also occurs in Job 20:23, which should be translated, "May this happen (note the apocopated jussive form יְהִי) when his belly is full! May he send (the form here is ambiguous, but since it is preceded and followed by jussive forms, it is best to interpret it as jussive) his raging anger on him! May he rain down his terror on him!"

Imperative

The imperative is a volitional form of the second person. Unlike the jussive, it does not have a prefix and it is not negated. The precise force of the imperative can vary, depending on contextual factors such as the speaker's position relative to the one(s) being addressed.

(1) command

הִנֵּה אִשְׁתְּךָ קַח וָלֵךְ, "Here is your wife; *take* (her) and *go!*" (Gen. 12:19)

Pharaoh commands Abram to take what belongs to him and leave. Sometimes the imperative can be used rhetorically or sarcastically:

בֹּאוּ בֵית־אֵל וּפִשְׁעוּ, "*Go* to Bethel and *sin!*" (Amos 4:4)

The Lord tells his people to sin, though in the very next chapter he exhorts them to repent (5:4–6, 14–15, 23–24). In this case the commands are sarcastic. Rather than expressing the Lord's desire, they are a commentary on the people's attitude. They insist on engaging in formal religion and adding hypocrisy to their already bulging list of sins. This use of the imperative is comparable to saying to a recalcitrant child who is bent on climbing a high tree, "Go ahead, be stubborn! Break your neck!" The imperative expresses the speaker's frustration rather than his will or desire.

The Lord's commission to Isaiah also employs the imperative in a sarcastic way. Isaiah's words to the people appear to be a command, "Continually hear, but don't perceive! Continually see, but don't understand!" (Isa. 6:9) As far as we know, Isaiah did not literally proclaim these exact words. The imperatival forms are employed rhetorically and anticipate the response Isaiah will receive. When all is said and done, Isaiah might as well preface and conclude every message with these ironic words, which, though imperatival in form, might be paraphrased as follows: "You continually hear, but don't understand; you continually see, but don't perceive." Isaiah might as well command them to be spiritually insensitive, because, as the preceding and following chapters make clear, the people are bent on that anyway.

In Isaiah 6:10 the Lord commands Isaiah, "Make the hearts of these people insensitive, make their ears dull, and blind their eyes!" As in verse 9 the imperatival forms should be taken as rhetorical and as anticipating the people's response. One might paraphrase: "Your preaching will desensitize the minds of these people, make their hearing dull, and blind their eyes." From the outset the Lord might as well command Isaiah to harden the people, because his preaching will end up having that effect due to their obsession with sin.

(2) advice

לְכְנָה שֹׁבְנָה אִשָּׁה לְבֵית אִמָּהּ, "*You should go back,* each of you to your mother's house" (Ruth 1:8)

Naomi uses imperatival forms in advising Orpah and Ruth to return to their homes.

(3) invitation or permission

לֵךְ אַתָּה מְלָךְ־עָלֵינוּ, "You *come, rule* over us" (Judg. 9:14)

In Jotham's parable the trees invite the thornbush to be their king.

עֲלֵה וּקְבֹר אֶת־אָבִיךְ, "*Go on up and bury* your father" (Gen. 50:6)

Pharaoh gives Joseph permission to bury Jacob in Canaan.

(4) request or prayer

הַסְתֵּר פָּנֶיךָ מֵחֲטָאָי וְכָל־עֲוֺנֹתַי מְחֵה, "*Please hide* your face from my sin; and *please blot out* all my evil deeds" (Ps. 51:9, Heb. v. 11)

The repentant psalmist begs God to forgive his sin.

Cohortative

The cohortative is the volitional form of the first person. It is almost identical to the imperfect, but in most cases has הָ- suffixed to the form. (Third he verbs and forms with pronominal suffixes are exceptions.)

(1) request or wish

Sometimes a speaker uses the cohortative to make a request of someone or express a wish.

אֶעֱלֶה־נָּא וְאֶקְבְּרָה אֶת־אָבִי, *"Please let me go up and bury* my father" (Gen. 50:5)

Joseph asks Pharaoh for permission to bury Jacob in Canaan. The first cohortative is marked by the suffixed particle נָא, the second by the typical suffixed הָ-.

אַל־אֵבוֹשָׁה, *"Let me* not *be humiliated"* (Ps. 25:2)

The psalmist uses the cohortative to express his request that he not be humiliated. The cohortative is marked by the preceding negative particle אַל and by the typical suffixed הָ-.

(2) resolve (intention, determination, desire)

A speaker sometimes uses the cohortative to express his or her intent or determination.

וַאֲבָרֲכָה מְבָרְכֶיךָ, *"I will bless* those who bless you" (Gen. 12:3)

The Lord informs Abram of his intention or determination to bless those who treat Abram well. The cohortative is marked by the typical suffixed הָ-.

אַל־אֶרְאֶה בְּמוֹת הַיָּלֶד, *"I refuse to watch* (lit., "I will not see") the boy die" (Gen. 21:16)

Hagar expresses her refusal (i.e., her determination/desire not) to watch her son die of hunger. The cohortative is marked by the preceding negative particle אַל.

(3) exhortation

Sometimes a speaker uses the cohortative to urge a group or opposing party to join in an activity.

נֵלְכָה וְנַעַבְדָה אֱלֹהִים אֲחֵרִים, *"Let's go and worship* other gods" (Deut. 13:7)

The Lord anticipates a time when a person might decide to encourage others in the family or community to worship other gods.

Volitional Forms in Sequence

Volitional forms often occur in succession. When the subject does not change, the forms are often synonymous/parallel (especially in poetic texts) or purely sequential. Sometimes the second form in the sequence indicates purpose or result.

Jussive + jussive

אֵל שַׁדַּי יְבָרֵךְ אֹתְךָ וְיַפְרְךָ וְיַרְבֶּךָ, "May El Shaddai *bless* you, and *make* you *fruitful*, and *multiply* you" (Gen. 28:3)

The second jussive in the sequence specifies the nature of the general blessing requested in the first. The second and third jussives are synonymous/parallel.

יַעַבְדוּךָ עַמִּים וְיִשְׁתַּחֲווּ לְךָ לְאֻמִּים, "*May* nations *serve* you; *may* peoples *bow down* to you" (Gen. 27:29)

The subjects of the parallel lines are different, but synonymous, and the jussives are parallel.

תֵּרֶד אֵשׁ מִן־הַשָּׁמַיִם וְתֹאכַל אֹתְךָ, "*May* fire *come down* from the sky *and devour* you" (2 Kings 1:10)

The successive jussives are purely sequential.

יָבוֹא־נָא עוֹד אֵלֵינוּ וְיוֹרֵנוּ, "*May he visit* us again, *so he can teach* us" (Judg. 13:8)

The second jussive indicates purpose. Manoah prays that the angel might come visit them again for the purpose of instructing them about how the child should be raised.

יָבֹא־נָא אֵלַי וְיֵדַע כִּי יֵשׁ נָבִיא בְּיִשְׂרָאֵל, "*Let him come* to me *so he may know* that there is a prophet in Israel" (2 Kings 5:8)

The second jussive indicates purpose. Elisha instructs the king to allow Naaman to visit, so that he might learn from firsthand experience that a genuine prophet lives in Israel.

Imperative + imperative

צַהֲלִי וָרֹנִּי יוֹשֶׁבֶת צִיּוֹן, "*Shout and cry out*, O resident of Zion" (Isa. 12:6)

The two imperatives are synonymous.

שִׁמְעוּ שָׁמַיִם וְהַאֲזִינִי אֶרֶץ, "*Listen* O heavens; *pay attention*, O earth" (Isa. 1:2)

In the poetic structure heavens and earth correspond and the imperatives are synonymous/parallel.

עֲלֵה בֵית־אֵל וְשֶׁב־שָׁם, "*Go up* to Bethel *and live* there" (Gen. 35:1)

The imperatives are purely sequential.

זֹאת עֲשׂוּ וִחְיוּ, "*Do* this *so that you might live*" (Gen. 42:18)

The second imperative indicates result or consequence. The idea is, "If you do this, then you will live" (see also Amos 5:4; cf. v. 14).

פַּתִּי אוֹתוֹ וּרְאִי בַּמֶּה כֹּחוֹ גָדוֹל, "*Seduce* him, *so you can discover* the source of his great strength" (Judg. 16:5)

The second imperative indicates purpose. The Philistines tell Delilah to seduce Samson with the intent of finding out the secret of his strength.

Cohortative + cohortative

נָגִילָה וְנִשְׂמְחָה בִּישׁוּעָתוֹ, "*Let us rejoice and be happy* because of his salvation" (Isa. 25:9)

The two cohortatives are synonymous.

וְנַהַרְגֵהוּ וְנַשְׁלִכֵהוּ בְּאַחַד הַבֹּרוֹת, "and *let's kill* him *and throw* him into one of the cisterns" (Gen. 37:20)

The cohortatives are purely sequential.

וְאֹכְלָה וַאֲבָרֶכְכָה, "*and I will eat so that I might bless* you" (Gen. 27:7)

The second cohortative indicates purpose. The subordinate nature of the second cohortative may not be obvious from this verse alone, but three other verses in the immediate context validate this analysis:

וְאֹכֵלָה בַּעֲבוּר תְּבָרֶכְךָ נַפְשִׁי, "and I will eat so that I may bless you" (Gen. 27:4)

The conjunction בַּעֲבוּר, "so that," links the cohortative ("I will eat") with the imperfect ("may bless"). Eating the ritual meal is necessary before the formal blessing can be bestowed.

וְאֹכְלָה מִצֵּידִי בַּעֲבוּר תְּבָרֲכַנִּי נַפְשֶׁךָ, "Eat some of my meat so that you may bless me" (Gen. 27:19)

The conjunction בַּעֲבוּר links the imperative ("eat") with the imperfect ("may bless"), again indicating a subordinate relationship between the two actions.

109

וְאֹכְלָה מִצַּיִד בְּנִי לְמַעַן תְּבָרֶכְךָ נַפְשִׁי, "and I will eat some meat, my son, so that I might bless you" (Gen. 27:25)

The conjunction לְמַעַן, "so that," links the cohortative ("I will eat") with the imperfect ("may bless"), indicating the meal is a prerequisite to pronouncing the blessing.

When the subject changes, the successive volitional forms can be parallel or sequential, but the second volitional form in the sequence frequently indicates purpose/result.

Jussive (or imperfect) ו imperative

וְיִתְפַּלֵּל בַּעַדְךָ וֶחְיֵה, "*Let him pray* for you, *so that you may live*" (Gen. 20:7)

וְיִתֵּן קֹלוֹת וּמָטָר וּדְעוּ וּרְאוּ כִּי־רָעַתְכֶם רַבָּה אֲשֶׁר עֲשִׂיתֶם בְּעֵינֵי יְהוָה, "*that he may produce* thunder and rain, *so you may know and see* that what you have done is very wicked in the sight of the LORD" (1 Sam. 12:17)

Jussive (or imperfect) + cohortative

תָּבוֹא־נָא תָמָר אֲחֹתִי וּתְלַבֵּב לְעֵינַי שְׁתֵּי לְבִבוֹת וְאֶבְרֶה מִיָּדָהּ, "*Please allow* my sister Tamar *to come and bake* two heart-shaped cakes in my sight, *so I may eat* from her hand" (2 Sam. 13:6)

Imperative + jussive (or imperfect)

הֲשִׁבֵהוּ אִתְּךָ אֶל־בֵּיתֶךָ וְיֹאכַל לֶחֶם וְיֵשְׁתְּ מָיִם, "and bring him back with you to your house *so he may eat* food *and drink* water" (1 Kings 13:18)

The two jussives are subordinate to the imperative and indicate the old man's purpose for inviting the prophet to his house.

Imperative + cohortative

הַטִּי־נָא כַדֵּךְ וְאֶשְׁתֶּה, "*Lower* your water jug, *so I may drink*" (Gen. 24:14)

וְתֶן־זֶרַע וְנִחְיֶה, "*Please give* us some seed, *so we may live*" (Gen. 47:19)

Cohortative + jussive (or imperfect)

אָקוּמָה וְאֵלְכָה וְאֶקְבְּצָה אֶל־אֲדֹנִי הַמֶּלֶךְ אֶת־כָּל־יִשְׂרָאֵל וְיִכְרְתוּ אִתְּךָ בְּרִית, "*I will get up and go and gather* to my lord the king all Israel, *so they may make* a covenant with you" (2 Sam. 3:21)

Cohortative + imperative

וְאֶתְּנָה לָכֶם אֶת־טוּב אֶרֶץ מִצְרַיִם וְאִכְלוּ אֶת־חֵלֶב הָאָרֶץ, "*I will give* you the best land in Egypt, *so you may eat* the best produce of the land" (Gen. 45:18)

Recognizing and analyzing a volitional sequence can often be significant to the interpretation of a passage.

(1) For example, in Genesis 1:26 a jussive (or imperfect) follows a cohortative:

וירדו כדמותנו בצלמנו אדם נעשׂה, "*Let us make* humankind in our image, according to our likeness, *so that they may rule.*"

The jussive likely indicates purpose following the cohortative. This suggests that the image of God, however it is defined, gives humankind the authority and/or capacity to rule over creation. Elsewhere in Genesis the combination cohortative + jussive also indicates purpose/result:

ותחי נפשׁי . . . שׁמה נא אמלטה, "*Please let me escape* . . . *so that* my life *may be spared*" (Gen. 19:20)

אתנו וישׁבו להם נאותה, "*Let's make an agreement* with them, *so they may live* with us" (Gen. 34:23)

(2) In Genesis 17:1–2 two cohortatives follow two imperatives:

מאד במאד אותך וארבה וביני ביני בריתי ואתנה תמים והיה לפני התהלך, "*Walk* before me *and be* blameless. *And I will ratify* my covenant between you and me, *and I will greatly multiply* you."

The imperatives in verse 1 are possibly sequential, though the second could indicate purpose/result.[28] It is likely that the cohortatives in verse 2 are sequential in relation to each other and that they indicate purpose/result in relation to the preceding imperatives. One could paraphrase the statement:

"*Walk* before me *and be* (or, *so that you might be*) blameless. *Then I will ratify* (or, *so that I might ratify*) my covenant between you and me, and *I will greatly multiply* you."

Understanding the sequence in this way means the promise of verse 2 is conditional on Abram's obedience to the command of verse 1.[29]

(3) In Genesis 12:1–2 a complex sequence of volitional forms appears:

ברכה וחיה שׁמך ואגדלה ואברכך גדול לגוי ואעשׂך . . . מארצך לך־לך
"*Go* from your land . . . *and I will make* you into a great nation, *and bless you and make* your name *great, and be* a blessing."

The volitives are arranged in a three-tiered structure:

28. A decision depends on whether the phrase "walk before" has a neutral sense ("live in my presence") or a positive connotation ("live faithfully in my presence"). If the latter is chosen, then the second imperative would indicate purpose/result.

29. Other instances in Genesis of a cohortative indicating purpose/result after an imperative include 19:5, 34; 23:4, 13; 24:14, 49, 56; 26:3; 27:4, 7, 9, 25; 30:25; 42:2, 34; 44:21; 47:19; 49:1. The purpose/result nuance is possible, but not as obvious, in 29:27; 30:28; 31:3; 32:9; 34:12.

Imperative ("Go") (v. 1)

Cohortatives with waw ("and I will make . . . bless . . . make great")
(v. 2a)

Imperative with waw ("and be") (v. 2b)

The cohortatives in verse 2 are best understood as synonymous/parallel. After the imperative, they (as a three-part unit) likely indicate purpose/result. The final imperative is subordinate to the preceding cohortatives (see also Gen. 18:5; 19:8, 34), indicating the ultimate purpose/result of Abram's moving. One could paraphrase the verses as follows:

> *"Go* from your land. . . . *Then I will make* you into a great nation, *and bless you and make* your name *great, with the result that you will be* a blessing."

Understanding the sequence in this way means that God's promise (expressed through the cohortatives in v. 2a) and the realization of the ultimate goal (expressed through the imperative in v. 2b) are conditional upon Abram's leaving his land.

Support for this interpretation comes from Genesis 45:18, where the same sequence of imperative + cohortative + imperative appears:

וְקְחוּ אֶת־אֲבִיכֶם וְאֶת־בָּתֵּיכֶם וּבֹאוּ אֵלָי וְאֶתְּנָה לָכֶם אֶת־טוּב אֶרֶץ מִצְרַיִם וְאִכְלוּ אֶת־חֵלֶב הָאָרֶץ, "*Go get* your father and your families *and come* to me. *And I will give* you the best land in Egypt, *and eat* the best produce of the land" (Gen. 45:18)

The three-tiered structure may be outlined as follows:

Imperatives ("Go get . . . and come") (v. 18a)[30]

Cohortative with waw ("And I will give") (v. 18b)

Imperative with waw ("and eat") (v. 18c)

After the imperative, the cohortative in verse 18b likely indicates purpose/result. The final imperative is subordinate to the preceding cohortative, indicating the ultimate purpose/result of Jacob's moving to Egypt. Pharaoh's offer (expressed by the cohortative in v. 18b) and the realization of the ultimate goal (expressed through the imperative in v. 18c) are conditional upon Jacob's accepting the invitation and coming to Egypt.

30. Actually the series of imperatives begins in v. 17.

Dependent Clauses (GKC, 471–506; W–O, 632–46)

A clause is a group of words containing a subject and a predicate and forming part of a compound or complex sentence. Clauses can be independent or dependent. An independent clause is grammatically self-contained and can be punctuated as a complete sentence. A dependent clause is grammatically subordinate to an independent (i.e., main) clause. For example, consider the following sentence: "After the rain stopped, we went to the store." "We went to the store" is an independent clause and the main clause in this sentence. "After the rain stopped" is a dependent (in this case, temporal) clause, subordinate to the main clause. In this section we examine the different types of dependent clauses in Hebrew. A discussion of independent clauses is reserved for the following chapter, which deals with Hebrew narrative structure.

Noun clauses

Noun clauses fill a noun slot in the sentence. As such, they may function as nominatives, genitives, or accusatives. Noun clauses are often introduced by אֲשֶׁר, כִּי, or אֵת.

(1) Nominative

וּלְשָׁאוּל הֻגַּד כִּי־נִמְלַט דָּוִד, "It was told to Saul *that David had escaped*" (1 Sam. 23:13)

The noun clause, which is introduced by כִּי, is the grammatical subject of the passive verb form הֻגַּד. One could translate, "(The fact) that David escaped was told to Saul."

(2) Genitive

כָּל־יְמֵי הִתְהַלַּכְנוּ אִתָּם, "all the days *we lived among them*" (lit., "all the days we walked about with them," 1 Sam. 25:15)

The noun clause consists of a hithpael perfect verb form and a preposition with pronominal suffix. The clause follows a construct plural noun form, and is therefore genitival.

(3) Accusative

וַתֵּרֶא הָאִשָּׁה כִּי טוֹב הָעֵץ לְמַאֲכָל, "and the woman saw *that the tree yielded fruit that could be eaten*" (lit., "and the woman saw that the tree was good for food," Gen. 3:6)

The noun clause, introduced by כִּי, is the object of the verb "saw."

Sometimes a noun clause is appositional to a noun, forming a double accusative:

וַיִּרְאוּ בְנֵי־הָאֱלֹהִים אֶת־בְּנוֹת הָאָדָם כִּי טֹבֹת הֵנָּה, "and the sons of God saw the daughters of men, that they were attractive" (Gen. 6:2)

The noun clause, introduced by כִּי, is juxtaposed with the direct object "daughters" (which is introduced by the accusative sign אֵת and is modified by the genitive "men"). "Daughters" identifies whom they saw, the noun clause specifies what they saw. It is best to combine the accusatives in translation: "and the sons of God saw that the daughters of men were attractive."

Relative clauses

Relative clauses modify a noun or pronoun. They are typically introduced by a relative pronoun, though they can be asyndetic (i.e., unmarked and implied), especially in poetry.

הַמָּקוֹם אֲשֶׁר אַתָּה עוֹמֵד עָלָיו אַדְמַת־קֹדֶשׁ הוּא, "the place *upon which you stand* is holy ground" (Exod. 3:5)

יֹאבַד יוֹם אִוָּלֶד בּוֹ, "May the day *in which I was born* perish" (Job 3:3)

Here the relative clause is asyndetic.

Temporal clauses

Temporal clauses provide the time frame of the main action or state. They are typically introduced by כִּי or by a temporal preposition.

וַיְהִי בִּהְיוֹתָם בַּשָּׂדֶה וַיָּקָם קַיִן אֶל־הֶבֶל אָחִיו וַיַּהַרְגֵהוּ, "*while they were in the field,* Cain attacked his brother Abel and killed him" (Gen. 4:8)

The temporal clause is here introduced by the preposition -בְּ, which is prefixed to the infinitive construct of הָיָה.

Conditional clauses

A conditional clause (the protasis of a conditional sentence) expresses a condition in relation to the main clause (the apodosis of a conditional sentence). Conditional clauses are typically introduced by a conditional particle such as כִּי, אִם, or לוּלֵי/לוּ. Real conditions are those already fulfilled or viewed as possible (at least for the sake of argument) by the speaker; unreal conditions (usually introduced by לוּ or לוּלֵי) are not fulfilled or are viewed as incapable of being fulfilled by the speaker.

אִם־תַּעֲשׂוּן כָּזֹאת כִּי אִם־נִקַּמְתִּי בָכֶם, "*Since you insist on acting this way,* I will get revenge against you" (Judg. 15:7)

Here the conditional clause (protasis) expresses a real condition that is already fulfilled and serves as the basis for future action.

אִם־תֵּלְכִי עִמִּי וְהָלָכְתִּי וְאִם־לֹא תֵלְכִי עִמִּי לֹא אֵלֵךְ, "*if you go with me,* I will go, but *if you will not go with me,* I will not go" (Judg. 4:8)

This sentence contains two conditional clauses. Each expresses a real condition which, though not yet realized, is viewed by the speaker as capable of being fulfilled.

לוּ הַחֲיִתֶם אוֹתָם לֹא הָרַגְתִּי אֶתְכֶם, "*If you had let them live* (but you didn't!), I would not kill you" (Judg. 8:19)

Here the conditional clause is unreal; it expresses a condition that was not fulfilled.

וְלוּ אָנֹכִי שֹׁקֵל עַל־כַּפַּי אֶלֶף כֶּסֶף לֹא־אֶשְׁלַח יָדִי אֶל־בֶּן־הַמֶּלֶךְ, "*Even if I were paid a thousand shekels,* I would not lift my hand against the king's son" (2 Sam. 18:12)

Here the conditional clause is unreal; it expresses a condition that is viewed by the speaker as purely hypothetical and incapable of being fulfilled (or as highly unlikely).

Concessive clauses

In a concessive clause the speaker concedes a fact in relation to an affirmation or denial. Concessive clauses typically are introduced by כִּי, אִם, גַּם כִּי, or עַל.

גַּם כִּי־תַרְבּוּ תְפִלָּה אֵינֶנִּי שֹׁמֵעַ, "*Though you offer many prayers,* I am not listening" (Isa. 1:15)

Exceptive or restrictive clauses

In an exceptive or restrictive clause the speaker expresses certain exceptions to or places certain limitations on the main action or state. These clauses are often introduced by אַךְ, אֶפֶס כִּי, בִּלְתִּי אִם, כִּי אִם, or רַק.

לֹא אֲשַׁלֵּחֲךָ כִּי אִם־בֵּרַכְתָּנִי, "I will not let you go *unless you bless me*" (Gen. 32:26)

Comparative clauses

Comparative clauses draw a comparison to the idea expressed in the main clause. They are typically introduced by כַּאֲשֶׁר, כְּמוֹ, or -כְּ.

כמו הרה תקריב ללדת תחיל תזעק בחבליה כן היינו מפניך יהוה, "*As when a pregnant woman gets ready to deliver and strains and yells out because of her labor pains*, so were we before you, O LORD" (Isa. 26:17)

Causal or explanatory clauses

Causal clauses express a cause or reason for the main action or state. They are typically introduced by אֲשֶׁר, יַעַן, עַל, כִּי, or one of the other causal prepositions.

ואירא כי־עירם אנכי, "I was afraid *because I was naked*" (Gen. 3:10)

אהיה אֲשֶׁר אהיה, "(Call me) 'I AM,' *because I am*" (Exod. 3:14)

This seemingly enigmatic statement has been interpreted in a variety of ways, one of which is reflected in the above translation. Genesis 31:48b–49 provides support for this interpretation, displaying the same structure as Exodus 3:14, namely, proper name + אֲשֶׁר + explanation for the name:

קרא שמו גלעד והמזפה אשר אמר יצף יהוה ביני ובינך, "He called its name Galeed and Mizpah, because he said, 'The LORD will keep watch between me and you.'"[31]

Purpose and result clauses

A purpose clause expresses the intended result of the main action. Purpose clauses are typically introduced by לְ- with an infinitive construct, לְמַעַן, בַּעֲבוּר, אֲשֶׁר, or, if negated, בִּלְתִּי or פֶּן.

אמרי־נא אחתי את למען ייטב־לי, "Say you are my sister, *so it may go well for me*" (Gen. 12:13)

---

31. For a more detailed defense of this interpretation, see T. N. D. Mettinger, *In Search of God*, trans. Frederick Cryer (Philadelphia: Fortress, 1988), 33–36. The name "Yahweh" is derived from an original root *hwh* or *hwy* (= Hebrew *hyh*), "to be." It is not certain if the form is basic (qal stem) or causative (hiphil). The basic form would highlight God's existence or presence, "he is," while the causative form would focus on his creative power, "he causes (something) to be, he creates." Exod. 3:14–16 suggests the former is correct. When Moses asks God his name, the Lord responds by identifying himself as "I AM" (qal form, first person; v. 14), which he then converts to "Yahweh" (third person; vv. 15–16) to facilitate reference. (It is far less confusing to refer to God as "he is" than to call him "I am." On the other hand it is much more natural for God to refer to himself as "I am" than to call himself "he is.") The context suggests that the name points to God's enabling and saving presence with his people, not to his mere existence (vv. 12, 15–17). I would paraphrase God's words to Moses in vv. 14–15 as follows: "Call me 'I am the ever present helper' because I am indeed the ever present helper. This is what you should say to the Israelites: 'I am the ever present helper has sent me to you'. . . . Say to the Israelites, 'He (who) is the ever present helper, the God of your fathers, the God of Abraham, the God of Isaac, and the God of Jacob has sent me to you.' This will be my name forever, by which I will be remembered from generation to generation."

נִבְנֶה־לָּנוּ עִיר וּמִגְדָּל . . . וְנַעֲשֶׂה־לָּנוּ שֵׁם פֶּן־נָפוּץ, "Let's build for ourselves a city and a tower . . . and make a name for ourselves, *so we might not be scattered*" (Gen. 11:4)

A result clause expresses the actual result of the main action. Result clauses are typically introduced by -לְ with the infinitive construct, לְמַעַן, כִּי, or אֲשֶׁר.

וְאִישׁ וְאָבִיו יֵלְכוּ אֶל־הַנַּעֲרָה לְמַעַן חַלֵּל אֶת־שֵׁם קָדְשִׁי, "and a man and his son visit a young woman, *thus profaning my holy name*" (Amos 2:7)

Distinguishing purpose and result is not always easy. For example, in Isaiah 28:13 we read: "So the LORD's word to them will sound like gibberish, senseless babbling, a syllable here, a syllable there. As a result (לְמַעַן), they will fall on their backside when they try to walk, and be injured, ensnared, and captured." Because the people have rejected the Lord's appeals (v. 12), a day will come when they will be so spiritually insensitive that prophetic preaching sounds like gibberish to them. If one takes לְמַעַן as indicating mere result or consequence, the interpretation is quite straightforward. Without this divine guidance, the people will be doomed to destruction. However, לְמַעַן often indicates purpose (intended result). If understood that way here, the interpretation of the passage becomes a bit more profound, theologically speaking. One might translate, "So the LORD's word to them will sound like gibberish . . . in order that they might fall. . . ." In this case, the rejection of the prophetic word leads to spiritual insensitivity by the Lord's design, so that he might expedite the people's destruction.

For Further Reading and Reference

Gibson, J. C. L. *Davidson's Introductory Hebrew Grammar: Syntax*. 4th ed. Edinburgh: T. & T. Clark, 1994.

Jouön, P. *A Grammar of Biblical Hebrew*. 2 vols. Trans. and rev. T. Muraoka. Rome: Pontifical Biblical Institute, 1991.

Kautzsch, E., ed. *Gesenius' Hebrew Grammar*. 2nd English ed. Trans. A. E. Cowley. Oxford: Clarendon, 1910.

McFall, Leslie. *The Enigma of the Hebrew Verbal System*. Sheffield: Almond, 1982.

Niccacci, Alviero. *The Syntax of the Verb in Classical Hebrew Prose*. Trans. W. G. E. Watson. Sheffield: JSOT, 1990.

Waltke, Bruce K., and M. O'Connor. *An Introduction to Biblical Hebrew Syntax*. Winona Lake, Ind.: Eisenbrauns, 1990.

Williams, Ronald J. *Hebrew Syntax: An Outline*. 2nd ed. Toronto: University of Toronto, 1976.

6 Beyond the Sentence

The Basic Structure of Hebrew Narrative and Poetry

Linguistic analysis of the Hebrew text must extend beyond words, phrases, subordinate clauses, and individual sentences. The interpreter must also look at the larger structure of the literary unit. In narrative literature this means, among other things, examining how sentences interrelate to form paragraphs and how paragraphs combine to form a story. When working in a poetic text, the interpreter must analyze the various ways in which the poet utilizes parallelism to construct a prayer, hymn, or speech.

Hebrew Narrative

Main Elements

Hebrew narrative structure consists of three main elements: (1) the framework, (2) nonstandard constructions that deviate from or interrupt the normal pattern of the narrative framework, and (3) quotations and dialogues embedded in the narrative.

The Narrative Framework

The framework of a narrative gives the story its basic structure. A narrative may begin in a variety of ways, but its basic structure consists of a series of main clauses displaying the following pattern: conjunction (waw-consecutive) + verb (the short prefixed form/preterite) + subject (if stated). When the verb is negated, the conjunction takes its normal form and the verb appears in the suffixed conjugation (perfect) after the negative particle, which is attached to the conjunction. Occasionally an imperfect (used in a customary past or past progressive sense) will follow the negative particle (see, e.g., Gen. 2:25; Judg. 6:4; 2 Sam. 2:28; 1 Kings 1:1).

Many grammarians call the basic verbal pattern used in narrative "the waw-consecutive with the imperfect." However, as explained in the preceding chapter, the evidence seems to indicate that this conjugation is distinct from the imperfect. We labeled it the "short prefixed form/preterite." To simplify matters, especially for those who use the older terminology, we will refer to the form in question as the *wayyiqtol* pattern in the following discussion.

Within a narrative framework, *wayyiqtol* forms can have a variety of functions within their literary context. Some of the most common of these are listed and discussed here.[1]

(1) introductory

Sometimes a narrative or scene within a narrative begins with a *wayyiqtol* form.

וַיֵּלֶךְ אִישׁ מִבֵּית לֵוִי וַיִּקַּח אֶת־בַּת־לֵוִי, "*And* a man *went* from the house of Levi and married a daughter of Levi" (Exod. 2:1)

A new narrative unit (the account of Moses' birth) within the larger story begins with the *wayyiqtol* form וַיֵּלֶךְ, "and he went."

The *wayyiqtol* form וַיְהִי, "and it so happened," often followed by a temporal clause, is frequently used to begin a new narrative or scene.[2]

וַיְהִי כִּי־הֵחֵל הָאָדָם לָרֹב עַל־פְּנֵי הָאֲדָמָה וּבָנוֹת יֻלְּדוּ לָהֶם, "*And it so happened*, when men began to multiply on the face of the earth, daughters were born to them" (Gen. 6:1)

וַיְהִי signals the beginning of a new narrative (the account of how the earth became morally corrupt) after the genealogy of chapter 5.

וַיְהִי בַּלַּיְלָה הַהוּא וַיֹּאמֶר לוֹ יְהוָה, "*And it so happened*, during that night the LORD said to him" (Judg. 6:25)

וַיְהִי signals a new scene in the unfolding narrative of Gideon's divine call to deliver Israel.

(2) sequential (and/or consequential)

Most often *wayyiqtol* forms introduce clauses describing events that occurred in temporal and/or logical sequence.

וַיִּשְׁלַח דָּוִד מַלְאָכִים וַיִּקָּחֶהָ וַתָּבוֹא אֵלָיו וַיִּשְׁכַּב עִמָּהּ . . . וַתָּשָׁב אֶל־בֵּיתָהּ

---

1. Not all *wayyiqtol* forms occur in the basic narrative framework. They can also appear in parenthetical sections introduced by a disjunctive clause (cf. Gen. 31:34) and in quotations (cf. Judg. 7:13).

2. We are not referring to cases where וַיְהִי appears as the main verb in the sentence and is translated, "and (subject) was." See, for example, its use in Gen. 5:31–32.

"and David sent messengers *and took her and she came* to him *and he had sex* with her . . . *and she returned* to her house"* (2 Sam. 11:4)

(3) resumptive

Sometimes a *wayyiqtol* form repeats (not necessarily verbatim) a statement made earlier in the narrative in order to resume the earlier story line after a parenthesis or to link a later narrative unit with an earlier one.

וַיִּקַּח יְהוָה אֱלֹהִים אֶת־הָאָדָם וַיַּנִּחֵהוּ בְגַן־עֵדֶן לְעָבְדָהּ וּלְשָׁמְרָהּ, *"and the* LORD *God took* the man *and placed* him in the garden of Eden to cultivate it and take care of it"* (Gen. 2:15)

This statement resumes the earlier narrative (see vv. 7–9) after the lengthy parenthesis in verses 10–14. The statement essentially repeats what was reported in verse 8b ("and he put there the man whom he had formed"), but assumes what was reported in verses 8a and 9. The narrative structure may be outlined as follows:

2:8 And the LORD God planted a garden . . . and placed there the man . . .

2:15 and the LORD God took and placed . . .

2:9 And the LORD God caused to grow . . . (2:10–14 is parenthetical)

2:16 and the LORD God commanded . . .

By essentially repeating one of the statements made in the section before the parenthesis, the narrator links this new part of the narrative with the earlier portion and lets us know he is ready to resume the main story line.

וַיְשַׁלַּח יְהוֹשֻׁעַ אֶת־הָעָם וַיֵּלְכוּ בְנֵי־יִשְׂרָאֵל אִישׁ לְנַחֲלָתוֹ לָרֶשֶׁת אֶת־הָאָרֶץ, *"and Joshua sent* the people *away, and the Israelites went,* each to his allotted land to take possession of the land"* (Judg. 2:6)

This statement goes back to a much earlier point in the larger discourse (see Josh. 24:28) after a lengthy narrative of what happened after Joshua's death (see Judg. 1:1–2:5). The statement essentially repeats Joshua 24:28. (There are other links between Judg. 2:7–9 and Josh. 24:28–31 as well. Judg. 2:8 essentially repeats Josh. 24:29, while Judg. 2:9 is virtually identical to Josh. 24:30; the summary statement in Josh. 24:31 is placed at a different point in the sequence, cf. Judg. 2:7.) Through this resumptive technique the narrator links the new narrative (2:10–23) with an earlier one (Josh. 24). One might outline the narrative structure of Josh. 24–Judg. 2 as follows:

A	B	A
Josh. 24:1–33	Judg. 1:1–2:5	Judg. 2:6–23

The overall discourse displays parallelism:

Prior to Joshua's death	Josh. 24:1–28	Judg. 2:6
Notice of Joshua's death	Josh. 24:29–30	Judg. 2:8–9
Parenthetical/summary	Josh. 24:31–33	Judg. 2:7
After Joshua's death	Judg. 1:1–2:5	Judg. 2:10–23

(4) reiterative

Sometimes a *wayyiqtol* form simply reiterates what was stated in the preceding clause.

ולא־זכר שר־המשקים את־יוסף <u>וישכחהו</u>, "and the chief cupbearer did not remember Joseph; *he forgot* him" (Gen. 40:23)

(5) specifying or focusing

Sometimes a *wayyiqtol* form specifies a more general statement that directly precedes it.

ויעשו בני־ישראל את־הרע בעיני יהוה <u>וישכחו</u> את־יהוה אלהיהם <u>ויעבדו</u> את־הבעלים ואת־האשרות, "and the Israelites did evil in the eyes of the LORD; *they forgot* the LORD their God *and served* the Baals and the Asherahs" (Judg. 3:7)

The second and third statements specify the first statement by telling how Israel "did evil in the eyes of the LORD."

ובנה מזבחת בבית יהוה . . . . <u>ויבן</u> מזבחות לכל־צבא השמים, "and he built altars in the LORD's temple . . . ; *he built* altars to all the host of heaven" (2 Kings 21:4–5a)

The *wayyiqtol* form introduces a statement that specifies the preceding general statement by describing what type of altars Manasseh built in the temple.

Sometimes a *wayyiqtol* form introduces a more detailed or focused account of an immediately preceding general statement.

ותלך ותבוא ותלקט בשדה אחרי הקצרים <u>ויקר</u> מקרה חלקת השדה לבעז, "and she went and came and gleaned in the field behind the reapers; *she just happened to be working* in the portion of the field belonging to Boaz" (Ruth 2:3)

The first half of the verse states in very general terms that Ruth went out and gleaned in the field. The *wayyiqtol* form וַיִּקֶר begins a more detailed account that tells us precisely where she was working, how she happened to be there, and what transpired during the course of the day's events.

(6) supplemental or parenthetical

Occasionally a *wayyiqtol* form, especially וַיְהִי, introduces a parenthetical note in the narrative. For example, 1 Kings 18:3 states that Ahab summoned his palace administrator Obadiah. Verse 5 then records Ahab's orders to Obadiah. But in between the narrator places a parenthetical note about Obadiah's loyalty to the Lord (v. 4). This parenthesis is introduced by וַיְהִי. For another example see 1 Chronicles 11:6, which inserts parenthetical information about Joab's role in the conquest of Jerusalem.

(7) explanatory

Sometimes a *wayyiqtol* form introduces an explanatory statement.

"The families of the tribe of Levi were not counted with them, for the LORD *said* to Moses (וַיְדַבֵּר יהוה אֶל־מֹשֶׁה), 'Do not count the tribe of Levites'" (Num. 1:47–49a)

After the general observation that the Levites were not counted, the *wayyiqtol* form וַיְדַבֵּר, "and he said," introduces a section (vv. 48–53) explaining the reason why they were not included in the census. (For another example, see Isa. 39:1, וַיִּשְׁמַע, "for he heard," which is equivalent to כִּי שָׁמַע in 2 Kings 20:12.)

(8) summarizing or concluding

Sometimes a *wayyiqtol* form introduces a statement that summarizes or concludes the preceding narrative.

וַיֶּחֱזַק דָּוִד מִן־הַפְּלִשְׁתִּי בַּקֶּלַע וּבָאֶבֶן וַיַּךְ אֶת־הַפְּלִשְׁתִּי וַיְמִיתֵהוּ, "*So* David defeated the Philistine with a sling and a stone, and he struck down the Philistine, and killed him" (1 Sam. 17:50)

This statement summarizes David's victory over the Philistine warrior, the details of which appear in the preceding verses.

וַתִּכָּנַע מוֹאָב בַּיּוֹם הַהוּא תַּחַת יַד יִשְׂרָאֵל וַתִּשְׁקֹט הָאָרֶץ שְׁמוֹנִים שָׁנָה, "*So* Moab *was subdued* in that day under the hand of Israel, and the land had rest for eighty years" (Judg. 3:30)

This statement brings to a conclusion the preceding narrative about Ehud's exploits.

Nonstandard Constructions

Hebrew narrative structure also includes nonstandard constructions that deviate from or interrupt the normal pattern of the narrative framework (i.e., the sequence of *wayyiqtol* forms). Often a clause will begin with a conjunction followed by a nonverb, frequently the subject of the clause.[3] Less often the conjunction is followed by the perfect, where a

---

3. Occasionally the waw will be omitted. See, for example, Judg. 20:31, 43.

wayyiqtol form would be expected.[4] Sometimes the construction עַל־כֵּן, "therefore," introduces an explanatory clause interrupting a narrative sequence.

Waw + Nonverb Constructions (Disjunctive Clauses)

Clauses introduced by waw + nonverb constructions (sometimes referred to as disjunctive clauses) have a variety of functions in their literary context. Some of the most common of these are listed and discussed here.

(1) introductory

Sometimes the waw + nonverb construction introduces a new theme or character into the narrative. In such cases it often serves as a structural marker, formally indicating a shift in scene or the beginning of a new narrative unit within the larger discourse.

וְהַנָּחָשׁ הָיָה ערום מכל חית השׂדה, "*Now the serpent was* more crafty than all the other wild animals" (Gen. 3:1)

The subject ("the serpent") is placed before the verb ("was"). The construction serves to introduce a new character to the story and marks a shift in scene.

וְהָאָדָם יָדַע אֶת־חוה אשתו, "*Now the man knew* his wife Eve" (Gen. 4:1)

The subject ("Adam") is placed before the verb ("knew"). The construction serves to introduce a new theme into the story and marks a shift in scene.

(2) supplemental

Sometimes a statement introduced by a waw + nonverb construction appears at the beginning of a narrative and supplies the background or setting of the story.

וְהָאָרֶץ הָיְתָה תהו ובהו וְחֹשֶׁךְ עַל־פְּנֵי תהום וְרוּחַ אֱלֹהִים מְרַחֶפֶת עַל־פְּנֵי המים, "Now the earth was unformed and unfilled, *and darkness (was)* over the surface of the deep, *and God's spirit* (or perhaps, "a godlike/mighty wind") *was hovering* over the surface of the deep" (Gen. 1:2)

---

4. We are not referring here to the waw-consecutive with perfect functioning like an imperfect. The waw-consecutive with perfect (functioning like an imperfect) will extend a disjunctive clause introduced by the waw + nonverb pattern, if the initial disjunctive clause uses an imperfect (usually in a customary past or past progressive sense). See, for example, Gen. 2:6 (note וְהִשְׁקָה following the introductory וְאֵד יַעֲלֶה) and 2:10 (note וְהָיָה following the introductory וּמִשָּׁם יִפָּרֵד). When so used, the waw-consecutive with perfect can be sequential, consequential, or complementary. See also Exod. 33:7; Judg. 6:5 (qere); 1 Sam. 2:19.

This verse uses the waw + subject construction three times to describe the setting for the creation account, which is set in motion in verse 3 with the *wayyiqtol* form וַיֹּאמֶר, "and (God) said."

וְכֹל שִׂיחַ הַשָּׂדֶה טֶרֶם יִהְיֶה בָאָרֶץ וְעֵשֶׂב הַשָּׂדֶה טֶרֶם יִצְמָח ... וְאֵד יַעֲלֶה מִן־הָאָרֶץ, "*Now no shrub of the field was* in the earth, *and no plant of the field had yet sprouted.* . . . *And a spring would bubble up* from the earth" (Gen. 2:5–6)

These verses use the waw + subject construction to describe the background for the following account of man's creation.

Often a disjunctive clause (statement introduced by a waw + nonverb construction) is parenthetical (i.e., embedded in the narrative) and provides pertinent background information about a character or event.

וּמַלְכִּי־צֶדֶק מֶלֶךְ שָׁלֵם הוֹצִיא לֶחֶם וָיָיִן וְהוּא כֹהֵן לְאֵל עֶלְיוֹן, "Now Melchizedek, king of Salem, brought out bread and wine (*now he [was]* a priest of God Most High)" (Gen. 14:18)

The initial waw + subject construction ("Now Melchizedek") introduces a new subject into the narrative. The second waw + subject construction introduces a parenthetical clause that supplies background information about this Melchizedek.

וְרָחֵל לָקְחָה אֶת־הַתְּרָפִים וַתְּשִׂמֵם בְּכַר הַגָּמָל וַתֵּשֶׁב עֲלֵיהֶם, "*Now Rachel had stolen* the idols, and had placed them in the saddlebag of the camel and had sat on them" (Gen. 31:34)

This parenthetical statement is inserted between the references to Laban entering Rachel's tent (v. 33b) and to his finding nothing there (v. 34b). It explains why Laban's search of Rachel's tent yielded no results. Note that two *wayyiqtol* forms are used after the initial perfect to describe the sequence of events reported by the parenthesis.

(3) circumstantial

Disjunctive clauses sometimes identify circumstances surrounding the action described in the main clause (such as time or manner). These clauses are especially important rhetorically and dramatically, for they help one visualize the scene or action being described. These circumstantial clauses may be translated as dependent clauses in English.

וַיֵּרָא אֵלָיו יְהוָה בְּאֵלֹנֵי מַמְרֵא וְהוּא יֹשֵׁב פֶּתַח־הָאֹהֶל כְּחֹם הַיּוֹם, "And the LORD appeared to him near the oaks of Mamre. (*Now* [this happened while] *he was sitting* at the entrance to the tent during the afternoon.) Or, one could translate, "And the LORD appeared to him near the oaks of Mamre, *while he was sitting*" (Gen. 18:1)

The waw + pronoun construction introduces a clause that tells what Abraham was doing and where he was at the time of the divine revelation.

וְכַדָּהּ עַל־שִׁכְמָהּ . . . וְהִנֵּה רִבְקָה יֹצֵאת, "Now, look, Rebekah was coming out . . . . (*Now* [as she did] *her jar [was]* on her shoulder.) Or, one could translate, "Now, look, Rebekah was coming out . . . , *with her jar* on her shoulder" (Gen. 24:15)

Here the waw + subject construction introduces a clause that helps us picture Rebekah at the time she met the servant.

(4) synchronic

Sometimes a waw + subject + verb construction introduces a clause that is juxtaposed with a preceding clause to indicate synchronic (simultaneous) action. In these cases, the preceding clause also has the subject before the verb.

הוּא־בָא עַד־לֶחִי וּפְלִשְׁתִּים הֵרִיעוּ לִקְרָאתוֹ, "As he arrived in Lehi, *the Philistines shouted out* to attack him" (Judg. 15:14)

If sequential action were in view, a *wayyiqtol* form would be used, but the waw + subject pattern juxtaposes the clause with the preceding one, where the pronominal subject precedes the main verb.

(5) contrastive

Sometimes a waw + nonverb construction introduces a subject or statement that stands in contrast to the preceding statement.

וַיָּבֵא קַיִן מִפְּרִי הָאֲדָמָה מִנְחָה לַיהוה וְהֶבֶל הֵבִיא גַם־הוּא מִבְּכֹרוֹת צֹאנוֹ וּמֵחֶלְבֵהֶן, "And Cain brought some of the produce of the ground to the Lord, *but Abel brought* some of the firstborn of his flock, including their fat parts" (Gen. 4:3–4a)

וַיִּשַׁע יהוה אֶל־הֶבֶל וְאֶל־מִנְחָתוֹ וְאֶל־קַיִן וְאֶל־מִנְחָתוֹ לֹא שָׁעָה, "And the Lord was pleased with Abel and his offering, *but with Cain and his offering* he was not pleased" (Gen. 4:4b–5)

(6) dramatic (or deictic)

The waw + nonverb construction, especially the combination waw + הִנֵּה, "look," is often used for dramatic effect to invite the audience to step into the story and see what a bystander or one of the characters saw. The narrator verbally points to something or someone he wants us to see.

וַיַּחֲלֹם וְהִנֵּה סֻלָּם מֻצָּב אַרְצָה וְרֹאשׁוֹ מַגִּיעַ הַשָּׁמָיְמָה וְהִנֵּה מַלְאֲכֵי אֱלֹהִים עֹלִים וְיֹרְדִים בּוֹ וְהִנֵּה יהוה נִצָּב עָלָיו, "and he had a dream—*and look*, (there was/is) a ramp placed on the earth, with its top reaching to heaven, *and look*, (there were/are) the angels of God going up and down it, *and look,* (there was/is) the Lord standing on it" (Gen. 28:12–13a)

In this passage the narrator invites the audience to see the vision through Jacob's eyes.

ויחרד האיש וילפת <u>והנה</u> אשה שכבת מרגלתיו, "and the man was startled and sat up—*and look,* (there was/is) a woman lying at his feet" (Ruth 3:8)

Here the narrator invites us to experience Boaz's surprise at finding a woman at his feet at the threshing floor in the middle of the night. The reference to "a woman" is proof that the perspective is Boaz's, for both the narrator and the audience already know it is Ruth, not just "a woman" (see v. 7).

Sometimes a disjunctive clause, by drawing attention to a character or action, signals a shift in scene or focus. Judges 20:31–48 illustrates nicely the use of this technique. (See the sample analysis at the end of this chapter.)

(7) concluding

Often a disjunctive clause signals formally the conclusion of a narrative or scene.

ויקברו אותו בין צרעה ובין אשתאל בקבר מנוח אביו <u>והוא</u> שפט את־ישראל עשרים שנה, "And they buried him between Zorah and Eshtaol in the tomb of his father Manoah. *Now he* had led Israel for 20 years" (Judg. 16:31)

As one can see from the preceding discussion, disjunctive clauses play an important role in narrative. Because they deviate from or interrupt the normal pattern (*wayyiqtol* sequence), they grab one's attention. The very structure of such clauses tends to highlight their content. For this reason, narrators can utilize this structure to heighten a story's dramatic dimension.

For example, in 2 Samuel 11:1–4 the narrator utilizes the waw + non-verb construction to heighten the tension of the unfolding drama.

(1) In the spring, when kings march to war,	ויהי לתשובת השנה לעת צאת המלאכים
David sent Joab, his servants, and all Israel,	וישלח דוד את־יואב ואת־עבדיו עמו ואת־כל־ישראל
and they defeated the Ammonites,	וישחתו את־בני עמון
and they besieged Rabbah,	ויצרו על־רבה
but David was staying in Jerusalem.	<u>ודוד יושב בירושלם</u>
(2) One evening	ויהי לעת הערב
David arose from his bed,	ויקם דוד מעל משכבו

127

and he walked around on the roof of the royal palace	ויתהלך על־גג בית־המלך
and he saw from the roof a woman bathing.	וירא אשה רחצת מעל הגג
(Now the woman was very attractive.)	<u>והאשה טובת מראה מאד</u>
(3) And David sent,	וישלח דוד
and he asked about the woman's identity,	וידרש לאשה
and he said: (quotation)	ויאמר (quotation)
(4) And David sent messengers,	וישלח דוד מלאכים
and he took her,	ויקחה
and she came into him,	ותבוא אליו
and he had sexual relations with her,	וישכב עמה
(she was purifying herself from her impurity)	<u>והיא מתקדשת מטמאתה</u>
and she returned to her house.	ותשב אל־ביתה

The first disjunctive clause ("but David . . .") contrasts David's inactivity with the military activity of Joab and the army. The construction draws attention to the fact that David seems to be in the wrong place at the wrong time. The second disjunctive clause ("Now the woman . . .") is parenthetical and provides pertinent information about the woman David saw from the roof. The construction highlights the statement, which adds more tension to the narrative by making it clear that David is now faced with sexual temptation. This is not some aging grandmother bathing in the house next door, but a very attractive and sexually desirable woman. The third disjunctive clause ("she was purifying . . .") is also parenthetical, informing the reader that Bathsheba (we know her name by this point, see v. 3) has just completed menstruation. Once more the construction highlights a statement that heightens the tension of the story. This statement makes it clear that David's liaison with Bathsheba takes place at a time when she is especially ripe for conception.[5] This is not "safe sex;" David is playing with fire. Will he get burned?

Non-Consecutive Waw + the Perfect

A less common nonstandard construction is the use of the perfect with waw in contexts where one might expect a *wayyiqtol*.[6] Grammarians have not examined this construction thoroughly enough, and some even

---

5. See P. Kyle McCarter Jr., *II Samuel* (Garden City, N.Y.: Doubleday, 1984), 286.
6. As noted above, we do not refer here to the use of the perfect with so-called waw-consecutive as a functional equivalent of an imperfect or imperative.

eliminate difficult to explain examples by arbitrary textual emendation (usually to an infinitive absolute or *wayyiqtol* form).[7] The categories proposed below may not be mutually exclusive; in some texts dual functions seem apparent.[8]

(1) introductory

Because the waw + perfect construction deviates from the normal *(wayyiqtol)* pattern, it grabs one's attention. For this reason a narrator can use it to mark formally a new narrative unit or signal a shift in scene.

וּבָא הַמֶּלֶךְ דָּוִד עַד־בַּחוּרִים, "*And* King David next *came* to Bahurim" (2 Sam. 16:5)

One might expect a *wayyiqtol* form at the beginning of verse 5, but the waw + perfect construction signals a shift in scene, from David's meeting with Ziba to his encounter with Shimei. (Note that the next shift in scene, which occurs in v. 15, is introduced by a waw + nonverb construction.)

Sometimes וְהָיָה, "and it so happened," formally introduces a new narrative unit or scene, like the functionally equivalent וַיְהִי.

וְהָיָה כִּי־קָם הַפְּלִשְׁתִּי וַיֵּלֶךְ וַיִּקְרַב לִקְרַאת דָּוִד, "*And it so happened* when the Philistine arose, he came and drew near to meet David" (1 Sam. 17:48)

וְהָיָה marks a shift from the verbal sparring recorded in verses 43–47 to the actual battle between the two warriors. (For another example of וְהָיָה marking a shift in scene, see 1 Sam. 25:20.)

(2) emphatic

Because the waw + perfect construction deviates from the normal *(wayyiqtol)* pattern, a narrator can use the construction to highlight a statement.

וְהֶאֱמִן בַּיהוה וַיַּחְשְׁבֶהָ לּוֹ צְדָקָה, "*And he believed* the Lord, and he reckoned it to him as righteousness" (Gen. 15:6)

One expects a *wayyiqtol* form to appear here, for Abram's response is part of a larger sequence of events that leads to the covenant ratification ceremony described at the end of the chapter. Three *wayyiqtol* forms appear in the preceding verse, while nine more appear in verses 6b–11. However, Abram's act of faith is the pivotal event of the chapter and is highlighted by the use of a nonstandard construction.

---

7. See, for example, GKC, 338–39.
8. The following discussion acknowledges dependence on Robert E. Longacre's study "*Weqatal* Forms in Biblical Hebrew Prose," in *Biblical Hebrew and Discourse Linguistics*, ed. Robert D. Bergen (Winona Lake, Ind.: Eisenbrauns, 1994), 50–98.

Second Kings 21:2–6, which describes in detail King Manasseh's paganism, illustrates nicely how a narrator can use the nonstandard waw + perfect for emphasis.

(2) And he did evil . . .	. . . ויעש הרע
(3) and he again built the high places . . .	. . . וישב ויבן את־הבמות
and he erected altars for Baal,	ויקם מזבחת לבעל
and he made an Asherah pole . . .	. . . ויעש אשרה
and he bowed down to all the host of heaven,	וישתחו לכל־צבא השמים
and he worshiped them.	ויעבד אתם
(4) *And he built* altars in the LORD's temple . . .	. . . וּבָנָה מזבחת בבית יהוה
(5) He built altars to all the host of heaven . . .	. . . ויבן מזבחות לכל־צבא השמים
(6) *And he passed* his son through the fire,	וְהֶעֱבִיר את־בנו באש
and he practiced divination,	וְעֹנֵן
and he interpreted omens	וְנִחֵשׁ
and he set up a ritual pit supervised by conjurers.	וְעָשָׂה אוב וידענים
He did a great deal of evil . . .	. . . הרבה לעשׂות הרע

After a series of six *wayyiqtol* forms in verse 3, verse 4 begins with a waw + perfect (וּבָנָה, "and he built"), when one would expect another *wayyiqtol*. This nonstandard construction highlights the statement, which describes how Manasseh went so far as to desecrate the Lord's temple. One might translate, "and he even built (pagan, cf. v. 5) altars in the temple." Another *wayyiqtol* follows at the beginning of verse 5 (note וַיִּבֶן, "and he built"), specifying that the altars mentioned in verse 4 were indeed pagan. Verse 6a then uses the construction waw + perfect in four successive clauses before a concluding summary statement. The nonstandard construction highlights the statements, which draw attention to Manasseh's extreme paganism. The structure of the passage may be outlined as follows:

Verse 2	Summary statement of Manasseh's paganism *(wayyiqtol)*
Verse 3	Manasseh's pagan policies (*wayyiqtol* forms)
Verses 4–5	A radical pagan policy (waw + perfect followed by specifying use of *wayyiqtol*)
Verse 6a	Other radical pagan acts (waw + perfect constructions)
Verse 6b	An emphatic (note הִרְבָּה) summary statement of Manasseh's paganism (perfect)

The summary statements in verses 2 and 6b form a bracket around the account. Just as the concluding summary statement in verse 6b is more emphatic than the introductory one of verse 2, so the second half of the account (vv. 4–6a) illustrates the king's paganism in a more heightened manner than the first half of the account (v. 3). The switch to the waw + perfect in verse 4 and the heaping up of nonstandard forms in verse 6a contributes to this intensification. To bring out the force of the structure, one might translate verse 4a, "He had the audacity to build altars in the LORD's temple," and verse 6a, "he even passed his son through the fire, practiced divination."

(3) specifying

Sometimes a waw + perfect introduces a statement that gives a specific instance or example to demonstrate the truth of a preceding, general statement.

וישׂראל אהב את־יוסף מכל־בניו . . . וַעֲשָׂה לו כתנת פסים, "Now Israel loved Joseph more than any of his other sons . . . ; *he made* for him a fine robe" (Gen. 37:3)

After the initial perfect (אָהַב, "loved"), one would expect the narrative to continue with a *wayyiqtol* form (namely, וַיַּעַשׂ; note the normal narrative sequence in v. 4). However, sequence is not the point here; the second verb gives a prime example of how Israel showed his favoritism toward Joseph. At the same time, the statement is emphatic, highlighting to what extent Israel went to express his favoritism. One could translate, "He even made for him a fine robe."

(4) complementary

Very often the waw + perfect form is used to indicate that actions are complementary and/or that they combine to form a whole.

וְהָלַךְ מדי שׁנה בשׁנה וְסָבַב בית־אל והגלגל והמצפה וְשָׁפַט את־ישׂראל, "*and he went* on an annual circuit, *and he traveled around* to Bethel, and Gilgal, and Mizpah, *and he judged* Israel" (1 Sam. 7:16)

The series of three waw + perfect constructions gives the procedural details of Samuel's annual trips. When he went, he traveled through specific areas and made legal decisions for the Israelite community.

וַיַּדַּח (Qere) ירבעם את־ישׂראל מאחרי יהוה וְהֶחֱטִיאָם חטאה גדלה, "and Jeroboam drove Israel away from following the LORD, *and he made* them commit a great sin" (2 Kings 17:21)

The second verb (waw + perfect) complements the preceding one; it refers to the same action but in a different way.

Other examples of the complementary use of the waw + perfect construction occur in 1 Samuel 17:20 (the army shouted as they marched); **131**

2 Samuel 12:16 (David's nighttime vigils on the floor accompanied his fasting); 13:18–19 (pushing Tamar out the door and locking it were complementary actions); 16:13 (throwing stones and hurling dirt would have been simultaneous actions); 1 Kings 13:3 (the sign accompanied the message, cf. v. 2); 2 Kings 18:3–4 (smashing the stones, cutting down the Asherah pole, and destroying the bronze serpent were the defining acts of Hezekiah's campaign against paganism).

Sometimes the waw + perfect construction can be both complementary and emphatic. For example, 1 Samuel 17:38 records how Saul tried to prepare David for battle: וילבש שאול את־דוד מדיו וְנָתַן קובע נחשת על־ראשׁו, "And Saul clothed David in his own armor, *and put* a bronze helmet on his head." One expects a *wayyiqtol* form here, since *wayyiqtol* forms appear both before and after this within the verse. The waw + perfect construction introduces a complementary action; Saul gives David both body armor and a helmet. However, the construction also has an emphatic function. It draws attention to the statement and highlights this particular action by Saul, which epitomizes his approach to this crisis. By putting a bronze helmet on David, Saul is trying to make David a "little Goliath." (Note that in v. 5 Goliath is described as having "a bronze helmet on his head." קוֹבַע and כּוֹבַע are alternative forms of the same term.) He just doesn't seem to get the point that divine intervention, not weaponry, will be the key in this battle (cf. v. 37). One might translate the statement, "And he even put a bronze helmet on his head!"

(5) consequential

Sometimes the waw + perfect construction introduces a consequence of what precedes.

וַיַעֲקֹב שמע כי טמא את־דינה בתו ובניו היו את־מקנהו בשדה וְהֶחֱרִשׁ יעקב עד־באם, "When Jacob heard that he (Shechem) had violated his (Jacob's) daughter Dinah, his (Jacob's) sons were taking care of the cattle in the field. *So he kept silent* until they came in" (Gen. 34:5)

ותקרא לסרני פלשתים לאמר עלו הפעם כי־הגיד לי (Qere) אֶת־כל־לבו וְעָלוּ אליה סרני פלשתים, "She summoned the lords of the Philistines, saying, 'Come up this time, for he has been completely honest with me.' *So* the lords of the Philistines *came up*" (Judg. 16:18)

(6) climactic or concluding

Sometimes the waw + perfect construction formally marks the end of a scene or the final action in a series of events.

וְהִכָּה בארם מכה גדולה, "*and he* thoroughly *defeated* Aram" (1 Kings 20:21b)

The waw + perfect construction introduces a concluding summary statement for the narrative that began in verse 1.

וְהַחֲרִישׁוּ הָעָם, *"and the people were silent"* (2 Kings 18:36a)

Verse 36, which begins with the waw + perfect construction, records the people's response to the Assyrian field commander's arrogant speech (vv. 17–35) and brings this segment of the unfolding story to an end.

וַיִּקַּח עֹבַדְיָהוּ מֵאָה נְבִאִים וַיַּחְבִּיאֵם חֲמִשִּׁים אִישׁ בַּמְּעָרָה וְכִלְכְּלָם לֶחֶם וָמָיִם, "and Obadiah took a hundred prophets and hid them in caves in two groups of fifty, *and he provided* them with food and water" (1 Kings 18:4)

The waw + perfect construction marks the final action in the series and signals the end of the brief parenthesis that began with וַיְהִי. (One could see this as an emphatic or complementary use of the construction.)

וְהִגְלָה אֶת־כָּל־יְרוּשָׁלַ͏ִם, *"and he carried away* all Jerusalem" (2 Kings 24:14)

This statement records the climactic act in the series of events outlined in verses 13–14. It may also be emphatic by reason of its climactic position.

Clauses Introduced by עַל־כֵּן

Sometimes עַל־כֵּן, "therefore," interrupts the narrative sequence by introducing an explanatory note that supplements the story or concludes an episode within it.

עַל־כֵּן יַעֲזָב־אִישׁ אֶת־אָבִיו וְאֶת־אִמּוֹ וְדָבַק בְּאִשְׁתּוֹ וְהָיוּ לְבָשָׂר אֶחָד, "This is why a man leaves his father and his mother and clings to his wife and they become one flesh" (Gen. 2:24)[9]

עַל־כֵּן קָרְאָה שְׁמוֹ דָּן, "therefore she named him Dan" (Gen. 30:6)

Quotations

Most narratives have quotations embedded within them. Quotations typically contain a wide variety of grammatical constructions, including, among others, conditional sentences (e.g., Judg. 4:8), volitional forms in sequence (e.g., Gen. 45:17–18), and perfects with waw-consecutive in sequence (e.g., 1 Sam. 10:2–6).

Sometimes quotations include *wayyiqtol* forms, though the sequences are not as extensive as one finds in the basic narrative framework. Within quotations *wayyiqtol* displays a variety of discourse functions, including several of the categories outlined earlier:

---

9. Note how the waw-consecutive with the perfect (וְדָבַק and וְהָיוּ) is used to follow up the imperfect (יַעֲזָב) that appears after עַל־כֵּן. All three verbs carry a characteristic or habitual present nuance here.

(1) sequential and/or consequential

"And he said, 'Look, I had a dream. I saw a stale cake of barley bread rolling into the Midianite camp. *And it came* (וַיָּבֹא) *to a tent, and hit it* (וַיַּכֵּהוּ), *and it fell over* (וַיִּפֹּל), *and turned it* upside down (וַיַּהַפְכֵהוּ)" (Judg. 7:13b)

When the person being quoted is giving a report or telling a story, one expects to see some typical narrative forms. In such cases the quotation is really a smaller narrative within a larger one.

(2) resumptive

"For to save lives God sent me on ahead of you, because there has been a famine in the midst of the land for the past two years, and for five more years there will be no planting or harvesting. *So* God *sent* me on ahead (וַיִּשְׁלָחֵנִי)" (Gen. 45:5b–7a)

The *wayyiqtol* form at the beginning of verse 7 resumes the statement made at the end of verse 5, after the parenthetical explanation about the length of the famine (v. 6).

(3) reiterative

"She said, 'Indeed I am a widow; my husband *is dead* (וַיָּמָת)'" (2 Sam. 14:5)

(4) specifying

"You know what Joab did . . . to the two commanders of Israel's armies, to Abner son of Ner and to Amasa son of Jether, *he killed* (וַיַּהַרְגֵם) them" (1 Kings 2:5)[10]

(5) restrictive

"I saw God face to face, *and yet* my life *was spared* (וַתִּנָּצֵל)" (Gen. 32:30, Eng.)

Within quotations one can also find disjunctive (waw + nonverb) clauses (e.g., Gen. 24:56) and the nonconsecutive waw + perfect construction. See, for example:

(1) Genesis 24:56: אַל־תְּאַחֲרוּ אֹתִי וַיהוה הִצְלִיחַ דַּרְכִּי שַׁלְּחוּנִי, "Do not detain me, *since the* Lord *has made my mission successful; send me on my way*"

The disjunctive clause is circumstantial, giving a reason or explanation for the preceding request.

(2) Judges 7:13b: וְנָפַל הָאֹהֶל, "The tent *just collapsed*"

10. For other examples of the specifying use of *wayyiqtol,* see Gen. 31:26; Exod. 1:18; Judg. 16:10; 1 Sam. 8:8; 1 Kings 1:44.

The waw + perfect construction concludes the Midianite's report of his dream. The statement is also emphatic, since it reiterates וַיִּפֹּל, "and it fell," earlier in the verse.

(3) 1 Samuel 2:2: וַאֲנִי זָקַנְתִּי וָשַׂבְתִּי, "I am old *and gray*"

In this case the waw + perfect complements the verb that immediately precedes. Being old and becoming gray-haired typically go together.

Sample Analyses

(1) Judges 3:12–30[11]

Verses 12–17 (prologue)

(12) Now the Israelites again did evil before the Lord, (introductory) (a)

so the Lord prompted Eglon king of Moab to attack Israel, (sequential) (b)

because they did evil before the Lord. (causal) (c)

(13) And he allied with the Ammonites and Amalek, (sequential) (a)

and came (sequential) (b)

and defeated Israel (sequential) (c)

and they seized the City of Date Palm Trees. (sequential) (d)

(14) And the Israelites were subject to Eglon king of Moab for eighteen years. (sequential) (a)

(15) And the Israelites cried out to the Lord (sequential) (a)

and the Lord raised up a deliverer for them—Ehud son of Gera the Benjaminite, a left-handed man. (sequential) (b)

And the Israelites sent him to Eglon king of Moab with their tribute payment. (sequential) (c)

(16) And Ehud made a sword. (sequential) (a)

(It had two edges and was eighteen inches long.) (supplemental) (b)

And he strapped it under his coat on his right thigh. (sequential) (c)

(17) And he brought the tribute payment to Eglon king of Moab. (sequential) (a)

Now Eglon was a very fat man. (supplemental) (b)

Comments:

(1) The narrative begins with a *wayyiqtol* form and the story line is then developed in a reportorial, matter-of-fact style by a succession of

---

11. Statements beginning with *wayyiqtol* (or with a negated perfect) are placed flush left in the translation. Statements beginning with nonstandard constructions are in bold print. Subordinate clauses are indented; quotations are placed in italics. The function or category of each clause is identified in parentheses following the translation of the clause. Syntactical notes and observations follow each paragraph.

thirteen *wayyiqtol* forms. The *wayyiqtol* form at the beginning of verse 12a is introductory, but it can also be viewed as sequential at the larger story level. It introduces a historical account that postdates the story of Othniel recorded in verses 7–11.

(2) The causal clause in verse 12c essentially repeats verse 12a and thereby sets verse 12 off as the introduction to the narrative which provides the theological framework for the story.

(3) The disjunctive clause in verse 16b gives supplemental information that will become more pertinent as the story unfolds.

(4) The disjunctive clause in verse 17b signals closure for the prologue. It also gives supplemental information that will become more pertinent as the story unfolds.

Verses 18–26 (central narrative unit)

(18)	And it so happened (introductory)	(a)
	when he had finished presenting the tribute payment, (temporal)	(b)
	he dismissed the people who had carried it. (sequential)	(c)
(19)	**But he went back once he reached the carved images** (contrastive)	(a)
	which are in Gilgal. (relative)	(b)
	And he said: (sequential)	(c)
	"I have secret message for you, O king."	(d)
	And he replied: (sequential)	(e)
	"Shh!"	(f)
	And all his attendants left. (sequential)	(g)
(20)	**When Ehud approached him,** (circumstantial)	(a)
	he was sitting in his ventilated upper room (synchronic)	(b)
	where he was all alone. (relative)	(c)
	And Ehud said: (sequential)	(d)
	"I have a divine message for you."	(e)
	And he got up from his throne. (sequential)	(f)
(21)	And Ehud reached with his left hand (sequential)	(a)
	and pulled the sword from his right thigh (sequential)	(b)
	and drove it into his belly. (sequential)	(c)
(22)	And the handle went in after the blade (sequential)	(a)
	and the fat closed around the blade (sequential)	(b)
	for he did not pull the sword out of his belly. (causal)	(c)
	And he went out into the vestibule. (variant of v. 23a/sequential)	(d)
(23)	And Ehud went out into the vestibule (variant of v. 22d/sequential)	(a)
	and he closed the doors of the upper room behind him (sequential)	(b)
	and he locked them. (complementary)	(c)

(24) **When he had left,** (circumstantial)   (a)

   his (Eglon's) servants entered (synchronic)   (b)

   and they looked. (sequential)   (c)

   And look, the doors of the upper room were locked. (dramatic)   (d)

   And they said: (sequential)   (e)

   "He must be relieving himself in the upper room."   (f)

(25) And they waited so long they became embarrassed. (sequential)   (a)

   And look, he did not open the doors of the upper room.   (b)
   (dramatic)

   And they took the key (sequential)   (c)

   and opened them. (sequential)   (d)

   And look, their master was lying on the floor dead. (dramatic)   (e)

(26) **Now Ehud escaped while they delayed.** (dramatic)   (a)

   When he passed by the carved images, (circumstantial)   (b)

   he escaped to Seirah. (sequential)   (c)

Comments:

(1) The temporal indicator וַיְהִי, "and it so happened," in verse 18a introduces the central section of the narrative.

(2) The disjunctive clause in verse 19a contrasts Ehud's movements with those of the servants.

(3) The disjunctive clauses in verses 20a, 24a, and 26a, all of which have Ehud as the stated or implied subject, divide the central section into distinct parts. In verses 18–19 Ehud makes sure he is alone with the king, in verses 20–23 he maneuvers the king into a vulnerable position and then assassinates him, in verses 24–25 the focus turns to the king's servants, and verse 26 reports Ehud's successful escape. The structure in verses 20ab and 24ab (where disjunctive clauses are paired) indicates synchronism of action. In verse 26a the disjunctive clause signals a shift in focus back to Ehud; the disjunctive clause in verse 26b is circumstantial, being subordinate to the main clause that follows.

(4) The waw + perfect construction in verse 23c is complementary (shutting and locking a door are actions that typically go together), but it may also indicate the climactic act in the sequence and signal a transition in focus.

(5) The dialogue in verses 19–20 slows the story down and helps build the drama. We already suspect what Ehud intends to do and have some idea of how his left-handedness may help him. But how will he get the king isolated and how will he ever be able to escape?

(6) Once the king rises from his throne, the story rushes along in headlong fashion as eight *wayyiqtol* forms appear in rapid succession, interrupted by one brief explanatory clause in verse 22c. The descriptive

details in verse 22 tend to slow the pace ever so slightly, but they also "drive home the point" (!) of the finality of the king's death. (Verses 22d and 23a appear to be variant readings. See the exegetical discussion in chapter 8.)

(7) The three disjunctives in verses 24d, 25b, and 25e (all beginning with וְהִנֵּה, "and look") dramatically invite the audience to share the servants' perspective. They also tend to slow the pace of the story (after all, Ehud needs time to escape) and resolve the tension. The servants' slow reaction and initial failure to suspect anything already suggest what we are told in verse 26—Ehud is going to get away with murder.

Verses 27–30 (epilogue)

(27) And it so happened (introductory)	(a)
when he arrived, (temporal)	(b)
he blew the trumpet in the Ephraimite hill country. (sequential)	(c)
And the Israelites went down with him from the hill country. (sequential)	(d)
Now he was in the lead. (supplemental or circumstantial)	(e)
(28) And he said to them: (sequential)	(a)
"Follow me, for the LORD is handing your enemies, Moab, over to you."	(b)
And they followed him down (sequential)	(c)
and captured the fords of the Jordan opposite Moab (sequential)	(d)
and did not allow anyone to cross. (sequential)	(e)
(29) And they struck down about ten thousand Moabites at that time, all of whom were strong, capable warriors, (specifying)	(a)
and no one escaped. (specifying)	(b)
(30) And Moab was subdued that day under the hand of Israel, (concluding)	(a)
and the land was undisturbed for eighty years. (sequential)	(b)

Comments:

(1) The temporal indicator וַיְהִי, "and it so happened," in verse 27a marks the transition to the epilogue, which tells how Ehud followed up his daring deed by mustering Israelite troops and defeating the Moabites.

(2) The disjunctive clause in verse 27e facilitates the transition from the hurried actions described in verse 27 to Ehud's speech reported in verse 28b. The *wayyiqtol* form following the speech (v. 28c), which repeats the verb יָרַד, "go down" (cf. v. 27d), sets the scene in motion again.

(3) The phrases "at that time" (v. 29a) and "that day" (v. 30a) begin to distance us from the events and signal closure, which is provided by the chronological note in verse 30b.

(2) Judges 20:29–48[12]

Verses 29–36a (condensed account)

(29) Israel hid men in ambush outside Gibeah. (introductory or sequential) (a)

(30) The Israelites marched against the Benjaminites the next (lit., third) day; (sequential) (a)

they took their positions against Gibeah just as they had done before. (sequential) (b)

(31) The Benjaminites attacked the army; (sequential) (a)

they were drawn away from the city. (dramatic) (b)

They began to strike down their enemy as before on the roads (one of which leads to Bethel and the other to Gibeah) (relative) (c)

and in the field—about thirty men. (sequential) (d)

(32) And the Benjaminites said: (sequential) (a)

"They are defeated just as before." (b)

But the Israelites said: (contrastive) (c)

"Let's retreat and lure them away from the city to the roads." (d)

(33) **Now all the Israelites got up from their places** (dramatic or circumstantial) (a)

and took their positions at Baal Tamar, (sequential) (b)

while the Israelites hiding in ambush jumped out of their places west of Gibeah. (synchronic) (c)

(34) And ten thousand men, well-trained warriors from all Israel, made a frontal assault against Gibeah, (sequential) (a)

The battle was fierce. (dramatic) (b)

Now they (i.e., the Benjaminites) **did not realize disaster was imminent.** (dramatic) (c)

(35) And the LORD annihilated Benjamin before Israel; (sequential) (a)

the Israelites struck down that day 25,100 sword-wielding Benjaminites. (specifying) (b)

(36) The Benjaminites saw they were defeated. (sequential) (a)

Comments:

(1) The perfect (without waw) in verse 31b introduces an emphatic statement. As far as the Benjaminites were concerned, they were attacking (v. 31a). But the nonstandard, asyndetic construction in verse 31b draws attention to Israel's perspective, which will be the telling one on this day.

12. All statements beginning with *wayyiqtol* (or with a negated perfect) are placed flush left in the translation. Statements beginning with nonstandard constructions are in bold print. Subordinate clauses are indented; quotations are placed in italics. The function or category of each clause is identified in parentheses following the translation of the clause. Syntactical notes and observations follow each paragraph.

(2) The disjunctive clause in verse 32c contrasts Israel's perspective with Benjamin's.

(3) The disjunctive clause in verse 33a signals a shift in scene from the Benjaminite attack to the Israelite counterattack and ambush. It is both dramatic and circumstantial (in relation to verse 33c). The disjunctive clause in verse 33c indicates synchronism of action (cf. verse 33a).

(4) The disjunctive clauses in verse 34bc signal a transition from the battle account per se to the report of Benjamin's demise.

(5) The *wayyiqtol* form in verse 35b has a specifying function after the general statement in verse 35a. It gives a more detailed report of the Lord's victory over Benjamin and focuses on the human, rather than theological, perspective.

Verses 36b–45 (expanded account)

(36, con't)

The Israelites retreated before Benjamin (specifying)	(b)
because they had confidence in the men hiding in ambush (causal)	(c)
whom they had stationed outside Gibeah. (relative)	(d)

(37) **The men hiding in ambush acted quickly** (dramatic) (a)
and rushed to Gibeah. (sequential) (b)
And the men hiding in ambush attacked (sequential) (c)
and put the sword to the entire city. (sequential) (d)

(38) **Now the Israelites and the men hiding in ambush had agreed that the latter would send up a smoke signal from the conquered city.** (supplemental) (a)

(39) **And the Israelites counterattacked.** (sequential) (a)
Now the Benjaminites had begun to strike down the Israelites— about thirty men, (dramatic and resumptive) (b)
because they said, (causal) (c)
"There's no doubt about it! They are totally defeated as in the earlier battle." (d)

(40) **Then the signal, the pillar of smoke, began to rise from the city** (dramatic and resumptive) (a)
and the Benjaminites turned around (sequential) (b)
and look, the whole city was going up in a cloud of smoke that rose up into the sky. (dramatic) (c)

(41) **Then the Israelites turned around** (dramatic and resumptive) (a)
and the Benjaminites panicked (sequential) (b)
because they could see that disaster was on their doorstep. (causal) (c)

(42) They retreated before the Israelites on the road leading to the wilderness, (sequential) (a)
but the battle overtook them (contrastive) (b)

as those from the surrounding cities struck them down. (c)
(circumstantial)

(43) **They surrounded the Benjaminites,** (dramatic) (a)

they chased them from Nohah, (dramatic) (b)

they annihilated them all the way to a spot east of Geba. (c)
(dramatic)

(44) 18,000 Benjaminites, all of them capable warriors, fell dead. (a)
(sequential or summarizing)

(45) The rest turned (sequential) (a)

and ran toward the wilderness, toward the cliff of Rimmon. (b)
(sequential)

And they (i.e., the Israelites) caught five thousand of them on the (c)
main roads. (sequential)

They stayed on their heels all the way to Gidom (sequential) (d)

and struck down two thousand more of them. (sequential) (e)

Comments:

(1) Verses 36b–48 recapitulate verses 29–36a.

(2) The *wayyiqtol* form in verse 36b has a specifying function; it introduces a more detailed account of the battle just reported in the preceding verses.

(3) The dramatic use of the disjunctive clause in verse 37a shifts the focus from the main battle to the actions of the men hiding in ambush.

(4) The disjunctive clause in verse 38a is parenthetical; it gives pertinent background information that explains the sudden change described in verse 39.

(5) The disjunctive clause in verse 39b shifts the focus back to Benjamin and chronologically takes us back to where verse 36 left off.

(6) The disjunctive clause in verse 40a shifts the focus to the scene in the city and chronologically takes us back to where verse 37 left off.

(7) The disjunctive clause in verse 40c, introduced with וְהִנֵּה, puts us in the Benjaminites' shoes and describes what they saw.

(8) The disjunctive clause in verse 41a briefly shifts the focus back to the main Israelite army and resumes verse 39a. Note how the narrator uses disjunctive clauses in verses 37–41 to shift focus abruptly and give us differing perspectives on the battle, much as camera shots from multiple angles are utilized in modern films.

(9) The disjunctive clause in verse 42b, which describes how the Benjaminites failed to escape, stands in contrast to verse 42a, which describes their efforts to do so. Verse 42b also begins the account of Benjamin's demise.

(10) The three clauses in verse 43 all begin with a perfect without a waw, creating a staccato style that tends to intensify the dramatic tone and highlight each individual action.

Verses 46–48 (epilogue)

(46) And it so happened (introductory)   (a)

      25,100 sword-wielding Benjaminites fell in battle that day, all of   (b)
them capable warriors. (summarizing)

(47) Six hundred survivors turned (resumptive)   (a)

      and ran away to the wilderness, to the cliff of Rimmon. (resumptive)   (b)

      And they stayed there four months. (sequential)   (c)

(48) **Now the Israelites returned to the Benjaminite towns** (contrastive)   (a)

      and put the sword to cities, animals, and everything they could find.   (b)
(sequential)

      They set fire to all the cities in their path. (concluding)   (c)

Comments

(1) The temporal indicator וַיְהִי in verse 46a introduces a summary statement that begins the story's epilogue.

(2) The first two clauses in verse 47 are resumptive (cf. verse 45ab).

(3) The disjunctive in verse 48a contrasts the actions of the defeated Benjaminites, described in verse 47, with those of the victorious Israelites and may also signal the conclusion of the story.

(4) The final clause (verse 48c) begins with גַּם, "also," and signals the end of the narrative.

An interpreter, when preparing to preach or teach a narrative text, should develop an outline of the text's structure similar to the ones presented above. In this way one may discern the story's contours, shifts in focus, and dramatic pace, as well as the narrator's emphases. Sensitivity to these features enables one to "retell" the story in a way that reflects the original author's purpose(s) and allows the narrative to engage the audience in accordance with its intended shape and design.

Hebrew Poetry

Poetic Parallelism

Simple Parallelism

The basic structural device used by biblical Hebrew poets is parallelism, where two statements are juxtaposed. The precise conceptual relationship between these statements can vary. The following list identifies and illustrates some of the ways the second line relates to the first:

(1) reiterative or synonymous

Sometimes the second line simply reiterates the first. The second line restates the idea of the first line, but uses synonymous terms. Psalm 18:5 provides an example:

The ropes of Sheol enveloped me,
the snares of Death confronted me.

חבלי שאול סבבוני
קדמוני מוקשי מות

The symmetry between the lines is syntactical as well as conceptual. The first line has a genitival construction followed by a suffixed verb. The order in the second line is reversed (or chiastic), with a suffixed verb preceding a genitival construction.

(2) specifying

Sometimes the second line specifies a preceding general statement. For example, Psalm 5:12 (Eng., Heb. v. 13) says:

For you do indeed bless the righteous, O LORD,   כי־אתה תברך צדיק יהוה
like a shield you protect (lit., "encircle") him with favor.   כצנה רצון תעטרנו

The first line refers in a general way to God's blessing on the righteous. The second line, utilizing a simile, more specifically identifies the form this blessing takes (God's shieldlike protection).

(3) complementary

Often the second line of a poetic couplet complements the first line in some way.

Sometimes the second line looks at a theme from a complementary angle. For example, consider Psalm 8:6 (Eng., Heb. v. 5):

You gave him a position just below God,   ותחסרהו מעט מאלהים
you crowned him with honor and majesty.   וכבוד והדר תעטרהו

The verse describes the exalted position of humankind as God's vice-regent. The first line speaks of humankind's status in relation to God, the second of the honor attached to such a position.

At other times the two poetic lines describe complementary actions. For example, Psalm 4:5 (Eng., Heb. v. 6) says:

Offer the proper sacrifices!   זבחו זבחי־צדק
Trust in the LORD!   ובטחו אל־יהוה

(4) explanatory

Sometimes the second line gives an explanation or reason for what is stated or described in the preceding line. For example, consider Psalm 4:8 (Eng., Heb. v. 9):

In peace I will lie down and sleep,   בשלום יחדו אשכבה ואישן
for you alone, LORD, give me security.   כי־אתה יהוה לבדד לבטח תושיבני

143

(5) progressive or consequential

Sometimes the second line makes a logical and/or temporal advance on the previous line. Consider Psalm 2:5:

Then he speaks to them in his anger,	אז ידבר אלימו באפו
and in his rage he terrifies them.	ובחרונו יבהלמו

The first line states that God speaks to the rebel kings angrily. The second line also mentions his anger, but makes the additional observation that the divine word frightens the kings. The first line describes the action, the second describes its effect.

In Psalm 4:3 (Eng., Heb. v. 4) the second line in the couplet states a logical consequence:

Realize that the LORD sets the godly apart for himself,	ודעו כי־הפלה יהוה חסיד לו
the LORD hears when I call to him.	יהוה ישמע בקראי אליו

The first line states a general theological truth which is the logical basis for the psalmist's statement of confidence in the second line.

(6) comparative

Sometimes the second line completes a comparative statement. For example, Psalm 4:7 (Eng., Heb. v. 8) says:

You make my heart happier	נתתה שמחה בלבי
than when their grain and wine are abundant.	מעת דגנם ותירושם רבו

The comparative מִן at the beginning of the second line introduces the object of comparison. The psalmist's God-given joy is greater than the happiness farmers experience from an abundant harvest.

Sometimes one of the lines (it need not be the second) in a couplet utilizes a metaphor or simile to illustrate the statement made in the accompanying line. For example, Psalm 5:9b (Eng., Heb. v. 10b) states:

Their throat is an open grave,	קבר־פתוח גרונם
they use their tongue to flatter.	לשונם יחליקון

In the second line the psalmist refers to those who use flattery to exploit and destroy others (cf. v. 9a). The metaphor in the first line expresses in a very vivid way the destructive nature of their words.

(7) contrastive

Sometimes, especially in didactic poetry, the second line makes a statement that contrasts with the first. For example, Proverbs 12:15 contrasts the self-sufficiency of a fool with a wise man's willingness to consider the advice of others:

The way of a fool seems right to him,   דרך אויל ישר בעיניו
but a wise man listens to advice.   ושמע לעצה חכם

Complex Parallelism

Sometimes a poet constructs an intricate structure involving more than two lines. For example, consider the structure of Psalm 5:4–6 (Eng., Heb. vv. 5–7):

(4a) For you are not a God who approves of wickedness,
(4b) an evil person cannot dwell with you.
(5a) Proud people cannot stand in your presence,
(5b) you hate all who commit sin.
(6a) You destroy those who speak lies,
(6b) the LORD despises a violent, deceitful person.

Verse 4a describes a divine attitude (the Lord does not approve of wickedness), while verse 4b states a logical consequence of this fact (an evil person cannot dwell with the Lord). Verse 5a restates this consequence, but also characterizes the evil person as proud. Verse 5b explains why proud persons are banned from the divine presence. In so doing it states more forcefully the point made in verse 4a and further characterizes the evil person as one who is committed to a sinful lifestyle. Verse 6a progresses beyond verse 5b by describing the action that results from the attitude, while verse 6b reiterates verses 4a and 5b by focusing on the divine attitude that produces the action. Both lines of verse 6 add more characteristics to the developing profile of the evildoer. He is dishonest, violent, and deceitful.

The parallelism can be viewed in several ways. In relation to 4a, 4b is progressive (it gives a logical consequence of the attitude just described). In relation to 4b, 5a is reiterative. In relation to 5a, 5b is explanatory (it gives an underlying reason for the truth just affirmed). In relation to 5b, 6a is progressive (it describes the action resulting from the attitude). In relation to 6a, 6b is explanatory (it gives an underlying reason for the action just described). At the same time, 4a and 5b (underlying reason) bracket 4b–5a (logical consequence), and 5b and 6b (underlying reason) bracket 6a (logical consequence). This interlocking structure can be outlined as follows:
[4a] (4b–5a) [5b] (6a) [6b]

Poetic Narrative

Biblical narrative sometimes takes a poetic shape, especially when the narrator celebrates God's saving intervention (see, e.g., Exod. 15 and   145

Judg. 5). Hebrew poetic narrative may utilize *wayyiqtol* forms, but it accommodates such use to the stylistic device of poetic parallelism. The *wayyiqtol* forms are often simply reiterative in the parallel structure, rather than sequential. Greater freedom in word order results in *wayyiqtol* forms being mixed with other verbal forms (perfects and short prefixed/preterite forms without waw-consecutive) to a greater degree than in regular prose style. The use of verbal forms in 2 Samuel 22:5–8, a segment of a poetic narrative about how God delivered the author from death, illustrates this style.

(5) The waves of Death surrounded me,
the torrents of Belial attacked me.

אֲפָפֻנִי מִשְׁבְּרֵי־מָוֶת
נַחֲלֵי בְלִיַּעַל יְבַעֲתֻנִי

Verse 5a uses a perfect; verse 5b a preterite without waw-consecutive. The subject precedes the verb in verse 5b, producing a chiastic structure within the verse (verb + subject // subject + verb). The parallelism is reiterative.

(6) The ropes of Sheol enveloped me,
the snares of Death confronted me.

חֶבְלֵי שְׁאוֹל סַבֻּנִי
קִדְּמֻנִי מֹקְשֵׁי־מָוֶת

Both lines use a perfect. The subject precedes the verb in verse 6a, producing a chiastic structure within the verse (subject + verb // verb + subject). The parallelism is again reiterative.

(7a) In my distress I cried out to the Lord,
to my God I cried out.

בַּצַּר־לִי אֶקְרָא יְהוָה
וְאֶל־אֱלֹהַי אֶקְרָא

Both lines use a preterite without waw-consecutive. The verb is preceded by a prepositional phrase in both cases. The parallelism is reiterative, but in relation to verses 5–6, the couplet is progressive.

(7b) He heard my voice from his temple,
my cry (entered) his ears.

וַיִּשְׁמַע מֵהֵיכָלוֹ קוֹלִי
וְשַׁוְעָתִי בְּאָזְנָיו

The first line uses *wayyiqtol*; the second is verbless. The *wayyiqtol* is sequential, describing God's response to the psalmist's cry for help. The second line reiterates the first, but the couplet is progressive in relation to verse 7a.

(8) The earth surged and quaked,
the foundations of the heavens trembled,
they surged because he was angry.

וַתִּגְעַשׁ וַתִּרְעַשׁ הָאָרֶץ
מוֹסְדוֹת הַשָּׁמַיִם יִרְגָּזוּ
וַיִּתְגָּעֲשׁוּ כִּי־חָרָה לוֹ

The first line uses two *wayyiqtol* forms. The first is sequential, describing how God began to intervene once he heard the psalmist's prayer. The second verb is reiterative; like the preceding verb, it describes the earth convulsing. The second line, where the subject precedes, uses a preterite without waw-consecutive. The *wayyiqtol* at the beginning of the third line is reiterative, the verb being synonymous to the preceding verb רָגַז. However, the rest of the line goes on to explain the reason for the cosmic disturbances just described.

For Further Reading and Reference

Bergen, Robert D., ed. *Biblical Hebrew and Discourse Linguistics*. Winona Lake, Ind.: Eisenbrauns, 1994.

Berlin, Adele. *The Dynamics of Biblical Parallelism*. Bloomington: Indiana University Press, 1985.

Dawson, David Allan. *Text-Linguistics and Biblical Hebrew*. Sheffield: JSOT, 1994.

Gibson, J. C. L. *Davidson's Introductory Hebrew Grammar: Syntax*. 4th ed. Edinburgh: T. & T. Clark, 1994.

Jouön, P. *A Grammar of Biblical Hebrew*. 2 vols. Trans. and rev. T. Muraoka. Rome: Pontifical Biblical Institute, 1991.

Kautzsch, E., ed. *Gesenius' Hebrew Grammar*. 2nd English ed. Trans. A. E. Cowley. Oxford: Clarendon, 1910.

Kugel, James. *The Idea of Biblical Poetry*. New Haven, Conn.: Yale University Press, 1981.

Longacre, Robert E. *Joseph: A Story of Divine Providence: A Text Theoretical and Textlinguistic Analysis of Genesis 37 and 39–48*. Winona Lake, Ind.: Eisenbrauns, 1988.

Niccacci, Alviero. *The Syntax of the Verb in Classical Hebrew Prose*. Trans. W. G. E. Watson. Sheffield: JSOT, 1990.

Waltke, Bruce K., and M. O'Connor. *An Introduction to Biblical Hebrew Syntax*. Winona Lake, Ind.: Eisenbrauns, 1990.

Watson, W. G. E. *Classical Hebrew Poetry*. Sheffield: JSOT, 1984.

Williams, Ronald J. *Hebrew Syntax: An Outline*. 2nd ed. Toronto: University of Toronto, 1976.

7 Getting Beneath the Surface

Narrative and Poetry as Literature

Interpretation involves more than text criticism, word studies, syntactical analysis, and evaluation of structure. The interpreter must go beneath the surface of what the text says and probe more deeply into what it meant in its ancient Israelite context, for this is the key to understanding what it means theologically for the people of God of all ages.

To appreciate fully the meaning of a text, one must understand the historical context from which it derives and the cultural realities that it reflects and assumes. An awareness of the cultural background of the Old Testament can only be acquired over a period of time as one reads a wide range of studies dealing with archaeological discoveries. (See the bibliography on the cultural background of the Old Testament at the end of this chapter.)

An interpreter should also become familiar with the main features of the Old Testament's two main literary genres—narrative and poetry. Stories highlight narrative, but this genre also incorporates other literary types, such as legal material, reports, and genealogies. The poetic genre encompasses several specific literary types, including psalms, proverbial sayings, and love songs. Most of the speeches recorded in the prophetic books take a poetic form, and poems are even embedded in narrative texts. This chapter includes a brief introduction to the literary analysis of both narrative and poetry. (For more detailed studies, see the bibliography at the end of this chapter.)

Narrative Literature

How Should One Approach Old Testament Narrative?

Many interpreters of Old Testament narrative continue to employ source criticism, form criticism, and redaction criticism. These approaches tend to question or deny the historicity of the text, focus on its origin and supposed evolution, and see embedded within it multiple sources and traditions, which are often delineated by alleged inconsistencies in content and   149 style and by supposed conflicting viewpoints. These approaches have been called into question by some critics and are even becoming obsolete in certain circles, for they do not adequately address the meaning of the text.

For the most part evangelicals have rightly repudiated these approaches because they tend to rob the biblical narratives of their unity and historicity. But evangelicals, assuming a defensive posture, have often become so obsessed with counterpunching the critics that they, too, fail to do justice to the narratives. Many focus on defending the historicity of the narratives or view them primarily as source material for reconstructing Israel's history. Apologetic and historical studies have their place, but they are ultimately deficient because they fail to grapple adequately with the literary dimension, message, and theology of the narratives. They bring to the narratives an agenda which is foreign to the viewpoint of the original author and thus fail to read the narratives as God intended.

In recent years many interpreters have turned to other approaches, such as canon criticism, literary criticism, structuralism, and reader–response criticism. These methods focus on the present form of the narratives and their arrangement in the canon, tend to see literary unity, and downplay the issue of historicity.

Evangelicals have responded more positively to these newer approaches because, relatively speaking, they have yielded more valuable results than the earlier critical methods. However, one should not applaud too loudly this dawning of a new day in biblical studies. Many of these newer studies and methods are reader-oriented, rather than author-text centered. Many literary critics, by their own admission, are not concerned with what the text meant. They prefer to articulate what the text means to them or to "deconstruct" its "sinister patriarchalism," and so on. Such interpreters impose their own agenda (whether it be Neo-Marxist, feminist, etc.) on the text. In this kind of pluralistic hermeneutical milieu there is no such thing as an authoritative divinely intended meaning, only several individual "meanings" created by a motley group of interpreters. Such studies reveal far more about the psychological profile, sociological context, and personal biases of the interpreter than the intent of the text's divine Author.

With many evangelicals, we propose an approach to biblical narrative that steers clear of the two extremes of modern critical methods and postmodern reader-oriented approaches. As noted earlier, a proper (dare we say, "sane") approach to the interpretation of narrative must take the historical and cultural context of the text seriously. The goal of interpretation is to discover the meaning intended by its author(s) in its original ancient Israelite context. This authoritative meaning then becomes the foundation for biblical theology and application.

Some well-meaning evangelicals deemphasize historical setting and cultural background, arguing that "meaning resides in the text." This affirmation is true so far as it goes, but one must remember that the text is rooted in a historical-cultural context that is inextricably linked to its meaning. To understand what the text meant, we must try to reconstruct this context to the best of our ability, utilizing the linguistic and archaeological evidence at our disposal. When a so-called text-centered interpreter fails to do this, one's approach easily degenerates into a reader-oriented analysis, for the interpreter's own biases inevitably warp one's interpretation.

A proper interpretive approach to narrative must also be literary in its focus. The narrative should not be viewed as a battlefield for apologetics or as a mere source for historical reconstruction. A literary approach must (1) demonstrate the literary and thematic unity of a narrative, (2) explain how every detail contributes to the narrative, and (3) show how the narrative fits into its larger literary context. Only in this way can we read the narratives as God intended and derive from them authoritative theological principles.

Basic Ingredients of a Story

Old Testament narrative, defined in its broadest sense, encompasses several literary forms (e.g., reports and genealogies, among others), but stories (in this case, true ones) are at the core of the genre. The stories contained in Old Testament narrative, like stories the world over, have three basic ingredients: setting, characterization, and plot.

Setting

We can analyze the setting of a story from different angles:[1]

(1) A story usually has a stated physical (or dramatic) setting. As we approach a story, we should ask: Where does the story take place? How does its physical setting contribute to it?

Details of physical setting are often just "props" on the literary stage, included to lend realism to the story or to create a certain mood. But at other times physical setting can have symbolic value and contribute to the story's theme. For example, in 2 Kings 1:9 the king's arrogant officer demands that the prophet Elijah "come down" from his perch "on the top of a hill." Elijah refuses to come down and instead calls fire down on the officer and his men. Elijah's elevated position symbolizes his authority as God's spokesman over the king and his messengers.

(2) A story also has a temporal setting. For example, the author of the Book of Ruth tells us that the story occurred during the general period of the Judges. This is important in understanding the story's theme, for it provides the dark moral and ethical background against which Ruth's

1. See Leland Ryken, *How to Read the Bible as Literature* (Grand Rapids: Zondervan, 1984), 35–37.

shining example of devotion is highlighted. Laban's deception of Jacob took place at evening (Gen. 29:23), when Jacob's eyes were blinded by the darkness, just as his own father's eyes had been blinded when Jacob masqueraded as Esau and stole his brother's blessing (Gen. 27).

(3) A story's historical-cultural setting can be very important. For example, to appreciate fully the story of Elijah's conflict with the prophets of Baal (1 Kings 17–18) one must read the story against the cultural background of Baalism, which was at this time a state religion in the northern kingdom (1 Kings 16:31–32). To ensure agricultural prosperity and human fertility, Israel decided to worship Baal, the Canaanite fertility god who, according to his devotees, controlled the rain and gave life. In response to Israel's idolatry, God sent a famine upon the land. According to pagan mythology, Baal was subject to Mot, the god of death, during times of famine. During the famine, while Baal was presumably trapped in the underworld and unable to exercise his royal responsibility to care for the needy, the Lord demonstrated (in Phoenicia, Baal's backyard!) his royal authority over fertility and life (see 1 Kings 17:7–24). At Mount Carmel the prophets of Baal were unable to "resurrect" their god by their frantic mourning rites, but the Lord proved that he, not Baal, really controls the elements of the storm and possesses the ability to bless Israel (see 1 Kings 18).

Characterization

A story's characters comprise another of its basic ingredients. When reading a biblical story, it is important to evaluate the characters. Data for analysis come in a variety of ways, including the author's direct description of a character, the response of other characters (which may or may not be fair, cf. 1 Sam. 17:28), as well as a character's names and epithets, self-characterization (which may or may not be honest), recorded thoughts, speech, and actions (but motives behind a character's speech and actions are sometimes difficult to determine). Sometimes an author will reveal his evaluation of a character through contrasts with another character (e.g., David and Saul), by contrasting a character's later actions with his earlier deeds (cf. Judah's attitude in Gen. 44:18–34 with his earlier words and actions), or by contrasting the character's actions with a cultural norm (see Jacob's actions in light of Laban's words in Gen. 29:26).

One can classify characters according to their extent of development. According to Berlin, round characters "are realistically portrayed; their emotions and motivations are either made explicit" or are "strongly hinted at." She adds: "We feel that we know them, understand them, and can, to a large extent, identify with them."[2] Flat characters, on the other

---

2. Adele Berlin, *Poetics and Interpretation of Biblical Narrative* (Winona Lake, Ind.: Eisenbrauns, 1994), 31–32.

hand, possess only one or two traits. Of course, it is sometimes overly simplistic to categorize a character as "round" and "flat." Extent of character development is actually a spectrum, with "round" and "flat" characters being at opposite ends. Often a character falls in between these two extremes.

One can also categorize characters according to their role in the story. Characters can be major or minor. A major character is one on whom the author focuses interest. A story can have more than one major character, but usually has only one central character, or protagonist. Protagonists can be sympathetic or unsympathetic, a hero or an anti-hero. Minor characters tend to have a purely functional role in the story. The labels "major" and "minor" are really opposite ends of a spectrum. Sometimes a character falls in between these two extremes.

One can combine the two main areas of classification (extent of development and role).[3] A major character who is round may be labeled full-fledged. Abraham, Jacob, Joseph, Saul, and David are full-fledged characters. The experience of full-fledged characters generally teaches us lessons, though they are not usually models to follow in all of their actions.

Major characters who are flat are types, who, in Berlin's words, possess "a limited and stereotyped range of traits" and represent "the class of people with these traits."[4] For example, Ehud the assassin (Judg. 3:12–30) is a type of the courageous leader. Types are often held up as an example to follow or avoid.

A minor character who is nevertheless round may be called a supporting actor/actress (Saul's son Jonathan is an example), while a minor character who is flat may be labeled an agent. Agents abound in the biblical stories; they are often stereotypical and may function as foils. Because their role tends to be purely functional, neither the experience nor behavior of minor characters usually carries a lesson for the reader. Bathsheba, as depicted in 2 Samuel 11–12, is a prime example of an agent. Her actual name is given in 11:3, but otherwise she is called "a/the woman" (11:2, 5), "the wife of Uriah" (11:3, 26; 12:10), "my/his wife" (11:11; 12:9). She is the stereotypical desirable woman who belongs to someone else and is an agent of temptation.

Sample Analyses of Characterization

The Prophet Jonah

(1) Jonah is initially disobedient to God's commission (cf. 1:3) and only obeys God's command (3:3) after being subjected to the most severe form of divine coercion,

---

3. See Pamela LaBreche, "A Methodology for the Analysis of Characterization in Old Testament Narrative" (Th.M. thesis, Dallas Theological Seminary, 1992), 14–17.

4. Berlin, *Poetics and Interpretation*, 32.

(2) is insensitive to God's mighty deeds in nature (1:5),

(3) affirms that God is the Creator of the sea and dry land (1:9), though he has tried to run away from God via the sea (1:3–4),

(4) is willing to die to save the sailors (or to avoid fulfilling his commission?) (1:12–13),

(5) though giving no sign of repentance, presumes he has been delivered by God (chapter 2),

(6) disdains idolaters and speaks of himself as superior to them (2:8–9),

(7) greatly resents God's forgiveness of Nineveh (4:1), though quite aware of God's compassionate and gracious nature (4:2),[5]

(8) asks to die, but acts as if he wants to live (4:3–9),

(9) and greatly appreciates God's provision for his physical comfort, but then displays resentment when that comfort is removed (4:8–9).

In contrast to Jonah, the sailors submit to God's sovereign will, show great moral sensitivity in dealing with Jonah, and display genuine fear of the Lord (chapter 1). The Ninevites, though spiritually ignorant (4:11), also respond positively to the Lord's sovereign intervention in their experience. Led by their king, they genuinely repent of their sins and throw themselves upon God's mercy (chapter 3).

From his own personal experience, as well as his theological tradition, Jonah knows God is gracious. He is more than willing to accept God's mercy when it is directed toward him, but he is unwilling to allow God to show that same mercy to the hated Ninevites. When the plant is destroyed and Jonah's physical comfort is at stake, Jonah's response is one of self-interest. However, he seems unwilling to let God act out of self-interest, even when the lives of thousands of spiritually ignorant people and innocent beasts are at stake.

Jonah is the central character, or protagonist, in the Book of Jonah. However, he is a flat character, whose only traits seem to be prejudice and selfishness. He is a type of the disobedient prophet, an unsympathetic anti-hero whose negative example serves to teach us an important lesson.

The Cast of the Story of Ehud (Judg. 3:12–30)[6]

Eglon is a major character who functions as the antagonist in the story. Though physically round (!), he is a flat literary character, a type of the oppressive foreign ruler.

Ehud is the central character and protagonist. However, his characterization is flat; he is a type of the ideal leader who possesses courage born out of faith. The author holds him up as the exemplar of the story.

---

5. Jonah quotes here from a traditional credal statement that originates in the context of God's forgiveness of unfaithful Israel. See Exod. 34:6 and Num. 14:18.

6. The characters in the story are analyzed in their order of appearance.

The tribute carriers are agents, as are the king's attendants. The latter are stereotypical lackeys whose obsession with protocol all but paralyzes them.

The Israelite and Moabite soldiers are agents, through whom the plot's conflict reaches its final resolution.

The Cast of the Book of Ruth[7]

One might expect Elimelech and his sons to play a major role in the story, but they are mere agents, men who die and leave their widows in a vulnerable position in a patriarchal culture.

Naomi is the protagonist or central character of the story. Her experience illustrates that even though one may have to endure suffering in a fallen world, in such circumstances God is not an enemy, but an ally who can bring order out of the chaos. Naomi's experience is instructive, but her behavior, however human and natural, is not necessarily exemplary.

Orpah is an agent, the stereotypical dutiful daughter-in-law who displays a degree of loyalty, but has her limits. She makes a superb foil for Ruth. If the loyalty of a relatively good person like Orpah has its limits, what does that say about the character of Ruth, whose allegiance can be limited only by the power of death?

Ruth is a major character who functions as a type of the devoted wife and daughter. Because of her extraordinary allegiance, which appears to be her dominant or even sole quality, she actually transcends the typical; perhaps we should call her "Super Wife and Daughter." Her behavior provides an example for the reader to follow. Yes, God cares for needy widows like Naomi, but he often does so through instruments like loyal Ruth.

The women of Bethlehem are agents who make a good sounding board for depressed Naomi and eventually correct her faulty perspective.

Boaz may be viewed as a major character in the story, but he probably ranks third in importance. He is a type of the rich, powerful landowner. But unlike some in this position, he takes his duties seriously. The appearance of the unnamed kinsman as a foil suggests that Boaz is not merely an agent, but a type and exemplar.

The foreman of Boaz's work crew is an agent; the field hands are mere "extras." Their character is not developed at all; they merely appear as human props on the stage.

The elders and people at the gate are agents, including the unnamed kinsman who refuses to take responsibility for Ruth. He stands as a foil for Boaz.

Obed is an agent, a divine blessing in human form over whom Naomi dotes and through whom God grants even greater blessings.

7. The characters in the story are analyzed in their order of appearance.

Plot

A story's third basic ingredient is its plot, which Ryken defines as "a coherent sequence of interrelated events, with a beginning, middle, and end." He adds, "It is, in other words, a *whole* or complete action."[8] Ryken goes on to explain that "the essence of a plot is a central conflict or set of conflicts moving toward a resolution." As Ryken explains, plots can display physical (e.g., David versus Goliath), character (e.g., Elijah versus Ahab/Jezebel), or moral/spiritual (e.g., Job versus chaos) conflicts. Moral/spiritual conflicts often take place within a character (e.g., Jacob). They frequently involve a test or challenge that arises in the midst of a crisis.[9]

Conflicts can be multidimensional. For example, Jacob is in conflict with Esau, then Laban. But his real conflict is with God and within himself, as he struggles to depend on the God of his fathers, rather than his own wits and schemes, for success in life. His wrestling match with God is a microcosm of this deeper conflict and brings it to resolution.

Plots can be categorized in a variety of ways. Some of the more common plot types include:[10]

(1) Tragedy (e.g., Saul's story): In a tragic plot the protagonist (who has great potential or opportunity) makes a wrong decision (usually because of a tragic, but very human, character flaw) and falls. Tragic plots bring tears of sorrow to our eyes.
(2) Punitive story (e.g., Ahab's story): Punitive plots make us cheer when the "bad guy" finally meets his just demise.
(3) Negative example story (e.g., Jonah's story): In this type of story a character's negative behavior is described. These stories bring a disapproving frown to our faces.

The preceding three plot types warn us about behavior patterns to avoid. Punitive plots also encourage us by reminding us that God is just.

(4) Comedy (e.g., Naomi's story): In a comic plot the protagonist encounters obstacles but eventually overcomes them through faith and/or divine intervention. Comic plots bring tears of joy to our eyes.
(5) Reward story (e.g., the story of the impoverished widow in 2 Kings 4:8–37): In this type of story God rewards a commendable deed. These stories make us cheer when the "good guy" is properly rewarded for his actions.

8. Ryken, *How to Read the Bible*, 40.
9. Ibid., 50–51.
10. Ibid., 53.

(6) Admiration story (e.g., Daniel's story): In this type of story a character's commendable behavior is described. These stories make us smile.

These three plot types inspire, challenge, and encourage us.

A narrator sometimes merges plot types. For example, Numbers 25 includes both a punitive story (vv. 1–5) and a reward story (vv. 6–13). The story of Jephthah's deliverance of Israel (Judg. 11) begins with a physical conflict between Jephthah and the Ammonites and appears to be resolved as a comic plot (vv. 4–33), but it then turns into a tragedy because of major flaws (inadequate faith and lack of wisdom) in Jephthah's character (vv. 34–40).

Plot structure varies, depending on the plot type and the nature of the conflict. When a test or inner conflict is at the heart of a story, the plot often follows this basic structure:

Setting
Test or challenge
Protagonist's response
Divine counterresponse and consequences
Closure

In a tragedy or negative example story, a character fails a test or responds negatively to a crisis. For example, the story of Cain's murder of Abel (Gen. 4:1–16) displays this structure:

Setting (vv. 1–5)
Challenge (vv. 6–7)
Cain's negative response (v. 8)
Divine counterresponse and consequences (vv. 9–15)
Closure (v. 16)

In a comedy or admiration story a character passes a test or responds positively to a crisis. For example, the story of Abraham's offering of his son Isaac (Gen. 22:1–19) exhibits this structure:

Setting (v. 1)
Test (v. 2)
Abraham's positive response (vv. 3–10)
Counterresponse and consequences (vv. 11–18)
Closure (v. 19)

Plots (especially the tragic and comic variety) sometimes develop according to the following basic pattern:

Setting
Action begins[11]
Conflict introduced
Conflict intensifies
A potential solution appears
Conflict subsides and moves toward resolution
Conflict is resolved
Action ends
Closure

A good story usually maintains a degree of tension, even after the plot reaches its peak. Pauses and plot twists, in addition to reflecting real life, also make for good drama. Consider the plot development of the Book of Ruth:

Setting (1:1a)
Action begins (1:1b–2)
Conflict introduced (1:3–5)
(Pause: Relief?) (1:6–7)
Conflict intensifies (1:8–23)
A potential solution appears (chapter 2)
Conflict moves toward resolution (3:1–11)
PLOT TWIST (3:12): Potential wrong ending (the reader feels a tension headache coming on)
Move toward resolution resumes (author offers a pain reliever) (3:13–18)
Conflict is resolved (but not before one more plot twist, cf. 4:4) (4:1–12)
Action ends (4:13–17)
Closure (4:18–22)

The final verses (4:13–22) drive home the main lessons of the story: God's care for needy people, his ability to overcome chaos, and the importance of devotion and faithfulness to duty.

Punitive stories often have a simple plot structure in which an evil deed is followed by divine punishment (e.g., 2 Kings 1). In similar fashion the plot structure of a reward story includes a commendable deed followed by divine reward (e.g., 2 Kings 4:1–7).

Hebrew narrative often combines plot structures. For example, the reward story of the Shunammite woman in 2 Kings 4:8–37 combines the simple deed–reward structure with the more complex conflict resolution

11. Early action in a story sometimes contributes more to characterization than plot per se. However, the character trait(s) revealed can be vital to the plot. See, for example, 1 Sam. 9, where Saul's search for the lost donkeys brings him to Samuel, but also reveals the hesitancy that will later prove fatal to his kingship.

structure outlined above, thereby creating a major plot twist and dramatic intensity:

Part One:
Setting (v. 8)
Commendable deed (vv. 9–10)
Divine reward (vv. 11–17)

Part Two:
Setting (v. 18a)
Action begins (v. 18b)
PLOT TWIST: Potential wrong ending as conflict is introduced (v. 19)
Conflict intensifies (v. 20)[12]
(Pause: What exactly does the Shunnamite have in mind?) (vv. 21–28)[13]
A potential solution appears (vv. 29–30)
PLOT TWIST: The conflict is not resolved (v. 31)
Conflict subsides and moves toward resolution (vv. 32–34)
Conflict is resolved (v. 35)
Action ends (vv. 36–37)

Some Literary Features of Hebrew Narrative

Point of View

Apart from quotations, we ordinarily assume that the narrative reflects the viewpoint of the narrator (who by inspiration writes with divine authority).[14] However, sometimes the narrator writes from the perspective of one of the characters and invites us to step into that character's shoes and view the situation from his or her perspective.

For example, when Genesis 32:24 informs us that Jacob wrestled with "a man," the perspective is Jacob's at the time when the struggle began. At this point he did not know with whom he was wrestling. (Neither do we, if we are reading the story for the first time.) The vagueness of the

---

12. Following vv. 8–17, the introduction of a conflict in vv. 19–20 is a plot twist that seems to transform a reward story into an unmitigated disaster.

13. The "pause" in vv. 21–28 increases the dramatic tension. While hinting at a potential resolution by focusing on the prophet, it delays any real resolution and then surprises us by informing us in vv. 27–28 that the seemingly calm Shunammite is bitterly disappointed and feels somewhat betrayed.

14. As God's spokesman the narrator appears to be omniscient. For example, he can invade the privacy of a person's thoughts (1 Sam. 20:26), knows about events and statements that would seem to be outside the scope of the ordinary source material utilized by the biblical authors (Judg. 3:24–25; 5:28–30), and has theological insight into the significance of events (Judg. 14:4). On the subject of the narrator's omniscience in Hebrew narrative, see Meir Sternberg, *The Poetics of Biblical Narrative* (Bloomington: Indiana University Press, 1987). Consult the index, p. 559, for pages dealing with this issue of the narrator's "omniscience."

character's perspective contributes to the drama of the event and arouses our curiosity. (Just who is this mysterious adversary? Is it Esau, or someone else?) By refusing to identify the opponent more specifically, the narrator allows us to relive some of the suspense that Jacob must have felt.

In Exodus 4:24 we read the odd statement, "Along the way, at the place where they lodged, the LORD confronted him (i.e., Moses) and attempted (or perhaps, "intended," the verb is the piel of בקשׁ) to kill him." Apparently the Lord was angry because Moses' son was uncircumcised; at any rate his anger was placated when Moses' wife circumcised the child. Can we take the statement "attempted/intended to kill him" at face value? God had just commissioned Moses to go to Egypt. Furthermore, if God wants or tries to kill someone, one might expect him to succeed! The account is probably written from Moses' perspective. When Moses had this fearful encounter with God, the details of which are omitted, it must have seemed to him as if God were trying to kill him. To emphasize the terror and seriousness of the encounter, the narrative is written from Moses' perspective.

In Ruth 2:3 the narrator, with tongue-in-cheek, informs us that Ruth "just happened by chance" to come to the field of Boaz. The narrator knows that Ruth's every step is guided by providence, but at this point he writes from Ruth's perspective. As far as she was concerned, she randomly picked a place to glean, but God had directed her to the field of Boaz, a relative who was capable of delivering the two widows from their plight. By reflecting Ruth's perspective the narrator emphasizes God's sovereignty. Ruth took the initiative in committing herself to Naomi; God took care of the rest.

The author often uses the interjection הִנֵּה ("look") to invite the reader to share a character's perspective. For example, in Ruth 3:8 Boaz, the "place of his feet" having been exposed, wakes up. We then read, "And look (הִנֵּה), a woman was lying at the place of his feet!" We already know the woman lying beside Boaz is Ruth (vv. 6–7), but from Boaz's confused perspective, she is just "a woman."[15]

Reported Speech

Dialogues and quotations play an important role in Hebrew narrative, for they can reveal much about a character and contribute in significant ways to plot development. Sometimes it is especially instructive to examine reported speech, where a character reports what another has said. Berlin, building on the work of Savran, divides such reports into verifiable and unverifiable categories.[16] Within the first category we sometimes see exact or verbatim repetition of the recorded original speech, but at other times the report is significantly altered.

---

15. For other examples of this use of הִנֵּה, see Gen. 28:12–13; 29:25; Judg. 3:24–25; 4:22b.
16. Berlin, *Poetics and Interpretation*, 97.

For example, Judges 8 tells how Gideon and his exhausted men pursued the fleeing Midianite kings across the Jordan. When they arrive in Succoth, they ask for provisions from the people of Succoth, but the city officials reject their request, saying: "You have not yet overpowered Zebah and Zalmunna. So why should we give bread to your army?" (v. 6). Gideon warns the leaders of the city that he will punish them when he returns from the chase (v. 7). When Gideon and his men return victoriously with Zebah and Zalmunna in tow, he confronts the leaders of Succoth and reminds them of their earlier words: "You insulted me, saying, 'You have not yet overpowered Zebah and Zalmunna. So why should we give bread to your exhausted men?'" (v. 15) For rhetorical effect Gideon changes their actual statement (cf. v. 6) by substituting "exhausted men" for "army." In this way he emphasizes the crisis his men were facing at the time of the request, highlights the insensitivity of the men of Succoth, and makes it clear that he is justified in punishing them (cf. v. 16).

In Genesis 3:2–3 the woman badly garbles God's earlier words to the man when she attempts to tell the serpent what God said. Among other alterations, she omits the emphatic infinitive absolute when describing God's provision (v. 2, cf. 2:16) and warning (v. 3, cf. 2:17), but adds the statement "and you must not touch it" to his prohibition. In this way she deemphasizes what God stressed and emphasizes what he did not. When God spoke, one was impressed with the abundant provision he had made available and his concern that the man understand the grave consequences of rebellion. The woman's report places God in a much harsher light and may explain in part why she seems so willing to rebel against him.

In the narrative of Samson's birth (Judg. 13) the angel announces to Manoah's barren wife that she will have a son (v. 4). After giving her dietary regulations to follow (v. 5), he informs her that the boy will be a Nazirite and that "he will begin the deliverance of Israel from the hands of the Philistines" (v. 5). When Samson's mother reports the news to her husband (vv. 6–7), she makes a glaring omission. She leaves out the reference to her son being God's deliverer. No wonder Manoah is confused about his son's role in life (v. 12). The story gives no indication that Samson ever understood his larger purpose in life. His struggles with the Philistines end up being a mere personal vendetta, not a holy war.

Repetition and Variation

Hebrew narrative sometimes appears to be unduly repetitive, but careful analysis usually reveals a rhetorical purpose for such repetition.[17] For ex-

---

17. On repetition in Hebrew narrative, see Sternberg, *Poetics*, 365–440, and Robert Alter, *The Art of Biblical Narrative* (New York: Basic Books, 1981), 88–113.

ample, the author of 2 Kings 1 uses repetition to emphasize God's disapproval of the king's paganism and the authority of God's prophet over the king. Three times we hear God's message to the king (as initially given to Elijah, vv. 3–4; as reported by the king's messengers to the king, v. 6; as delivered by Elijah directly to the king, v. 16). Through the repetition one cannot miss the reason for God's judgment on the king.

Three times in 2 Kings 1 we read of an encounter between Elijah and a royal military official (vv. 9–15). The first two panels are virtually identical (though notice the more official introduction to and emphatic form of the command in v. 11b); the repetition makes it clear that the king does not truly respect the Lord's prophet. The repetition also heightens the reader's anticipation and sets the stage for the dramatic finale. Significant variation occurs in the third panel and draws our attention to one of the narrative's main themes—God's prophets must be shown proper respect.

The story of Samson's seduction (Judg. 16:6–21) displays four panels and effectively utilizes repetition and variation to build suspense and highlight Samson's stupidity. It may be outlined as follows:

Panel 1 (vv. 6–9)

Delilah's request (v. 6)
Samson's response (v. 7)
The failed plot (vv. 8–9)

Panel 2 (vv. 10–12)

Delilah's complaint and request (v. 10)
Samson's response (v. 11)
The failed plot (v. 12)

Panel 3 (vv. 13–14)[18]

Delilah's complaint and request (v. 13)
Samson's response (v. 14a)
The failed plot (v. 14b)

Panel 4 (vv. 15–21)

Delilah's complaint and request (vv. 15–16)
Samson's response (v. 17)
The successful plot (vv. 18–21)

There are several reasons why Delilah might believe the false explanations Samson offers in the first three panels. The suggestion that he

18. We assume that the longer version of the story, as preserved in the Septuagint, is original. See our text-critical discussion of this passage in chapter 3.

could be subdued by seven fresh thongs (v. 7) has an authentic ring to it, for seven is a highly symbolic number which might suggest magical or supernatural power. In the second panel he advises the use of "new" (i.e., strong) ropes and places the emphatic infinitive absolute (cf. NIV "securely") before the verb "tie," suggesting an element of certainty. In the third panel he again uses the number "seven," presents a substantially different proposal involving his hair (he's moving closer to the truth!), and offers more detailed instructions which she might think were too elaborate to be a hoax.

As is typical with paneled stories of this type, several literary variations from the repetitive pattern of the earlier panels mark out the culminating panel. In the fourth panel Delilah's argument is far more persuasive than before as she questions the sincerity of Samson's love for her and nags him day after day. We already know Samson is vulnerable to this kind of argumentation and suspect the worst.[19] The narrator's observation that her nagging tired him "to death" hints at the final outcome of her efforts and is dripping with irony, for his capitulation to her nagging will literally cause his death.

Samson's response is also far different in the final panel. Rather than using the simple pattern, "If you do . . . , I'll become as weak as any other man," he now prefaces his response with an authentic explanation about his personal background, changes the verb form in the protasis of the conditional sentence to a perfect (note אִם־גֻּלַּחְתִּי in v. 17, in contrast to the imperfects he used earlier), adds the words "my strength would leave me," and changes "like any other man" (כְּאַחַד הָאָדָם) to "like all men" (כְּכָל־הָאָדָם).

Delilah's response to Samson's explanation and the Philistines' response to her report also differ significantly in the fourth panel. This time, the narrator informs us, Delilah is absolutely convinced that he is telling the truth, and her words to the Philistines reflect that. They, too, seem sure that she is right, for they arrive with their money in hand.[20]

Contrast and Analogy

Narrators sometimes employ literary foils to contrast and highlight characters and/or actions. Ryken defines a foil as follows: "A foil is literally something that 'sets off' or heightens what is most important in a story. It is usually a *contrast*, though it can also consist of a *parallel* that reinforces something else. The commonest type of foil is a character who ac-

19. In Judg. 14:16–17 the Timnite girl employs the same tactic; the narrator uses the same verb (note צוק in both 14:17 and 16:16) to describe her persistence.

20. Paneled structures of this type are frequent in literature that is designed to be heard, rather than read. See H. Van Dyke Parunak, "Oral Typesetting: Some Uses of Biblical Structure," *Biblica* 62 (1981): 153–68. For modern parallels in children's literature, see "The Three Little Pigs" and "Three Billy Goats Gruff."

centuates the protagonist, but sometimes an event or thread of action can serve as a foil to the main plot."[21]

For example, in the Book of Jonah the sailors and Ninevites are foils for Jonah. Their proper response to divine revelation contrasts with Jonah's disobedience to his divine commission. In the Book of Ruth, Orpah functions as a foil for Ruth and the unnamed kinsman is a foil for Boaz. In each case the contrast highlights the superior moral qualities of the major character.

In the Book of Judges Caleb's kindness toward his daughter Acsah, expressed through a gift symbolizing fertility (Judg. 1:14–15), is a foil for Jephthah's treatment of his daughter, which dooms her to infertility and death (Judg. 11:29–40). The contrast draws attention to the moral decline that has taken place in Israel by Jephthah's time.

In Judges–1 Samuel the unnamed mothers of Samson (Judg. 13) and Micah (Judg. 17) are foils for Hannah (1 Sam. 1). In contrast to Samson's mother, whose miraculously conceived Nazirite son failed to realize his potential, Hannah supernaturally gave birth to a Nazirite son through whom the Lord restored effective leadership to Israel. In contrast to Micah's mother, whose misguided zeal gave rise to a polluted, unauthorized cult, Hannah's devotion to the Lord led to the revival of genuine Yahwism through the spiritual direction provided by her son Samuel.

The three accounts even begin in the same way:

Judges 13:2 ויהי איש אחד מצרעה . . . ושמו מנוח
"Now there was a certain man from Zorah . . . whose name was Manoah"

Judges 17:1 ויהי־איש מהר־אפרים ושמו מיכיהו
"Now there was a man from the hill country of Ephraim whose name was Micaiah"

1 Samuel 1:1 ויהי איש אחד מן־הרמתים צופים מהר אפרים ושמו אלקנה
"Now there was a certain man from Ramathaim . . . whose name was Elkanah"

At first glance the formula "now there was a (certain) man from (geographical name) . . . whose name was (personal name)" seems to be merely a stylized way of introducing a new pericope. However, in Judges–1 Samuel this formula appears only in these three passages and in 1 Samuel 9:1, where Saul's family background is introduced. Like Samson, Saul contrasts with Samuel.[22] This suggests that the introduc-

---

21. Ryken, *How to Read the Bible*, 54.

22. For some of the parallels between Samson and Saul, see my article "The Role of Women in the Rhetorical Strategy of the Book of Judges," in *Integrity of Heart, Skillfulness of Hands: Biblical and Leadership Studies in Honor of Donald K. Campbell*, ed. Charles H. Dyer and Roy B. Zuck (Grand Rapids: Baker, 1994), 47–48, n. 34.

tory formula is a linking device at the macrostructural or larger discourse level.

Parallelism of characters and/or events is very common. Sometimes an earlier occurrence foreshadows a later event of greater magnitude. For example, in Exodus 2:17–19 the refugee Moses drives off some bullies and delivers Reuel's daughters. This seemingly minor incident foreshadows how the Lord would deliver oppressed Israel through Moses.

In Judges 14 Samson, through the power of God's Spirit, kills a roaring lion (vv. 5–6) and then, sometime later, eats some honey from the lion's carcass (vv. 8–9). Both of these events reveal characteristics about Samson and foreshadow key episodes in the story. Samson's killing the lion shows what he is capable of accomplishing in God's strength. Later in the story the Philistines attack Samson like a lion.[23] Their shouts correspond to the lion's roar. God's Spirit once again rushes on him.[24] Samson supernaturally defeats one thousand Philistines, just as he supernaturally killed the lion. Samson's eating the honey indicates that he has a tough time controlling his physical desires and lusts and suggests that satisfying his physical desires may be more important to him than his status as a Nazirite. It also foreshadows his fall, which comes as a result of his unbridled lust for sex. The sweet honey foreshadows the feminine charms of Delilah, who uses her tremendous hold over Samson to bring him down. Samson can resist and defeat lions, but he has trouble with sweet honey.

Parallelism often highlights irony. For example, the Canaanite king Adoni-Bezek, who mutilated seventy other kings and then recognized God's talionic justice in his own punishment (Judg. 1:5–7), seems to find his match in the Israelite Abimelech, who murdered his seventy half brothers and experienced God's retributive justice (Judg. 9). The parallel draws attention to the tragic fact that an Israelite leader has become quite "Canaanite" in his mentality.

One can often detect parallelism on a larger scale. For example, the sequence of cultic impropriety (involving an ephod) followed by anarchy and civil war in Judges 8–9 is repeated in Judges 17–21. The parallelism illustrates one of the book's main themes—Israel is in an ever-deepening moral rut that becomes increasingly injurious to the nation's well-being and more and more threatening to its existence. Similarly, Jephthah's misplaced oath (which led to the death of his own daughter) and his mini-civil war with the Ephraimites (Judg. 11–12) foreshadow the bloody full-scale war with Benjamin in which many women, like Jephthah's daughter, became victims of a misplaced oath and male brutality (Judg. 19–21).

23. Note Hebrew לִקְרָאתוֹ in both 14:5 and 15:14.
24. Note Hebrew צָלַח in both 14:6 and 15:14.

Discerning the presence of parallelism often helps one evaluate a character and his career. For example, young David is portrayed in 1 Samuel 17 as a new giant killer—the second coming of Joshua, Caleb, and Othniel, as it were. However, later, when he looks on a woman with lust in his eye,[25] he is transformed into a new Samson whose failures usher in (at least literarily, if not chronologically) a period of civil strife (cf. 2 Sam. 11–20 with Judg. 17–21). By the end of David's story we get the uneasy feeling that Israel has not made as much moral progress as we may have thought. When even the king does what is right in his own eyes, chaos is inevitable.

Ambiguity and Omission

Often a narrative omits information that the reader might wish had been provided.[26] Undoubtedly the text sometimes appears to be ambiguous or elliptical because we are so far removed from the original context. Readers who shared the author's culture and experiences may have intuitively understood implications or aspects of the story that to us are unclear. However, ambiguity or omission is sometimes intentional. In many cases the author does not provide clarification or information because apparently it is not important to his goal and/or because ambiguity or omission fits his literary purpose.

For example, readers of 2 Samuel 11 often want to know more about the background of David's affair with Bathsheba. How did Bathsheba feel when David propositioned her? Did she try to get the king's attention in the first place? Did she resist when he invited her to the royal palace? The author leaves our questions unanswered and instead focuses on David's actions. Why? Not because Bathsheba had no feelings, but because they are irrelevant to his purposes. He wants to emphasize the king's culpability. To delve into Bathsheba's psyche might be interesting to us, but it is not relevant to the point the narrator wants to make. Furthermore, the author introduces Bathsheba out of the blue; there is nothing in the earlier context that might suggest answers to our questions and facilitate filling the informational gaps. As interpreters we should honor the boundaries set by the author, avoid speculation, and focus on what the text does say.

However, it is legitimate to attempt to fill gaps in a story if the context provides genuine clues. For example, 2 Kings 9:30–31 records Jezebel's response to Jehu, who has just murdered King Joram, Jezebel's son. Oddly enough, she puts on some eye liner, sets her hair, and looks out her

---

25. The statement "he saw a woman," appears in both 2 Sam. 11:2 and Judg. 16:1, but nowhere in between.

26. Most stories, of course, utilize temporary ambiguity or omission for dramatic effect. For example, the author of Gen. 32:22-32 waits to tell us that Jacob's foe is God himself, undoubtedly to heighten our curiosity.

window as if ready to seduce the assassin when he arrives (see Jer. 4:30). But when Jehu enters the city gate, Jezebel asks him this sarcastic, insulting question: "Is everything fine with you, Zimri, you murderer of your master?" With this question she associates Jehu with another assassin, Zimri, who approximately forty-four years before had murdered King Elah, only to meet a violent death just a few days later (1 Kings 16:9–20). On the surface Jezebel's actions seem contradictory. She beautifies herself as if to seduce Jehu, but then insults and indirectly threatens him with this comparison to Zimri. Upon further reflection, however, her actions reveal a clear underlying motive that is consistent with characteristics she has demonstrated earlier in the story, namely, excessive arrogance, unquenchable thirst for power (as evidenced by her hatred for the Lord's prophets, who represented an authority higher than her own), and the ability to connive (see 1 Kings 21). She wants to retain her power, not to mention her life. By beautifying herself, she appeals to Jehu's sexual impulses; by threatening him, she reminds him that he is in the same precarious position as Zimri. But, if he makes Jezebel his queen, he can secure his tenuous position.[27] Her looks say, "Wouldn't you like to have me sexually?" At the same time her words say, "You need me politically, you assassin!" In other words she is saying through her appearance and words, "You want me; you need me! So take me as your lover and queen!"

Diversity of Literary Forms within Narrative Literature

As noted above, stories are at the core of Old Testament narrative, but the genre encompasses and utilizes other literary forms as well, including among others genealogies and reports. (A report is generally much shorter than a story and, unlike a story, lacks a plot.) Literary analysis must account for all the material in a narrative, explaining how it contributes to the author's literary strategy and purpose.

For example, the Book of Ruth, a short story with a well-developed plot structure, concludes with a genealogy, which seems like a rather anticlimactic way for the narrative to end. But closer inspection shows how the genealogy relates to its context. By tracing the family line of Perez through Boaz and on to David, the narrator demonstrates that the prayers of blessing offered earlier in the chapter were fulfilled. God made Boaz famous and gave him an unbroken line of male descendants, culminating in the great king David. The genealogy reminds us that God does indeed bless the faithful, often beyond their lifetime and more than they can imagine.

A genealogy also plays an important role in the developing story of humankind in the opening chapters of Genesis. Genesis 5, with its lengthy

---

27. See Richard G. Smith, "Jehu's Revolt in Deuteronomic Perspective" (Th.M. thesis, Dallas Theological Seminary, 1996), 88–92.

litany of birth, life, and death, brings together two major themes from the earlier chapters. As humankind seeks to carry out the mandate to be fruitful, God's edict of judgment, bringing with it death, tarnishes and frustrates the ideal.

Reports also play an important role in many narratives. For example, the Books of Kings contain several stories, but also include several annalistic style reports of kings' reigns that lack plot structure. The list of reports in 2 Kings 15 traces in rapid fashion Israel's decline, as a series of assassinations, atrocities, and foreign invasions bring the nation and its sinful leadership to the brink of chaos and annihilation. In so doing it contributes to the overall message of the narrative.

In Judges 10:1–5 one finds two short reports separating the stories of Abimelech and Jephthah. These reports have an important role to play in the larger narrative. The story of Abimelech (Judg. 9) is a fast-paced account filled with action and violence. It tells how chaos engulfed the nation as a power-hungry ruler tried to establish a Canaanite style of rule within Israel. By the end of the story, the audience needs relief, both literarily and emotionally. The reports in 10:1–5 provide this relief by giving a capsulized account of the careers of Abimelech's successors, Tola and Jair, and by indicating that some semblance of order and leadership was reestablished in Israel and Transjordan. However, the earlier formulaic conclusion, which mentioned the land having peace (cf. 3:11, 30; 5:31; 8:28), does not appear here or later. Abimelech's quest for power marked a transition for Israel. Genuine peace was no longer possible.

Three more brief reports appear in Judges 12:8–15, separating the stories of Jephthah and Samson. Jephthah's career brought civil strife, but these reports inform us that at least no new Abimelech emerged from the clash between Gilead and Ephraim. Instead there were thirty-one years of stability. As in 10:1–5, this list of "minor judges" gives the audience a break after the action-packed account which precedes. The emphasis on numerous offspring and interclan marriage suggests Israel is experiencing a degree of divine blessing and tribal unity, though we do not read of genuine peace being restored.

Placement and Sequence in Old Testament Narrative

To understand fully the significance of a narrative one must examine its placement within the larger whole of which it is a part. Just as one cannot assess the significance of a scene in a movie apart from the film's overall plot and message, so one must attempt to understand how each individual narrative in a biblical book or complex of books (e.g., Joshua–Kings) contributes to and is impacted by its larger context.

For example, the story of Judah and Tamar (Gen. 38) seems at first to be misplaced and to interrupt the story of Joseph. However, this section of Genesis should not be titled "The Story of Joseph," but "A Story of Two

Brothers." Initially Judah is a foil for Joseph; in the end he becomes a paradigm of God's redemptive work. Judah is transformed from a self-righteous, jealous man ready to kill his father's favorite son into a realistic, self-sacrificing son who is willing to give up his own freedom and future for the sake of his father and his father's new favorite son. God's providential work in Judah's life runs concurrently with his sovereign direction of Joseph's steps and contributes to his overall goal of forming the great nation he promised Abraham.

The sequence of narrative units is also important, for it contributes to both the plot and theme of the larger story. For example, the Deborah–Barak narrative (Judg. 4), which follows the Othniel–Ehud narratives (Judg. 3:7–30) and precedes the Gideon story (Judg. 6–8), is strategically placed. Its introduction of a woman leader in juxtaposition to a hesitant male leader signals a decline in the quality of male leadership in Israel. Barak is no Othniel or Ehud (let alone Caleb or Joshua) and his hesitancy foreshadows that of Gideon, who combines insufficient faith with lack of wisdom. Gideon's shortcomings mix together in an explosive and destructive way in Jephthah. Israelite male leadership then collapses entirely, as Samson takes Gideon's lack of wisdom to an unprecedented level. To summarize, the Deborah–Barak narrative marks a move away from the leadership ideal depicted in Judges 3. Barak paves the way for Gideon, who in turn becomes a paradigm for Jephthah and Samson.

Poetic Literature

Poetic Style and Techniques

Much of the Old Testament is written in poetic form, including Psalms, Proverbs, and a good portion of the prophetic writings. A poem is a literary composition in parallelistic verse which conveys experiences, ideas, and emotions in a vivid and imaginative way and utilizes imagery more extensively than prose does.

Comparison

Imagery is vivid, figurative language that grabs one's attention and seizes one's emotions as it paints word pictures. One of the most common ways for a poet to create an image is through comparison. Comparisons are often directly stated. The most basic form of comparison is a simile, in which the author compares two objects using the preposition -כְּ, "like, as." For example, the author of Psalm 1 says that the godly man "is like a tree planted by streams of water" (v. 3, note כְּעֵץ, "like a tree"), but sinners are "like chaff" (v. 4, כַּמֹּץ). The psalmist could have simply and prosaically declared: "The godly will prosper, sinners will not." However, by using the imagery of a well-watered tree and wind-blown chaff, he conveys this two-sided truth in a much more vivid and emotionally gripping way that should motivate one to desire godliness.

Sometimes a poet states a comparison more forcefully, by eliminating the comparative preposition and using an equative sentence. For example, the author of Psalm 5, describing how the wicked use words to destroy, says: "Their throat is an open grave" (v. 9, Eng.). It's as if the poet would rather not have you think in terms of a comparison at all. Instead he wants you to see their throat as if it were actually an open grave. Of course, the effectiveness of this image also depends on the connotative power of "grave," which intuitively suggests death. (Metonymy and symbolism are also at work here. Something typically associated with death, the grave, stands for the reality of death.)

Very often comparisons are implied, rather than stated. For example, the author of Psalm 22, describing the life-threatening crisis he faces, laments: "Many bulls surround me, strong bulls of Bashan encircle me. They open their mouths at me, the lions that rip and roar" (vv. 12–13, Eng.). The psalmist has not wandered into a bull-fighting arena or African veldt exhibit! No, with a touch of hyperbole he describes his human enemies as if they were wild animals (cf. v. 16, Eng.). He does not make a formal comparison, for he wants us to envision his enemies as wild animals so that we might understand how fierce they are and how helpless and vulnerable he feels. By not mentioning the reality behind the metaphor, the psalmist gives the image greater rhetorical power.

Comparisons are especially effective when they involve irony. For example, Isaiah pictures the exiles returning to Zion on a road specially constructed for them. He says: "They will enter Zion with a happy shout, unending joy will be upon their heads" (35:10; 51:11). Obviously joy cannot be upon someone's head. The prophet must be painting a word picture. Perhaps he wants us to see the returning exiles crowned, as it were, with joy. Just as a crown is an obvious symbol of the status of the one wearing it, so the joy of the exiles will be an obvious indicator of their status as the Lord's ransomed people. Be that as it may, the power of this image is not so much in the implied comparison that may be involved, but in the irony of the statement. The picture of "joy" being on one's head appears to be an ironic twist on the idiom "earth/dust on the head" (cf. 2 Sam 1:2; 13:19; 15:32; Job 2:12), which occurs in contexts where one mourns. The returning exiles, in contrast to mourners who put dust on their heads, will be crowned with joy, as it were. In contexts of mourning one expects the phrase "upon the head" to be preceded by "earth/dust." But to highlight the radical transformation of the exiles' condition, the poet takes the phrase "on the head," moves it into a context of celebration, and slips "joy" into the slot abandoned by "earth/dust."

Having utilized a comparison, a poet will sometimes extend the metaphor. For example, the author of Psalm 23, having affirmed, "The Lord is my shepherd," speaks from a sheep's perspective and extends the pastoral metaphor. Like a shepherd, the Lord provides food and water, the essentials of life. The divine shepherd guides him down correct paths and protects him when he must travel through dark ravines where predators may lurk. (For a more detailed analysis of Psalm 23, see chapter 8.)

Isaiah compares judgment to drinking wine (51:17; cf. v. 21, where he explains his use of the imagery) and then extends this metaphor throughout the remainder of the oracle. Mother Jerusalem and her sons stagger because of this wine of judgment (vv. 18–20), but someday her enemies will be forced to drink from the cup and will stagger in the streets (vv. 22–23).

Personification

Personification is a form of comparison in which personal characteristics and/or actions are attributed to an impersonal object. For example, Isaiah describes a day when "the mountains and hills will shout for joy" and "all the trees of the field will clap their hands" as they celebrate the return of the exiles (55:12). In this case personification merges with hyperbole to emphasize that the exiles' redemption will be no mere run-of-the-mill occurrence. It will be an extraordinary event that gives cause for widespread celebration.

Isaiah 35:10 pictures happiness and joy overtaking the exiles, while grief and suffering flee. By personifying these abstract qualities and utilizing verbs of motion, the prophet vividly emphasizes the sudden transformation that will occur in the exiles' circumstances.

Personification is prominent in Proverbs 1–9. For example, in Proverbs 8 personified wisdom calls out to those passing by. She speaks of herself as a special creation of God that preceded the creation of the universe. She was present with God when he created the world, lending her skill to the task (vv. 22–31). In Proverbs 9 wisdom and folly appear as women who make their respective appeals to humankind. Wisdom compares herself to a hostess who has prepared a fine meal for her guests (vv. 2–5); folly is likened to an adulteress who promises great enjoyment, but delivers only death (vv. 17–18).

While techniques such as personification are typical of poetic literature, narrators also employ them occasionally. For example, the author of the Book of Jonah, describing the powerful storm that prevented Jonah from escaping to Tarshish, says: "Even the ship thought it would be shattered" (1:4).[28] It is very odd to see a verb of thinking used with an inanimate ship as subject. Some critics have pointed to this as an example of the alleged fictional quality of the story; others skirt the problem

---

28. Note how the disjunctive clause structure, waw + subject + verb, is used here to highlight the statement.

by translating the verb "threatened to." Both approaches are literarily calloused. The reality here was probably the creaking of the ship as the wind and waves blasted against it. But the author is not so pedestrian in his description. He uses personification to emphasize that everything—the sea, the ship, the sailors—seems to be responding to God's intervention—except for Jonah, who would have slept through it all if not awakened by the sailor's strangely familiar words, "Get up! Cry out!" (v. 6).

Anthropomorphic Language

Biblical poets frequently depict God in anthropomorphic terms, as if he possessed a physical body complete with hands, arms, eyes, and so on. They also cast God in typically human roles, such as shepherd (Ps. 23), king (Ps. 146), warrior (Isa. 63:1–6), farmer (Isa. 5:1–7), romantic lover (Hos. 2:14–15, Eng.), and father (Isa. 1:2). Some philosophical types, concerned that such metaphors might be misleading, are often quick to place a disclaimer on such texts, "That's an anthropomorphism! God isn't really (they would probably employ the word "ontologically" at this point) like that!" However, such disclaimers miss the point God is trying to make! God wants to reveal himself in terms we can understand. We should focus on what the metaphorical language communicates about God, rather than issuing a disclaimer that it is technically incorrect. For example, when we read of God's "hands" and "eyes" we should think, "God is active and aware," not "The text is misleading here for God is a spirit."

Metonymy

As noted in our earlier discussion of semantics, metonymy is a figure of speech where a word or phrase is substituted for another that is closely associated with it. For example, in the statement, "The candidates had their eye on the White House," the phrase "the White House" stands by metonymy for "the presidency." Because metonymies usually involve concepts and realities that typically go together, they can easily become idiomatic. Good poets are creative in their use of metonymy and avoid overusing clichés and idioms that lack adequate rhetorical punch.

Biblical poets often use metonymy for rhetorical effect. For example, the author of Psalm 30 asks rhetorically, "Does dust praise you?" (v. 9., Eng.). He refers here to the dust of the grave, more specifically, to a decomposed human corpse. In verse 11 (Eng.) he uses another metonymy when he declares, "You removed my sackcloth and clothed me in joy." One does not literally "wear" joy; joy is a metonymy here for the festive garments that replaced the sackcloth. The author of Psalm 51 also speaks metonymically when he prays, "Let me hear happiness and joy" (v. 8, Eng.). One does not literally "hear" happiness and joy; the underlying reality is likely a pronouncement of forgiveness which will produce joy within the psalmist's heart. By focusing on the effect, rather than the cause, the psalmist draws attention to the emotional dimension of his experience.

Of course such use of metonymy is not limited to the poetic genre. One also discovers metonymy in narrative, especially in quotations. For example, 1 Chronicles 11:15–19 tells how three of David's elite warriors risked their lives to get him some water to drink. When David mentioned that he was thirsty and would love to have a drink from the cistern near Bethlehem's gate, these warriors broke through Philistine lines, retrieved some water from that very cistern, and brought it back to David at Adullam. David was so overcome by their loyalty that he refused to drink the water and instead poured it out as a drink offering to the Lord. In explaining his actions, David asked rhetorically, "Should I drink the blood of these men who risked their lives"? (v. 19). As David looked at the water, he saw a different form of liquid—the life's blood of the men who risked their lives to retrieve it. As far as David was concerned, drinking the water would be an abomination, for in so doing he would be treating their heroic deed too lightly. By utilizing this metonymy (substituting for "water" the life's "blood" of those who retrieved it), David reveals his perspective in a vivid and emotionally stirring way.

Symbolic Language

A symbol represents something or someone by association, resemblance, or convention. A material object often symbolizes something that is abstract or not presently visible. For example, traditionally a cross has symbolized the death of Christ and by extension the Christian faith.

Language can also be symbolic, especially terms and phrases that refer to symbolic material objects. For example, consider the phrase "the arm of the Lord." Because a warrior uses his arm to wield a weapon and kill his enemies, the warrior's "arm" becomes symbolic (via metonymy) of strength and prowess in battle. When this metonymic language is applied to the Lord, the phrase "the arm of the Lord" symbolizes the Lord's military power (cf. Isa. 51:9–10; 63:5–6).

Sometimes symbolic language is deeply rooted in culture. For example, the sea monster Leviathan appears in Ugaritic myth as an ally or embodiment of Yam, the god of the sea. Like Yam, this multiheaded, serpentine creature symbolizes the chaotic forces that challenge the order maintained by Baal. Biblical poets borrow this symbol from myth and use it to symbolize the watery chaos overcome by Yahweh at creation (Ps. 74:14) and the heavenly-earthly coalition that opposes his rule in the eschaton (Isa. 27:1; cf. 24:21).

Archetypal Language

An archetype is an original model or type after which other similar things are patterned. Biblical poets, especially the prophets, frequently employ

173

archetypal language. Prophetic visions of the future are marked by geographical and cultural features which would be meaningful to the prophet and his contemporaries. When partial or complete fulfillment of the vision transcends the prophet's time and the geographical and cultural realities it assumes, various aspects of the vision take on an archetypal character.[29]

For example, consider the prophets' messages about the future of Assyria. Both Nahum and Zephaniah (see 2:13–15) prophesied that the once mighty Assyrian Empire would fall. This prophecy was literally fulfilled in 612–609 B.C. Other prophets, however, cast Assyria in a different eschatological role. Micah foresaw the coming of a new David, an ideal king who would protect Israel from hostile enemies. After describing the splendor of this king, he says: "When the Assyrians invade our land and march against our fortresses, we will raise against him seven shepherds, eight leaders. They will strike the land of Assyria with a sword, the land of Nimrod with a drawn sword. He (the ideal king) will deliver us from the Assyrians, when they invade our land and march into our territory" (5:5b–6, Eng.). Only the most hyperliteral interpreter would suggest that a literal revived Assyrian Empire will reappear during the messianic king's reign and threaten Israel. Assyria is an archetype here. In terms that would be powerful and inspiring to Micah's audience, the prophet assures them that a day is coming, unlike the late eighth century B.C., when God's people would no longer have to worry about threats from powerful, hostile Assyria-like nations.

Isaiah also employs Assyria as an archetype, but in an entirely different sense. Isaiah looks forward to a day when the two megapowers of his day, Egypt and Assyria, would become peaceful allies and join with Israel in worshiping the Lord. He describes that day this way: "In that day there will be a roadway from Egypt to Assyria, the Assyrians will travel to Egypt, and the Egyptians will travel to Assyria. Egypt and Assyria will worship together. In that day Israel will be the third member of the group, along with Egypt and Assyria, and will be a recipient of blessing in the midst of the earth. The Lord of Hosts will bless them, saying: 'Blessed be my people Egypt, and the work of my hands, Assyria, and my special possession, Israel'" (19:23–25). Assyria and Egypt are archetypes here of the powerful, warring kingdoms of the earth which will one day lay down their weapons and finally acknowledge the Lord as their God (cf. Isa. 2:2–4).

Stereotypical Language

Stereotypical language consists of conventional, formulaic descriptions that are often deeply rooted in culture and tradition. Such language

---

29. Perhaps the prophets did not always understand that their visions would transcend such realities. Be that as it may, what the prophet may have assumed would be literal, in the progress of revelation and history proves to be archetypal from the divine Author's perspective.

sometimes comes to be so entrenched and emotionally charged that any major deviation is unacceptable. For example, in modern American culture we expect a fairly stereotypical description of Santa Claus's annual visit. Santa is fat, dressed in red, has a big white beard, rides a sleigh pulled by at least three reindeer capable of flight, yells "Ho! Ho! Ho! Merry Christmas!", and makes his entry down a chimney carrying a sack of toys on his back. Minor additions, such as the appearance of red-nosed Rudolph among the team, are allowed, but not major or systemic alterations. Let's say we modernize the tradition: Santa now appears slim, dressed in green, and is well-shaven. He drives a minivan, taps on a horn that plays a few bars of "Rudolph the Red-Nosed Reindeer," rings the front door bell, and leaves the toys on the front steps. Such an appearance by Santa might be allowed one time in a television comedy, but true fans of Christmas would not accept this modernized adaptation as a permanent substitute for the tradition. It simply would not contribute to the mood and spirit of Christmas like the stereotypical version of Santa's arrival does. After all, Santa, to really be Santa, has to arrive a certain way!

Old Testament poets employ stereotypical language on occasion. For example, they describe the coming of God to do battle in a fairly standard manner. The poetic theophanic description of the divine warrior usually consists of several typical elements. The Lord marches or descends, displaying his anger in tangible ways and shooting arrows. His appearance is accompanied by elements of the storm, such as dark clouds, heavy rain, thunder, lightning, and hail. His terrifying appearance radically impacts the cosmos; the earth quakes and the Lord's enemies melt with fear or run for their lives.[30] The elements of this theophanic motif are rooted in history; the Lord sometimes revealed himself in such ways, for example, at Sinai. But culture has also contributed to the description. Ancient Near Eastern warrior kings utilized such imagery in their literary bravado and Ugaritic myth depicted the fertility god Baal as coming in the storm to do battle with his enemies. In the ancient Near East, any warrior-king worth his salt, especially a divine one, must appear in style with the proper cosmic fanfare and effect. In describing the Lord, the divine warrior-king par excellence, the biblical poets employed this stereotypical description.

Another example of stereotypical language is the prophets' description of cities and lands devastated by divine judgment. The city/land so judged is typically reduced to a perpetual ruin inhabited by a menagerie of fowl, rodents, and other scavengers (see, e.g., Isa. 13:20–22; 34:9–15; Zeph. 2:13–15). This stereotypical description has its basis in the reality of ancient warfare and has literary parallels in ancient Near Eastern curse lists. For a city to be thoroughly destroyed, a certain scenario must follow the devastation.

30. See, among others, Judg. 5:4–5; 2 Sam. 22:8–16; Pss. 77:16–18; 97:2–5; 144:5–6; Isa. 29:6; 30:27–33; Mic. 1:3–4; Nah. 1:2–6; Hab. 3:3–15.

Hyperbole

Old Testament poets frequently utilize hyperbole, or exaggeration for the sake of rhetorical effect and emphasis, especially in their visions of the future. For example, Amos employs hyperbole to emphasize the agricultural abundance that will characterize the eschatological age (9:13). He sees a time when the crops will be so abundant the reapers will not have time to harvest them all before the next planting season. The grape harvest will be so large that the vats will overflow and juice will run down the hillsides!

Isaiah, using light as a symbol of divine deliverance and renewed blessing, describes future conditions this way: "The light of the full moon will be like the sun's glare, and the sun's glare will be seven times brighter, like the light of seven days, when the Lord binds up his people's fractured bones, and heals their severe wound" (Isa. 30:26). Because light is purely symbolic here, Isaiah can hyperbolically describe the sun's light as increasing in intensity sevenfold. This blinding light reflects the underlying reality of the divine presence, which will be far more apparent in the eschaton than in Isaiah's day. In 60:19–20 the prophet carries hyperbole even further: "The sun will no longer be your source of light by day, and the brightness of the moon will no longer shine on you. The Lord will become your permanent source of light, your God will be your glory. Your sun will never set, or your moon disappear. For the Lord will become your permanent source of light." Once again light symbolizes divine deliverance and renewed blessing. To emphasize the dominating reality of the divine presence in the eschaton, the prophet describes the normal light sources as being eliminated and replaced by the Lord.

Zechariah utilizes hyperbole in his description of eschatological Jerusalem. He overhears an angelic dialogue, in which an angel reports that it is unnecessary to measure the city's dimensions, for it will be an unwalled city. He then quotes God as saying: "I will be a wall of fire around it" (2:5, Eng.). Walls, because of their defensive function in ancient cities, symbolized protection and security. Isaiah depicted eschatological Jerusalem as having walls, built, ironically, by once hostile nations (see 60:10–11). But Zechariah goes way beyond this relatively pedestrian description. He indicates that no walls will be built, because God himself, taking the form of fire, will personally guarantee the city's security! Both prophets indicate that Jerusalem will be secure, Isaiah in the expected way with a note of irony added, Zechariah in a powerfully ironic and hyperbolic manner.

Sample Literary Analyses of Poetic Texts

Isaiah 40:1–11

This prophetic oracle announces that the Lord will return to destitute Jerusalem. The prophet utilizes several poetic techniques. Jerusalem is personified as a woman (vv. 1–2), who is told that her time of hardship is over. She is then cast in the role of a herald who is commanded to climb a mountain and tell the good news to the rest of the towns of Judah (v. 9). The Lord is likened to (the comparison is implied, not stated) a victorious warrior returning from battle with the spoils of victory (v. 10), which probably represent the rescued exiles, as verse 11 suggests. In verse 11 the prophet uses a simile as he compares the Lord to a shepherd who cares for his flock, which represents the returning exiles. The anthropomorphic language draws attention to the power of God which establishes his rule and provides security for his people. The oracle also employs simile in verse 6 when it compares frail, short-lived human beings to the grass that quickly withers and likens the promises (lit., "faithfulness") of people to the quickly fading flowers of the field.

Hosea 5:8–15

In this judgment oracle the Lord announces he will judge Israel and Judah. Playing the dual role of a watchman and a military general, the Lord calls for the ram's horn to sound the alarm and for the Israelite army to prepare for battle (v. 8). The language of verse 8 is metonymic; sounding an alarm and shouting are preliminary to a battle and would signal an impending conflict. In verse 10a the Lord compares Judah's corrupt leaders to those who "move boundary stones," a metonymic idiom for stealing land (see Deut. 19:14; 27:17; Job 24:2; Prov. 22:28; 23:10) that alludes here to the leaders' oppressive socioeconomic policies. In verse 10b the Lord announces, "I will pour out my anger on them like water." "Anger" is a metonymic idiom for judgment; the simile emphasizes the relentless and inescapable character of the rainlike judgment. The Lord utilizes another simile in verse 12, where he compares himself, in his role as judge, to a moth and its decaying effect on clothes. Here the point is that God has already slowly, but surely, begun to "eat away" at the fabric of Israel's and Judah's national strength. In verse 13 Israel's and Judah's present condition is likened to an illness involving open sores or boils (note מָזוֹר). (Here the comparison is implied, rather than directly stated.) This picture of festering ulcers also draws attention to the gradual, but effective, character of divine judgment up to this point. This gradual form of judgment was about to terminate, however. The Lord was now ready to judge swiftly and severely. Utilizing a simile, he compares himself to a great lion in verse 14a. He then extends the metaphor in verse 14b, as he depicts himself tearing his prey to pieces and dragging it off.

Psalm 46

The author of Psalm 46 celebrates the Lord's protection of his people. In verses 2–3 (Eng.) the psalmist pictures an apparent natural catastrophe marked by landslides, huge tidal waves, and an earthquake. In verse 6

(Eng.) we discover that the language is metaphorical. The surging sea of verse 3a symbolizes aggressive nations that seek to inundate the world with chaos (cf. Isa. 17:12–13), while the toppling, shaking mountains of verses 2–3 symbolize the once seemingly stable kingdoms that fall in the face of this onslaught. God's people need not fear the chaos that threatens the world order, for God protects them, like a high tower (v. 7, an equative sentence is utilized to draw the comparison). The Lord dwells within the "city of God" (v. 4, a metonymic idiom for Jerusalem) and keeps it secure from enemies. All he has to do is issue a battle cry (v. 6, i.e., "lift his voice," a metonymic idiom) and armies (metonymically symbolized by their weapons in v. 9) are destroyed.

This divine intervention comes at the "break of day" (v. 5). Here the threat may be compared (by implication) to the dark of night, but the morning light (symbolizing salvation) dispels the darkness and eliminates the danger. The phrase לִפְנוֹת בֹּקֶר, "at the turn of morning" refers to daybreak (cf. Judg. 19:26), corresponding to its counterpart לִפְנוֹת עֶרֶב, "at the turn of evening (i.e., dusk, sunset)" (cf. Gen. 24:63; Deut. 23:11). However, this construction occurs in only two other passages, Judges 19:26 and Exodus 14:27. The latter passage tells how the Lord destroyed the Egyptian army at the Red Sea at the "turn of morning." One wonders if the psalmist may be alluding to the Exodus tradition. However, if the psalm postdates the miraculous deliverance of Jerusalem from the Assyrians in 701 B.C., that event may be in the background, for it was the morning after the killer angel's visit to the Assyrian camp that the people saw the corpses of the Assyrians outside the city walls (2 Kings 19:35; cf. Isa. 17:14).

In contrast to the surging waters of the sea (v. 3), the psalmist pictures a "river," the tributaries of which flow through Jerusalem (v. 4). Given the geographical realities, the description is obviously not a literal one; the river and its branches must be metaphorical. Since a river is a source of water and consequently fertility and life, it is likely that the river and its branches symbolize God's abundant provision and blessing.[31]

Diversity of Literary Types and Forms within Poetic Literature

As noted above, the poetic genre encompasses several specific literary types, including psalms, proverbial sayings, and prophetic speeches. These literary types share the basic features of poetry (parallelism and an abundance of imagery), but they differ thematically and, in many ways, stylistically. Each literary type also exhibits its own distinctive forms.

---

31. Perhaps the imagery is rooted literarily in Isaiah's contrast between the flood waters (symbolizing Assyria) and the "gently flowing waters of Shiloah" (Isa. 8:6–8). The psalmist's portrait may have inspired Ezekiel and Zechariah, both of whom pictured water (neither uses the term נָהָר, however) flowing out of Jerusalem in the eschaton. In Ezek. 47:1–12 this symbolic stream flows into the Dead Sea; in Zechariah the symbolic water flows both eastward and westward.

Forms of Prayer and Praise

Ancient Israelites frequently utilized certain standard forms when they worshiped God. The most widely attested literary form in the Book of Psalms, the Old Testament's prayer and hymnbook, is the psalm of petition (sometimes labeled a lament). Such prayers typically include an introductory appeal, a description of the psalmist's plight (the lament), which is designed to move God emotionally and motivate him to respond positively to the psalmist's request, and the formal petition, in which the psalmist asks God to deliver him from his crisis. Additional motivating arguments are sometimes attached to the petition.

Often the psalmist will also declare his confidence in God and his assurance that deliverance is on the way. Some have theorized that this change in mood from petition to confidence can be attributed to a formal divine oracle of assurance, in which God promises to deliver the psalmist. Such oracles occasionally appear in psalms (see Pss. 12:5, Eng.; 60:6–8, Eng.). It is possible that many of the petitionary psalms were written after such oracles were delivered. If so, they recall the original petition, assume a divine response to the prayer, and look with assurance to the realization of the divine promise.

Psalm 6 is a good example of the typical prayer form utilized by the psalmists. Its form may be outlined as follows:

(1) Introductory appeal (v. 1, Eng.): The psalmist asks God not to discipline him severely.

(2) Petition mixed with lament as motivation (vv. 2–3): God should intervene on the psalmist's behalf because he is suffering unbearable pain.

(3) Petition with motivation (vv. 4–5): The psalmist appeals to God's character and reputation. If God intervenes, he will enhance his reputation because others will hear of his faithfulness. If the psalmist dies, God will receive no praise.

(4) Lament (vv. 6–7): The psalmist again attempts to motivate a positive response by describing his intense suffering.

(5) Confidence (vv. 8–10): The psalmist "gets in the face" of his enemies, for he is confident that God has heard his request and will turn back his adversaries. The twofold statement "the Lord has heard" may allude to an oracle of assurance given in response to the petition of the preceding verses.

After the Lord had actually intervened and delivered, an ancient Israelite would sometimes offer a song of thanks. Such songs typically begin with some type of declaration about the propriety of praise. They then recall the psalmist's crisis, his petition for help, and God's mighty act of deliverance. While this poetic narrative is the core of the song, it usually includes other elements, such as an invitation to join the psalmist in praise, an exhortation, instruction about God's character, and/or a vow to praise the Lord in the future.

Psalm 30 is a typical song of thanks; it displays the following structure:

(1) Introductory declaration (v. 1, Eng.): The psalmist declares his intention to praise the Lord because the Lord delivered him.
(2) Brief poetic narrative (vv. 2–3): The psalmist recalls his crisis, call for help, and God's positive response.
(3) Invitation to praise and instruction (vv. 4–5): The psalmist invites God's people to join him in praise because the psalmist's experience demonstrates God's merciful character.
(4) Expanded poetic narrative (vv. 6–12a): The psalmist gives a more detailed account of his experience and includes the petition he offered during his crisis.
(5) Vow to praise (v. 12b): The psalmist promises to demonstrate his gratitude and glorify God by continuing to praise him in the future.

The hymn is another widely attested form in the Book of Psalms. The structure of hymns is very simple; they include an opening call to praise and a list of reasons why God is praiseworthy. For example, Psalm 113 begins with a call to praise (vv. 1–3) followed by several reasons why God is praiseworthy (vv. 4–9). The concluding call to praise (v. 9b, "Praise the Lord") forms an inclusio with the introductory appeal.

While the basic forms of prayer and praise are fairly standardized, the psalmists utilize them in a very flexible manner. They often highlight certain elements. In one prayer the lament may be primary (see, e.g., Ps. 88), while in another confidence is the dominant mood (see, e.g., Ps. 4).[32] One song of thanks may have a lengthy poetic narrative (see, e.g., Ps. 18), while instruction overshadows the narrative in another (see, e.g., Ps. 32). The psalmists sometimes modify, alter, and/or combine forms. For example, Psalm 33 begins as a hymn, but the second half of the psalm blends praise with instruction and ends with a statement of confidence and a petition. On several occasions the theme of confidence, a motif of psalms of petition, permeates an entire psalm, producing a form called the song of confidence (e.g., Ps. 23).

Proverbial Forms

Within the Book of Proverbs one detects two major literary forms. The first of these, instruction, takes the form of an exhortation, to which are attached motivating statements designed to encourage one to follow the

---

32. The author of Ps. 4, following a brief petition (v. 1, Eng.), spends the rest of his time rebuking observers (vv. 2–5), praising God (vv. 6–7), and affirming his confidence (v. 8).

teacher's instruction. For example, in Proverbs 23:10–11 the speaker exhorts his listeners not to take advantage of the helpless and then uses a warning as motivation.

The exhortation can be a moral imperative, similar to the laws of the Old Testament or the exhortations of the prophets (see 3:29–30). However, the majority of the exhortations in the Book of Proverbs fall into the category of good practical advice (see 20:13).

The motivating statements attached to the exhortations usually take one of three forms—general observation, personal consequences, or theological principle. Let's suppose I'm exhorting my son Doug not to steal. I could say: "Doug, don't steal, because thieves end up in prison." The motivating statement in this case is a general observation which describes the typical outcome of a certain type of behavior. The proverbs frequently use this kind of motivation (see 23:20–21, 26–28).

A second approach is to make the warning more personal. I could say: "Doug, don't steal, because, if you do, you'll end up in prison." Here the motivating statement describes the outcome of an action for the specific individual being addressed. The proverbs also use this form of motivation (see 22:24–25; 23:9).

But there is a third approach. I could say: "Doug, don't steal, because God despises thieves." Here the motivating statement is a general theological principle, which though not necessarily observable to the average Joe on the street, has been revealed by God to human beings. Examples of this kind of motivation also appear in the proverbs (see 22:22–23; 24:17–18).

The instruction form need not be restricted to a brief saying. In Proverbs 1–9 a series of speeches follow the pattern of instruction. For example, Proverbs 5:1–14 exhibits the following structure:

Introductory exhortation (v. 1, practical advice) + motivation (vv. 2–6, combining personal consequences and general observation)
Exhortation (vv. 7–8, practical advice) + motivation (vv. 9–14, personal consequences)

The second basic form of proverbial saying is the descriptive proverb. Descriptive proverbs lack an exhortation; they take the form of general statements, which can be theological and/or empirical in nature.

Theological descriptive proverbs are based primarily on God's revelation, rather than experience or observation of the world (see 16:4). Though there is no stated exhortation, there is a recommended course of action implied. For example, in 20:10 the speaker observes that God despises economic deception. If God despises such actions, one would be wise to avoid them.

Empirical descriptive proverbs are based on experience or observation of the world (see 16:18, 26). Sometimes a recommended course of action is implied. For example, in 20:4 the speaker observes that a lazy man does not make adequate provision for the future and ends up hungry. If this is true, one would be wise to work hard and make provision for the future. In some descriptive proverbs, there appears to be no recommended course of action. The statement is just an observation on how things are. For example, in 20:14 the speaker observes that buyers tend to downgrade the value of a product in front of the seller, but once they make the purchase, they brag about what a great deal they got. Even though there is no exhortation or implicit recommended course of action in such proverbs, awareness of the principle/observation is useful because it can enable one to live more skillfully. If you know how buyers characteristically operate, you can function more effectively as a seller in the marketplace.

Prophetic Forms

Though the prophetic books contain narrative material (see, e.g., Isa. 7; Jer. 26–29, 32–45; Amos 7:10–17; Jonah), prophetic speeches in poetic style dominate most of these books. The prophets utilized a variety of standard forms in constructing their speeches.

One of the most widely attested prophetic speech forms is the judgment oracle, which usually consists of two elements, an accusation and formal announcement of judgment. For example, each of Amos's eight judgment oracles against the nations (see chapters 1–2) includes a stereotypical introduction ("For three sins, even for four, I will not turn back"), a formal accusation that gives the reason(s) for divine judgment, and a formal announcement of divine judgment, in which God declares his intention to intervene in judgment and describes the effects of that intervention:

Oracle	Introduction	Accusation	Announcement
Damascus (1:3–5)	v. 3a	v. 3b	vv. 4–5
Gaza (1:6–8)	v. 6a	v. 6b	vv. 7–8
Tyre (1:9–10)	v. 9a	v. 9b	v. 10
Edom (1:11–12)	v. 11a	v. 11b	v. 12
Ammon (1:13–15)	v. 13a	v. 13b	vv. 14–15
Moab (2:1–3)	v. 1a	v. 1b	vv. 2–3
Judah (2:4–5)	v. 4a	v. 4b	v. 5
Israel (2:6–16)	v. 6a	vv. 6b–12	vv. 13–16

The woe oracle is a specific type of judgment oracle. It begins with the interjection הוֹי, "woe," and then addresses or identifies the guilty individual/group. Usually the accusation is hinted at or stated here; sometimes the accusatory element is then developed in more detail before the formal announcement of judgment. For example, the woe oracle in Micah 2:1–5 exhibits the following structure: (a) introductory woe + identification of guilty group (v. 1a), (b) expansion of accusation (vv. 1b–2), (c) formal announcement of judgment (vv. 3–5).

Another widely attested prophetic speech form is the exhortation or call to repentance. This form consists of an appeal, to which are attached motivating arguments, often taking the form of promises and/or threats. Such an exhortation appears in Joel 2:12–14, where the appeal (vv. 12–13a) is supported by motivating arguments that focus on God's gracious character (v. 13b) and the possibility of divine mercy and renewed blessing (v. 14). The exhortations in Amos 5:4–6 use the possibility of survival (note "and live" in vv. 4b and 6a) and the threat of judgment (vv. 5b, 6b) to motivate the appeal (note "seek me/the LORD" in vv. 4b, 6a).

The prophets' messages were not entirely doom and gloom. For them judgment was God's way of purifying his covenant community and they anticipated a time of renewed blessing when the smoke of judgment cleared. Prophetic oracles of deliverance typically describe God's saving intervention and/or depict the future age of divine blessing, often in hyperbolic terms (see, e.g., Isa. 4:2–6; 9:1–7 [Eng.]; 11:1–9, 10–16; Amos 9:13–15).

The prophets did not utilize forms in an inflexible or rigid manner. Loose patterns like those noted above are standard, but the rhetorically conscious and adept prophets obviously felt free to alter speech forms. For example, in Isaiah 5:8–30 the prophet strings together a series of six woe oracles. The first two display the usual pattern, with an accusatory element being followed by a formal announcement of judgment (see vv. 8/9–10 and 11–12/13–17), but oracles 3 through 5 omit the announcement (see vv. 18–19, 20, 21). The sixth and final oracle returns to the standard pattern, the accusatory woe pronouncement (vv. 22–23) being followed by a lengthy and terrifying judgment announcement (vv. 24a, 25–30) that has embedded within it a more generalized accusation (v. 24b). This lack of symmetry is not due to some kind of error in textual transmission, nor is it evidence of a complex redactional history. Such ridiculous explanations, offered by some form/redaction critics, are symptomatic of such critics' lack of literary sensitivity and evidence of how rhetorically impoverished their methods really are. From a rhetorical perspective the reason for this lack of symmetry is obvious. The prophet, having established the usual pattern in his first two oracles, deviates from it in oracles 3–5 to grab his audience's attention and to highlight the people's guilt. Woes 3–6 strike the ear like a series of hammer blows, forcing the audience to focus on the nation's sin. As this theme of sin and guilt rapidly snowballs, it also creates a foreboding mood. One familiar with the usual pattern (already utilized in oracles 1–2) expects Isaiah to top off this series of intentionally truncated, rapidly spoken accusatory woes with a whopper of a judgment announcement, and the prophet does not disappoint us.

Prophets almost always embellish their speeches with a unique rhetorical touch. They might combine and/or alter forms and then add some nonstandard ingredients for special effect. For example, the speech in Amos 5:1–17 includes a judgment oracle (vv. 10–12), two sets of exhortations (vv. 4–6, 14–15), two formal announcements of judgment (unaccompanied by or only loosely attached to an accusation, vv. 3, 16–17), and several nonstandard elements, including a funeral lament (vv. 1–2), an accusatory address appended to the first hortatory section (v. 7), a hymnic style description of the sovereign divine judge (vv. 8–9), and a proverbial style observation (v. 13).

Placement and Sequence in Poetic Literature

Generally speaking, the placement and sequence of literary units in poetic literature does not exhibit the design one detects in narrative. Psalms, Proverbs, and the prophetic books are, for the most part, anthological. The Book of Psalms is a collection of prayers and hymns; it exhibits no overarching design that might impact one's interpretation of any individual psalm. The bulk of the Book of Proverbs is a collection of individual sayings that appear to be randomly arranged. At times the prophetic books do exhibit some degree of literary structure, but often the arrangement is based on very loose associations between themes and/or catch-words. For this reason, when one is interpreting poetic literature, the whole anthology in its final canonical shape should usually be viewed as the primary context of any given psalm, saying, or speech. What immediately precedes or follows a passage may or may not be of relevance in interpreting that text.

For Further Reading and Reference

The Cultural Background of the Old Testament

Aharoni, Yohanan. *The Land of the Bible: A Historical Geography.* 2nd. ed. Trans. and rev. A. F. Rainey. Philadelphia: Westminster, 1979.

Aharoni, Yohanan, and Michael Avi-Yonah. *The Macmillan Bible Atlas.* 3rd ed. New York: Macmillan, 1993.

Albrektson, Bertil. *History and the Gods: An Essay on the Idea of Historical Events as Divine Manifestations in the Ancient Near East and in Israel.* Lund: CWK Gleerup, 1967.

Borowski, Oded. *Agriculture in Iron Age Israel.* Winona Lake, Ind.: Eisenbrauns, 1987.

Cogan, Mordechai. *Imperialism and Religion: Assyria, Judah and Israel in the Eighth and Seventh Centuries B.C.E.* Missoula, Mont.: Scholars, 1974.

Day, John. *God's Conflict with the Dragon and the Sea.* New York: Cambridge University Press, 1985.

Dearman, John Andrew. *Property Rights in the Eighth-Century Prophets.* Atlanta: Scholars, 1987.

deVaux, Roland. *Ancient Israel.* 2 vols. New York: McGraw-Hill, 1965.

Kaminsky, Joel S. *Corporate Responsibility in the Hebrew Bible.* Sheffield: Sheffield Academic Press, 1995.

Keel, Othmar. *The Symbolism of the Biblical World: Ancient Near Eastern Iconography and the Book of Psalms.* New York: Seabury, 1978.

King, Philip J. *Amos, Hosea, Micah—An Archaeological Commentary.* Philadelphia: Westminster, 1988.

Lichtheim, Miriam. *Ancient Egyptian Literature.* 3 vols. Berkeley: University of California Press, 1975–80.

McCurley, Foster R. *Ancient Myths and Biblical Faith: Scriptural Transformations.* Philadelphia: Fortress, 1983.

Mettinger, Tryggve N. D. *In Search of God: The Meaning and Message of the Everlasting Names.* Philadelphia: Fortress, 1988.

Patterson, Richard D. "The Widow, the Orphan, and the Poor in the Old Testament and the Extra-Biblical Literature." *Bib Sac* 130 (1973): 23–34.

Pritchard, James. *Ancient Near Eastern Texts Relating to the Old Testament.* Princeton, N.J.: Princeton University Press, 1969.

Ringgren, Helmer. *Religions of the Ancient Near East.* Trans. John Sturdy. Philadelphia: Westminster, 1973.

Stadelmann, Luis I. J. *The Hebrew Conception of the World.* Rome: Pontifical Biblical Institute, 1970.

Walton, John H. *Ancient Israelite Literature in Its Cultural Context: A Survey of Parallels Between Biblical and Ancient Near Eastern Texts.* Grand Rapids: Zondervan, 1989.

Weinfeld, Moshe. *Social Justice in Ancient Israel and in the Ancient Near East.* Jerusalem: Magnes, 1995.

———. "The Covenant of Grant in the Old Testament and in the Ancient Near East." *Journal of the American Oriental Society* 90 (1970): 184–203.

Wolff, Hans Walter. *Anthropology of the Old Testament.* Trans. Margaret Kohl. Philadelphia: Fortress, 1974.

Wright, Christopher J. H. *An Eye for An Eye: The Place of Old Testament Ethics Today.* Downers Grove, Ill.: InterVarsity, 1983.

———. *God's People in God's Land: Family, Land, and Property in the Old Testament.* Grand Rapids: Eerdmans, 1990.

Yadin, Yigael. *The Art of Warfare in Biblical Lands*. New York: McGraw-Hill, 1963.

Hebrew Narrative and Poetic Art

Alter, Robert. *The Art of Biblical Narrative*. New York: Basic Books, 1981.

———. *The Art of Biblical Poetry*. New York: Basic Books, 1985.

———. *The World of Biblical Literature*. New York: Basic Books, 1992.

Bar-Efrat, Shimon. *Narrative Art in the Bible*. Sheffield: Almond, 1989.

Berlin, Adele. *Poetics and Interpretation of Biblical Narrative*. Winona Lake, Ind.: Eisenbrauns, 1994.

———. *The Dynamics of Biblical Parallelism*. Bloomington: Indiana University Press, 1985.

Brichto, Herbert Chaim. *Toward a Grammar of Biblical Poetics: Tales of the Prophets*. New York: Oxford University Press, 1992.

Caird, G. B. *The Language and Imagery of the Bible*. Philadelphia: Westminster, 1980.

Jeansonne, Sharon Pace. *The Women of Genesis*. Minneapolis: Fortress, 1990.

Kugel, James. *The Idea of Biblical Poetry*. New Haven, Conn.: Yale University Press, 1981.

Long, V. Philips. *The Art of Biblical History*. Grand Rapids: Zondervan, 1994.

Longman, Tremper, III. *Literary Approaches to Biblical Interpretation*. Grand Rapids: Zondervan, 1987.

Ryken, Leland. *How to Read the Bible as Literature*. Grand Rapids: Zondervan, 1984.

Sternberg, Meir. *The Poetics of Biblical Narrative*. Bloomington: Indiana University Press, 1987.

Trible, Phyllis. *Rhetorical Criticism: Context, Method, and the Book of Jonah*. Minneapolis: Fortress, 1994.

Watson, W. G. E. *Classical Hebrew Poetry*. Sheffield: JSOT, 1984.

Webb, Barry G. *The Book of Judges: An Integrated Reading*. Sheffield: JSOT, 1987.

8 Pulling It All Together

An Exegetical Method Outlined and Illustrated

This chapter outlines an exegetical method and illustrates the process through worked examples from three passages. At first you may think the proposed method is too mechanical, involved, and time-consuming. But interpretation is a skill that demands practice. Think of the process outlined here as exegetical practice. As you practice, you will discover your skills sharpening. As time goes on, you will learn to distinguish between the routine and nonroutine, and to identify those elements that are most important. Doing exegesis will become more natural and less mechanical, and you should find that it will take less time to produce better-quality work. Better yet, developing a good interpretive foundation will provide greater depth and credibility to your messages and lessons, and give you more confidence as you preach and teach.

A Basic Method Outlined

Preparing for the Expedition

Before one begins the exegetical expedition, it is important to prepare adequately for the journey. As noted in the previous chapter the interpreter must bring to the study of the text an awareness of the historical and cultural context of ancient Israel in general and, if possible, of the specific passage in view. The exegete must also possess an awareness of and sensitivity to the main literary features and techniques of each of the two basic literary genres—narrative and poetry. Without knowing how these genres "work," the interpreter can easily miss the message of the story, song, or speech.

Step 1: Viewing the Forest

One should begin the exegetical process by looking at the whole forest, rather than the individual trees. *When working in Hebrew narrative (i.e., nonpoetic passages), mark out the literary unit and then develop a tentative outline of each literary unit's structure/paragraph divisions.* Look for shifts in scene, focus, and/or theme. As we have seen in the earlier chapter on narrative structure, such shifts are often marked in formal way. Look for repeated or parallel expressions (cf. Gen. 4:1, 17, 25 and 6:22; 7:5, 9) and introductory or concluding formulas, such as headings (cf. Gen. 5:1; 6:9), introductory temporal indicators (cf. Gen. 5:3; 6:1), introductory or concluding disjunctive clauses (cf. Gen. 3:1; 4:1; 6:8), and concluding summary statements (cf. Gen. 10:32; 11:9).

When working in a poetic text, develop a tentative outline of the psalm or speech according to its logical/thematic units or formal elements. (See chapter 7 for a discussion of the standard forms used in hymnic, didactic, and prophetic literature.)

Step 2: Entering the Woods

When working in narrative, develop a working translation of the passage and then outline the basic structure of each paragraph by delineating the narrative framework, nonstandard constructions, and quotations/dialogues embedded within the narrative. Using the categories listed in chapter 6, analyze the function of each main clause in the narrative framework, each nonstandard construction, and the various grammatical constructions within quotations. Make as many observations as possible on how the narrative structure contributes to the narrator's rhetorical strategy.

When working in poetry, develop a working translation of the passage and then identify the type of parallelism in each verse. For a list of some of the major categories, see chapter 6. Look for special arrangements of couplets, such as the one discussed earlier in Psalm 5:4–6 (Eng.).

Step 3: Looking at the Trees

In steps 1–2 we have moved from the literary unit/paragraph level to the verse/sentence level. Now we are prepared to look at the individual trees in more detail. Step 3, which is the most time-consuming step in the process, includes lexical, syntactical, and text-critical analysis. These issues are often interrelated and cannot be separated in some artificial way. A decision in one area will often impact one's decision in another. Also each verse is not necessarily self-contained; usually one cannot solve an interpretive problem without ranging through the verses that immediately precede and/or follow. What follows is a checklist to aid you in making observations; it should not be viewed as a sequence of steps to be followed in a mechanical way.

(a) *Isolate nouns and adjectives/participles.* Identify important (often nonroutine) uses of the singular/plural and the various noun cases (especially genitival relationships). Where ambiguous and/or important, identify whether adjectives/participles are attributive or predicative. If predicative, determine the time frame from the context.

(b) *Isolate all pronouns (including suffixes) and identify the antecedent for each.* In determining antecedents take into account the gender and number of the relevant Hebrew forms. Pronouns usually must agree with their antecedents in gender and number. When dealing with second-person pronouns, remember that Hebrew is more precise than English.

(c) *Take note of all articles, prepositions, and conjunctions.* Identify any important and/or nonroutine uses of the article, prepositions, and/or conjunctions.

(d) *Isolate all infinitives.* Determine whether the infinitive is absolute or construct and then identify its function in the sentence.

(e) *Parse every verb form.* If the subject is not stated or obvious, make sure you determine its identity. Since verbal stem is as much a semantic issue as a syntactical one, it may be dealt with in conjunction with lexical analysis (see the next item in the list). Categorize the aspectual function of each form. (See chapter 5 for categories.) Many times this will be a routine task (e.g., most perfects and *wayyiqtol* forms in a narrative framework describe completed action in the past.) Be especially alert for nonroutine or ambiguous uses.

(f) *Determine the precise contextual nuance of each word and/or phrase.* In most cases this will be a fairly routine procedure, easily accomplished with the aid of a good lexicon. However, certain words or phrases will be problematic. With an adequately attested word, you should survey the range of meaning and then try to pinpoint its specific nuance of meaning in light of the context. Avoid the "semantic sins" listed earlier and be alert for idiomatic and metaphorical uses. If the word is especially important or highly debated, you may want to do your own usage survey and develop your own semantic categories before making a decision about the word's nuance in your passage.

(g) *Isolate key words* that are repeated in the text and/or are particularly important in understanding the text's meaning and theme. Explain how the key word contributes to the text's theme. Look for any instances of wordplay and explain how this technique contributes to the author's rhetorical strategy and message. It may be important to locate allusions or references to earlier texts of Scripture and to determine the author's purpose for utilizing this technique.

(h) *Examine the text-critical problems* listed by BHS or discussed in a critical commentary. Determine which problems are important and choose or reconstruct an original reading. Important text-critical problems are those where one's choice of variant readings affects the meaning or emphasis of the passage in a significant or noteworthy way. (One might think that text critical analysis would logically be placed at the beginning of the checklist, but in actual practice one is better able to appreciate and solve text-critical problems once one is familiar with the text at the semantic and syntactical levels.)

(i) *Identify subordinate clauses and analyze those that are important and/or nonroutine.* This step will be more involved when you are working in narrative, where such clauses are more common than in poetry. (This step can also include the analysis of adverbs and adverbial prepositional phrases.)

(j) *Study several up-to-date translations of the passage and read two or three good critical commentaries on the text,* looking for insight on issues surfaced through the above process and for important problems overlooked in the above procedure. Revise earlier conclusions if need be, and work through problems you overlooked.

Step 4: Synthesizing Observations

Make any needed revisions in the conclusions you developed in steps 1–2 (in light of step 3).

Translate the passage in a modern, up-to-date style that reveals the various decisions you have made in the preceding steps. Make sure you consult and evaluate other translations, especially those that are popular among your congregation/students.

Step 5: Looking Beneath the Surface

When dealing with hymnic, didactic, and prophetic literature, the very nature of the interpretive task forces one to give attention to all details. However, in narrative it is sometimes easy to focus on the main story line and gloss over seemingly insignificant details. But it is very important that you *explain how every detail of the text fits its context literarily and contributes to the message of the passage.*

Make sure you *explain how metaphorical language contributes to the rhetoric and message of the passage.* (Metaphorical language is more common in poetic texts.)

Step 6: Leaving the Woods

Narrative texts typically utilize a plot structure that reflects an overriding theme or set of themes. When working in narrative texts, *develop the plot structure of the story or episode* and show how each paragraph contributes to this structure. (One should also include here a literary analysis of setting.) *Summarize the main literary/theological theme(s) and lesson(s) of the story.* This will often entail an analysis of characterization. Who are the most significant characters, what role do they play, and how should they be evaluated from a moral perspective?

Hymnic, didactic, and prophetic texts normally exhibit a logical argument or structure (the proverbial sentence literature is an exception). In such texts *summarize the main point of each thematic unit and then relate each thematic unit to its immediate and following contexts. Summarize the main literary/theological theme(s) of the entire chapter or literary unit.*

Step 7: Viewing the Forest Again

In narrative relate the literary/theological theme(s) of the story to the surrounding context and/or developing larger story.

In anthological texts (the basic structure of hymnic, didactic, and prophetic collections or books), where there is not a running story line or episodic arrangement as in narrative, *relate the literary/theological theme(s) of the literary unit to the overriding theme(s) of the anthology as a whole.*

Worked Examples

(1) Ehud Gets Away with Murder (Judges 3:12–30)

Step 1

This is the story of how Ehud led a successful revolt and freed Israel from Moabite oppression. The phrase "and the Israelites again did evil" (v. 12) marks the beginning of this narrative unit. This is a recurring statement (sometimes "again" is omitted) which introduces the major story units of Judges 3–16 (see 3:7, 12; 4:1; 6:1; 10:6; 13:1). The reference to the land being "undisturbed" for a number of years (in this case, eighty) is a recurring conclusion to the major story units of Judges 3–8 (see 3:11, 30; 5:31; 8:28).

This story has three main subunits or paragraphs: a prologue (vv. 12–17), a central section (vv. 18–26), and an epilogue (vv. 27–30). As noted above, the prologue (vv. 12–17) begins with a standard recurring introductory formula. Its conclusion is signaled by a disjunctive clause (v. 17). The central section (vv. 18–26) begins with the temporal indicator וַיְהִי, "and it so happened." The reference to Ehud's successful escape (v. 26) gives this section thematic closure. The epilogue (vv. 27–30) begins with the temporal indicator וַיְהִי (v. 27) and concludes with the standard recurring statement about the land being undisturbed (v. 30).

Step 2

The narrative structure of the passage is outlined in chapter 6.

Steps 3–5

The following notes should be viewed as illustrative of the process, not as an exhaustive analysis. We do not include the parsing of every verb or 191 label aspectual function when it is routine. The many *wayyiqtol* verbal forms in the narrative framework have a preterite function; they describe completed action in a past time frame. In our semantic analysis we do not duplicate information that is readily available in the major lexicons or stop to define words that are used in common, well-attested ways. Our translation reveals our decisions in such routine matters. We also omit notes on geographical references (e.g., the City of the Date Palm Trees in v. 13). For geographical sites, see a Bible encyclopedia or atlas. The translation below differs from the one given in chapter 6, which is more "wooden" to facilitate clause analysis. The translation below is more idiomatic and paraphrastic to reflect interpretive decisions.

Verses 12–14

(12) Now the Israelites again did evil before the LORD, so the LORD prompted Eglon king of Moab to attack Israel, because they did evil before the LORD. (13) He allied with the Ammonites and Amalek, and came and defeated Israel; they seized the City of Date Palm Trees. (14) The Israelites were subject to Eglon king of Moab for eighteen years.

(1) The opening verb וַיֹּסִפוּ (v. 12) is a hiphil *wayyiqtol*, 3mp, from יָסַף, "add, increase." The hiphil stem of this verb is used idiomatically with the following infinitive construct (לַעֲשׂוֹת) to indicate that the action is repeated. (see step 3, d–f)

(2) The object of the infinitive is הָרַע, "[the] evil," which is always followed by the phrase "in the eyes of the LORD" in Judges (2:11; 3:7, 12; 4:1; 6:1; 10:6; 13:1). This idiom refers specifically to the moral evil of idolatry (cf. 2:11; 3:7; 10:6), explaining why the article is prefixed to the noun. (step 3, c, f)

(3) The verb וַיְחַזֵּק (v. 12) is a piel *wayyiqtol* 3ms, from חָזַק, "be firm, strong." The piel (which is factitive) of this verb has several attested semantic nuances. BDB (304) lists our text under their first category, "make strong (physically)," while K–B (303) places it under the category "strengthen," in the sense of "encourage" (the third category in BDB's list of nuances). Either sense is acceptable here. The statement could mean that the Lord strengthened Eglon militarily so that he gained confidence and attacked Israel. Or it could mean that the Lord encouraged or prompted Eglon to attack. (The piel of חָזַק is used with the preposition עַל only here and in Neh. 3:19, where the verb has the nuance "repair" and is not instructive for understanding Judg. 3:12.) (step 3, e–f)

(4) The causal clause at the end of verse 12 essentially repeats the lead sentence and thereby sets the verse off as the introduction to the narrative which provides the theological framework for the story. (step 3, g, i)

(5) The fourth of the four *wayyiqtol* verb forms in verse 13 is 3mp, in contrast to the first three, which are singular. The BHS editor (see note "a"), with support from the Septuagint and Vulgate, suggests that the

form be changed to singular, but this is an obvious attempt to harmonize the form with those that precede. The Hebrew text is fully capable of standing as is. Whereas Eglon is the subject of the first three verbs, the subject shifts in the final clause to Eglon and his allies, the Ammonites and Amalek. (step 3, b, e, h)

(6) The reference to Amalekite involvement in Eglon's campaign (v. 13) is sadly ironic, for Moses had instructed Israel to annihilate the Amalekites because of the way they had treated God's people (Deut. 25:17–19; cf. Exod. 17:8–16). Israel's failure in this regard was coming back to haunt them. (step 5)

Verses 15–17

(15) The Israelites cried out to the LORD and the LORD raised up a deliverer for them—Ehud son of Gera the Benjaminite, a left-handed man. The Israelites sent him to Eglon king of Moab with their tribute payment. (16) Ehud made a sword. (It had two edges and was eighteen inches long.) He strapped it under his coat on his right thigh. (17) He brought the tribute payment to Eglon king of Moab. (Now Eglon was a very fat man.)

(7) The phrase אִטֵּר יַד־יְמִינוֹ (v. 15) apparently means "left-handed" (see v. 21). It occurs only here and in Judges 20:16, where it describes seven hundred Benjaminite slingshot specialists who were particularly adept. Apparently the phrase carries a literal meaning, "bound with respect to his right hand." (A verb אָטַר appears in Ps. 69:15 [Eng., Heb. v. 16] with the meaning "close up, shut.") Because of this some have speculated that Ehud was handicapped and unable to use his right hand. But the use of the phrase to describe the contingent of Benjaminite slingers makes this theory highly unlikely. Apparently since right-handedness was considered normal, "bound in the right hand" became an idiomatic way of referring to left-handedness. The normal way of referring to left-handedness in Hebrew is to use the phrase יַד שְׂמֹאל, "left hand" (see, e.g., Judg. 3:21; 7:20) or simply שְׂמֹאל, "left" (see, e.g., Judg. 16:29), but a language sometimes uses different expressions for the same idea (see, e.g., English "lefthander," "southpaw," "portsider," all of which are used to describe a lefthanded pitcher in baseball). (step 3, f)[1]

(8) מִנְחָה (v. 17) often refers to an offering in a cultic context, but in this political context it refers to tribute payment (see BDB, 585; K–B, 601). (step 3, f)

---

1. Baruch Halpern contends that the phrase does not refer generally to one who is left-handed, but rather to a specially trained left-handed, or even ambidextrous, warrior. He theorizes that the Benjaminites trained several of their young men to be left-handed by restricting the use of their right hand from an early age so they could use their left hand with facility. The practice is known in antiquity; left-handed warriors had a distinct military advantage, especially when attacking city gates. See his article, "The Assassination of Eglon," *Bible Review* (December 1988): 35.

(9) The details given in verses 15–17 (Ehud's left-handedness, the length of his sword, the fact that he strapped it on his right thigh, Eglon's obesity) become important as the story unfolds. But it is obvious that the narrator is already building the tension; we suspect Ehud may have something "up his sleeve" (or should we say "thigh"). Ehud is tricky, armed, and dangerous; Eglon is obese, immobile, and vulnerable. The depiction of Eglon may also suggest he is pampered and has been getting fat on Israel's wealth (notice the threefold reference to tribute in vv. 15–18). His name may even take on significance at this point. The name sounds like עֵגֶל, "calf," and the וֹ- ending may be adjectival (see W–O, 92, on the different functions of this ending in Hebrew), suggesting the meaning "calflike." In this case, the author depicts the oppressive king as obese and "calflike"; he has been fattened for the slaughter. (step 5)

Verses 18–19

(18) When he had finished presenting the tribute payment, he dismissed the people who had carried it. (19) But he went back once he reached the carved images in Gilgal. He said: "I have secret message for you, O king." And he (the king) replied: "Shh!" And all his attendants left.

(10) The significance of the reference to the "idols" (פְּסִילִים, v. 19) is uncertain. Perhaps they were a well known geographical marker that separated Israelite turf from occupied territory. Once Ehud reaches them after the assassination, he seems to be scot-free (v. 26). (step 5)

(11) On the lips of Ehud the phrase דְּבַר־סֵתֶר (v. 19) may be a double entendre. On the surface the phrase means "secret word/message" (lit., "word of secrecy," the genitive being attributive) and this is undoubtedly how Eglon understood it. But דָּבָר can refer to more than just a word or verbal message. Sometimes it carries the nuance "matter, affair, dealing" (Judg. 18:7, 28) or "business, task, mission" (see Josh. 2:14). From Ehud's perspective the phrase may refer to his "secret task/mission," namely, his plan to assassinate Eglon in private. (step 3, f–g)

Verses 20–23

(20) When Ehud approached him, he was sitting all alone in his ventilated upper room. When Ehud said: "I have a divine oracle for you," he got up from his throne. (21) Ehud then reached with his left hand, pulled the sword from his right thigh, and drove it into his belly. (22) The handle went in after the blade and the fat closed around the blade, because he did not pull the sword out of his belly. (23) Ehud went out into the vestibule, closed the doors of the upper room behind him, and locked them.

(12) The phrase עֲלִיַּת הַמְּקֵרָה (v. 20) means literally, "upper room of cooling," that is, "cool/ventilated upper room." (step 3, f)

(13) The phrase דְּבַר־(הָ)אֱלֹהִים, "word of God" (v. 20) refers elsewhere to a prophetic oracle (see 1 Sam. 9:27; 2 Sam. 16:23; 1 Kings 12:22; 1 Chron. 17:3; see also "the word of the Lord God of Israel" in 2 Kings 14:25 and "the word of our God" in Isa. 40:8), the lone exception being in 1 Chronicles 26:32, where the phrase לְכָל־דְּבַר הָאֱלֹהִים refers to "all matters pertaining to God." (step 3, f)

(14) The verb תָּקַע (v. 21) is used with a variety of objects. Here it refers to driving or thrusting a sword. (step 3, f)

(15) The noun נִצָּב, "handle" (v. 22) occurs only here in the Old Testament, but the meaning is clear from the context (note "after the blade"). An Arabic cognate is also attested. (See BDB, 662; K–B, 715) (step 3, f)

(16) The meaning of הַפַּרְשְׁדֹנָה (v. 22, the noun has the article prefixed and a directive ending suffixed) is uncertain, for it occurs only here in the Old Testament. The word may be a technical architectural term, referring to an area into which Ehud moved as he left the king and began his escape. In this case Ehud is the subject of the preceding verb יֵצֵא.[2] Some understand the form to mean "out his back," and understand the "sword," mentioned in the preceding causal clause, as the subject. But the verb יֵצֵא is masculine, while חֶרֶב, "sword," is feminine. One expects agreement in gender (cf. Ezek. 33:4, 6), especially when the subject is supplied from the preceding clause. For this reason, it would be better, if one sees this as referring to the sword, to understand לַהַב, "blade," as the subject of the verb. Another option is to relate the noun to פֶּרֶשׁ, "feces, excrement," and understand the form as the subject of the verb. (This would certainly explain the servants' statement in v. 24!) But the ה and final ָה - (which would have to be taken as a feminine ending in this case) are problematic. One could eliminate the ה as a virtual dittograph of the immediately following ו. (step 3, f, h)

(17) The meaning of הַמִּסְדְּרוֹנָה (v. 23, this noun, like the one at the end of v. 22 has the article prefixed and a directive ending suffixed) is uncertain. Since it is preceded by the verb "go out" and the next clause refers to Ehud closing doors, the noun is probably an architectural term referring to the room (perhaps a vestibule, see K–B, 604) immediately outside the upper room. But how could Ehud lock the doors of the upper chamber without arousing suspicion? As verse 24 indicates, this vestibule separated the upper room from an outer chamber where the king's servants were located (see note 19 below). So Ehud could have locked the doors of the upper room without being seen. He would have then left the vestibule, walked right past the guards in the outer chamber, and left the same way he came in. (step 3, f, g)

(18) There has been some debate over Ehud's escape route. Did he lock the doors of the upper chamber from the inside and then escape

---

2. If one follows this line of interpretation, then the statement at the end of v. 22 and the one beginning v. 23 are variants.

through a back door, window, or latrine?[3] Or did he simply leave the upper chamber the same way he entered, locking the doors behind him, as we suggested in the preceding note?

We must examine the statement וַיִּסְגֹּר דַּלְתוֹת הָעֲלִיָּה בַּעֲדוֹ before proposing an answer. The verb סָגַר, "shut, close," is used in ten different passages with the preposition בַּעַד. Five times the word "door" does not appear after the verb and בַּעַד introduces the object that is "shut in":

> Genesis 7:16: ויסגר יהוה בעדו, "and the LORD shut him (Noah) in"
> Judges 3:22: ויסגר החלב בעד הלהב, "and the fat closed around the blade"
> Judges 9:51: ויסגרו בעדם, "and they shut themselves in"
> 1 Samuel 1:6: סגר יהוה בעד רחמה, "the LORD closed up her womb"
> 2 Kings 4:21: ותסגר בעדו, "and she shut him in"

In the other five passages סָגַר takes "door(s)" as its object and is then followed by בַּעַד in the sense of "behind, after":

> Judges 3:23: ויצא . . . ויסגר דלתות העליה בעדו, "and he went out . . . and closed the doors of the upper room behind him"
> 2 Kings 4:4: ובאת וסגרת הדלת בעדך ובעד בניך, "and enter and close the door behind you and behind your sons"
> 2 Kings 4:5: ותלך מאתו ותסגר הדלת בעדה ובעד בניה, "and she went with him and closed the door behind her and behind her sons"
> 2 Kings 4:33: ויבא ויסגר הדלת בעד שניהם, "and he entered and closed the door behind both of them"
> Isaiah 26:20: בא בחדריך וסגר דלתך בעדך, "enter your inner rooms and close your door (sg., Qere; Kethib has the plural "doors") behind you"

In 2 Kings 4:4–5, 33 and Isaiah 26:20 "closing the door behind" clearly refers to locking oneself inside the room. For this reason some argue that the statement in Judges 3:23 must refer to Ehud locking himself inside the upper chamber, meaning that he would have had to escape through a window, back door, or the like. However, note that in each of the other four texts the statement is preceded by a reference to the subject *entering* the room. When one closes a door after entering a room, one shuts oneself in the room. But Judges 3:23 is unique. Here the statement is preceded by a reference to Ehud *going out*. When one closes a door after leaving a room, one is not shutting oneself inside the room. So a close examination of the evidence reveals that there are no precise syntactical parallels to Judges 3:23. However, because the verb "go out" appears, it

3. See Halpern, "Assassination of Eglon," 35–41.

seems that Ehud locked the doors of the upper chamber after he stepped out into an adjoining room. (step 3, f)

Verses 24–26

(24) When he left, his (Eglon's) servants entered and noticed that the doors of the upper room were locked. They said: "He must be relieving himself in the upper room." (25) They waited so long they became embarrassed. He still did not open the doors of the upper room. So they took the key and opened them. Then they saw their master lying dead on the floor. (26) In the meantime Ehud escaped while they delayed. Once he passed by the carved images, he escaped to Seirah.

(19) The construction at the beginning of verse 24 indicates synchronic action. It also supports the explanation of Ehud's escape outlined above. As Ehud passed by the servants in the outer chamber, they reasoned correctly that his business with the king was finished and entered the vestibule adjoining the upper chamber. Notice how the verb בא implies that they entered a room, but this could not have been the upper chamber, for its doors were locked and they only entered it later (v. 25). This indicates that there was a room separating the upper chamber from the room where they were waiting during Ehud's interview with the king. (step 5, see also step 2)

(20) The statement מֵסִיךְ הוּא אֶת־רַגְלָיו (v. 24) means literally, "he was covering his feet (i.e., with his garments)" (cf. 1 Sam. 24:4; see BDB, 697; K–B, 754). It is apparently an idiomatic euphemism for urination/defecation, comparable to the English expression, "dropped his drawers." (step 3, f)

(21) The verb יָחִילוּ (v. 25) appears to be from a hollow root חיל/חול. BDB (297) defines it here as "be in severe pain, anguish" (from anxious longing). BHS textual note "a" labels the reading of the text "doubtful" ("dub") and suggests that we "perhaps" ("frt") read וַיְיַחֲלוּ (a piel form from the verbal root יחל) or ("vel") וַיּוֹחִילוּ (a hiphil form from the same root, יחל). (K–B, 311, 407, favors the latter emendation.) In either case the form would be translated, "they waited." (A similar problem occurs in Gen. 8:10, 12, where BHS note "a" suggests emending וַיָּחֶל, "and he was in anguish" [??] to וַיְיַחֶל, "and he waited.") The verb יָחַל does occur with עַד, "until," elsewhere (see 1 Sam. 10:8; Job 14:14); חיל/חול does not. If the hiphil form of יָחַל is original, the MT consonantal text either has the prefix vowel defectively written or has accidentally omitted a waw after the yod prefix (virtual haplography; yod and waw are very similar in later script phases). If the piel of יָחַל is original, then MT has inverted the second yod (the initial root letter after the verbal prefix) and the heth. (step 3, f, h)

(22) The form אֲדֹנֵיהֶם, "their master" (v. 25) consists of a plural noun with the pronominal suffix. Why is the plural form of the noun used,

even though it refers to an individual (Eglon)? אָדוֹן, "master," is often pluralized, as here, to indicate respect or honor (see BDB, 11). The plural does not necessarily mean that the referent is actually honorable or worthy of respect; it simply reflects, as here, the reality of his authority over his servants. He was their "sovereign master." (step 3, a)

(23) In this context the active participle נֹפֵל (v. 25) does not mean "was falling." (It is highly unlikely that Eglon's body remained standing for such a long time and then tumbled to the floor just as the servants walked in!) Followed by אַרְצָה, "to the ground," and in conjunction with מֵת, "dead," נֹפֵל carries the nuance, "was lying prostrate on the ground," (See Judg. 4:22, where נֹפֵל is also followed by מֵת. In 1 Sam. 5:3–4 and 2 Chron. 20:24 it occurs with אַרְצָה.) This is probably a metonymic use of the verb "fall," where the term actually refers to the effect of falling. (step 3, a, f)

Verses 27–30

(27) When he arrived, he blew the trumpet in the Ephraimite hill country. The Israelites went down with him from the hill country. Now he was in the lead (28) and he said to them: "Follow me, for the Lord is handing your enemies, the Moabites, over to you." They followed him down and captured the fords of the Jordan opposite Moab; they did not allow anyone to cross. (29) They struck down about ten thousand Moabites at that time, all of whom were strong, capable warriors; no one escaped. (30) So Moab was subdued that day under the hand of Israel, and the land was undisturbed for eighty years.

(24) The verb תָּקַע (used earlier of "thrusting" a sword, v. 21) here refers to "blowing" a horn (v. 27). The repetition is not accidental. The sword thrust killed the Moabite leader; the horn blast rallies Israel to finish what Ehud started. These two actions are defining moments in Ehud's revolt. (step 3, f–g)

(25) In verse 28 BHS note "a" suggests, with support from Greek witnesses that attest to the original Septuagintal reading, altering רִדְפוּ, "follow," to רְדוּ, "go down." They observe that the clause immediately following the quotation says "they went down (וַיֵּרְדוּ) after" Ehud, rather than "they followed after him." אַחֲרֵי only occurs four times with יָרַד in the Old Testament, but it follows רָדַף forty-five times (see, e.g., Judg. 1:6; 4:16; 7:23; 8:5, 12). A scribe could have easily substituted the more common expression for the relatively rare one. However, the phrase "follow after" (רָדַף אַחֲרֵי) is used forty-three times of pursuing someone with hostile intent. Only once is it used in a nonhostile sense of "follow after" (see 2 Kings 5:21, where Gehazi runs after Naaman). In a context where Ehud is leading his men, it is unlikely that a scribe would substitute this idiom. Though rare, רָדַף אַחֲרֵי is attested and should be retained in verse 28. It is more likely that the Septuagint translator harmonized the reading to the immediately following context. (step 3, f, g)

(26) When rallying his troops for battle, Ehud announces that the Lord "has given" (נָתַן) the enemy into their hands (v. 28). The very common idiom "give into the hand of" (נָתַן בְּיָד) means "to deliver over to the power of," or "to enable to conquer." Ehud uses the perfect aspect here to describe a future action or state. The action, though not completed in reality, is described as such from Ehud's perspective for dramatic effect. He wishes to emphasize to his troops that victory is a "done deal." This dramatic future use of the perfect נָתַן appears elsewhere in Judges in rhetorically charged rallying cries (Judg. 4:14; 7:15) and divine oracles of deliverance (Judg. 1:2; 7:9; 18:10; see also Josh. 6:2; 8:1). It is used once in a response to an omen where the interpreter wishes to emphasize the disaster which the sign symbolizes (Judg. 7:14). (step 3, e–f)

(27) The adjective שָׁמֵן (v. 29), used here of warriors, means "robust, strong" (see BDB, 1032). (step 3, f)

(28) The expression "the land was undisturbed" (v. 30, וַתִּשְׁקֹט הָאָרֶץ) means the land was free from invasion and warfare (see Judg. 3:11; 5:31; 8:28; 2 Chron. 14:1, 6; Isa. 14:7). (step 3, f)

Step 6

The background for this story is God's moral conflict with Israel (v. 12). God's response to Israel's sin introduces a conflict between his instrument of punishment (the king of Moab) and his covenant people (vv. 13–14). This conflict intensifies as God enables Eglon to defeat and oppress Israel, but Israel's cry for help activates divine deliverance and a potential resolution to the conflict appears in the person of Ehud, who is specifically called a "deliverer" (v. 15). The plot begins to move toward resolution, as we discover that Ehud has access to the oppressive Moabite king and has something deadly "up his sleeve" (vv. 16–17a). The reference to Eglon's obesity (v. 17b), which brings the first paragraph to its conclusion, hints at the king's vulnerability, but also reminds us of his oppressive rule. The plot is moving toward resolution, but tension is also mounting as we wonder if Ehud will really be able to accomplish Israel's deliverance.

Perhaps this Ehud has help? No, he sends the tribute bearers away and enters the king's presence alone (v. 18)! Ah, but he's shrewd and knows how to position his prey for the kill (vv. 19–20). He's a quick and effective assassin who disposes of his victim without even a peep. He even has an escape plan (vv. 21–23), but will it work? Yes, the dull-witted Moabite attendants delay long enough for Ehud to get away with murder (vv. 24–26). In this second paragraph the plot ascends, reaches, and starts down its peak. A measure of resolution has been achieved, but what will happen next?

The final paragraph brings the conflict to complete resolution. If we are still uncertain about what will happen, Ehud is not. He rallies his forces, traps the Moabites, and annihilates them (vv. 27–29). Israel's conflict with Moab ends, and the nation's conflict with God has subsided, at least temporarily (v. 30).

The story's main character, Ehud, is not full-fledged, but typical. Though he is not directly commissioned by God or supernaturally empowered by the divine spirit, he emerges as a heroic leader who mixes faith with skill as he seizes the moment and exploits the opportunity granted him by divine providence. Some of the details of the story may be offensive to our modern Western sensibilities, but we dare not judge it by our cultural standards. Israel's situation was dire, and Ehud utilized the means and opportunity available to him to deliver his people from bondage. One can almost hear an ancient Israelite audience cheering as Ehud boldly enters the palace under the guise of a loyal subject, outwits and slaughters the king, tricks the guards, and leads Israel to an overwhelming victory. One may summarize the theme/lesson of this admiration story as follows: The Lord can use men of faith and initiative to accomplish great things for his people.

Step 7

In the literary context of the entire book, Ehud's story plays an important role. Like the other episodes in the central part of the book, it reminds us that God will not tolerate sin among his people. But it also assures us that he is willing to respond to their suffering and is able to deliver them through the instrumentality of an individual. Like Othniel before him, daring Ehud carries on the tradition of the ideal leader established by Joshua and Caleb, a tradition that will slowly but surely fade in the persons of Barak, Gideon, Jephthah, and Samson.[4]

(2) The Lord Takes Israel to Court (Isaiah 1:2–20)

Step 1

The first literary unit in the Book of Isaiah is a so-called covenant lawsuit in which the Lord issues his sinful people an ultimatum. The first line of the speech (v. 2a) concludes with the words כִּי יְהוָה דִּבֵּר, "for the LORD speaks," while the last line of the speech (v. 20) ends with כִּי פִּי יְהוָה דִּבֵּר, "indeed the mouth of the LORD has spoken." These almost identical formulas bracket the speech.

The unit may be divided into three parts: (a) accusation (vv. 2–3); (b) lament and admonition (vv. 4–9); (c) reproof, exhortation, and ultimatum (vv. 10–20). In verses 2–3 the prophet summons witnesses (v. 2a)

---

4. See my article, "The Role of Women in the Rhetorical Strategy of the Book of Judges," in *Integrity of Heart, Skillfulness of Hands: Biblical and Leadership Studies in Honor of Donald K. Campbell,* ed. Charles H. Dyer and Roy B. Zuck (Grand Rapids: Baker, 1994), 34–49.

to hear the Lord's formal accusation against his rebellious people (vv. 2b–3). In verses 4–9 the prophet laments the nation's condition (v. 4), attempts to reason with the people (vv. 5–8), and speaks on their behalf (v. 9). In verses 10–20 the prophet summons the people (v. 10) to hear the Lord's reproof of their empty formalism (vv. 11–15), his call to repentance (vv. 16–17), and his ultimatum (vv. 18–20).

Step 2

The following translation reflects the poetic structure of the passage. Following each couplet is an explanatory note analyzing the nature of the parallelism.

Verses 2–3

(2) Listen, O heavens!
Pay attention, O earth!
For the LORD speaks.

The first two lines are essentially synonymous; in both the prophet issues a call to covenantal witnesses. Since the stereotypical phrase "heavens and earth" is broken up in the parallel structure, one could classify the second line as complementary. One witness is summoned in the first line, its companion in the second. The third line is explanatory; it provides a reason why the witnesses need to report.

I raised children and brought them up,
but they have rebelled against me.

The second line contrasts the children's response to their father's efforts. Note that a disjunctive clause structure is employed (waw + subject + verb) to highlight this.

(3) An ox recognizes its owner,
a donkey the feeding trough of its owner;
Israel does not recognize,
my people do not understand.

The parallelism is complex. In this double couplet the first two lines are complementary (two different animals are used to illustrate the same point). Lines 3–4 are synonymous, but the second couplet (lines 3–4) forms a contrast with the first (lines 1–2).

Verses 4–9

(4) Woe to the sinful nation,
people weighed down by evil,
offspring who do wrong,
children who act wickedly.

201

"People," "offspring," and "children," stand in apposition to "nation," and each line emphasizes the sin of the covenant community. However, two distinct couplets are discernible. The first (lines 1–2) describes the community as a nation/people; the second views them as offspring/children. In each couplet the second line reiterates the first; the second couplet is complementary in relation to the first.

> They have abandoned the LORD,
> and rejected the sovereign king of Israel.
> They have turned back.

The first two lines of this triplet are synonymous; the third line is complementary; without supplying an object, it describes their rejection of the Lord as "turning back."

> (5) Why do you insist on being battered?
> Why do you continue to rebel?

Both lines express rhetorical questions. (The interrogative "why" is elliptical [unstated, but implied] in the second line.) The parallelism is complementary. The first line focuses on the people's condition, the second on what produces it. Their situation is viewed from two perspectives—its surface characteristic and its underlying cause.

> Your whole head is wounded,
> your whole body weak.

The prophet describes their battered condition from complementary angles, focusing first on the head and then the body.

> (6) From the sole of your foot to your head, there is no spot unharmed,
> there are only bruises, cuts, and open wounds.

The first line makes the point that the body is injured from head to toe; the second line specifies by giving a more detailed description of their condition.

> They have not been cleansed or bandaged,
> nor have they been treated with olive oil.

The parallelism is complementary. The first line refers to two aspects of treating a wound (cleansing and bandaging), the second line adds a third (application of medicine).

> (7) Your land is devastated,
> your cities burned with fire.

Once again the parallelism is complementary; the first line describes the invasion's effect on the land, the second focuses on the cities.

Right before your eyes invaders are devouring your land,
they devastate it as only invaders can do.

The parallelism is best labeled complementary. The first line emphasizes how the invaders devour the land (i.e., its crops); the second makes the point that this devastation is typical of such invaders.

(8) Daughter Zion is left isolated,
like a hut in a vineyard,
or a shelter in a cucumber field,
she is a besieged city.

The parallelism is complex. In the Hebrew text the opening line is followed by three parallel lines, each beginning with the comparative preposition. While the first two of these are true similes, the third points to the reality of Zion's condition (see exegetical note 25 below). In reality the first and fourth lines correspond, with the fourth specifying why Zion finds herself isolated. The second and third lines contain complementary similes which metaphorically depict Zion's condition. (So we could say that lines 2–3 are comparative in relation to line 1.)

(9) If the LORD of armies had not left us some survivors,
we would have quickly become like Sodom,
we would have become like Gomorrah.

In this case the prophet uses a conditional sentence, the first line being the protasis ("if" statement), the second and third the apodosis ("then" statement). The second and third lines are loosely synonymous. Since the stereotypical phrase "Sodom and Gomorrah" is broken up in the parallel structure, one could classify the third line as complementary to the second. One city is used as a simile in the second line, its companion city in the third.

Verses 10–20

(10) Listen to the LORD's word, you leaders of Sodom!
Pay attention to our God's instruction, you people of Gomorrah!

The parallelism is loosely synonymous or complementary. As in verse 9 the stereotypical phrase "Sodom and Gomorrah" is broken up in the parallel structure. Also the first line mentions leaders, the second people.

(11) What good to me are your many sacrifices? says the LORD.
I am stuffed with the burnt sacrifices of rams and the suet of steers,
the blood of bulls, lambs, and goats I do not want.

The parallelism is complex. Lines 2–3 give a reason for the rhetorical question of line 1. Line 3 is progressive or consequential in relation to line 2. Because the Lord is stuffed full with sacrificial animals, he has no desire for any more to be brought to him. In the chiastic structure of lines 2–3 the verbs at the beginning and end highlight God's displeasure, while the heaping up of references to animals, fat, and blood in between hints at why God wants no more of their sacrifices. They have, as it were, piled the food on his table and he needs no more.

(12) When you enter my presence,
who asks you to trample on my courts like this?

There is no true parallelism here, only a formal correspondence between the two lines. The first line is a temporal clause, subordinate to the rhetorical question in the second line.

(13) Don't bring any more meaningless offerings!
I consider your incense detestable.

The second line gives a reason for the command in the first line.

As for new moon festivals, sabbaths, and convocations—
I cannot tolerate sin-stained celebrations.

The parallelism is purely formal; the nouns in the first line stand in apposition to "assembly and sin" in the second.

(14) I hate your new moon festivals and assemblies,
they are a burden I'm tired of carrying.

In the first line the Lord declares his hatred for their festivals; the second line explains why he finds them so loathsome.

(15) When you spread out your hands in prayer, I look the other way,
when you offer many prayers, I do not listen.
Your hands are covered with blood.

The second line, in which the Lord states he will not hear their prayers, complements the first, in which he declares that he will not take notice of them when they pray. The third line is explanatory; it gives the reason for the Lord's refusal to respond to their prayers.

(16) Wash! Cleanse yourselves!
Remove your sinful deeds from my sight!

The second line specifies; it explains what is meant by the general commands in the first line.

Stop sinning!
(17) Learn to do what is right!

The second line complements the first by giving the "other side of the coin," as it were.

Promote justice!
Give the oppressed reason to celebrate!

The second line gives the specific way in which they can promote justice.

Take up the cause of the orphan!
Defend the rights of the widow!

The lines are loosely synonymous, but since the stereotypical phrase "widow and orphan" is broken up in the parallel structure, one could classify the second line as complementary to the first.

(18) Come, let's reason through your options, says the LORD.
Though your sins have stained you like the color red,
you can become white like snow;
though they are as easy to see as the color scarlet,
you can become white like wool.

The exhortation in the first line is introductory and outside the parallel structure. The parallelism of lines 2–5 is complex. The second couplet (lines 4–5) reiterates the first (lines 2–3), though it uses a different simile (wool) within the larger metaphor. Within each couplet, the first statement is concessive (lines 2, 4) and subordinated to the second (lines 3, 5).

(19) If you have a willing attitude and obey,
you will eat the good crops of the land.
(20) But if you refuse and rebel,
you will be devoured by the sword.
Indeed the mouth of the LORD has spoken.

The concluding line gives closure to the whole unit and is outside the parallel structure. The parallelism of lines 1–4 is complex. The second couplet (lines 3–4) contrasts with the first (lines 1–2). Each couplet is a conditional sentence with protasis (lines 1, 3) and apodosis (lines 2, 4).

Steps 3–5

After each note, we indicate which step or steps the note pertains to. (For step 4, the translation of the text, see the preceding section.) The notes should be considered as illustrative of the process, not as an exhaustive analysis. We do not include the parsing of every verb or label aspectual function when it is routine, nor do we duplicate information that is readily available in the major lexicons or stop to define words that are used in common, well-attested ways. The above translation reveals our decisions in such routine matters.

Verses 2–3

(1) At the beginning of the speech (v. 2) the prophet commands the personified heavens and earth to listen to the Lord's accusation against his people. What is the significance of this? The prophet is probably alluding here to the covenantal tradition. When finalizing the covenantal arrangement between the Lord and Israel, Moses had warned the people that the heavens and earth would be witnesses against the people if they violated the agreement (see Deut. 4:26; 30:19; 31:28; 32:1). By summoning these witnesses, Isaiah already hints that a covenant violation has occurred and that the Lord is ready to take legal action. (step 3, g)

(2) דִּבֶּר (v. 2) here introduces the following accusation, so the perfect states factually that an action is occurring in the present (simple present use). (step 3, e)

(3) The Lord metaphorically refers to the Israelites as בָּנִים, "sons," or "children" (v. 2), placing himself in the role of a father. Both the piel of גָּדַל, "be great," and polel (a hollow verb's equivalent of a piel) of רוּם, "be raised," are used here in a factitive sense, meaning, "to rear, raise." (step 3, e–f)

(4) The idiom בְּ- פָּשַׁע (v. 2) means "rebel against." It frequently refers in political contexts to a subject nation revolting against an overlord, but its use is appropriate here, where children rebel against parental authority, especially when a covenantal relationship underlies the familial metaphor. (step 3, f)

(5) In the proverbial-like statement at the beginning of verse 3, the perfect of יָדַע expresses a well-known truth (characteristic present use). (step 3, e)

(6) In the second half of verse 3 the perfects state factually Israel's characteristic attitude. יָדַע has no expressed object, but the parallelism suggests that Israel fails to recognize the Lord as the one who provides for their needs. As Israel's provider, he corresponds to the ox's master and the donkey's feeding trough. (step 3, e–f)

Verses 4–9

(7) The interjection הוֹי, "ah, woe" (v. 4), was used in funeral laments (see 1 Kings 13:30; Jer. 22:18; 34:5) and in certain contexts (such as prophetic judgment speeches) carries the connotation of death. In highly dramatic fashion the prophet acts out Israel's funeral in advance, emphasizing that their demise is inevitable if they do not repent soon. (step 3, f)

(8) In the phrase עַם כֶּבֶד עָוֹן, literally, "heavy-of-sin people" (v. 4), the genitive עָוֹן specifies what is characterized by the adjective כֶּבֶד ("heavy with respect to sin"). (step 3, a)

(9) The participle מְרֵעִים (v. 4) might be construed as a genitive of source (i.e., "the offspring produced by evildoers," cf. Isa. 14:20), but in this passage God is pictured as their father. In the corresponding expression בָּנִים מַשְׁחִיתִים, "sons who act corruptly," the participle is an attributive adjective (not genitival; note that "sons" is in the absolute, not construct form) and describes a characteristic of the sons. So it is preferable to take מְרֵעִים as descriptive of the offspring, not their parents. In this case מְרֵעִים is probably appositional (possibly a genitive of apposition, see W–O, 53, who classify it as a genitive of species). The hiphil of רָעַע, "be evil," is used here with an exhibitive force, "exhibit/do evil." (step 3, a, e–f)

(10) The precise force of the piel of נָאַץ, "spurn, reject" (v. 4) is not entirely clear. The qal of this verb is transitive, and is used of spurning individuals (always human beings, not God personally) and wise advice, including God's counsel (Ps. 107:11). The piel is used with a variety of objects, including God himself (several times), his offerings (1 Sam. 2:17), his word (Isa. 5:24; Jer. 23:17), his people (Isa. 60:14), and his name (Ps. 74:10, 18). It appears that the piel (perhaps a resultative use) is specialized and reserved for contexts where God is rejected, whether directly or indirectly (the lone exception being Ps. 107:11). (step 3, e–f)

(11) The divine title קְדוֹשׁ יִשְׂרָאֵל, "Holy One of Israel" (v. 4) is one of Isaiah's favorites. It pictures the Lord as the sovereign king who rules over his covenant people and exercises moral authority over them. The basic sense of the word "holy" is "special, unique, set apart from that which is commonplace." As we discover in Isaiah 6, the Lord's holiness is first and foremost his transcendent sovereignty as ruler of the world. He is "set apart" from the world over which he rules. Note the emphasis on the elevated position of his throne in 6:1 and his designation as "the king" in 6:5. At the same time, his holiness encompasses his moral authority, which derives from his royal position. As king he has the right to dictate to his subjects how they are to live; indeed his very own character sets the standard for proper behavior. He is "set apart" from his subjects in a moral sense as well. He sets the standard; they fall short of it. Note that Isaiah laments he is morally unworthy to be in the king's presence (6:5). (step 3, f)

(12) The last line of verse 4 (נָזֹרוּ אָחוֹר) is problematic. The Septuagint omits it, but if this shorter text is the original, there is no apparent reason why a scribe would add such a difficult statement. It seems more likely that the Greek translator omitted it because it was so difficult. According to BDB (266), נָזֹרוּ (a niphal perfect) is from the root זוּר, "be a stranger." K–B (267) offers the basic definition "turn aside" for this verbal root and suggests translating the line, "become estranged." The niphal appears in

207

only one other passage, Ezekiel 14:5, where the Lord laments that the Israelites have "turned aside" from him to follow after idols. Perhaps the best way to translate the construction in Isaiah 1:4 would be, "they have turned back" (i.e., from him). (step 3, e–f, h)

(13) The verb תֻכּוּ (v. 5) is a hophal imperfect, 2mp, from נָכָה, "beat." It is addressed to the wayward "sons" of verse 4. The imperfect is subjective here, indicating the subject's desire or intention. (step 3, e)

(14) The hiphil of יָסַף (v. 5) is used idiomatically to indicate repeated action. With the accusative סָרָה, "rebellion," one can translate it, "persist in rebellion," or "continue to rebel." (step 3, f)

(15) The preposition -לְ prefixed to חֳלִי designates a condition (see BDB, 516, 5. j). The statement would read literally, "all the head is in a state of illness," which we have paraphrased, "your head has a massive wound." Verses 5–6 use the image of a battered and injured person to illustrate the devastation that Israel has experienced as a result of divine judgment. (steps 3, c, 5)

(16) לֵבָב, "heart" (v. 5), here stands for bodily strength and energy (see Jer. 8:18; Lam. 1:22, for parallel uses of "heart" with דַּוָּי, "faint"). (step 3, f)

(17) The adjective טְרִיָּה (v. 6) is used only here and in Judges 15:15, where it refers to the "fresh" (i.e., not decayed and brittle) donkey's jawbone that Samson used as a weapon against the Philistines. In verse 6, where it modifies מַכָּה, "wound," it must refer to an open or fresh wound, as opposed to one that has started to dry up and scab over. (step 3, f)

(18) The verbal root of זֹרוּ (v. 6) is debated. BDB (266) derives it from the hollow root זוּר, "press," while K–B (283) takes it as an otherwise unattested geminate root זָרַר. In either case the meaning seems apparent; the wounds have not been treated with compresses. (step 3, f)

(19) The three perfects in the last couplet of verse 6 state factually a condition that was present at the time Isaiah spoke (simple present use). (step 3, e)

(20) The feminine noun אַדְמָה (v. 7, it has a 2mp pronominal suffix) is an accusative absolute, resumed by the 3fs suffix on the accusative sign at the end of the sentence. (step 3, a)

(21) זָרִים refers here to foreign invaders (probably the Assyrians). In the most basic sense זָרַ/זָרָה refers to something that is unauthorized or to someone who is outside one's social sphere, as specifically defined by the context. For example, a אִשָּׁה זָרָה, "strange woman," is a woman who is not one's wife (i.e., she is outside his family). In verse 7 the זָרִים are outside Israel's context, that is, they are foreigners. (step 3, f)

(22) The last line of verse 7 reads literally, "and (there is) devastation like an overthrow by foreigners." The comparative preposition (כְּ) has the rhetorical nuance, "in every way like." The point is that the land has all the earmarks of a destructive foreign invasion because that is what has indeed happened. One could paraphrase, "it is desolate as it can only

be when foreigners destroy."[5] Many (see, e.g., BHS note "a") prefer to emend "foreigners" here to "Sodom," though there is no external attestation for such a reading in the manuscripts or ancient versions. Such an emendation finds support from the following context (vv. 9–10) and usage of the preceding noun מַהְפֵּכָה, "overthrow." In its five other uses, this noun is associated with the destruction of Sodom. (If one accepts the emendation, then one might translate, "the devastation resembles the destruction of Sodom.") However, the usage of the noun is too limited to demand the emendation. (step 3, c, h)

(23) In the phrase בַת־צִיּוֹן (v. 8), the genitive "Zion" is appositional, identifying precisely the daughter in view. By picturing Zion as a daughter, the prophet emphasizes her helplessness and vulnerability before the enemy. (step 3, a, f)

(24) The similes in verse 8 suggest isolation. Invaders have swept through the land; Jerusalem is left isolated and besieged. Based on what we know of the historical background of Isaiah's time, Assyria's invasion of Judah in 701 B.C. seems to be in view. (step 5)

(25) The phrase כְּעִיר נְצוּרָה reads literally, "like a city besieged." This third comparative clause identifies the reality behind the preceding similes, which are purely metaphorical. In this case the comparative preposition, as in verse 7, has the force, "in every way like," indicating that all the earmarks of a siege are visible because that is indeed what is taking place. (See note 22 above.) נְצוּרָה is a qal passive participle, fs of נָצַר, "guard," but since this verb is not often used of a siege (see BDB, 666), some prefer to repoint the form as נְצוּרָה, a niphal participle, fs from צוּר, "besiege" (see BHS note "b"). Since this latter verb is not attested elsewhere in the niphal (see BDB, 848), it seems preferable to retain the Hebrew text. (step 3, c, h)

(26) לוּלֵי, "if not" (v. 9) introduces an unreal condition, that is, a situation that is viewed as unfulfilled by the speaker. (step 3, i)

(27) The divine title יהוה צְבָאוֹת, traditionally translated "the Lord of Hosts," pictures God as a sovereign king who has at his disposal a multitude of attendants, messengers, and warriors. In some contexts, like this one, the military dimension of his rulership is highlighted. In this case, the title pictures him as one who leads armies into battle against his enemies.[6] (step 3, f)

(28) The syntactical function of כִּמְעַט, "quickly" (lit., "like a little") (v. 9) is uncertain. The accentuation in the Hebrew text suggests that it goes with what precedes, in which case one might translate, "If the Lord of armies had not left us a few survivors." However, in Psalm 94:17, which provides the closest syntactical parallel to Isaiah 1:9, כִּמְעַט appears

---

5. On this use of the preposition in general, see GKC, 376, para. 118x.

6. For a discussion of the title and its significance, see T. N. D. Mettinger, *In Search of God*, trans. Frederick Cryer (Philadelphia: Fortress, 1988), 134–35.

to go with what follows: לּולֵי יהוה עזרתה לי כִּמְעַט שָׁכְנָה דוּמָה נַפְשִׁי, "if the LORD had not helped me, I would have quickly dwelt in silence." (step 3, i)

(29) The reference to Sodom and Gomorrah emphasizes the degree of Judah's devastation. Sodom and Gomorrah became paradigmatic for divine judgment. (steps 3, g, 5)

Verses 10–20

(30) By sarcastically addressing Judah's leaders and people as "rulers of Sodom" and "people of Gomorrah" (v. 10), the prophet emphasizes the degree of their sin, for these cities were paradigmatic of rebellion against God. Judah was like Sodom and Gomorrah morally; that is why Judah's destruction resembled the devastation of those two ancient cities (cf. v. 9). (steps 3, g, 5)

(31) When followed by אֱלֹהִים, תּוֹרָה (v. 10) usually refers to the Mosaic Law (see, e.g., Josh. 24:26), but here, where it refers to the rebuke and call to repentance that follow, it has the nuance "corrective instruction." (step 3, f)

(32) The verb שָׂבַע, "be satisfied, full" (v. 11) is often used of eating and/ or drinking one's fill (see BDB, 959). Here sacrifices are viewed, in typical ancient Near Eastern fashion, as food for the deity. The Lord declares that he has had more than enough suet to eat and blood to drink. The perfect (see also חָפַצְתִּי at the end of the verse) here states factually God's attitude toward Isaiah's contemporaries (simple present use), not a characteristic reaction to sacrifice, as some, seeking to pit the prophets against the priests, have argued. The context clearly points to a specific audience at a specific point in time. (step 3, e–f)

(33) The rhetorical question in verse 12 sarcastically makes the point that God does not require this parade of livestock. The verb "trample" probably refers to the eager worshipers and their sacrificial animals walking around in the temple area. (step 5)

(34) The hiphil of יָסַף (v. 13) is used idiomatically to indicate repeated action. With the infinitive הָבִיא, "bring," one can translate it, "no longer bring." The imperfect has a subjective, prohibitive force here. (step 3, e–f)

(35) שָׁוְא, "empty" (v. 13) is a genitive of attribute. Modifying "offering," it has the nuance "worthless, ineffective" (see BDB, 996). (step 3, a, f)

(36) קְטֹרֶת, "incense" (v. 13) is a nominative absolute, resumed by the feminine singular pronoun הִיא. (step 3, a)

(37) Preceded by the negative particle, the verb אוּכַל (from יָכֹל, "be able") (v. 13) here has the nuance "I am unable to endure," or "I am intolerant of." (step 3, f)

(38) אָוֶן וַעֲצָרָה, "sin and assembly" (v. 13), must not be understood as two distinct objects of divine intolerance. In this case the conjunction indicates accompaniment, that is, "sin along/together with assembly." Their attempts at worship during their religious assemblies are unacceptable to God because the people's everyday actions in the socioeco-

nomic realm are stained by sin and prove they have no genuine devotion to God (see vv. 16–17). (step 3, c)

(39) The perfects in verse 14 express the Lord's attitude at the time he spoke (simple present use). (step 3, e)

(40) The phrase "spread out the hands" (פָּרַשׂ כַּפַּיִם, v. 15) is a metonymic idiom for praying; it reflects a typical prayer posture, especially when one is seeking favor. Usually the qal form of the verb is used; but here the piel appears (resultative use?). (The only other use of the piel of פָּרַשׂ with כַּפַּיִם is in Jer. 4:31, where personified Zion spreads out her hands and laments her fate.) (step 3, e–f)

(41) The phrase "hide the eyes" (hiphil of עָלַם followed by עֵינַיִם, v. 15) is a metonymic idiom meaning "ignore" (see Lev. 20:4; 1 Sam. 12:3; Prov. 28:27; Ezek. 22:26). The imperfect is used of God's characteristic response to their prayers. (step 3, e–f)

(42) The final statement of verse 15 ("your hands are covered with blood") has a different meaning than one might initially think. In light of the preceding context (see v. 11), one might understand this statement as referring to the sacrificial blood of animals which covers their hands and epitomizes their empty ritualism. But the following context, which alludes to their acts of social injustice, suggests that human blood is in view. By depriving the poor and destitute of proper legal recourse and adequate access to the economic system, the oppressors have, for all intents and purposes, "killed" their victims by subjecting them to abject poverty, hunger, and exploitation. Elsewhere in Isaiah the plural form of "blood" (דָּמִים) refers to human bloodshed (see 4:4; 9:5 [Eng.]; 26:21; 33:15). (The singular דָּם is used in 1:11.) (step 3, f)

(43) The hithpael of זָכָה, "be pure" (v. 16) occurs only here; it has a reflexive force. The imagery of washing in the first line of verse 16 fits nicely with the last statement of verse 15: their hands are covered with the blood of their human victims; that blood needs to be washed away. The idea is not that they should try to cover up or hide their evil deeds, but that they should seek forgiveness (see v. 18). (steps 3, e, 5)

(44) דָּרַשׁ, "seek" (v. 17) is used metonymically to mean "promote." BDB (205) defines this use "seek with application, study, follow, practise." (step 3, f)

(45) The precise meaning of אַשְּׁרוּ חָמוֹץ (v. 17) is uncertain. The form חָמוֹץ occurs only here. It is usually interpreted as a noun meaning "oppressor." Cognates appear in Semitic (see K–B, 329), and a related verb occurs in Psalm 71:4, where the psalmist asks to be delivered from evil oppressors (the participial form חוֹמֵץ is employed). If חָמוֹץ is retained in Isaiah 1:17 and defined as "oppressor," then the piel of אִשֵּׁר would have to mean, "set right, reprove," a nuance that it never has elsewhere. Because of the morphological and semantic problems surrounding the traditional reading, many (see, e.g., BHS note "a") suggest emending חָמוֹץ, 211

to חָמוּץ, "oppressed" (a passive participle from חָמֵץ, "oppress"). One can then take the piel of אָשַׁר in its well-attested sense of "make happy" (the factitive-delocutive piel, meaning "call/pronounce happy," would be metonymic here, referring to actually effecting happiness). The parallelism favors this interpretation, for the next two lines speak of positive actions on behalf of the destitute. (step 3, e–f, h)

(46) The niphal וְנִוָּכְחָה (v. 18) is reciprocal; the plural cohortative is hortatory. (With the conjunction prefixed to it after the imperative, one could take the form as indicating purpose, but the imperative of הָלַךְ has become equivalent to an attention-getting interjection.) Traditionally the form has been translated "let us reason together," which makes sense in this context, where the Lord lays out a very logical argument. However, the verb יָכַח (usually hiphil) frequently appears in a legal context (note Gen. 20:16 and Job 23:7, the only other passages where the niphal occurs). The Lord is not just reasoning; he is concluding his case against the nation by delivering an ultimatum that lays out their two options. (step 3, e–f)

(47) In verse 18b אִם has in both instances a concessive force, "even though," as in Isaiah 10:22 (see GKC, 498, para. 160a). The imperfects that follow אִם in the protases (יַאְדִּימוּ, יִהְיוּ) indicate a present reality from the speaker's perspective (present progressive use). The imperfects in the concluding apodoses (יִהְיוּ, יַלְבִּינוּ) are subjective and indicate possibility or potential. The hiphil forms יַאְדִּימוּ, "are red," and יַלְבִּינוּ, "can become white," are exhibitive. (step 3, c, e)

The point is not that the sins will be covered up, though still retained. The metaphorical language must be allowed some flexibility and should not be pressed into a rigid literalistic mold. חֲטָאֵיכֶם, "your sins," is metonymic for the guilt of sin (see BDB, 308). The people's sins are as obvious as the color red; they are stained guilt-red with sin, as it were. But cleansing (see v. 16a) is possible if repentance is forthcoming (vv. 16b–17). The guilt of the people's sin can be removed; the red can be transformed to white, as it were. (steps 3, f, 5)

(48) In verses 19–20 the imperfects in the protases of the conditional sentences indicate hypothetical situations (hypothetical future use; the perfects with waw-consecutive also have this force), while the imperfects in the apodoses describe future developments contingent on the fulfillment of the protases (contingent future use). The use of אָכַל in both apodoses draws attention to the two options before the people: they can obey and experience God's blessing (i.e., "eat the good [crops] of the land), or they can persist in rebellion and experience his judgment (i.e., "be devoured by the sword"). (step 3, e, g)

Step 6

The legal tone of this message is apparent from the outset, as the prophet summons witnesses to hear the Lord's accusation against his people

(v. 2a). They have rebelled against him and he will not ignore his people's disobedience and ingratitude (vv. 2b–3).

Before summoning the defendant to appear (cf. v. 10), the prophet stops to reason with his countrymen. He points out that they have already experienced severe divine discipline, which should have been a warning signal to them (vv. 4–9).

Having attempted to reason with the people, he now summons them to appear before the Lord (v. 10), who breaks down their potential defense by pointing out that their religious acts and rituals do not insulate them from divine judgment. No, such formalism merely adds hypocrisy to their list of sins (vv. 11–15). The people will only experience divine forgiveness if they repudiate their oppressive policies and promote social justice (vv. 16–17). The choice is theirs—obey and be blessed, or persist in rebellion and be destroyed (vv. 18–20).

One could summarize the overall message of this speech as follows: God will discipline, confront, and, if need be, judge his people when they try to substitute religious formalism for genuine obedience and brotherly love.

Step 7

Isaiah probably preached this message in 701 B.C., when the Assyrians overran Judah and threatened Jerusalem. Though it originates in the latter part of the prophet's career, it is an appropriate introduction to the anthology that follows. Through Isaiah's preaching, God had hardened his stubborn people (see Isa. 6) and brought devastating punishment upon them. Now he was giving them a door of opportunity, through which King Hezekiah walked (see Isa. 36–37). But even Hezekiah showed the symptoms of Israel's spiritual disease, and Isaiah prophesied a time of exile (see Isa. 39). Rhetorically positioning himself among these future exiles, he spoke at length to them and urged them to turn back to God (see Isa. 40–66, especially chapter 55). In the context of the exilic perspective of the anthology as a whole, the ultimatum of 1:2–20, while originating in the crisis of 701 B.C., is a powerful call to God's alienated covenant people to transform their ways and enjoy his renewed blessings.

(3) Divine Provision and Protection (Psalm 23)

Step 1

This famous psalm of confidence has two major parts. In verses 1–4 the psalmist pictures the Lord as a shepherd who provides for his needs and protects him from danger. The psalmist declares, "The LORD is my shepherd," and then extends and develops that metaphor, speaking as if he were a sheep. In verses 5–6 the metaphor changes as the psalmist depicts a great royal banquet hosted by the Lord. The psalmist is a guest of honor, much to the frustration of his enemies. He is a recipient of divine favor, who enjoys unlimited access to the divine palace and presence.

Step 2

The psalm has poetic cadence, but its style is closer to free verse than the more structured parallelism so characteristic of most psalms. The following translation attempts to reflect the poetic structure of the passage. Following each couplet is an explanatory note analyzing the nature of the parallelism.

Verses 1–4

(1) The LORD is my shepherd,
I lack nothing.

The parallelism is progressive; the second line states a logical consequence of the first. Verse 2 goes on to specify the meaning of verse 1b.

(2) He takes me to lush pastures,
he leads me to refreshing water.
(3) He restores my strength.

Lines 1–2 of this triplet are complementary (both deal with the basic essentials of life—the first with food, the second with water). The third is progressive; it summarizes the consequence of the actions described in lines 1–2.

He leads me down the right paths,
for the sake of his reputation.

There is no true parallelism here, only a formal correspondence between the two lines. The second line contains a purpose clause which is subordinate to the main clause in the first line.

(4) Even when I must walk through a dark ravine,
I fear no danger,
for you are with me,
your rod and your staff keep me calm.

There is no true parallelism between lines 1 and 2. The first line contains a temporal clause which is subordinate to the main clause in line 2. Line 3 is explanatory in relation to line 2; it explains why the psalmist is unafraid. Line 4 gives a more specific explanation for this lack of fear.

Verses 5–6

(5) You prepare a feast before me
in plain sight of my enemies.

Once again there is no true parallelism here, only a formal correspondence. The prepositional phrase in the second line is subordinate to the main clause in the first line.

> You refresh my head with oil,
> my cup is full of wine.

The parallelism is complementary, as the psalmist describes two banquet scenes that illustrate his favored status before the host.

> (6) Certainly your goodness and faithfulness will chase after me all the days of my life,
> and I will live in the LORD's palace for the rest of my life.

The parallelism is complementary; the psalmist gives a two-part description of the Lord's lifelong favor toward him.

Steps 3–5

As before, we combine steps 3–5 in the following analysis of the text. (For step 4, the translation of the text, see the preceding section.) After each note, we indicate which step or steps the note pertains to. The notes should be considered as illustrative of the process, not as an exhaustive analysis. We do not include the parsing of every verb or label aspectual function when it is routine, nor do we duplicate information that is readily available in the major lexicons or stop to define words that are used in common, well-attested ways. The translation above reveals our decisions in such routine matters.

Verses 1–4

(1) The opening metaphor (v. 1a) suggests that the psalmist is assuming the role of a sheep. In verses 1b–4 the psalmist extends the metaphor and explains exactly how the Lord is like a shepherd to him. At the surface level the language can be understood in terms of a shepherd's relationship to his sheep. Our translation reflects this level. But, of course, each statement also points to an underlying reality which our exegesis seeks to bring to the surface. (step 5)

(2) The imperfect אֶחְסָר (v. 1) is best understood as expressing the psalmist's ongoing experience as a result of having the Lord as his shepherd (habitual present use). The next verse explains more specifically what he means by this statement. (step 3, e)

(3) The verb יַרְבִּיצֵנִי (v. 2) literally reads, "he makes me lie down." The hiphil has a causative-modal nuance (see W–O, 445–46, on this use of the hiphil) here, meaning "allows me to lie down" (see also Jer. 33:12). The point is that the shepherd takes the sheep to rich pastures and lets them eat and rest there. Both imperfects in verse 2 are habitual present. (step 3, e)

(4) Both genitives in verse 2 indicate an attribute of the noun they modify. דֶּשֶׁא characterizes the pastures as "lush" (i.e., rich with vegetation), while מְנֻחוֹת probably characterizes the water as refreshing (see BDB, 630). In this case the plural indicates an abstract quality. Some take מְנֻחוֹת in the sense of "still, calm" (i.e., as describing calm pools in contrast to dangerous torrents) but it is unlikely that such a pastoral scene is in view. Shepherds usually watered their sheep at wells (cf. Gen. 29:2–3; Exod. 2:16–19). Another option is to take מְנֻחוֹת as "resting places" (see K–B, 600) and to translate, "water of/at the resting places" (genitive of location, see W–O, 147–48). (step 3, a, e)

(5) Within the framework of the metaphor, the psalmist/sheep is declaring in verse 2 that his shepherd provides the essentials for physical life. At a deeper level the psalmist may be referring to more than just physical provision, though that would certainly be included. (step 5)

(6) The appearance of נַפְשִׁי, traditionally translated "my soul," might suggest a spiritualized interpretation for the first line of verse 3. However, at the surface level of the shepherd/sheep metaphor, this is unlikely. נֶפֶשׁ with a pronominal suffix is often equivalent to a pronoun, especially in poetry (see BDB, 660, cat. 4). In this context, where the statement most naturally refers to the physical provision just described, the form is best translated simply "me." The accompanying verb (a polel form [factitive use] of שׁוּב), if referring to the physical provision just described, carries the nuance "refresh, restore strength." Note the TEV/GNB translation, "he gives me new strength," which captures nicely the force of the statement in light of verse 2.[7] (step 3, e–f)

(7) The imperfects in verse 3 (יְשׁוֹבֵב and יַנְחֵנִי), like those in verses 1–2, are habitual present, highlighting what is typical of the shepherd/sheep relationship. (step 3, e)

(8) The attributive genitive צֶדֶק (v. 3) is traditionally translated "righteousness" here, as if designating a moral or ethical quality. But this seems unlikely, for it modifies מַעְגְּלֵי, "paths." Within the shepherd/sheep metaphor, the phrase likely refers to "right" or "correct" paths, that is, ones that lead to pastures, wells, or the fold. While צֶדֶק usually does carry a moral or ethical nuance, it can occasionally refer to less abstract things, such as weights and offerings (see BDB, 841). Of course, beneath the metaphor there is an underlying reality. In light of the context, which emphasizes divine provision and protection, the psalmist is probably referring to God's providential guidance. The psalmist is confident that God takes him down paths that will ultimately lead to something beneficial, not destructive. (steps 3, a, f, 5)

---

7. BDB interprets the use of נֶפֶשׁ in Ps. 23:3 differently. They understand נֶפֶשׁ here as the "seat of the emotions, taking the accompanying verb in the sense of "refresh, cheer." See p. 661, cat. 6.g.

(9) The noun שֵׁם, "name" (v. 3), refers here to the shepherd's reputation. (English "name" is often used the same way.) The statement לְמַעַן שְׁמוֹ, "for the sake of his name," makes excellent sense within the framework of the shepherd/sheep metaphor. Shepherds, who sometimes hired out their services, were undoubtedly concerned about their vocational reputation. To maintain their reputation as competent shepherds, they had to know the "lay of the land" and make sure they led the sheep down the right paths to the proper destinations. The underlying reality is a profound theological truth: God must look out for the best interests of the one he has promised to protect, because if he fails to do so, his faithfulness could legitimately be called into question and his reputation damaged. (steps 3, f, 5)

(10) צַלְמָוֶת (v. 4) has traditionally been understood as a compound noun, meaning "shadow of death" (צֵל + מָוֶת)(see BDB, 853). Other authorities (see, e.g., K–B, 1029) prefer to vocalize the form צַלְמוּת and understand it as an abstract noun (from a root צלם) meaning "darkness" (note the translation of TEV/GNB, "deepest darkness"). An examination of the word's usage favors the latter derivation. It is frequently associated with darkness/night and contrasted with light/morning (see Job 3:5; 10:21–22; 12:22; 24:17; 28:3; 34:22; Ps. 107:10, 14; Isa. 9:1; Jer. 13:16; Amos 5:8). In some cases the darkness described is associated with the realm of death (Job 10:21–22; 38:17), but this is a metaphorical application of the word and does not reflect the inherent meaning of the word. If the word does indeed mean "darkness," it modifies גַּיְא, "valley, ravine," quite naturally. At the metaphorical level, verse 4 pictures the shepherd taking his sheep through a dark ravine where predators might lurk. The life-threatening situations faced by the psalmist are the underlying reality. (steps 3, f, 5)

(11) The imperfects in verse 4, like those in verses 1–3, are habitual present. (step 3, e)

(12) רָע (v. 4) is traditionally translated "evil" here, perhaps suggesting a moral or ethical nuance. But at the level of the metaphor, the word means "danger, injury, harm" (see, e.g., REB and NJB), as a sheep might experience from a predator. The life-threatening dangers faced by the psalmist, especially the enemies mentioned in verse 5, are the underlying reality. (steps 3, f, 5)

(13) The piel of נחם (v. 4), when used with a human object, means "comfort, console." But here, within the metaphorical framework, it refers to the way in which a shepherd uses his implements to assure the sheep of his presence and calm their nerves. The underlying reality is the emotional stability God provides the psalmist during life-threatening situations. (steps 3, f, 5)

(14) The imperfect in verse 5a carries on the habitual present nuance of the earlier imperfect forms. However, in verse 5b the psalmist

switches to a perfect (דִּשַּׁנְתָּ), which may have a characteristic present force. But then again the perfect is conspicuous here and may be present perfect in sense, indicating that the divine host typically pours oil on his head prior to seating him at the banquet table. (step 3, e)

(15) The verb דִּשֵּׁן (the piel is factitive) (v. 5) is often translated "anoint," but this is misleading, for it might suggest a symbolic act of initiation into royal status. One would expect the verb מָשַׁח in this case; דִּשֵּׁן here describes an act of hospitality extended to guests and carries the nuance "refresh" (see K–B, 234). In Proverbs 15:30 it stands parallel to "make happy" and refers to the effect that good news has on the inner being of its recipient. (step 3, e–f)

(16) The rare noun רְוָיָה (v. 5) is derived from the well-attested verb רָוָה, "be saturated, drink one's fill." In this context, where it describes a cup, it must mean "filled up." (step 3, f)

(17) In verse 5 the metaphor switches. (It would be very odd for a sheep to have its head anointed and be served wine.) The background for the imagery is probably the royal banquet. Ancient Near Eastern texts describe such banquets in terms similar to those employed by the psalmist.[8] The reality behind the imagery is the Lord's favor. Through his blessings and protection he demonstrates to everyone, including dangerous enemies, that the psalmist has a special relationship to him. (step 5)

(18) The noun חֶסֶד (v. 6) has been the subject of several monographs. Gordon Clark concludes that חֶסֶד "is not merely an attitude or an emotion; it is an emotion that leads to an activity beneficial to the recipient." He explains that an act of חֶסֶד is "a benificent action performed, in the context of a deep and enduring commitment between two persons or parties, by one who is able to render assistance to the needy party who in the circumstances is unable to help him- or herself."[9] K–B (336–37) defines the word as "loyalty," or "faithfulness." Other appropriate glosses might be "commitment" and "devotion." (step 3, f)

(19) As we pointed out in chapter 4, the use of רָדַף, "pursue, chase" (v. 6), with טוֹב וָחֶסֶד as subject is ironic. This is the only place in the entire Old Testament where either of these nouns appears as the subject of this verb רָדַף, "pursue." This verb is often used to describe the hostile actions of enemies. One might expect the psalmists' enemies (cf. v. 5) to chase him, but ironically God's "goodness and faithfulness" (which are personified and stand by metonymy for God himself) pursue him instead. The

8. See Michael L. Barré and John S. Kselman, "New Exodus, Covenant, and Restoration in Psalm 23," in *The Word of the Lord Shall Go Forth: Essays in Honor of David Noel Freedman*, ed. Carol F. Meyers and M. O'Connor (Winona Lake, Ind.: Eisenbrauns, 1983), 104–5.

9. Gordon R. Clark, *The Word* Hesed *in the Hebrew Bible* (Sheffield: Sheffield Academic Press, 1993), 267.

word "pursue" is used outside of its normal context in an ironic manner and creates a unique, but pleasant word picture of God's favor (or a kind God) "chasing down" the one whom he loves. (step 5)

(20) The verb form וְשַׁבְתִּי (v. 6) is a qal perfect (with waw-consecutive), 1cs, from שׁוּב, "return," and should be translated, "and I will return." But this makes no sense when construed with the following phrase, "in the house of the Lord." שׁוּב appears only here with the following phrase בְּבֵית. The form should be emended to וְשִׁבְתִּי (an infinitive construct from יָשַׁב, "live," with pronominal suffix) or to וְיָשַׁבְתִּי (a qal perfect with waw consecutive, 1cs, from יָשַׁב) (see BHS note "c"). In either case one could then translate, "and I will live (in the house of the Lord)." The phrase "in the house" frequently follows the verb יָשַׁב in the Old Testament. (step 3, h)

(21) The phrase "house of the Lord" may be purely metaphorical here, referring to the royal palace where the royal host of verse 5 holds his banquet and lives. If one takes the phrase more literally, it would refer to the earthly tabernacle (if one accepts Davidic authorship) or the temple (see Judg. 19:18; 1 Sam. 1:7, 24; 2 Sam. 12:20; 1 Kings 7:12, 40, 45, 51). (step 3, f)

(22) The final phrase, אֹרֶךְ יָמִים, "length of days" (v. 6), is often translated "forever." However, this phrase, when used elsewhere of men, usually refers to a lengthy period of time, such as one's lifetime, and does not mean "forever." (See K–B, 88, and Deut. 30:20; Job 12:12; Ps. 91:16; Prov. 3:2, 16; Lam. 5:20.).[10] Furthermore, the parallel phrase "all the days of my life" suggests this more limited meaning. (step 3, f)

Step 6

In the first part of the psalm (vv. 1–4), the psalmist confidently affirms that the Lord is his shepherd. Like a shepherd, the Lord provides for his needs and protects him from disaster, ultimately because his own divine reputation is at stake. The second part of the psalm (vv. 5–6) develops the theme of protection as well, but here the psalmist also emphasizes the Lord's favor and access to the divine presence. One could summarize the main theme of the psalm as follows: The Lord is a faithful guardian of his people, who provides for their needs, protects them from enemies, grants them his favor, and allows them access to his presence.

Step 7

The Psalter depicts the Lord as the sovereign king of the universe. The author of Psalm 23 describes how this great king protects his people be-

---

10. Ps. 21:4, where the phrase is followed by "forever and ever," may be an exception, though the juxtaposition of the phrases may be an example of intensification, where the second phrase goes beyond the limits of the first, rather than synonymity. Even if one takes both expressions as referring to eternal life, the language is part of the king's hyperbolic description of the Lord's blessings and should not be taken literally.

cause of his allegiance to them and his concern for maintaining his reputation as a faithful guardian. The struggle between God's people and their enemies is a prominent theme in the psalms and a major concern of the psalmists, but the author of Psalm 23 is confident that the king insulates his own from disaster and ruin.

9 Making It Contemporary

Crossing the Bridge from Exegesis to Exposition

The preceding chapters outline an exegetical process designed to unearth the meaning of the text in its original literary context. But the urgency of modern ministry demands that we not remain standing in the soil of antiquity. We do not have the luxury of being mere linguists, historians, and literary critics. God's word is relevant for God's people in all ages. Our responsibility is to make the ancient text come alive, so that it can impact the thinking and behavior of people living, struggling, suffering, and dying in the here and now.

It is relatively easy to teach or preach from the New Testament epistles. After all, they are addressed to Christians, and their hortatory style and didactic nature make their relevance rather obvious and facilitate practical application for a modern audience. However, when one turns to the Old Testament, one confronts a much greater challenge. These ancient texts are not addressed to Christians, nor do they pertain directly to the New Testament church. Even when a passage is hortatory (as in the prophets), hymnic (as in many of the psalms), or didactic (as in the wisdom literature), it has an ancient Israelite aura about it that tends to cloud its modern relevance. The narratives of the Old Testament seem even more obscure. While these stories are usually exciting and even humorous to read, a relevant message for a modern audience living in a far different culture does not readily emerge from their ancient soil.

So how do we go about accomplishing the task? This chapter discusses how to develop an exposition of an Old Testament text that is rooted in its original meaning but is also timely, hard-hitting, and relevant. As I have done throughout the book, I will mix a relatively brief discussion of theory with a sizable dose of illustrations. Let's begin with narrative, and then move on to the poetic genre.

Exposition of Narrative

Let the Story Impose Its Will on You, Not Vice-Versa

Preachers often use Old Testament stories simply for their illustrative value. In this approach a preacher bases the message on another passage (usually from the New Testament) and then utilizes an Old Testament story, or a character or an incident from a story, to illustrate the lesson being taught. This is certainly valid, for New Testament authors frequently utilize Old Testament stories for illustrative purposes. For example, Hebrews 11 includes a lengthy list of Old Testament characters whose experiences illustrate what faith in God can accomplish.

However, just because a story can be used to illustrate a principle does not mean that the primary or even secondary intent of the story, in its original literary context, is to teach that truth. For example, the author of Hebrews includes among his examples of faith Gideon, Barak, Samson, and Jephthah (11:32). All four possessed a measure of faith and won great victories over Israel's enemies. They are apt examples of the principle the author develops in Hebrews 11. However, is this the same principle that the author of Judges is developing in Judges 4–16? Hardly! The author of Judges traces the decline of Israelite leadership. Starting with an ideal, represented by Joshua, Caleb, Othniel, and Ehud, he shows how subsequent Israelite leaders lacked the wisdom and faith necessary to carry on this leadership standard. This steady decline parallels the overall moral decline in Israel and culminates in societal disintegration and chaos. In their original literary context, Gideon, Barak, Samson, and Jephthah are prime illustrations of what was wrong with Israel, not paradigms of faith! Yes, they had a degree of faith, but not the quality of faith that makes an effective leader.[1]

When one makes an Old Testament story the base text for a message, the theme of the message should derive from that text, not somewhere else. Though purporting to explain what an Old Testament story means, a preacher will sometimes ignore the point of the story in its original literary setting and instead impose an entirely different theme upon it. Here's how it often happens. A preacher wants to preach from the Old Testament. He doesn't take the time to determine what the story is saying in its original context, or, having determined what it meant back then, he decides that message is irrelevant for today. However, the story does illustrate a biblical theme found elsewhere. Rather than choosing that other passage as his target text and using the Old Testament to illustrate

---

1. See my article, "The Role of Women in the Rhetorical Strategy of the Book of Judges," in *Integrity of Heart, Skillfulness of Hands: Biblical and Leadership Studies in Honor of Donald K. Campbell*, ed. Charles H. Dyer and Roy B. Zuck (Grand Rapids: Baker, 1994), 34–49.

the theme, our hypothetical preacher pulls a sleight of hand trick, imposes a foreign theme on the text, and gives the impression that the original author intended to teach this lesson. Of course, such sermons, since they find their inspiration in a biblical text, often challenge an audience. But they are not truly biblical, for they do not convey the point God was and is trying to make through the story. We could say about such a message, "Good point, wrong text!"

For example, I once heard a preacher present the story of David and Jonathan as if the author of Samuel actually wanted to teach us what true friendship entails. If one wants to use this story to illustrate some principles about friendship, fine. But the target text should come from somewhere else, perhaps Proverbs 17:17 or 18:24. In its literary context the account of David's friendship with Jonathan is not designed to teach principles about friendship. Throughout this section of 1–2 Samuel the author validates David as God's chosen king and demonstrates that Saul has been rejected by God. Even Saul's own son recognizes what God is doing, but not Saul! Jonathan appears as a foil for Saul. Because of his pride and lust for power, Saul resists God's program and tries to kill God's chosen king. In contrast to this, Jonathan, who stood in line to inherit his father's throne and could have joined him in his quest to kill David, acknowledges God's choice of David and demonstrates that his allegiance to David (and to God!) is stronger than any personal ambition he might have. If the author intends for his audience to emulate Jonathan in some way, perhaps the point is this: One must fully support God's program, rather than allowing pride and personal ambition to stand in the way of and impede what God is trying to accomplish. This was a very relevant message for Israel (especially the tribe of Benjamin) in the aftermath of David's rise to kingship that finds expression in the New Testament and remains a timely principle for today as well.

As I have described how some abuse narrative texts, did I step on some toes or hit a little too close to home? Were you inclined to say, "Been there, done that!" I'll be honest with you—we all have at one time or another. But to be true to the original author's intention, we must resist the temptation to make the story say something it wasn't designed to teach. To be truly biblical we need to be faithful to the text's literary context.

Developing a Principle and Application

How do we make sure we do so? It begins with solid exegesis, including analysis of the text's historical-cultural background and its literary dimension (see steps 1–5 in the method outlined in chapter 8). From one's exegetical study the text's primary theme(s) in its original context should emerge (see steps 6–7 in the method outlined in chapter 8). One can then transform the main theme into a general theological principle that would be true now, as well as then. The next step is to derive from this principle an applicational point which stresses how we should think and/ or act.

For example, let's consider Ehud's story. In the preceding chapter we summarized the general theological principle of the Ehud story in its larger literary context as follows: "The Lord uses men of faith and initiative to accomplish great things for his people." But stating the principle is not enough. We should also produce an applicational idea that deals with thought and/or behavior. For the Ehud story, such an applicational idea might be stated: "We should exercise faith and initiative, for when we do, God can accomplish great things for his people through us." Of course in developing this into a sermon for a modern audience, one would have to broaden the principle to include women (even Judges does this, see Judg. 4–5), explain what faith and initiative might look like today (these characteristics are no longer demonstrated by assassinating oppressive rulers!), and give illustrations of what God is accomplishing today through such people (today's battles are spiritual, not physical).

Multiple Perspectives in Old Testament Narrative

Sometimes it is difficult, and even artificial, to reduce a story to a single principle. One can often read Old Testament narratives from different perspectives. These perspectives, rather than being contradictory, actually complement one another and contribute to the narrative's overall message. For example, from one perspective Samson's story is a great tragedy. With Samson's death in the rubble of the Philistine temple, the decline in Israelite leadership which began with Barak is complete. Deficient faith and lack of wisdom culminate in spiritual ignorance and utter folly and usher in a period of chaos characterized by a leadership void. In many respects Samson represents Israel. Despite his miraculous beginning and tremendous God-given potential, he misses his calling to be God's consecrated servant and instead succumbs to the allurements of a temptress. He becomes a humiliated prisoner on foreign soil, but in the end is vindicated by God when he desperately begs for divine intervention.

But Samson's story can also be viewed as a great testimony to the providence of God, who begins delivering his people, even when they do not ask to be delivered, through a deliverer whose divinely ordained role is never recognized by his parents, Israel, or even himself. However, in approaching the story in this more positive way, it is important to note that the truth of God's sovereignty does not absolve people from seeking his will and striving to be holy. Later generations can take great comfort in the Samson story as they see God's relentless commitment to his people and his providential working. But remember that the participants in the story—Israel and Samson—did not experience the full benefit of God's intervention. God is always at work, accomplishing great things for his people, but his people only experience the full benefits of his providence if they are actively seeking him.

Starting with the Big Picture

In contrast to the relatively short story of Ehud's revolt, Samson's tragic story contains several episodes. When working with longer stories like this, you should begin with an exposition of the whole story. Then in separate sermons you can go back and develop the individual episodes in more detail and relate the subthemes to the overall theme. Think of the biblical stories as being similar to a modern movie. When you watch a movie, you don't pause the VCR at the end of every scene and ask, "Now what is the significance of that scene? How can we apply that to our lives?" Those questions are meaningless until one has seen the whole movie. However, once the whole movie has been viewed and analyzed, you can then watch it again and appreciate more fully how each scene contributes to the whole. The same is true for biblical stories. Those who preach a story episode by episode without a sense of the whole usually miss the point of the episodes and the story. A sermon that gives an overview of the story and its main theme(s) should precede sermons that focus on individual scenes.

Let's use the Book of Ruth as an example. An exegetical and literary study of the Book of Ruth in its historical and literary context reveals two closely related theological principles, reflecting the book's dual focus on Naomi and Ruth (see our discussion of characterization in Ruth in chapter 7). If we focus on Naomi's experience, this principle emerges: "God cares for his needy people; he is their ally in this chaotic world." If we focus on Ruth, this principle is apparent: "God richly rewards people who demonstrate sacrificial love and in so doing become his instruments in helping the needy." To highlight their modern relevance for sermonic purposes, we should transform these principles into applicational statements: (1) "When we suffer in this chaotic world, we can take comfort in the reality that God is our ally." (2) "We should love those in need, for God meets their needs through us and richly rewards our efforts." We could preach two separate introductory sermons on the book or merge these applicational statements into one. Either way we should begin our exposition of the book with a sermon (or two) that presents the overall message and point(s) of the book.

Having done that, we can now delve more deeply into the individual episodes and develop certain facets and subthemes of the story in detail. For example, we could do at least three more expositions from Ruth:

225

Ruth 1

In this chapter we see a glowing example of sacrificial love at work. Against the dark moral and ethical backdrop of the Judges period, the foreigner Ruth emerges as a paradigm of loyal love and of the kind of person the Lord is looking for to populate his covenant community. Though Ruth could have taken her blessing for good deeds rendered (v. 8) and gone back to the security of her own home and people, she trades in her blessing for a potential curse and attaches herself by oath (vv. 16–17) to a woman who views herself as a special object of divine wrath (v. 20) and has no appreciation at all for Ruth's devotion (v. 21; note especially, "the LORD has brought me back empty").

Principle: Genuine love is risky and sacrificial.

Applicational idea: In contrast to the paganism all around us, we should demonstrate genuine love by taking risks and placing the needs of others above our own.

Ruth 2:1–4:10

On the surface Ruth's love for Naomi does not seem to be able to accomplish much of tangible value; after all Ruth is a widow and a resident alien—not exactly a position brimming with power and leverage in the socioeconomic context of ancient Israel. But God takes her love, providentially guides her steps, and brings renewed fertility and life where there seemed to be only barrenness and death.

Principle: Our sovereign God is active in the lives of those who demonstrate genuine love for others.

Applicational idea: We can be confident that our sovereign God will use our expressions of genuine love to meet needs as he providentially guides our footsteps.

Ruth 4:11–22

Throughout the book individuals offer prayers of blessing on behalf of those who perform worthy deeds. That pattern continues here, as observers ask for divine blessing on Boaz and Ruth. The book's conclusion explains how God answered those prayers in an especially marvelous way.

Principle: God's rewards for those who sacrificially love others sometimes exceed their wildest imagination and transcend their lifetime.

Applicational idea: We can be confident that God will richly reward our sacrificial love for others, sometimes in ways we may not have anticipated and in ways we may only fully appreciate in retrospect.

Retelling the Story

What format should a sermon on a narrative text follow? In my fairly extensive experience of preaching Old Testament narrative texts, I have found that the best way to develop a biblical story sermonically is to re-tell the story. I am not talking about a dry restating of the events and facts. That would bore everyone to death, especially those who are already familiar with the story. I am talking about a lively, insightful, contemporized retelling of the story that is sensitive to its historical and cultural background, brings out its literary qualities, highlights its inner connections, and develops its theme. When a story is retold well, those who are unfamiliar with it should find it fascinating, and even those who think they know it well will probably gain a new appreciation for it.

Sample Expositions of Narrative Texts

Since a picture is better than a thousand words, I have included below four expositions of narrative texts. The first two expositions (on Exod. 3 and Judg. 13–16, respectively) are more sermonic than didactic in form, so the exegetical work that undergirds the exposition may not be as "visible" as it would be in a lesson prepared for a Sunday school class or Bible study. Though exegesis must undergird a sermon in order to give it credibility, time limitations prevent the preacher from presenting the results of that exegesis as extensively as one would do in a lesson.

The third exposition (on Gen. 25–35) gives an overview of Jacob's story. If one were doing a series on Genesis, this message would be foundational for other, more focused messages on individual episodes. Because the exposition covers such a large literary unit, it only hits the highlights and certain key verses.

The fourth exposition (on Judg. 9) is more didactic, illustrating what a manuscript for a Sunday school lesson or Bible study might look like. In this exposition the exegesis is more visible and illustrations and more pointed applications are kept to a minimum. The format is more like a lecture, but, even so, the exposition identifies overall principles and applications in its conclusion.

(1) Moses and Yahweh Meet for the First Time (Exod. 3:1–20)[2]

Pharaoh Don't Know Diddly!

During the summers of 1952 and 1953 sportswriter Roger Kahn covered the Brooklyn Dodgers baseball team for the *New York Herald Tribune*. Day after day he rubbed shoulders with the players and got to know them all quite well. Fifteen years later he decided to track them down and see how the years had treated them. He set out with notebook and tape re-

---

2. I wrote this sermon about five years ago, when the "Bo Knows" Nike commercials were the TV rage. If you don't remember those, you must have been on another planet and won't appreciate the title of the message or the analogy between Amenhotep and Bo Jackson. Though it is now a bit dated, I kept this material in this exposition to illustrate how to "contemporize" historical background material so that it is both informative and engaging.

corder and traveled all over the country in search of a group of men he affectionately called "the Boys of Summer." What he found was staggering and when he put his findings into book form it became a national best seller. Kahn's Boys of Summer, once robust and full of youthful vigor, had, almost to a man, experienced the ravages of time and encountered personal tragedy.

In some ways the saddest of Kahn's case studies was Billy Cox, the third baseman on those great Dodger teams. In his day Billy Cox was the finest defensive third baseman in the game; he possessed almost super human eye–hand coordination and reflexes. Game after game he would dive through the air, spear a line drive, and hear the roar of thousands of fans. To find Billy Cox, Kahn had to drive out into rural Pennsylvania to the little town of Newport. When he inquired about Billy's whereabouts he discovered that Billy had recently changed jobs from bartender at the American Legion to bartender at the Owls Club. When Kahn finally found Billy, Billy suggested they go to the VFW bar to talk. It seemed as if Billy spent most of his waking hours in bars. No longer was Billy the slim athlete of 1953, and half of the middle finger on his throwing hand was missing. As the two of them sat in the bar, strange scenes began to unfold. Some nearby patrons of the bar began using crass terms to describe African Americans. An enraged woman came storming into the bar, started hitting a man on the head with a purse, and shouted, "I know about the redhead." Cox got up and began to hit a few billiard balls at a nearby pool table, muttering to himself things like, "Get the [bleep] down." Kahn records his thoughts at that moment: "No one present, I thought, except myself . . . could have realized that this broad-shouldered, horse-faced fellow tapping billiard balls, missing half a finger on one hand, sad-eyed, among people who would never be more than strangers, was the most glorious glove on the most glorious team that ever played baseball in the sunlight of Brooklyn."[3] Billy Cox had become a classic example of a has-been. The glory days he had experienced were so far in the past he must have wondered sometimes if they had ever really happened at all.

That's kind of the way it was with Moses. Many years before he had lived in a king's palace in Egypt. However, the day came when he had to flee into the desert for his life, leaving behind the glory and riches of Egypt. For many long years he lived out in a desert on the back side of the world, working as a shepherd for a Midianite priest named Jethro.

But then a strange thing happened. We read about it in Exodus 3. Put yourself in Moses' sandals for a moment.[4] You're tending your flock near a mountain called Horeb. Suddenly you see a strange sight—a burning

---

3. Roger Kahn, *The Boys of Summer* (New York: The New American Library, 1973), 382.

4. The author uses הִנֵּה in v. 2b, inviting us to view the sight of the burning bush through Moses' eyes.

bush, which, despite being enveloped by flames, is not consumed. This sight caught Moses' attention; as he moved closer, he heard a voice declaring, "Moses! Moses!" He replied, "I'm here." The voice continued: "Don't come any closer. Take off your sandals, for you are standing on holy ground. I am the God of your father, the God of Abraham, the God of Isaac and the God of Jacob." At this point Moses covered his face, for he knew viewing God can be dangerous to one's health. The Lord continued: "I have indeed seen how my people are suffering in Egypt. I have heard them crying out because of what their slave drivers do to them. I am certainly aware of the pain they're experiencing. So I have come down to rescue them from the power of the Egyptians and to lead them up out of that land to a good, wide land. . . . So now, go. I am sending you to Pharaoh to bring my people the Israelites out of Egypt" (cf. Exod. 3:1–10).

Now be honest; if you were Moses, what would you say at this point? Moses' response seems quite appropriate. He said: "Who am I, that I should go to Pharaoh and bring the Israelites out of Egypt?" (Exod. 3:11). Good question, Moses! Let's face it, on the surface this command seems preposterous and even downright ludicrous. How in the world can a lowly shepherd, a has-been, a nobody, deliver an entire nation from Pharaoh, the most powerful ruler on the face of the earth? To really appreciate the apparent absurdity of this, we need to look more closely at Moses and at Pharaoh.

In the ensuing dialogue between God and Moses, recorded in Exodus 3–4, Moses emerges as a pathetic character whose self-confidence is shot and whose self-image is nonexistent. After offering a series of objections to God's commission, he finally admits: "O Lord, I have never been eloquent, neither in the past nor during this conversation with your servant. I'm not articulate" (lit., "I am heavy of mouth and heavy of tongue," Exod. 4:10). When God counters, Moses begs God to send someone else: "O Lord, please send someone else" (Exod. 4:13). Moses is an extremely unlikely candidate for the task of delivering Israel from Egypt.

When we take a closer look at Pharaoh, God's proposal looks even more ridiculous. As you may know, biblical historians argue about the precise date of Israel's Exodus from Egypt. I personally agree with the many evangelical scholars who date the Exodus around the year 1446 B.C. If this dating scheme is correct, the Pharaoh at this time was Amenhotep II.[5] Amenhotep ruled over a land with a longstanding tradition of greatness. Amenhotep had already demonstrated his prowess as a warrior by conducting one, maybe two, successful military expeditions. He had been groomed from birth to one day rule Egypt and lead its armies. Among other things, he was trained in horsemanship, ar-

---

5. See Eugene H. Merrill, *Kingdom of Priests: A History of Old Testament Israel* (Grand Rapids: Baker, 1987), 63.

chery, and rowing. An Egyptian inscription from the time of Amenhotep describes the king as follows:

> Now then his majesty appeared as king, as a beautiful youth who was well developed and had completed eighteen years upon his thighs in strength. He was one who knew all the works of Mont; he had no equal on the field of battle. He was one who knew horses; there was not his like in this numerous army. Not one among them could draw his bow; he could not be approached in running.
>
> Strong of arms, untiring when he took the oar, he rowed at the stern of his falcon-boat as the stroke-oar for two hundred men. Pausing after they had rowed half a mile, they were weak, limp in body, and breathless, while his majesty was strong under his oar of twenty cubits in length. He stopped and landed his falcon-boat only after he had done three miles of rowing without interrupting his stroke. Faces shone as they saw him do this.
>
> He drew three hundred strong bows, comparing the workmanship of the men who had crafted them, so as to tell the unskilled from the skilled. He also came to do the following which is brought to your attention. Entering his northern garden, he found erected for him four targets of Asiatic copper, of one palm in thickness, with a distance of twenty cubits between one post and the next. Then his majesty appeared on the chariot like Mont in his might. He drew his bow while holding four arrows together in his fist. Thus he rode northward shooting at them, like Mont in his panoply, each arrow coming out at the back of its target while he attacked the next post. It was a deed never yet done, never yet heard reported: shooting an arrow at a target of copper, so that it came out of it and dropped to the ground—(done) only by the King rich in glory, whom Amun made strong, the King of Upper and Lower Egypt, Aakheprure, a fighter like Mont.[6]

Amenhotep's father, Thutmose III, had this to say about his son: "He will make a ruler of the whole land whom no one can attack. . . . It is the god who inspires him to act, so as to become the protector of Egypt, the ruler of the land."[7]

Certainly these descriptions of Amenhotep and his exploits are exaggerated, but, as one Egyptologist observes, "the claims of royal prowess have a basis in fact, for several other monuments of this king extol him as sportsman, and his mummy is that of an exceptionally tall and strongly built man."[8]

Amenhotep II was the Bo Jackson of ancient Egypt. I can see it now—the Nike marketing department enters a time tunnel along with a few other folks. As they're swept back into ancient Egypt, they devise this commercial. We see Amenhotep riding a horse, and then the camera

---

6. See Miriam Lichtheim, *Ancient Egyptian Literature* (Berkeley: University of California Press, 1974), 2:41–42.

7. Ibid., 2:42.

8. Ibid., 2:39.

pans to Prince Charles sitting on his polo horse. Charles says: "Amenho knows horses." We then see Amenhotep running swiftly, and Carl Lewis appears and says: "Amenho knows running." The scene shifts to the archery range where Kevin Costner, dressed as Robin Hood, declares: "Amenho knows the bow and arrow." Finally we see Amenhotep rowing a boat in the Nile, and the crew team from one of our Ivy League schools appears and says, "Amenho knows how to row."

On the surface inarticulate, aged, seemingly washed up Moses from just east of nowhere land versus athletic, proud Amenhotep, warrior-king of the greatest nation on earth, looks like one of the greatest mismatches in history.

And it was. Amenhotep never stood a chance! That's right, Amenhotep never stood a chance. This ancient Egyptian Nike commercial is going to end with God (minus the guitar and backup band!) saying: "Amenho may know horses, Amenho may know running, Amenho may know the bow and arrow, and Amenho may know how to row, but as far as I'm concerned, Amenho don't know diddly." You see, there is a very important element which we've been leaving out. Moses is not going down to Egypt alone. In Exodus 3:12 God says to Moses, "I will be with you," and God's presence is going to make all the difference. In fact, we should have already picked up on this, for in verse 8 the Lord said, "I have come down to rescue them."

After assuring Moses of his presence, God tried to encourage him and challenge his faith at the same time. He says: "This will be the confirming sign that I have sent you: When you lead the people out of Egypt, you all (the verb is plural in the Hebrew) will worship God on this very mountain" (Exod. 3:12b). God offered Moses a confirming sign, but this sign is not something miraculous that generates faith right there on the spot. God simply assumed Moses would accomplish his mission and lead the people to this mountain; at that point Moses would remember this conversation and realize God was with him.

Without commenting on this promise of a future sign, Moses anticipates a problem. When the Israelites ask for the name of the God who sent him, what should he say? (see Exod. 3:13).

God takes this opportunity to once again emphasize that he will be with Moses (see Exod. 3:14–15). God gives Himself a new name, "I AM" (or, in its third person form, Yahweh = "He Is"). But what is the point of this name "I AM/He Is"? Is God emphasizing that he is the eternally existing one? That's probably not the point in this context, where God draws special attention to his active presence and willingness to help his people. God is "I AM" in the sense that he is the ever-present one who is ready and willing to help his needy people. Here's my paraphrase of verses 14–15: "Call me 'I Am The Ever Present Helper,' because I am indeed the ever present helper. Tell the Israelites, 'I Am The Ever Present Helper' sent me to you . . . Tell the Israelites, 'He Who Is The Ever Present Helper,' the God of your ancestors—the God of Abraham, the God of Isaac and the God of Jacob sent me to you. This will be my permanent name; this is how I will be known to future generations."

But what's the big deal about having Yahweh, "He Who Is The Ever Present Helper," with you? The immediate context tells us why that's important.

(1) First of all, this Yahweh, "He Who Is The Ever Present Helper," is the *faithful* God of the patriarchs. Four times in chapters 3–4 (cf. 3:6, 15–16; 4:5) the Lord identifies himself as the "God of Abraham, Isaac, and Jacob." He is not an unknown God—he already has a track record. He was present with the ancestors of Moses and Israel, revealing himself in tangible ways, directing their paths, and, most important, promising them great blessings. As verse 17 mentions, he promised the patriarchs a land of their own; now he comes to the patriarchs' descendants ready to fulfill that promise and prove that he is a faithful God.

(2) Second, this Yahweh is also a *compassionate* God who is moved by his people's suffering (recall 3:7–8a) and watches with great interest what is being done to them in Egypt (see 3:16).

(3) Last, but not least, this Yahweh is the incomparably *powerful* God who is capable of performing supernatural deeds. As verses 18–19 indicate, he intends to incite a conflict with Pharaoh by suggesting that he, not Pharaoh, has ultimate authority over the Hebrews. When Pharaoh refuses to comply with Yahweh's request to let his people worship him, he will forcefully intervene. In verse 20 he announces: "I will stretch out my hand and strike down the Egyptians through all the mighty acts I will perform among them. Then he will send you away!"

So you see, Moses versus Amenhotep really was a mismatch. Amenhotep didn't have a chance in the world because Moses was not alone. Amenhotep would really be fighting Moses' traveling companion, Yahweh, "The Ever Present Helper," Yahweh the faithful God who makes and fulfills promises, Yahweh the compassionate God who takes notice of his needy people, Yahweh the almighty God who exercises his incomparable power on their behalf.

From this dialogue between Yahweh and Moses, a theological principle emerges: God is present with his people when he sends them on a mission. This means that God's people, when called to carry out a difficult assignment, should tackle the challenge with confidence, knowing that God's presence makes success certain.

Maybe you're thinking at this point—that's all very inspiring, but how does all this relate to me? I don't have a special commission from God, nor do I, like Moses, have a special staff that turns into a snake. God isn't going to do any miracles through me, I assure you that.

But wait a minute—the followers of Christ in the present age do have a special commission from God to go out into the world and make disciples by evangelizing the lost and then teaching them to obey the commands of Jesus (cf. Matt. 28:18–20a). If we have decided to accept Jesus' offer of salvation and become his followers, then we have the responsibility to carry out his wishes. He has commissioned us to make disciples. That involves evangelism, but also includes helping others to progress as disciples until they become mature believers.

There are three major hurdles that we face in carrying out this commission. The first is our complacency and self-centered approach to life. We'd rather just stay in our own little world and enjoy ourselves. We don't like to venture out of our comfort zones. But if we're going to follow Jesus, that option is not available to us. We have to accept the challenge and go.

The second obstacle, once we face up to the challenge, is fear. Maybe your specific assignment is to carry the message into your campus or workplace. No matter what the specific circumstances might be, the obstacles are seemingly insurmountable and the prospects kind of frightening. In some ways this commission is more challenging than that of Moses. That's why God doesn't leave us on our own. The Gospel of Matthew closes with these words from Jesus: "And surely I am with you always, to the very end of the age." Jesus' presence is absolutely essential because two verses earlier he informs us that "all authority in heaven and on earth has been given to" him.

As we go out to fulfill this commission, we need Jesus' authoritative presence. We're going out into a hostile world where there is an all-out war going on between God and the forces of darkness. And we're being sent into the very heart of the battle. The enemy looks at us and he's not very impressed—in his opinion we're as pitiful as dusty, heavy-tongued Moses. But begrudgingly the enemy has come to the point where he is impressed with King Jesus, who sits at the right hand of the Father and possesses all authority in heaven and on earth, because the enemy knows that authority and power are the name of the game in the cosmic war.

In the summer of 1745 Charles Edward Stuart landed in the western Highlands of Scotland. Though he had only a handful of followers, he came with a big vision. Charles's goal was to restore the Stuart dynasty to its rightful place on the combined thrones of England and Scotland. Fifty-seven years before his grandfather James VII (of Scotland) and II (of England) had been forced to abdicate and for many years Charles's father, James VIII and III, had been living in exile. Now Charles, the young, handsome crown prince, had arrived to restore the family's honor and royal position. Charles had a well-defined strategy. He would rally the loyal Highland clans, who would provide a formidable core for his army. Over the past one hundred years these Highland warriors had been very successful in battle, as they charged headlong into the enemy lines with their wild pipe tunes skirling and their broadswords flashing. Charles would march victoriously through the lowlands and on into England. The people would celebrate his arrival and rejoice in the return of their divinely ordained monarchy, the Stuart dynasty. Seeing this groundswell of support, the French would invade England from the south and help Charles take London.

At first everything proceeded according to plan. Many clansmen rallied to his standard at Glenfinnan and they marched virtually unopposed into Edinburgh, where Charles declared his father James the rightful ruler of Scotland. At Prestonpans his Highlanders in a matter of minutes literally dismembered a government army with their broadswords, leaving the bloody turf littered with the heads and limbs of horses and men. On into England they marched, but the expected support did not come. The great majority of the people no longer recognized the authority of the Stuarts. Three government armies blocked the way to London. Outnumbered by 6 to 1, disillusioned Charles and his loyal Highlanders were forced to retreat into northern Scotland, a government army at their heels.

Finally on a raw, icy day in April 1746 Charles and his hungry, weary, half-naked, ill-equipped army stood on Culloden Moor, face-to-face with a very well equipped government army that had learned the secret of stopping the broadsword charge—well-aimed, continuous artillery fire. The cannons opened fire, first with grapeshot, then the cannon balls. The restless Highlanders charged but they were cut to shreds by the artillery and musket fire. Charles's big vision had turned into a horrible nightmare. He had a strategy, his men had skill and determination, but he lacked what he really needed—royal authority and the power that goes with it.

Without Jesus' authority we'd be as doomed as Charles was. But Jesus has given us his authority and, consequently, we can enter into the conflict with confidence.

Once we step out of our self-centered little world and then overcome our fear by focusing on the authority that we possess because of our relationship to Jesus, there's still a third obstacle. Once we face up to the challenge and start to fulfill our commission, there's a tendency, especially if we experience some success, to become self-sufficient. There are many who will tell you that the key to success is your vision, or your intellect and formal training, or your skills and strategies. But if you begin to trust in your abilities, you may be in for a rude awakening. As we learn from the life of Jacob, God has a way of taking proud, self-sufficient people down and reminding them of who's really in control. Ministry is a war zone. Without God's authority and power, you're a goner. Out beyond the doors of your cozy little corner of the world is the cold, cruel cosmos and an enemy who is ready to aim his big guns at you and cut you to bits. Your only hope is Jesus, Son of David, who sits enthroned at the right hand of the Father. King Jesus is building his church, the new covenant community, and he has declared that the power of hell will not prevail against it. The realities of the war demand from us not some arrogant trust in our vision and skills, but rather utter, humble, day-to-day dependence on the authority and enabling presence of King Jesus, who after all is Yahweh, the God of Moses, the ever-present helper who is faithful, compassionate, and so powerful that he can spit in the enemy's eye and say, "Just try to stop me."

(2) The Rise and Fall of Samson (Judges 13–16)

Lion Killer with a Sweet Tooth

Let's play word association! When I say the name "Samson," what word or phrase comes to your mind? Many will say "Delilah," the Bible's most famous temptress and Samson's last lover. Others will say "long hair" or "super strong." When I think of Samson, the name Jethro Bodeen comes to mind. You recall Jethro, one of the main characters on the "Beverly Hillbillies," who, much like Samson, was a big strong babe hound who obviously got trapped at the end of the line the day the brains were handed out.

The story of Samson is one of the Bible's most famous. Most of us are familiar with its main contours and details. It begins with great promise. An angel tells a barren woman she will have a son who will be a special servant of God. She names him Samson, meaning "sun-like," or "solar-like," suggesting brightness and joy. It ends on a tragic note, as Samson is blinded and perishes in darkness with a death wish on his lips in the rubble of a Philistine temple. Along the way there's all kinds of excitement, including a fight with a lion and several bouts between Samson and the hated Philistines. Then, of course, there's the Delilah affair, which robs Samson of his strength, his eyesight, his dignity, and eventually his life. But beyond the details, what's the story really all about? How do the details fit together to form a theme? Why did God include this story in the Bible? What are we supposed to learn from it?

Like a lot of biblical stories, Samson's story can be viewed from different perspectives. For example, you can read the story of Samson as a great illustration of God's power and mercy. Through one very imperfect man God begins to deliver his people from the Philistines even when they're not particularly interested in being delivered.

But I want to look at the story as a great tragedy which tells how a man called by God for a very special purpose fails to realize his potential. Samson was a specially endowed servant of God, what they called a Nazirite in ancient Israel. But he never had a clear-cut mission in life. He didn't understand what being a Nazirite really meant for him. Instead of

235

being a great leader with a vision, he brings to a culmination the steady decline in Israelite leadership narrated in the Book of Judges.

Let's take a closer look at the story and then talk about its relevance for us. Samson's story can be divided into four episodes, roughly corresponding to the chapter divisions in Judges 13–16.

Chapter 13 tells of Samson's miraculous birth. We could entitle it, "Miracle Baby," but a better title might be "Does Anybody Here Have a Clue?"

Before we talk about the details of Samson's birth, however, we need to set the stage. Israel has been under the oppressive hand of the cruel Philistines for forty years. Elsewhere in Judges, such oppression prompts Israel to cry out to the Lord for deliverance, but this time we don't read of such a response. Israel didn't like the Philistines, but they were intimidated by them and apparently they had come to the point where they accepted Philistine rule. They didn't seem to care if God delivered them; maybe they thought he couldn't.

But God decides to deliver them anyway, and he decides to do it through one man. He sends an angel to a barren woman, the wife of Manoah (we'll call her Mrs. Manoah), and announces that she is going to have a son (see Judg. 13:3–5). Being barren was considered a curse in this culture, so Mrs. Manoah is understandably excited to discover she is going to be a mother. She rushes to tell her husband what has happened (see Judg. 13:6–7). Now compare her report with what the angel actually said. Do you see any glaring omissions? She focuses on the first part of the angel's message—on what she is supposed to do. In her excitement she doesn't tell Manoah the second part of the angel's message—about why God is making her son a Nazirite. She omits the reference to her son being God's deliverer. It's as if she didn't even hear that part of the angel's message.

No wonder her husband, Manoah, doesn't seem to have a clue about the boy's career. When the angel returns, he asks: "Now, when your announcement comes true, how should the child be raised and what should he do?" (see Judg. 13:12). Oddly enough the angel doesn't answer his question. He says in verse 13: "Your wife should pay careful attention to *everything* (emphasis) that I have said." I think he's telling Manoah that his wife needs to recall all that was said before and that the answer to his question can be found there. Then he simply repeats what Mrs. Manoah focused on—the dietary rules she is to follow. He says nothing about Samson's role as a deliverer. Why he did not repeat all of his earlier message is not clear. He only repeats what she heard and reported; he refuses to repeat what she missed. I guess the lesson here is: When God speaks, listen closely because he may refuse to repeat himself if you ignore a portion of his message. The seeds of confusion have been sown. Mrs. Manoah seems to have ignored her son's real purpose in life, Manoah is left in the dark, and Samson is going to grow up as a Nazirite without a clearly defined mission.

Samson is born, raised as a Nazirite, and in due time God's Spirit comes upon him (see Judg. 13:24–25). That brings us to chapter 14, which we might entitle "A Wedding without a Honeymoon" or "The Foreshadowing of Samson's Fate."

On a visit to the town of Timnah Samson sees a Philistine girl who really catches his eye. When he informs his parents that he intends to marry her, they are disturbed. They say: "Certainly you can find a wife among our relatives or among all our people. You should not have to go and get a wife from the uncircumcised Philistines" (see Judg. 14:3a). We are inclined to agree with them. After all, why can't Samson marry a nice Israelite girl? But Samson persists: "Get her for me, because she's the right one for me!" (see Judg. 14:3b).

Verse 4 then shocks us by notifying us that Samson's desire for the Philistine girl is God's doing! Samson has no clear cut vision of himself as Israel's deliverer, so the Lord is going to have to push him in that direction. He knows what Samson is like, and he also knows that if he can get Samson involved with the Philistines, sparks will fly, Samson will come into conflict with the Philistines, and through that conflict Samson can begin the deliverance of Israel. Why didn't God just come down and commission him, you ask? I don't know. He had expected Samson's parents to instill within him his life's goal, but when they failed to do that, God decides to work more indirectly.

A bit later, on his way to visit this Philistine girl, Samson is attacked by a lion, but the Spirit of the Lord empowers him and he rips the lion in two with his bare hands (see Judg. 14:5b–6a). Still later, as he journeys to Timnah a third time in order to marry the Philistine girl, he stops to take a look at the lion's carcass and he finds some honey inside the dead lion's body. Now a Nazirite is not supposed to touch anything that is dead, but Samson wants some of that tasty, sweet honey. In fact, he may even consider it a good omen on the eve of his wedding, for eating honey is used in the Song of Solomon as a symbol of sexual fulfillment (cf. 4:11; 5:1). Samson can't resist the temptation, so he reaches down, scoops some of the honey into his hands, and eats it.

What is the meaning of all this? How do these events fit into the story? What is their significance? The answer is quite simple—they reveal something about Samson's God-given abilities, his character, and his destiny.

Samson's killing the lion shows what he's capable of accomplishing in God's strength. It also foreshadows his great victory over a Philistine army. Jump ahead to chapter 15 and look at verse 14. The Philistines attack Samson like a lion. Their shouts correspond to the lion's roar. God's Spirit once again rushes on him. Samson supernaturally defeats one thousand Philistines, just as he supernaturally killed the lion. With God on his side, Samson can defeat lions!

What about eating the honey? What's its significance? His eating the honey indicates that he has a tough time controlling his physical desires and lusts. His willingness to eat the honey shows that he considers the satisfaction of his physical desires to be more important than his status as a Nazirite. It also foreshadows his fall, which will come as a result of his unbridled lust for sex. The sweet honey foreshadows the feminine charms of Delilah, who will use her tremendous hold over Samson to bring him down. Samson can resist and defeat lions, but he has trouble with sweet honey. And the rest of the story illustrates this all too well.

Samson arrives in Timnah for his wedding and the weeklong feast begins. Samson decides he can take advantage of the Philistines, so he proposes a wager. If the Philistines can guess a riddle, he will pay them thirty sets of clothes; if they can't, they will pay him thirty sets of clothes. The riddle is a tough one, because it's based on his experience of seeing the honey in the lion's carcass—not something you see every day (see Judg. 14:14). Samson, however, has underestimated the Philistines' cunning and his own weakness with women. The Philistines threaten Samson's bride. If she doesn't get the answer for them, they'll kill her and her family. She sobs and pleads with Samson (note especially v. 16) and he finally gives in, she tells them the answer, they win the bet, Samson angrily leaves the feast, kills thirty Philistines, takes their clothes, returns to pay his debt, and then goes home without consummating his marriage to the girl. God's plan is working to perfection. Samson is developing a hatred for Philistines and further conflict with the Philistines seems to be a very real possibility.

That brings us to chapter 15, the third episode in the story, which we might entitle "The Lion Killer Becomes The Terminator." Samson still likes his little Philistine honey and he decides to return to Timnah to claim her. He arrives with a young goat for a meal (the ancient Israelite equivalent of a box of chocolates) and demands that he be allowed to go see his bride in her bedroom. Her father refuses (see Judg. 15:2). Samson is furious and feels he is justified in seeking revenge (see Judg. 15:3). Somehow he captures three hundred foxes (maybe wild dogs), ties them tail to tail in pairs, fastens burning torches to each pair, and lets them loose in the Philistines' grain fields. The Philistines kill the Timnite girl and her father and then they come after Samson, who has retreated to a cave to hide out. Samson's own countrymen, fellow Israelites, are upset with him (see Judg. 15:11–12). This is proof of what we said earlier. Israel is intimidated by the Philistines and content with being their subjects. They're not looking for a deliverer. They tie Samson up and lead him out to the Philistines, who come shouting toward him. He rips off the ropes, grabs the donkey's jawbone, and wipes out one thousand Philistines through God's power.

God's program is really in full gear now. Samson and the Philistines are now mortal enemies. God has given Samson another vivid example of what he can accomplish through God's help, and Samson even recognizes God as his deliverer. All Samson needs to do is connect the dots. If God can deliver Samson from the Philistines, then he can use Samson to deliver Israel from them as well. We expect the next step to be an all-out war of liberation as Samson realizes his mission as Israel's deliverer, but that's not what happens. The last verse of chapter 15 seems to bring the story to an abrupt end (see Judg. 15:20). Elsewhere in Judges when we see this kind of statement, we also see attached to it a notice of the individual's death (cf. 10:2, 3–5; 12:7, 9b–10, 11–12, 14b–15). That's what we're expecting and that's what chapter 16 gives us—in narrative, rather than epitaph form.

Chapter 16 is the detailed account of how Samson descends into the grave. We could entitle it "Too Much Honey Can Be Dangerous to Your Health." Instead of Samson finally coming to grips with his role as deliverer of Israel, we see him visiting a Philistine prostitute in Gaza. We know from the Book of Proverbs that prostitutes are one of the gateways to death. Despite the Philistines' efforts to trap him, he escapes unscathed, carrying the entire city gate with him.

But you can only flirt with danger so many times. Samson gets involved with Delilah, whose name means either "possessor of dangling curls" or "flirtatious." As the story progresses through its successive panels, it is obvious that Samson should have been suspicious and realized Delilah was a threat to his well-being. But he's addicted to sex, and when Delilah begins to question his love and nags him (cf. 16:15–16), he decides keeping her is more important than anything else, even his Nazirite status. He tells her the secret of his success—his long hair. Well, you know the story. She shaves his hair, his strength leaves him, the Philistines capture him and put out his eyes.

This wasn't the first time Samson had violated his Nazirite commitment. Why then did his strength leave him this time, and not earlier when he touched the dead lion and ate the honey? Was there something magical about his hair? When Samson touched the dead lion, his concept of his destiny was undeveloped, through no fault of his own. He knew he was a Nazirite, but he didn't know why. Israel wasn't looking for a deliverer and apparently Samson's parents weren't either. His career was just beginning and God was willing to work with him patiently. However, after his great victory over the Philistines at Jawbone Hill, Samson should have realized his God-given strength was for some larger purpose than mere personal vengeance and he should have begun to develop some concept of his role as a deliverer. Certainly he should have stayed away from Philistine women. As he confessed to Delilah, his long hair was a visible reminder of his special relationship with God. His identity and destiny were inextricably linked to his long hair. But when he told her the secret of his success, he was in essence saying: "Your happiness and my sexual satisfaction are more important than my divine calling." God could not tolerate that kind of attitude and he abandoned him. The story ends with Samson wishing for his own death in order to exact vengeance on the Philistines (see Judg. 16:28). Even at the end, Samson doesn't get it. He kills Philistines out of personal revenge, not because he sees himself as God's deliverer. His physical blindness ironically symbolizes a spiritual blindness that characterized his life. He never really understood God's purpose for him.

With Samson's death in the rubble of the Philistine temple, the decline in Israelite leadership which began with Barak is complete. Deficient faith and lack of wisdom culminate in spiritual ignorance and utter folly, ushering in a period of chaos characterized by a leadership void. In many respects Samson represents Israel. Despite his miraculous beginning and tremendous God-given potential, he misses his calling to be God's consecrated servant and instead succumbs to the allurements of foreign women. He becomes a humiliated prisoner on foreign soil.

What's the point of the story, when it is viewed as a tragedy? On the surface Samson's story reminds us that falling prey to temptation can prevent God's people from realizing their full potential for God. Even worse, it can bring embarrassment, humiliation, pain, and death. The lesson for us seems simple: If we want to realize our full potential for God, we must avoid giving in to temptation.

Of course, that's easier said than done! But Samson's story also holds the key for success. There's an even more fundamental, underlying principle in this story that yields a more profound application. Let's probe more deeply into why Samson failed. Samson knew he was a Nazirite and he knew that meant he needed to follow certain rules. But that wasn't enough. He needed to know that God had made him a Nazirite for a larger purpose—to deliver Israel. Without knowledge of and commitment to that larger purpose, his awareness of his Nazirite status was not enough to sustain him when temptation came his way. The rules must have seemed arbitrary to him, especially when that delicious honey—both literal and nonliteral—was there waiting to be eaten. Without an understanding of his larger purpose as Israel's deliverer, he viewed his struggles with the Philistines as a mere personal vendetta or blood feud. He should have seen his battles with the Philistines as a holy war. Instead he viewed them strictly as an opportunity to get revenge against people he hated.

A lot of Christians are like Samson. How? They realize they have a special relationship with God through his Son, Jesus Christ. They also realize that because of this relationship God makes certain demands upon their behavior. They may even experience God's work in their life in some remarkable ways. Just as Samson's status as a Nazirite meant that he wasn't supposed to eat or drink certain things, so Christians realize they are not supposed to do certain things. But if your ideas about being a Christian never get beyond this level, you're missing the whole point of what it means to be a Christian.

That's what happens to a lot of Christians, especially young Christians, especially young Christians who grow up in the sometimes overly legalistic setting of the fundamentalist-evangelical subculture. They identify themselves as Christians, but fail to realize why God called them to be Christians. So they view Christianity primarily as a set of rules—a list of do's and don't's. Then when they're tempted to eat the sweet honey that the world offers in a variety of forms, they don't have what it takes to resist. Seen in isolation their Christian rules seem arbitrary and designed to keep them from having fun in life. Samson needed to know that he was set apart to be Israel's deliverer. If he had known that, the purpose of the Nazirite rules would have been clear to him. He would have realized that the dietary rules and the long hair marked him out as a special person with a special divinely determined destiny.

Christians need to know they have such a destiny. What is that destiny? The New Testament spells it out in various places. (See, for example, Matt. 28:18–20; John 15:16a; Col. 1:10–12; 1 Peter 2:9–12.) God has called us to make disciples, to bear fruit, to be his special holy people who preview what his kingdom of light will be like. You are on a mission for him. That's your primary purpose in life. He's not asking you to keep a bunch of rules so you can pass some kind of test or become a religious holy person. His commands about how we are to live fit into the larger purpose he has for us. If we live the way he asks us to live, we model his character to the world and our lifestyle becomes a testimony to the watching world of his standards. When we understand this larger purpose, the lifestyle prescribed in the New Testament begins to make sense and we are able to resist the forces that tempt us to compromise God's standards. But trying to keep God's rules without a knowledge of God's larger purpose in your life doesn't work.

Most of you have probably seen the movie *Karate Kid,* which tells of the friendship between Mr. Miyagi and "Daniel Son." Daniel wants to learn karate for self-protection, Mr. Miyagi agrees to teach him, but then doesn't seem to keep his promise. He makes Daniel wax his car ("wax on, wax off"), he makes him sand his wooden deck ("right a circle, left a circle"), he makes him paint his fence ("up, down, it's all in the wrist, long strokes"), he makes him paint his house ("side to side"). He makes Daniel use the same hand motions as he does these things. Daniel gets sick of this tedious work, he accuses Mr. Miyagi of making him a slave.

He says he hasn't learned a thing about karate, and announces he's going home. But then Mr. Miyagi shows him how the hand movements he's used in waxing, sanding, and painting are really the basic defensive moves of karate. ("Show me sand the floor; show me wax on, wax off; show me paint the fence, up down"). Daniel's eyes widen as he suddenly realizes how the tedious work contributes to his goal and his attitude is revolutionized.

Just as Daniel needed to understand the larger purpose of the tedious work, so Samson needed to understand how his status as a Nazirite contributed to his life's purpose. Tragically that never happened and he failed to realize his full potential as God's servant. Ancient Israel, whom Samson epitomized, also needed such a vision. God expected them to impact the nations in a positive way (see Exod. 19:6; Lev. 19:1; Deut. 4:4–8), but they lost sight of their larger purpose in the world and became just like the pagans around them. Christians need a vision of their larger purpose as well. If you just try to go through life with the attitude, "I'm a Christian and that means I don't do these things," you'll probably not make it. You may end up another Samson. You need to put your Christian life in proper perspective. God didn't make you a Christian so you can be a monk. He made you a Christian so you can be his spokesperson and servant—his light in a dark world. All the detailed things he tells you to do or not to do fit into that larger plan. So, when temptation comes—when you're tempted to eat the forbidden honey, don't say, "I can't do that, because I'm a Christian and Christians don't do that." Instead say, "I'm on a special assignment from the king himself. I don't do that because it would divert me from that assignment and compromise my purpose in life. I'm here to show the world what the kingdom of light looks like and to attract others to it."

We're all potential lion-killers with a sweet tooth. God can and wants to accomplish great things through us. But our sweet tooth can keep us from realizing our full potential. One of the keys to success is remembering the big picture—the larger purpose he has for us.

(3) Jacob Struggles Up the Spiritual Ladder (Genesis 25–35)

From Self-Sufficient Schemer to Dependent Servant: The Transformation of a Trickster

Americans tend to elevate self-sufficiency and independence to a virtue. We admire those who achieve success through hard work and ingenuity. Sometimes we think of a real man as one who refuses help from others (including God), tackles the world head on, and rises to prominence by sheer will power. Sometimes we think of a successful woman as one who rejects traditional domestic roles, courageously barges into the male-dominated corporate world, and by sheer determination, skill, and genius makes her mark as a professional.

Unfortunately this independent striving to get ahead sometimes throws ethics and principle to the wind and takes a dog-eat-dog philosophy which says, "I'll do whatever is necessary, including knifing the other guy or gal in the back, to get ahead." Of course, such an attitude is not new. We find it throughout history, including biblical history.

We perhaps see it most vividly in the story of Jacob, a self-sufficient schemer who was initially unwilling to commit himself wholeheartedly to God, but was more than ready to lie and cheat others out of what was theirs in order to promote his own interests. The story of Jacob reminds us of something we often forget—God does not consider this independent, win-at-all-costs attitude a virtue, and does not want his people to live this way. He's looking for submissive, dependent followers, who recognize his moral authority and trust him to provide the necessities of life. Jacob had to learn this lesson the hard way, and we can profit from reviewing his story.

One of the highlights of Old Testament history is recorded in Genesis 35. Jacob has returned to the Promised Land after a long period of exile in a foreign country. His sons Simeon and Levi have just massacred the entire male population of the city of Shechem, risking the wrath of their Canaanite neighbors and jeopardizing the lives of Jacob and his family. At this point the Lord comes to Jacob and instructs him to leave Shechem and go to Bethel, the place where years before, as he prepared to flee from the Promised Land to escape the wrath of his brother Esau, the Lord had appeared to him in a glorious vision (see Gen. 35:1–7).

Jacob's trip from Shechem to Bethel is far more than just a trip from one town to another. For Jacob it is a turning point with great symbolic value—in Shechem Jacob leaves behind self-sufficiency and half-hearted commitment; in Bethel he truly becomes Israel, the one who worships God as the only source of blessing. God confirms his promise to Abraham and Isaac, and Jacob becomes the bearer of that promise and thereby the key figure in God's program for mankind at this point in time. But to really appreciate what transpires here we must back up and look at some of the experiences that have brought Jacob to this moment. For Jacob it was a long, rocky road with difficult lessons along the way.

Sibling Rivalry

"Heel-Grabber" pulls off the original Manhattan Island ripoff (Gen. 25:19–34)

Jacob was born with a propensity to grab what belonged to others. In fact, when he came out of his mother's womb he was holding his twin brother's heel, as if trying to catch and pass him. They appropriately named him "Jacob," probably because the name "Jacob" sounds like the Hebrew word for "heel." But there is something ominous in the name, for it means "he deceives."

Jacob proved to be worthy of this name, for he later used cunning and deceit to cheat his brother Esau out of his birthright. One day Esau came in from hunting, tired and hungry. Jacob was cooking some stew, and when Esau asked for some, Jacob was ready to exploit the situation. Rather than kindly giving his brother a bowl of stew, he bargained with him: a bowl of stew for Esau's birthright as the firstborn. Esau foolishly made the deal, one which challenges the purchase of Manhattan Island as the biggest ripoff in world history. Jacob had taken advantage of his brother in a moment of weakness, when his physical appetites were in control of his reason.

Pulling the wool over the old man's eyes (Gen. 27:1–40)

Still later Jacob, at the instigation of his mother, stole Esau's paternal blessing as well, by tricking his aged, nearly blind father into thinking he was indeed Esau. Once again, he took advantage of another's weakness to selfishly further his own interests. Esau was understandably distraught. He said, "Isn't he appropriately named 'Jacob'? He has deceived me these two times!" (27:36). Yes, Esau, his name fits him perfectly—he deceives!

Billy the Kid Meets Jesse James

Bargaining with God (27:41–28:22)

Esau had murder on his mind and Jacob was forced to run for his life from his angry brother. He sets out for Haran to live with his uncle Laban, his mother Rebekah's brother. On the way, he spends a night at Bethel, where God appears to him in a dream and promises to be with him. However, he's not entirely sure he wants to commit himself wholeheartedly to this God just yet. He makes a bargain with God (see 28:20–22). Jacob eventually arrives in Haran, and at this point his past starts to catch up with him and God begins to teach him a very important lesson.

Past crimes reenacted (29:1–30)

In Uncle Laban, Jacob meets the mirror image of himself. Jacob falls head over heels for Laban's beautiful daughter Rachel. He makes a deal with Laban—he'll work for Laban for seven years in exchange for Rachel's hand in marriage. To Jacob this seems like a real bargain. With the deal completed, Jacob demands his wife be given him (see 29:21). At this point Jacob is a man driven by his hormones; he has one specific thing on his mind. So the wedding is arranged. After the feast, in the evening, his bride comes to him and Jacob, consumed by passion, has relations with her, without really stopping to verify that it's Rachel. Now put yourself in Jacob's shoes. In the morning you roll over and lo and behold, there is *Leah*, Rachel's older sister. In fact that's the way the text says it in verse 25: "Look! It was Leah!" When Jacob accuses Laban of deceiving him, Laban replies that it is the country's custom to give the first-born before the younger (see 29:26). Do you see what has happened here? Jacob's crimes against Esau have been reenacted, only this time Jacob is the victim. God puts him in Esau's shoes and lets him know how it feels to be cheated. The parallels between this account of Jacob's being deceived and the earlier accounts of his own deceptive acts are striking:

(1) In 29:14a Laban emphasizes, "You are my own flesh and blood," sort of like Esau and Jacob. One would think that trust, not deceit, would characterize such a relationship. But being a blood relative to Esau didn't keep Jacob from resorting to deceit and it doesn't stop Laban either.

(2) Like Esau when he comes in from the field tired and hungry, Jacob is tricked at a moment when his passions are in control (note his statement in 29:21b and the author's report in 29:23b). Here is a man so obsessed with satisfying his physical appetites he can't be concerned about details.

(3) Like Isaac, whose poor eyesight "kept him in the dark" as to what Jacob was doing when he robbed Esau's blessing, so Jacob was deceived by Laban in the darkness of evening (cf. 29:23a).

(4) Compare "deceived" in 29:25 with "deceitfully" in 27:35. They translate the same Hebrew root. The same word characterizes both Jacob's and Laban's deceitful deeds.

(5) Finally, Laban's words in 29:26 are a reminder to Jacob that his treatment of his older brother had been inappropriate. In fact, it was Jacob's very disregard for custom that made him vulnerable to Laban's deceit. He should have realized this basic custom about the special privilege of the firstborn, but he had forgotten about that dusty tradition and trampled it underfoot. But it was, ironically, his brazen disregard for this custom that proved to be his downfall.

Jacob had learned lesson number one: In God's world what goes around eventually comes around. God, the just ruler of the world, in his providence gives people what they deserve and punishes them in a way that it is appropriate.

Spared by divine providence (29:31–31:55)

As time passes God, in fulfillment of Isaac's blessing and his own promise to the patriarchs, begins to richly bless Jacob, despite Laban's continual dishonesty. If God hadn't been there to intervene supernaturally and providentially, Laban would have taken Jacob to the cleaners. In Laban Jacob has met his match, just like a gunfighter in the Old West who eventually encounters another gunslinger who's faster on the draw than himself. Billy the Kid had met Jesse James, as it were. Jacob summarizes the situation this way (see 31:6–7). Finally Jacob leaves, undoubtedly a bit wiser, for he has begun to learn another important lesson: The key to true success in life is not one's own schemes and efforts, but God's gracious blessing and providential protection.

The Long Road Home

Preparing to face the music (32:1–21)

The ghosts of Jacob's past are still chasing him, however. For Jacob it's time to face the music. Before returning to the Promised Land, he decides to contact his brother Esau as a sign of good will. The word arrives that Esau is already coming to meet him, along with four hundred men! Jacob takes measures to protect his family and he prepares gifts for Esau in hopes that he might appease his brother's wrath. He also prays to God, reminding God of His promise to bless him (see 32:9–12). One senses that there is a growing dependence on God within Jacob, even if it has been cultivated in the soil of fear and desperation.

Wrestling with God at the Jabbok River (32:22–32)

The night before he meets Esau, Jacob has a strange experience. At the Jabbok River he meets what appears to him to be a man. Jacob engages in a nightlong wrestling match with this unidentified "man." Now remember, Jacob is very, very strong. (Recall Gen. 29:1–14, which tells how Jacob, his adrenaline surging at the sight of Rachel, rolled the heavy stone from the well and watered Laban's sheep. Jacob is no weak mommy's boy!) As daylight approaches, the man, sensing that he is not going to win with standard wrestling maneuvers and holds, supernaturally injures Jacob's hip. Now suspecting the identity of the man, Jacob holds on for dear life and demands that the man bless him. The man gives him a new name, Israel. God has had to fight with Jacob to get his attention and win his full-fledged allegiance. The name Israel will serve as a reminder of his struggle with God, for the name sounds like a verb that means "God fights." God blesses him and Jacob then names the place Peniel, "Face of God," because he knows that he has just encountered God in physical form.

Now this demand for a blessing may seem presumptuous, but in the context of the story it is not. After all, God has promised to bless him (see Gen. 28) and here Jacob lays hold of that promise. His demand for a blessing is really a demonstration of his dependence on God. In fact, this entire episode is a microcosm of Jacob's life to this point. His nightlong struggle with one whom he perceives as being a man epitomizes Jacob's years of conflict with Esau and then Laban. Little did he realize that he was really fighting God. His desperate plea to the man, once he realizes his true identity, epitomizes his newfound reliance on God.

Time to eat crow (33:1–20)

As Jacob limps away from his all-night tussle, the morning dawns and Esau appears. It's time for Jacob to eat crow, to swallow his pride and face up to his past sins against his brother. One of the words of blessing which he stole from his brother reads as follows: "may the sons of your mother bow down to you" (see 27:29). Now, ironically, we see just the opposite. In spite of possessing the blessing for which he schemed, Jacob now bows down to Esau—seven times! (33:3)—and in 33:10 he offers Esau a gift (lit. a "blessing"). Once again the tables are turned. But Esau, who has been greatly blessed himself, kisses his brother and they are reconciled. God's blessing, not his own scheming, has preserved Jacob.

Chips off the Old Block Outdo Daddy (Gen. 34:1–31)

Jacob then moves to Shechem, where he purchases some land from the Canaanites and begins to live among them. When one of the Canaanites violates his daughter Dinah, Jacob's sons show they are chips off the old block and have inherited their father's propensity to deceive. They agree to a marriage between the young man and Dinah, but first the Shechemites must agree to be circumcised. The Shechemites agree and are circumcised, but while they are lying around in pain, Simeon and Levi slaughter them. This is Dale Carnegie reversed: How to Make Enemies and Alienate People.

A Defining Moment in Jacob's Life (Gen. 35:1–15)

And that brings us back to where we started—chapter 35. At God's command, Jacob leaves Shechem. But before leaving, he buries the idols that some in his company possessed. When Jacob leaves Shechem he puts behind him things that hinder his relationship to God—deceitful actions and other gods. When he goes to Bethel he separates himself from all that and, in fulfillment of his earlier vow at Bethel, he, in essence, says, "From now on I will trust God, not my schemes, and I will worship him alone, not the gods of the peoples round about." Through some very difficult experiences, whereby God forced Jacob to face his past, God has taught Jacob that it is only through his blessing that one achieves success and accomplishes God's will. Jacob is going to carry the promise given to Abraham, and God wants the bearer of that promise to be, first and foremost, a man who depends on him and trusts his promise. So, as Jacob limps along the road from Shechem to Bethel, his hands covered with dirt from digging holes to bury idols, we have one of the high points of the Old Testament. A self-sufficient schemer and trickster has been transformed into a dependent servant—and dependent servants are the kind of people God wants to use to further his purposes in the world.

The story of Jacob carries a lesson for us all. It reminds us that we must submit to and depend upon God, not our own wits and abilities, as we seek to find meaning and fulfillment in life. Jacob had a faulty view of life. He actually believed that success depended on his own ability to manipulate and control the world around him. Consequently he became a self-centered person and would even resort to deceit if it was expedient. We tend to be like that—we strive for success with a self-sufficient attitude, forgetting that all our efforts will be futile if God is not blessing them and protecting us. But sooner or later we will encounter something that's too big for us to control. God will get our attention through a Laban and remind us that he's really driving the vehicle down the road of life. Rather than trying to steer the car ourselves, we need to let him be sovereign and submit to his will and depend on his power and blessing.

(4) The Rise and Fall of "King" Abimelech (Judges 8:33–10:5)

The Thornbush Who Wanted to Rule the Forest: "My Father Is King" Takes His Name at Face Value

The story of Abimelech is the sequel to the Gideon narrative. Together with 6:1–8:32, it may be viewed as one large literary unit parallel to 3:7–11, 12–31; 4:1–5:31; 10:6–12:13; 13:1–16:31. The sequel is introduced by a reference to Israel's turning back to the Baals. The introduction sets the stage for the main narrative by giving the background for Abimelech's rise to power, while the conclusion records how a semblance of stability was restored to the land following his death.

The main narrative has three major units. Verses 1–6 tell how Abimelech formed an alliance with the citizens of Shechem and murdered his brothers. References to Abimelech and Shechem appear in verses 1 and 6, forming an inclusio for the unit. Verses 7–21 record Jotham's parable. References to Jotham's movements bracket the unit. In both the introduction and conclusion to his speech he addresses Shechem's nobles (vv. 7b, 20). Abimelech again becomes the focus of the narrative in verse 22, which introduces the third unit. This long account begins and ends with statements about the Lord's intervention (vv. 23–24, 56–57). The main portion of the narrative (vv. 25–55) tells how the Lord providentially brought about Abimelech's demise and Shechem's destruction. This section is divided into two parts. Verses 25–44 tell of Gaal's rebellion and of Abimelech's activities outside the gates of Shechem. Verses 45–55 focus on Abimelech's campaigns against cities and their towers.

Recipe for Murder and Chaos

Israel Returns to Baal-Worship (8:33–35)

Israel quickly returned to Baal worship following Gideon's death. More specifically, they began to worship Baal-Berith (lit., "Baal of the covenant"), a local manifestation of the Canaanite storm-god. In so doing they failed to "remember" the Lord (cf. Deut. 8:18, which exhorts Israel to remember the Lord, who is Israel's source of material prosperity and their covenant-keeping God), who had delivered them from the various enemies that surrounded them. The passage refers to the earlier accounts in the book. Yahweh delivered Israel from northern foes (Aram-Naharaim and Hazor), eastern peoples (Moab and Ammon), westerners

(Philistines), southerners (Amalek), and the Midianites (who lived east and south of Israel).

Israel's ingratitude toward God was mirrored in their inappropriate treatment of Gideon's family, which reaches its culmination in the mass execution of Gideon's sons. Gideon's "other" name, Jerub-Baal ("let Baal contend"), appears in verse 35 (and nine times in chapter 9, where the name Gideon is completely absent), perhaps to bring out the irony and absurdity of Israel's actions. Gideon's experience demonstrated the Lord's power and Baal's weakness. Gideon delivered Israel from terrible oppression through the Lord's power. He also desecrated Baal's altar at Ophrah and then carried a name with him through most of his adult life that was a challenge and an affront to the Canaanite deity. Baal's failure to contend with Gideon is evidence of his weakness. Nevertheless, Israel rejected the Lord and his chosen servant Gideon in exchange for Baal, proving once again that sin is truly irrational!

Israel also wanted a king who would give them security. Mix paganized thinking with a leadership void and you have a situation that is ripe for power-hungry megalomaniacs to exploit. Enter Abimelech!

Abimelech Murders His Brothers (9:1–6)

To understand fully what happens in chapter 9, we must go back to 8:30–31. The situation described there had all the potential for a severe power struggle. Gideon, despite turning down the people's offer of kingship, acts like a king by marrying many wives and fathering seventy sons. When he also fathers a son by a Shechemite concubine, he brings into the world a potentially jealous and dangerous rival for his seventy sons. By naming this son Abimelech (which means "my father is king"!), Gideon reveals his own hidden aspirations and leaves the son with a false and potentially self-destructive legacy. His pagan behavior diluted his orthodox creed of its strength and set a dangerous pattern for his son to follow.

When Abimelech grows up, he takes his name seriously and decides to make its implications a reality. Appealing to the fact that he is related (through his mother) by blood to the Shechemites, he proposes that it would be more efficient for one man, rather than seventy men, to rule over Shechem. (The implication is that Gideon's sons have assumed some type of leadership position over Shechem.) Impressed by his appeal to their close blood ties, the Shechemites declare their allegiance to Abimelech by giving him seventy pieces of silver (corresponding to the number of Abimelech's half brothers) from the temple reserves of their god Baal-Berith. Abimelech takes the money and hires a group of "empty and reckless" men as his royal guard. (The Hebrew word translated "empty" is used elsewhere of a group of mercenaries/bandits [Judg. 11:3], a person who would indecently expose himself [2 Sam. 6:20], and men who support a coup against a king [2 Chron. 13:7].) He then goes to Ophrah and slaughters his half brothers on one stone. Jotham, the youngest, escapes and goes into hiding. Meanwhile Abimelech returns to Shechem, where the nobles of the city crown him king. The seeds planted by Gideon have taken root. Israel (cf. v. 22) now has as its king a murderer who is financed from the treasury of a pagan god and is supported by a gang of thugs. The whole scenario is Canaanite to the core. Of all the characters who have appeared thus far on the pages of Judges, Abimelech most resembles the Canaanite king Adoni-Bezek, who had mutilated and humiliated seventy rival kings (cf. 1:7a). Abimelech has gone even further, murdering his seventy brothers.

The fact that this enthronement occurs in Shechem is tragically ironic, for it was in Shechem that Joshua led Israel in a covenant renewal ceremony and set up a stone under an oak tree as a perpetual reminder of what had occurred there (see Josh. 24:26). Abimelech's enthronement takes place beside an oak and a pagan pillar. Many years before Jacob had buried the family's idols in Shechem under an oak tree (see Gen. 35:4). A town that was traditionally associated with renewed loyalty to the Lord has now become the site of an enthronement that represents a blatant rejection of his kingship.

The steps to chaos are clearly outlined. Assimilation to a pagan environment and way of thinking leads to spiritual insensitivity and ingratitude for God's blessings. This in turn leads to outright worship of false gods and an attraction to leaders who are motivated by power, but have no ethical dimension.[9]

A Curse Cracks a Skull

Jotham's Parable (9:7–21)

When the news of Abimelech's enthronement reached Jotham, he ascended Mount Gerizim and proclaimed a message to the nobles of Shechem. The location is ironic, for it was on Mount Gerizim that half the tribes of Israel stood for the recital of the covenantal blessings following the invasion of the promised land (Josh. 8:33; cf. Deut. 11:29; 27:12). The mountain was traditionally associated with the blessing of God. Now it would be the site of a curse which would tear the nation's social fabric in pieces.

Jotham begins his speech with a parable about the trees (= the people of Israel and Shechem in particular) seeking a king. One by one the most likely candidates for royalty—the olive tree, fig tree, and grape vine—turn down the offer. Their main concern is to yield their produce for the

---

9. A followup exposition, focusing on 8:33–9:6, might develop this principle: "The type of leader you choose may speak volumes about your loyalty to God." An applicational statement might be: "If the leaders you follow look a lot like the pagan world around you, you may be more pagan than you realize."

benefit of gods (or God) and men, not to sway in the wind as king over the trees. Finally the trees turn in desperation to the thornbush, which is clearly unqualified to rule over the trees. The thornbush tentatively agrees to the deal, but emphasizes that the trees must take refuge in its shade. ("Shade" is a metaphor in the Bible and ancient Near Eastern literature for a ruler's sovereign authority and protection. See Isa. 30:2; Ezek. 31:6, 12, 17.) The statement is absurd, for the thornbush is incapable of casting any significant shadow. This offer of power has obviously gone to the thornbush's head, for it then warns that if the trees do not follow through on their offer, it will destroy even the grandest of them—the cedars of Lebanon—with fire. The parable draws attention to Abimelech's utter lack of qualifications, his inability to provide genuine protection, his thirst for power, and his destructive potential.

Jotham next confronts the Shechemites with their treatment of Jerub-Baal's family. If they have dealt fairly with his father, they are certainly deserving of a blessing, but he makes it clear that such a prospect is absurd because of their murderous deeds. Still maintaining a tone of objectivity, he then presents the alternative. If they have not dealt fairly with Jerub-Baal, he prays that Abimelech and the Shechemites might destroy one another. The language of the curse is very similar to the words spoken by the thornbush to the trees (v. 15). The implication is that the Shechemites, like Jotham's brothers, will be victimized by Abimelech's destructive capacity, which in the end will cause the power-hungry thornbush itself to go up in smoke.

God Fulfills Jotham's Curse (9:22–57)

Jotham fades from the scene, escaping to Beer, while Abimelech rules for three years over Israel. The reference to Israel is surprising, for up to this point the narrative has led us to believe this was simply a local affair involving Shechem and its environs. But apparently all Israel came to recognize Abimelech as its leader. The notice is at first a bit alarming, for it suggests that Abimelech is growing more successful and that Jotham's curse may fall harmlessly to the ground.

But the narrator does not keep us in suspense very long. In verse 23 we see God directly intervening by sending an evil spirit to stir up hostility between Abimelech and Shechem. Verse 24 then informs us that God's purpose in doing so is to avenge the shed blood of Jerub-Baal's seventy sons. The name Elohim (God) is used here and in verses 56–57 because God appears in this chapter as the righteous, sovereign judge. The name Yahweh, "the Lord," is hardly appropriate for Israel has rejected him (cf. 8:34) and the loyalty that is to characterize covenantal life has disappeared (cf. 8:35). This incident is just one of several in which God employs the services of evil spirits to expedite judgment upon sinners (1 Sam. 16:14; 18:10; 19:10; 1 Chron. 21:1 [cf. 2 Sam. 24:1]). In this case the spirit incited the Shechemites to rebel against Abimelech. The following narrative outlines the details.

The Shechemites decided to rob travelers and merchants as they passed by the city on the trade routes. In some way, probably financially, this harmed Abimelech, who eventually received a report of the Shechemites' rebellion.

This is the second in a series of reports that God providentially uses to bring about Shechem's demise. In verse 7 the report of Abimelech's enthronement prompts Jotham to pronounce a curse on Shechem. Here another report informs Abimelech of Shechem's treacherous actions. In verse 31 Zebul sends messengers to Abimelech telling him of Gaal's attempted coup, prompting Abimelech to come to Shechem. According to verse 42, the movements of the Shechemites are reported to Abimelech, causing him to press the attack against the city itself. Finally, in verse 47, Abimelech learns that the nobles have fled to the city tower, so he sets it on fire, killing a thousand Shechemites.

In bringing about the destruction of Shechem, God uses two characters, Gaal son of Ebed and Zebul, the governor of the city. Gaal (whose name can be related by popular etymology to a verb meaning "abhor, loathe") is a loathsome individual who is even more repulsive than Abimelech. He and his brothers decide to celebrate the grape harvest in the temple of their god (Baal-Berith?). Emboldened by wine, they curse Abimelech and Gaal then challenges Abimelech's authority and boasts that he would "get rid of him" if only the Shechemites would support him militarily. Zebul (meaning "prince"), Abimelech's governor in Shechem, reports Gaal's words to Abimelech and advises him to launch a surprise attack against the city. Abimelech follows his advice, surprises Gaal and the Shechemites, routs them in battle, and drives them back into the city. Having played their role in the drama, Gaal's clan is driven from the city by Abimelech's loyal deputy, Zebul.

The next day the people of Shechem, naively thinking that the conflict is over, go out to their fields. Abimelech's honor is not yet vindicated, however. He divides his troops into three companies (cf. 7:16), attacks the people, invades the city, kills its people, and spreads salt on its fields (possibly a symbolic act in conjunction with a curse of infertility, cf. Deut. 29:23; Jer. 17:6).

Shechem's nobles retreat to the city stronghold, which is associated with the temple of El-Berith (lit., "God of the covenant," but here El is probably the Canaanite high god who rules over the divine assembly and imparts authority to Baal). Abimelech gets some branches from nearby Mount Zalmon, boldly charges up to the wall of the stronghold, piles the wood against it, and sets it on fire, killing about a thousand people. The thornbush has consumed the cedars (cf. v. 15) and the first part of Jotham's curse has been realized (v. 20).

Abimelech is not satisfied with the destruction of Shechem. He attacks the town of Thebez, perhaps because it had allied with Shechem and Abimelech needed to reestablish his authority in the region. The people of Thebez flee into a tower and climb up to the roof. Abimelech shows the same bold recklessness he did at Shechem as he storms the tower to set it on fire. However, his past successes have bred vulnerability and this time his daring is his undoing. An unidentified woman throws a millstone down from the tower and cracks open Abimelech's skull. The text emphasizes her singularity and by using the verb "threw" suggests an heroic act of strength comparable to that of a warrior. Vain and arrogant to the very end, Abimelech quickly instructs his servant to run him through with a sword so that people will not remember him as one who was killed in battle by a woman. The text informs us that "he died" (cf. 4:21), but there is no record of his being buried. This omission contrasts with obituaries that appear before (8:32) and after this (10:2, 5; see also 12:7, 10–11, 15; 16:31).

A comparison of this account with Sisera's death is instructive. In the earlier account a woman (Jael) delivered Israel from a foreign oppressor; here a woman delivers Israel again (once more, ironically, by a fatal blow to the head with an unconventional weapon; cf. 5:26 with 9:53), only this time from an oppressive Israelite.[10] The quality of Israelite leadership had steadily regressed as the brave warrior Othniel was replaced by hesitant Barak and unwise and timid Gideon, who in turn gave way to the "anti-judge" Abimelech, a power-hungry and bloodthirsty initiator of civil discord. The changing roles of the women are symptomatic of this decline. Unlike Acsah, who inspired worthy and brave deeds, women were forced to assume the role of warrior, first to deliver the nation from a foreign oppressor (Sisera) and then from a power-hungry countryman (Abimelech).

This portion of the narrative ends where it began (cf. vv. 23–24) with a theological commentary on the events recorded in the chapter. By providentially bringing about Abimelech's death and Shechem's destruction God was repaying them for what they did to Gideon's sons. In so doing he also demonstrated once more that he is the just king of the world, who carries out justice on behalf of individuals who have been wronged and are powerless before their oppressors. When they appeal to his justice by uttering a curse, he will bring that curse to fulfillment.[11]

---

10. D. W. Gooding remarks: "Things have seriously deteriorated when the bondage from which Israel has to be delivered in this fashion is no longer bondage to some foreign power but a bondage to one of Israel's own number who, instead of being a deliverer of Israel, has installed himself as a tyrant, and is maintaining his tyranny by ruthless destruction." See his article, "The Composition of the Book of Judges," *Eretz-Israel* 16 (1982): 74*–75*.

11. On the other hand, he ignores and does not fulfill unjust or undeserved curses. See Prov. 26:2.

Conclusion: Stability Restored (10:1–5)

The story of Abimelech is a fast-paced account filled with action and violence. It tells how chaos engulfed the nation as a power-hungry ruler seeks to establish a Canaanite style of rule within the nation. The reader needs relief—both literarily and emotionally. The conclusion provides this by giving a rather capsulized and pedestrian account of the careers of Abimelech's successors, Tola and Jair, and by indicating that some semblance of order was reestablished in Israel and Transjordan. However, the earlier formulaic conclusion, which mentioned the land having peace (3:11, 30; 5:31; 8:28), does not appear here or later. Abimelech's quest for power marks a transition for Israel. Genuine peace is no longer possible.

The story of Abimelech is a reminder of what can happen when God's people turn to paganism and their leaders act unwisely and inconsistently. Gideon declared God's kingship, but sent a false signal to both the people and his son when he acted like a typical Canaanite king. Abimelech took his father's actions to new depths and exploited the people's faulty view of kingship and rejection of God.

However, God remains sovereign even during the worst of times. He preserved Jotham and brought his justified curse to pass. In the process he intervened supernaturally (by sending the evil spirit to stir up strife) and manipulated people and circumstances in order to accomplish his just purposes. Through a series of reports he drew Abimelech to Shechem and brought about the destruction of that sinful city. By giving Abimelech temporary success, God placed him in a vulnerable position where his daring became his downfall. By using a woman to kill Abimelech, God once more showed he can accomplish his purposes through unlikely instruments.

Two related principles emerge from the story. When viewed in the context of Israel's moral decline during the period of the Judges, the story yields this principle: "When unwise leaders plant the seeds of discord in the soil of paganism, power-hungry megalomaniacs can easily spring up within God's covenant community. Such leaders and the people who find them attractive produce chaos and can do long-term damage to God's people." We might draw this application: "We must remain loyal to God, for turning to pagan practices and leaders is self-destructive and does harm to God's covenant community."

When one views the story as another example of how God preserves his people through the chaos of the Judges period, a related principle emerges: "God is just and will destroy those who abuse others and spread strife through the covenant community. In response to the appeals of innocent victims, he eventually eliminates the culprits through supernatural and providential means." In any given corner of God's worldwide covenant community, there will usually be power-hungry Abimelechs and innocent Jothams. Keeping this in mind, we can draw at least two related applications from this second principle: (1) "If your pagan attitudes and actions are threatening God's covenant community, you better watch out for falling rocks!" (2) "If power-hungry pagans are causing chaos in your little corner of God's covenant community, trust in our just and sovereign God for deliverance and vindication."

Exposition of Poetry

As with narrative literature, the exposition of poetic texts should begin with solid exegesis, including analysis of the text's historical-cultural background and its literary dimension (see steps 1–5 in the method outlined in chapter 8). As noted earlier, hymnic, didactic, and prophetic texts frequently exhibit a logical argument or structure. From one's exegetical study the main point of each thematic unit within the psalm or speech should emerge, as well as the text's primary theme in its original context (see steps 6–7 in the method outlined in chapter 8). The preacher/teacher can then transform the main points and overall theme into general theological principles that would be true now, as well as then. The next step is to derive from the overall principle of the passage an applicational point which addresses our attitudes and behavior.

Of course, this approach cannot be consistently utilized in Proverbs, where, apart from the speeches in chapters 1–9 and 31:10–31, randomly arranged individual sayings appear. Rather than preaching through such sentence literature in a verse-by-verse fashion, it is better in our modern context to deal with the material thematically, collecting the various proverbs on a given topic and organizing them into a series of principles related to the general theme. (Such an approach is illustrated below.)

Some Hermeneutical Guidelines for the Exposition of Specific Literary Types

Prayer and Praise

The biblical psalms give us a record of how ancient Israel spoke to God. On the surface these prayers and songs are people's word to God, but through the mystery of inspiration they are also, like all Scripture, God's word to people. As such, the psalms give us inspired models of how to talk and sing to God.

A close examination of the psalms reveals there is no standard way to approach God in prayer and song. The psalms of petition (or lament) are cries for help from the depths. Suffering psalmists protest their circumstances, plead with God for deliverance, and express their faith and hope.[12] The authors of the songs of thanks, having been rescued from the depths, stand safely on the shore and express their gratitude for God's intervention. In the songs of confidence the psalmists look danger in the eye and declare their trust in God as their protector. The writers of the hymns stand on the mountaintop and affirm God's sovereignty over the world and his goodness to his people.

Because the psalms display such variety, an expositor should be careful not to elevate one pattern over the others. One psalm might be appropriate for those who are suffering, while another might be more suitable for those who have just experienced God's intervention.[13]

For example, in preaching or teaching Psalm 23, we should say, "We *can* be confident in the face of danger, for God is our faithful guardian, who provides for our needs, protects us from enemies, grants us his favor, and allows us access to his presence." We should not phrase the application, "We *should/must* be confident. . . ," for the psalms remind us there are times when God's people are so overwhelmed by trouble they are compelled to protest their situation and are unable to exude confidence. For example, the author of Psalm 88 protests his suffering as he continues to plead for deliverance. Though regarding God as his enemy, he holds on to him for dear life, because he has enough faith left to realize that God is his only hope. One might draw this application from Psalm 88: "We can protest our situation to God when we feel that he is our enemy, for even in the midst of intense suffering he remains our only hope."

Because they testify to God's providential and direct involvement in ancient Israel's experience, the psalms are a rich source of biblical theology. However, as you develop theological principles from individual psalms, you should keep a couple of important facts in mind:

(1) The psalms often generalize and utilize hyperbole. For example, the hymns of the Psalter picture God as the sovereign king of the universe who promotes justice and cares for the needy of the earth, including the poor, barren women, starving prisoners, orphans, and widows (see, e.g., Pss. 113 and 146). Though there was ample evidence of God's just rule in Israel's experience, reality often collides with these affirmations in our experience. The world yields numerous examples of injustice and oppression, forcing many to conclude that God does not exist or that he is unconcerned about human suffering. It would seem that the hymnic affirmations of the psalms express an ideal. Rather than describing

---

12. Leslie Allen observes that the "laments are the voices of men and women who have been there before us and have wrestled with the agonizing eclipse of the stability that was synonymous with life." He adds: "In the laments there is no triumphalism that can readily exorcize the evil. Nor is there a stoic passivity that grits its teeth and rests patiently in the inscrutable will of God. Instead, one finds the gamut of human emotions that make up the sequence of human reactions to crisis." See his *Word Biblical Themes: Psalms* (Waco, Tex.: Word, 1987), 37–38.

13. In this regard see Allen's insightful discussion in ibid., 33–41.

reality as we know it, they focus on what could, should, and someday will be true. This ideal is rooted in the psalmists' faith in God's sovereignty and will be realized when God establishes his kingdom on earth (see Pss. 96:11–13; 98:7–9).[14]

(2) The psalmists expect God's physical protection in the here-and-now. Since New Testament Christians are not guaranteed such protection, the psalmists' declarations may seem like mere wishful thinking to us. However, the principle that God protects his people is always true. In the Old Testament era his protection apparently took a more tangible form; in the New Testament it is more spiritual in nature.

For example, the author of Psalm 23 confidently affirmed that the Lord is a faithful guardian of his people, who provides for their needs, protects them from enemies, grants them his favor, and allows them access to his presence. Evidently the psalmist experienced and anticipated these blessings in this life. Though Christians sometimes suffer cruel oppression and are even executed for their faith, the principle of the psalm still holds true, once it is placed in its larger theological context (cf. Rom. 8:28–39).

Proverbial Wisdom

The purpose of the Book of Proverbs is to impart wisdom, which may be defined as insight and skill for living life effectively, uprightly, and, most important, in a way that pleases God (cf. Prov. 1:1–5). The Book of Proverbs makes certain basic assumptions about the character of genuine wisdom, where it originates, and how one goes about acquiring it:

(1) Genuine wisdom originates with God (Prov. 2:6). In fact, God's own creative work is characterized by wisdom in that it displays order and operates by certain laws and principles (Prov. 3:19–20; 8:22–31). If genuine wisdom comes from God, then it is distinct from mere human wisdom (Prov. 3:5–6; 14:12).

(2) The quest for genuine, God-given wisdom has a departure point: the fear of the Lord (Prov. 1:7; 9:10). The way of wisdom is not a mere pathway of intellectual pursuit. To begin to pursue genuine wisdom one must come to grips with who God is (the Holy One) and respond to him with fear. What is meant by the phrase "fear of the Lord"? According to Proverbs 3:5–7, fearing the Lord involves humbly relying on him, rather than one's own understanding or wisdom. Fearing the Lord also means shunning evil, seeking to live uprightly, and refusing to envy the wicked (Prov. 14:2; 23:17).

(3) In addition to submitting humbly to the Lord's moral authority, the one who seeks genuine wisdom must have a teachable spirit. The

---

14. For a more detailed and nuanced discussion of this problem, see my "A Theology of the Psalms," in *A Biblical Theology of the Old Testament,* ed. Roy B. Zuck (Chicago: Moody, 1991), 274–76.

wise man or woman thrives on instruction, advice, and even correction (Prov. 9:8–9; 13:10).

(4) Wisdom is more valuable than material wealth, for its rewards include material wealth and a great deal more (Prov. 3:13–18, 21–26).

This fourth principle is especially problematic for modern Christians. Israel's sages seem to expect God's material blessings in the here-and-now. However, New Testament Christians are not guaranteed such blessings. Look at Jesus, the embodiment of genuine wisdom. He lived wisely, but was relatively poor, encountered opposition, and ended up dying on a cross. However, God will eventually reward his people. In the Old Testament era his blessings took more tangible, material form during one's lifetime; in the New Testament they are usually more spiritual in nature and reserved primarily for the future. One should also remember that even within the ancient Israelite wisdom tradition itself, certain qualifications were placed on the overly optimistic theology of Proverbs. Ecclesiastes reminds us that life is often unfair and seemingly meaningless, while Job's experience teaches us that even the righteous sometimes suffer intensely without ever fully understanding why.

Modern interpreters also struggle with other difficult hermeneutical issues in Proverbs. Do proverbs state truths that inexorably work themselves out with no exceptions? Or, do they state general principles to which there are sometimes exceptions? Should the motivating statements attached to some proverbs be understood as unconditional promises/warnings from God? Certainly some statements of a clearly theological nature must be understood as unconditional (see, e.g., Prov. 22:22–23; 23:17–18). However, in most cases proverbial sayings reflect what is typical or normal without suggesting or implying that there are never exceptions. For example, Proverbs 20:13 seems to guarantee that hard work will pay off, while laziness will lead to poverty. Under normal circumstances, this principle will prove to be true, as common sense and experience reveal. However, if the land experienced famine or military invasion, one would lose one's crop, no matter how hard one had worked. At that point, both the diligent and lazy would be in the same boat.

Prophecy

The messages of the prophets are especially relevant to contemporary audiences. The prophetic judgment speeches challenge us to love God and our neighbor, while the salvation oracles remind us that God punishes evil, rewards obedience, and will someday establish his kingdom on earth in fulfillment of his ancient covenantal promises to his people.

When doing exposition in the prophets, the preacher/teacher should keep in mind a couple of important hermeneutical guidelines:

(1) When working with judgment speeches, don't assume your audience is guilty of the same crimes as ancient Israel. Furthermore, never

arrogantly assume the confrontational, sarcastic posture of an Old Testament prophet, who, unlike the modern preacher, was directly commissioned by God and energized in a special way by the divine Spirit. We and the people in our churches, like ancient Israel, are certainly prone to turn from God to idols and neglect our responsibilities to others, but it would be presumptuous to assume that a modern congregation is collectively guilty of such deeds and is tottering on the brink of destruction! When preaching/teaching from the prophetic judgment speeches, it is better to focus on the theological principle of the text, emphasize the need to avoid Israel's example, and, within the redemptive context of the New Testament, highlight the importance of self-examination and, if needed, repentance.

As an example of how modern preachers can misapply prophetic judgment speeches, consider the way in which some utilize Isaiah's, Micah's, or Amos's diatribes against social injustice. In the cultural context of ancient Israel/Judah, these eighth-century B.C. prophets were denouncing a huge royal bureaucracy that had commandeered the economic and legal system and, through unjust policies and corrupt courts, was depriving the rural agricultural class of its God-given property rights, in direct violation of the Law of Moses. In other words, within a covenantal theocratic context, the prophets were confronting those who wielded economic and legal power in Israelite/Judahite society. Without apparently understanding the original socioeconomic context of the prophets' messages, some modern preachers use these prophetic texts as a springboard from which to denounce the "evils of capitalism," an economic system foreign to ancient Israel.[15] Some even try to make middle-class congregations feel guilty for the poverty that exists in modern America, as if their congregation, most of whom are struggling to make ends meet and are far-removed from the center of our modern power structures, are somehow responsible for the less than utopian economic conditions that exist in some quarters of American society.

Among the sample expositions to follow, we include a sermon on Isaiah 1:2–20 that attempts to draw a more legitimate and relevant application from such a prophetic speech. Most of the people in our churches are not oppressing others as Israel's and Judah's leaders were in the eighth century B.C. But, just as Israel's/Judah's bureaucrats neglected their God-given leadership responsibilities, some modern Christians neglect their responsibilities within their God-given relationships (primarily within the context of the family and church). For such individuals the theological principles of the prophetic diatribes against social injustice are particularly relevant and should be especially challenging.

---

15. For a discussion of the socioeconomic structures of ancient Israel, see John Andrew Dearman, *Property Rights in the Eighth-Century Prophets* (Atlanta: Scholars, 1988), 148.

(2) When preaching/teaching from the prophets' salvation oracles, don't sensationalize the message or assume the role of a crystal-ball gazer. The primary purpose of prophetic visions of the future is not to satisfy our curiosity about coming events or to test our ability to decode cryptic sayings. These visions were designed instead to stimulate faith in God's sovereignty and assure God's people that the sovereign divine king will keep his promises and vindicate them. An obsession with details, especially when married to a hyperliteralistic hermeneutic that overlooks the historical-cultural context of the message and fails to recognize the presence of symbolic, archetypal, and hyperbolic language (see our discussion in chapter 7), has led over the years to some preposterous interpretations of the prophetic messages. Dealing with details is important, but only in so far as it contributes to an understanding of the overall theological principle of the passage and leads to a meaningful application of that principle.

Sample Expositions of Poetic Passages

For illustrative purposes, I have included below four expositions of poetic texts. The first is a sermon on a relatively short prophetic speech (Isa. 1:2–20), while the second is a sermon on a larger prophetic unit, the Book of Habakkuk. The third and fourth expositions are more didactic than sermonic. The third is a lesson on Psalm 44, while the fourth illustrates how one might develop a topical exposition on a theme (in this case money) from Proverbs.

(1) Yahweh Takes His People to Court (Isaiah 1:2–20)

Obedience, Not Sacrifice

In 1845 former slave Frederick Douglass, having obtained his freedom a short time before, wrote of American Christianity:

> I love the pure, peaceable, and impartial Christianity of Christ: I therefore hate the corrupt, slaveholding, women-whipping, cradle-plundering, partial and hypocritical Christianity of this land. Indeed, I can see no reason, but the most deceitful one, for calling the religion of this land Christianity. I look upon it as the climax of all misnomers, the boldest of all frauds, and the grossest of all libels. . . . I am filled with unutterable loathing when I contemplate the religious pomp and show, together with the horrible inconsistencies, which every where surround me. . . . The man who wields the blood-clotted cowskin during the week fills the pulpit on Sunday, and claims to be a minister of the meek and lowly Jesus. The man who robs me of my earnings at the end of the week meets me as a class-leader on Sunday morning, to show me the way of life, and the path of salvation. He who sells my sister, for purposes of prostitution, stands forth as the pious advocate of purity. He who proclaims it a religious duty to read the Bible denies me the right of learning to read the name of the God who made me. . . . The

warm defender of the sacredness of the family relation is the same that scatters whole families,—sundering husbands and wives, parents and children, sisters and brothers,—leaving the hut vacant, and the hearth desolate.[16]

After further describing the hypocrisy of antebellum "Christianity," Douglass compared American Christians to the Pharisees of Jesus' day:

They attend with Pharisaical strictness to the outward forms of religion, and at the same time neglect the weightier matters of the law, judgment, mercy, and faith. They are always ready to sacrifice, but seldom to show mercy. They are they who are represented as professing to love God whom they have not seen, whilst they hate their brother whom they have seen. They love the heathen on the other side of the globe. They can pray for him, pay money to have the Bible put into his hand, and missionaries to instruct him; while they despise and totally neglect the heathen at their own doors.[17]

Religious individuals have always been susceptible to an insidious disease known as hypocrisy. It overtakes those who gradually divorce their faith from daily practice. In its final stages it is characterized by an extremely pious veneer, which Jesus compared to a whitewashed tomb (Matt. 23:27). In terms of formal, God-directed activity, religious hypocrites often go through all the right motions with an intensity that puts others to shame. They bring their offerings according to the divinely prescribed regulations. They pray and sing. But when they leave the sanctuary there is something missing. As they go through their daily routine they fail to implement God's commands about interpersonal relationships and social responsibilities. Somehow they fail to understand a very important biblical principle: *No vital relationship with God is possible apart from obedience to God's commands concerning responsibilities to one's fellow human beings.*

The vertical relationship (how we relate to God) needs a foundation (proper relationships with other people) or it will topple to the ground. Jesus reminded the Pharisees of this, "Woe to you, teachers of the law and Pharisees, you hypocrites! You give a tenth of your spices. . . . But you have neglected the more important matters of the law—justice, mercy and faithfulness. You should have practiced the latter, without neglecting the former" (Matt. 23:23). James reminded his readers of the same fact: "If anyone considers himself religious and yet does not keep a tight rein on his tongue, he deceives himself and his religion is worthless. Religion that God our Father accepts as pure and faultless is this: to look after orphans and widows in their distress and to keep oneself from being

---

16. *Narrative of the Life of Frederick Douglass, An American Slave,* Dolphin Books edition (Garden City, N.Y.: Doubleday, 1963), 117–18.
17. Ibid., 120–21.

polluted by the world" (James 1:26–27). In fact this principle permeates Scripture. One of its most powerful expressions is in Isaiah 1:2–20.

In this text the issue of Israel's relationship to God is central. It becomes apparent from the outset that this relationship has been seriously disrupted. Israel has broken the Mosaic covenant (vv. 2–3) and already has begun to experience the serious consequences of such rebellion (vv. 4–9). The relationship is in desperate need of restoration. However, that restoration cannot be realized through outward religious acts such as sacrifice and prayer (vv. 10–15). Only active obedience can bring vitality back to the relationship (vv. 16–20).

The passage begins with a courtroom scene (vv. 2–3). The Lord appears in the role of prosecutor, Israel is the defendant, and the heavens and earth are summoned as witnesses. At the time when God instituted the covenant with Israel these personified elements of nature were witnesses to the agreement (cf. Deut. 30:19). Now the Lord calls upon them to testify that Israel has not been faithful to its oath.

The Lord confronts his people with their ingratitude and disobedience. Despite his fatherly care, Israel has rejected him. As Israel's Father the Lord has done everything within his power to meet his children's needs and bring them to adulthood. The language used here is reminiscent of Deuteronomy 1:31, in which Moses recalls that the Lord "carried" the people through the wilderness "as a father carries his son." One would expect a son, as he reflected on such kindness, to be grateful and seek to please his father. In Israel's case, just the opposite occurred. They rebelled against his authority.

Such obstinance, like all sin, was irrational and inexplicable. Even the most brutish of animals (the ox and donkey) are capable of recognizing their owner as the source of food. In violation of this general principle, Israel refused to acknowledge the Lord as the source of its benefits.

Israel was already experiencing the consequences of its sin (vv. 4–9). The judgments, or "curses," threatened in Deuteronomy were being carried out, bringing Israel to the point of extinction. This *divine discipline should have been a warning signal to the disobedient and motivated them to immediate repentance.*

The section begins with the sound of death. The little word "Ah" was a cry of mourning heard at funerals (cf. 1 Kings 13:30; Jer. 22:18–19; Amos 5:16). When an Israelite heard this word, images of death would have appeared in her or his mind's eye. To use dynamic equivalents, he would have seen flowers, a casket, weeping friends and relatives, and a somber-looking member of the clergy. By prefacing his remarks with this word, the prophet suggests that the rebellious nation's funeral is imminent.

The reason for this impending doom is reiterated in verse 4 in strong language. Israel is loaded down with guilt and characterized by evil and corrupt actions. They have rejected (cf. "forsaken," "spurned," "turned their backs on") the transcendent King of Israel (cf. "Holy One of Israel") whose authority is binding upon them.

In its near-fatal condition Israel is like a severely battered human body that has been deprived of medical attention (vv. 5–6). The reality behind the vivid figurative language is described in verses 7–9. The nation has been invaded by a foreign army (probably the Assyrians under Sennacherib, ca. 701 B.C.), which has burned its cities and stripped the land of its produce.[18] Only the preservation of besieged Jerusalem (called here the "Daughter of Zion") has kept the nation from being totally annihilated like the ancient cities of Sodom and Gomorrah, paradigms of God's powerful and devastating judgment (cf. Isa. 13:19; Jer. 49:18; 50:40; Amos 4:11; Zeph. 2:9).

Two observations should be made about the nature of the judgment described here. First, it represents the implementation of the covenant "curses." The language of verses 5–9 reflects Deuteronomy 28–29. The appropriation of the nation's agricultural wealth (Deut. 28:33, 51), the siege of its cities (Deut. 28:52), its reduction to a small remnant (Deut. 28:62), and the comparison of its fate to that of Sodom and Gomorrah (Deut. 29:23) were all threatened by Moses. One is reminded from this that God's threats are not idle. Even if his patient love allows him to bear with his people for hundreds of years, persistent disobedience will eventually be punished in precisely the way he threatened.

Second, the judgment described here is perfectly appropriate. This is expressed in the Hebrew text through wordplay. The word translated "turned their backs" (lit., "estranged themselves") in verse 4 is related to and sounds like the term translated "foreigners" (and "strangers") in verse 7. Appropriately, then, those who have "estranged" themselves from the Lord are being punished by "strangers" sent by the Lord. In this way one is reminded that God's judgment is always perfectly just.

Having established the fact of Israel's guilt and dire need for restoration, the Lord moves next to the prerequisite for restoration. He begins by refuting the nation's potential defense. *Their outward religious acts,* which they apparently viewed as the essential element in their relationship with the Lord, *could not bring restoration. In fact they only heightened the people's guilt* by adding hypocrisy to the list of their sins.

By addressing the people as inhabitants of Sodom and Gomorrah (v. 10), the Lord sets the tone for this part of his argument. The people may be religious in their own eyes, but as far as he is concerned, they are no different in character than were the vile residents of those wicked cities (cf. 3:9 as well).

One quickly sees from the detailed description of the nation's religious life (vv. 11–15) that the people were heavily involved in formal worship.

18. For Sennacherib's own description of the invasion see James Pritchard, ed., *The Ancient Near East,* 2 vols. (Princeton, N.J.: Princeton University Press, 1975), 1:200–201.

They brought an abundance of sacrifices to the temple, faithfully observed the religious feasts, and offered prayers.

One sees just as quickly that the Lord is highly offended by all of this activity. The multiplication of sacrifices (apparently viewed here as food for God) has brought him to the point of vomiting. He detests the incense of their sacrifices as much as he does child sacrifice or idolatry.[19] Their assemblies in the temple are a heavy burden to him, which he loathes. He refuses to listen to the people's prayers because the very hands which they spread toward heaven are covered with the blood of fellow Israelites, as well as that of sacrificial animals.

Moshe Greenberg has perceptively described the logic of the Lord's argument in these verses:

> This vehement, unconditional repudiation of the whole of Israel's established worship has several premises: first, that in all its forms, worship is, like prayer, a social transaction between persons, with no magical virtue or intrinsic efficacy. It is rather a gesture of submission and like all gestures a formality whose meaning depends ultimately on the total moral evaluation the recipient makes of the one who gestures; for the recipient to esteem the gesturer there must be some moral identification between them. (I should regard a gesture of good will made to me by my sworn enemy as a trick.) For worship to find favor in God's eyes, the worshiper must identify himself with ('know' in the biblical idiom; e.g., Jer. 22:15f) God in the one way possible for man—by imitating his moral conduct (compare also Hos. 4:1f. and Jer. 9:23). Gestures of submission made by villains are an abomination to God.[20]

The allusion to violent crime in verse 15 provides the transition to the climax of the Lord's argument. In the final verses (16–20) he delivers an ultimatum to Israel in which the prerequisite for restoration is expressed. *Active obedience to the Lord's commands concerning social responsibilities is essential* for survival.

Through a series of commands the Lord appeals to Israel to change its ways (vv. 16–17). This is figuratively expressed by the command to "wash" and "make . . . clean." This cleansing would be realized by abandoning evil deeds of social injustice. Such deeds were a blatant violation of the standards set by the Lord, Israel's just king, to regulate covenant life (cf. Deut. 24:17). Injustice was also a practical denial of the nation's redemptive heritage. Each Israelite's treatment of a covenant brother was to follow the pattern set by the Lord when he redeemed Israel from Egypt, not that of their Egyptian oppressors (Deut. 24:18).

19. The word תּוֹעֵבָה, "detestable" (v. 13), is used of the Lord's attitude toward child sacrifice (Deut. 12:31) and idolatry in general (Deut. 13:15).

20. Moshe Greenberg, *Biblical Prose Prayer* (Berkeley: University of California Press, 1983), 55–56.

The people were also to take up the cause of the socially oppressed (such as widows and orphans). The latter task would involve purifying the corrupt legal system, which was an instrument used to exploit the poor.

The Lord concludes his argument with a gracious word of assurance and a reminder that Israel's response to his appeal will determine its future (vv. 18–20). According to verse 18, forgiveness is still available to sin-stained Israel. The nation's sins, likened to a garment that is dyed red, can still be transformed into pure white. This apparently means that their sins, although deserving of punishment, will not be held against them if they repent. The future of Israel's relationship to the Lord hinges on its response to this appeal for social justice. Obedience will bring a restoration of the Lord's blessing in the form of peace and agricultural prosperity. The land will again produce crops and the people, protected from invading armies, will be able to enjoy the fruits of their labor. However, continuation in rebellion will bring the final stroke of judgment. Ironically, instead of eating the best from the land, they themselves will be devoured ("eat," v. 19, and "devoured," v. 20, are the same Hebrew word) by the sword of an enemy invader.

In summary, for Israel obedience to all the demands of the covenant, especially those regulating social life and responsibilities to the poor, was essential for a vital relationship with their covenant Lord. Failure in this regard had brought the nation to the brink of total destruction. Outward religious acts could not heal the rift. Only active obedience could restore the relationship.

As observed earlier, the basic principle of this passage permeates Scripture: *No vital relationship with God is possible apart from obedience to God's commands concerning responsibilities to other people.* In the New Testament the principle is applied to various contexts. James made fulfillment of social obligations one of his twin pillars of true religion. According to Paul, these extend to unbelievers as well as Christians (Gal. 6:10). The principle appears in Jesus' teaching on interpersonal relationships. For example, one cannot expect divine forgiveness unless he has forgiven others (Matt. 6:14–15). One is not to present an offering to God at the altar unless he or she has reconciled all differences with his or her brother or sister (Matt. 5:23–24). According to the apostle John, one who withholds material goods from his brother cannot have a genuine relationship with God (1 John 3:17). Peter applies the principle to the marriage relationship. The husband who fails to treat his wife with respect will find his prayers to God hindered (1 Peter 3:7). It is clear, then, that proper treatment of others is foundational to one's relationship with God. Those who attempt to worship God apart from that foundation are, like ancient Israel, self-deceived and destined for severe judgment.

(2) Habakkuk Debates with God

Waiting for Justice

Eleven-year-old Liliane Gerenstein was living in the wrong place at the wrong time. For her it was the wrong place (German-occupied France) and the wrong time (April 1944) because she was Jewish. Already she had been separated from her parents, who were on their way to the Auschwitz death camp. From her room in a small children's home where she and forty other Jewish children had found at least temporary refuge she wrote down the following prayer:

> God? How good you are, how kind, and if one had to count the number of goodnesses and kindnesses You have done us he would never finish. God? It is You who command. It is You who are justice, it is You who reward the good and punish the evil. God? It is thanks to You that I had lovely things that others do not have. God? After that, I ask you one thing only: MAKE MY PARENTS COME BACK, MY POOR PARENTS, PROTECT THEM (even more than you protect me) SO THAT I CAN SEE THEM AGAIN AS SOON AS POSSIBLE. MAKE THEM COME BACK AGAIN. Ah! I could say that I had such a good mother and a good father! I have such faith in you that I thank You in advance.[21]

By the time Liliane voiced this prayer her mother was dead. Her father had somehow escaped the train bound for Auschwitz and was on his way to Sweden, but he would never see Liliane again. A few days later two trucks roared into the courtyard of the children's home. Ten German SS men got out. They broke into the kitchen while the children were eating their breakfast, rounded the children up, and took them to a cellar of a prison in Lyons.[22] Klaus Barbie, head of Gestapo Department IV in Lyons telegramed to Gestapo headquarters in Paris:

> Subject: The Jewish children's home. In the early morning hours the Jewish children's home "The Children's Colony" was terminated. A total of 41 children from 3–13 in age were removed. Cash or any other kind of possessions could not be secured. Transport is arranged on April 7, 1944.[23]

Shortly after this the children were transported to Auschwitz, where Liliane and her brother Maurice died in the gas chamber.

We live in a world where good rarely triumphs over evil. And we don't have to go back to 1944 or cross an ocean for illustrations. A liberal press harps away day after day about alleged violations of various groups' civil rights, at the same time turning a deaf ear to the death cries of millions of aborted babies, violently and ruthlessly wrenched and torn from their

---

21. See Barbara Goldsmith, "The Woman Who Avenged the Children of Izieu," *Parade Magazine*, 22 January 1984, 6.

22. Ibid., 4.

23. Ibid.

mothers' wombs by self-serving butchers who rationalize their actions by pious appeals to the great American principle of human rights.

For the Christian all of this poses a severe problem, for the Bible affirms that justice is the very foundation of God's throne (Ps. 97:2). If God is perfectly just and is sovereign over his world, why do we see so much injustice? Why does the prayer of a helpless and innocent eleven-year-old girl go unanswered? A well-known Old Testament scholar and professor at a seminary in New York City once challenged his students:

> Every morning when you wake up, before you reaffirm your faith in the majesty of a loving God, before you say *I believe* for another day, read the *Daily News* with its record of the latest crimes and tragedies of mankind and then see if you can honestly say it again.[24]

His challenge to his students draws attention to the apparent contradiction with which we are faced. Our experience seems to conflict with our theology. For some the tension is too great and they despair. For example, the contemporary Jewish writer Elie Wiesel describes his reaction to seeing children burned alive at Auschwitz: "Never shall I forget those moments which murdered my God and my soul and turned my dreams to dust. Never shall I forget these things, even if I am condemned to live as long as God Himself. Never."[25] One of Wiesel's biographers explains the significance of Wiesel's words:

> Ever since that first night, Wiesel has struggled with two irreconcilable realities—the reality of God and the reality of Auschwitz. Either seems to cancel out the other, and yet neither will disappear. Either in isolation could be managed—Auschwitz and no God, or God and no Auschwitz. But Auschwitz *and* God, God *and* Auschwitz? That is the unbearable reality that haunts sleep and wakefulness.[26]

If we're taking the time to observe the world around us and if we're honest, we must admit that on occasion we find ourselves asking, "Is God really just?" And taking it one step further, "Is God really faithful?"

The prophet Habakkuk faced these same questions head on and his experience is instructive for us. Let's consider together the message of this short, often neglected, but rich and profound book. The Book of Habakkuk does not answer all of our questions about the problem of evil,

---

24. The quotation comes from James Muilenburg. See Frederick Buechner, "James Muilenburg as Man and Scholar," in *Hearing and Speaking the Word: Selections from the Works of James Muilenburg*, ed. Thomas F. Best (Chico, Calif.: Scholars, 1984), [8].

25. Elie Wiesel, *Night* (New York: Avon Books, 1969), 44, as quoted in Stephen Gottschalk, "Theodicy after Auschwitz and the Reality of God," *Union Seminary Quarterly Review* 41, nos. 3 & 4 (1987): 77.

26. Robert McAfee Brown, *Elie Wiesel: Messenger to All Humanity* (Notre Dame, Ind.: University of Notre Dame Press, 1983), 54, as quoted in Gottschalk, "Theodicy," 77.

but it does encourage us and give us hope as we attempt to remain sane in the midst of a corrupt, unjust world. It reminds us that *God will ultimately judge evildoers and vindicate his people.*

Habakkuk lived in the late seventh century B.C., in those final dark days of the kingdom of Judah. Despite King Josiah's admirable attempts at social reform, the swift, downward spiral initiated by Manasseh's blatant acts of injustice earlier in the seventh century had continued (cf. 2 Kings 23:35; Jer. 22:13–19; 26:1–23). As Habakkuk looked around he saw injustice on every side. And when he cried out to God to intervene and hear and save, he received no answer:

> How long, LORD, must I cry for help? But you do not listen! I call out to you, "Violence!" But you do not intervene! Why do you force me to experience injustice? Why do you put up with wrongdoing? Destruction and violence confront me; conflict is present and one must endure strife. For this reason the law lacks power; justice is never carried out. Indeed the wicked intimidate the innocent. For this reason justice is perverted. (Hab. 1:2–4)

Notice the accumulation of words that refer to violent acts of injustice—"violence, injustice, wrongdoing, destruction, conflict, strife." God's Law (his covenant demands regulating Israel's life, including socioeconomic matters) had become "paralyzed." The word used here (translated "lacks power" above) is also used in Psalm 77:2 with reference to a hand which has fallen asleep. You know what it feels like to have your hand or foot fall asleep. As long as the hand or foot is numb it is ineffective. That had happened to God's Law in Habakkuk's day. The justice demanded by the Law never prevailed. The wicked outnumbered the just and controlled the legal system, with the result that justice was "perverted," that is, all bent and twisted out of shape. And through it all God was silent.

But finally God spoke. However, his words (cf. 1:5–11) were astonishing beyond belief. His solution to the problem of injustice in Judah was to raise up the Babylonians and send them to destroy Judah and carry the people away into exile. This was not quite the answer Habakkuk was expecting, not quite the savior that he had in mind. This would be like a fundamentalist, card-carrying member of the Conservative coalition being told by God on a national day of prayer that an invading foreign army, not a conservative sweep of the congressional races, would be the divine solution to the sin of abortion in America. Habakkuk was learning an important principle: *God's justice does not always appear just on the surface.*

But don't miss the justice in all of this. The Babylonians, according to verse 6, seized "dwelling places that do not belong to them," just like the unjust upper classes of Judah had been doing. According to verse 7, the Babylonians "decided for themselves what is right." How appropriate that those who showed no regard for God's principles of justice would be swept away by the Babylonians' own arbitrary brand of "justice." Notice also verse 9, which says that the Babylonians would come ready to do "violence." This same word appears back in verses 2–3 to describe the unjust oppressors of Judah. How appropriate that the violent of Judah were destined to die a violent death at the hands of the Babylonians!

Habakkuk undoubtedly caught the point. He responds:

> LORD, you have been active from ancient times; my holy God, you are immortal. LORD, you have made them your instrument of judgment; Protector, you have appointed them as your instrument of punishment. You are too just to tolerate evil; you are unable to condone wrongdoing. (1:12–13a)

In verse 12 he acknowledges that the Babylonians were appointed by God to judge and punish. This demonstrates once again that the eternal God is indeed holy and so Habakkuk addresses God as such in verse 12, calling him "my holy God." In verse 13 Habakkuk affirms that God is too pure to tolerate wrong. His confidence in God's justice has obviously advanced beyond where it was in verses 2–4.

But another problem has been raised. Granted that the unjust in Judah deserve punishment—but why would God use a nation even more wicked than Judah as an instrument of punishment? Habakkuk asks: "So why do you put up with such treacherous people? Why do you say nothing when the wicked devour those who are relatively innocent?" (1:13b).

The Babylonians arrogantly and ruthlessly extended their empire. Should Judah, though sinful, be destroyed by *these* people? In solving the problem of injustice in the land of Judah, wasn't the Lord actually spreading injustice to a worldwide level? Though he still has questions, Habakkuk has learned a lesson. He decides to wait eagerly for God's response (cf. 2:1).

Once more the Lord answers him, instructing him to record a vision (2:2) of what will transpire (2:3). The Lord also instructs him to wait for the fulfillment of the vision because it is certain to come (2:3b). This "vision," which is actually a prophecy of judgment, begins with a contrast between the proud Babylonians and loyal followers of the Lord: "Look, the one whose desires are not upright will faint from exhaustion, but the one who is innocent will be preserved by his integrity" (2:4). Verse 4 introduces the two main themes of the remainder of the book—the pride of the Babylonians, the consequences of which are outlined in detail in the remainder of chapter 2, and the destiny of the righteous, which comes into clearer focus in chapter 3.

First, let's look at God's message of judgment against the proud Babylonians, recorded in 2:5–20. The greedy Babylonians are compared in verse 6 to a dishonest loan shark. But God warns: "Your creditors will suddenly attack. Those who terrify you will spring into action, and they will rob you" (2:7). Suddenly Babylon's "creditors" will rise up against it and then Babylon will be plundered just as it plundered others (2:8). Verses 15–16 portray in vivid language the poetic justice God will bring upon Babylon. Babylon is pictured as one who keeps on forcing its neighbors to drink wine so that it can shame them. But what goes around comes around. According to verse 16, a day is coming when God will make the Babylonians drink from that same cup of intoxicating wine. In that day the Babylonians' lifeless gods, alluded to in verses 18–19, will be unable to rescue them from the righteous punishment of the sovereign God of the universe (2:20).

In the first two chapters of this book God has shown Habakkuk that *divine justice will ultimately prevail.* Using the Babylonians as his instrument, God will judge Judah for its neglect of God's Law. He will then judge the arrogant Babylonians for their sins against others.

But what about the faithful followers of the Lord? Would they be caught up in these judgments and destroyed? Would Judah come to an end forever? These were questions that were on Habakkuk's mind. In 2:4 God promises that the "righteous" will be preserved through the coming judgment by their integrity or faithfulness, that is, their unwavering devotion to God and his requirements.

With this promise from God in hand, Habakkuk prays in 3:2: "Lord, I have heard the report of what you did; I am awed, Lord, by what you accomplished. In our time repeat those deeds, in our time reveal them again. But when you cause turmoil, remember to show us mercy." He opens by telling God that he is aware of the Lord's mighty deeds in Israel's history. He then asks that God renew these deeds and concludes by requesting that God "remember mercy" as he judges and punishes. In other words, in the face of impending judgment Habakkuk holds God to his promise. As God brings judgment upon the evildoers, Habakkuk asks that he show mercy to the faithful and ultimately deliver his covenant people from their oppressors as he had done so many times before.

God answers Habakkuk this time with a picture, not words. In verses 3–15 Habakkuk describes this picture. Habakkuk saw God coming as a mighty warrior to deliver Israel. God comes from Teman and Mount Paran, that is, from the south, the direction of Mount Sinai. As he approaches, all the nations and nature itself tremble in fear before him. He shoots his arrows and hurls his spear, annihilating the enemies of his people. Even the sun and the moon stand still before him. Throughout this vision there are allusions to past historical events. For example, according to verse 11, the sun and moon stand still, just as they did when Joshua defeated the Amorites at Gibeon (Josh. 10:12–14). God's future intervention is described here in terms of past acts, emphasizing that he is still alive and active on behalf of his people.

At this point Habakkuk has seen it all. The Lord has given him a panorama of the future from Judah's judgment at the hands of the Babylonians (chapter 1) to the Lord's ultimate vindication of his people (chapter 3). But now the prophet has to face the historical realization of the prophesied events. As he considers the prospect of the immediate future he shudders with terror, for he has to wait patiently for the prophesied events to run their course. The prophet must endure the dark night of Judah's judgment before salvation arrives: He says:

> I listened and my stomach churned, the sound made my lips quiver. My frame went limp, as if my bones were decaying, and I shook as I tried to walk. I long for the day of distress to come upon the people who attack us. (3:16)

Yet Habakkuk had received a positive answer to his prayer. He had asked the Lord to renew his mighty acts and to show mercy in the midst of judgment. Through the vision of chapter 3 he gained assurance that the God of the Exodus and Conquest would indeed act again in the future. *The just God is alive and well!* Though the Babylonians would invade the land, the Lord would ultimately deliver and restore his people. This assurance enabled Habakkuk to express unwavering confidence in the Lord:

> When the fig tree does not bud, and there are no grapes on the vines; when the olive trees do not produce, and the fields yield no crops; when the sheep disappear from the pen, and there are no cattle in the stalls, I will rejoice because of the LORD; I will be happy because of the God who delivers me. The sovereign LORD is my source of strength. He gives me the agility of a deer; he enables me to negotiate the rugged terrain. (3:17–19)

Though the coming invasion would bring the destruction of crops and livestock, making food difficult to come by, Habakkuk would rejoice in the Lord, whom he recognized as his deliverer and source of strength. Habakkuk compares himself to a deer, which is capable of quickly and safely moving about in steep, rocky heights. Just as the deer travels through difficult terrain without stumbling or suffering injury, so Habakkuk would endure the hardships of the coming invasion, sustained by his trust in the sovereign Lord. Habakkuk had learned that *faith in God's justice can sustain the righteous.*

In James Michener's novel *Poland*, in a chapter about the German occupation of Poland during World War II, entitled "The Terror," two Poles, Szymon Bukowski and an aging professor named Tomczyk, are together in a prison cell. The Germans torture them daily. Szymon cannot understand what sustains the professor through this ordeal. One day, after a particularly brutal beating, the old professor explains the source of his strength to Szymon:

271

> It is not my responsibility to bring retribution to these men. We have . . . a God to whom we allocate that task and we must believe that He notes every action in this cellar and will in due course make honest restitution. . . . And it does not matter, son, whether we are alive to see the restitution or not. It will come as surely as day follows night, and we are now in the night. It will surely come. That we must never doubt. . . . God sees everything that happens in that room, and it is to Him that we look for deliverance.[27]

Like the old professor, Habakkuk had come to a place where he confidently trusted in the justice of God. Although we cannot understand or explain why God allows certain things to happen or why he seemingly so often turns a deaf ear to those in dire need, we can be sure that someday he will execute justice against the Klaus Barbies and the Babylonians of this world. At the same time, he will never abandon his faithful followers or sweep them away indiscriminately in his righteous judgment on sinful men and societies. We can be confident that *God will ultimately judge evildoers and vindicate his people.* Realization of this basic truth can sustain us through the dark night of the present hour, when suffering and injustice seem so widespread and God seems so silent. Come what may we can affirm with Habakkuk: "I will rejoice because of the LORD. . . . The sovereign LORD is my source of strength."

(3) Israel Faces a Dilemma (Psalm 44)

When Creed Collides with Reality

It's become a pretty common scenario in modern America. A young couple, intoxicated by romantic expectations, gets married and vows to be faithful to each other until death separates them. Before too long they have a couple of kids and begin to raise what appears to be a happy little family. The husband works hard to put bread on the table and establishes a reputation, within his family and in the community, as a faithful husband and a good provider. However, twenty to twenty-five years later, as the last of the kids leaves the nest, this faithful husband and good provider, who's seemingly always come through, at the job and at home, becomes disillusioned with life. He develops a friendship with another woman, perhaps one of the gals at the office, and before long he's involved in an adulterous relationship or "affair," as it's euphemistically referred to by our amoral society. Suddenly he announces to his wife that he's getting a divorce.

Perhaps one of the most difficult experiences in all of life is when someone you're trusting in, someone who has promised to be faithful to you, fails to come through. This is especially perplexing when this person has come through in the past and seemingly demonstrated his or her faithfulness. How do you respond in such a situation? Some might say,

27. James A. Michener, *Poland* (New York: Random House, 1983), 427.

wisely I think, "Well, don't jump to conclusions. Give them the benefit of the doubt. Maybe there's a good reason for the delay or maybe the failure is only apparent." However, sometimes the circumstances so obviously suggest a breakdown in faithfulness and the pain caused by the other person's failure is so intense, that one is forced to conclude the worst.

Psalm 44 was written in such a context. The nation of Judah had just suffered a humiliating defeat on the battlefield. Many people had been carried away by the enemy to be sold into slavery. For the people of Judah a head-on collision had occurred between the brutal reality of their circumstances and the theological ideals they had inherited from their ancestors and had long cherished. God had always come through in the past—their fathers had told them of the early days when God brought them miraculously into the land and again and again they themselves had affirmed God's greatness and faithfulness in their hymns. Furthermore, as far as they could tell, they had been faithful to God's covenant. Everyone knew that God had promised to bless the nation abundantly if they remained faithful to him. But now they found themselves humiliated before their enemies. At best God seemed to be asleep. At worst he had proven to be unfaithful to his promises.

In the midst of their suffering, embarrassment, and confusion, God's Spirit, the ultimate author of all Scripture, mysteriously moved God's people to offer up this psalm to God, who, in his providence, made sure that it was included in the Book of Psalms as a model for hurting and perplexed believers of all generations to appropriate.

The psalm has four major sections. The first section, verses 1–8, when heard in isolation, sounds very positive and confident. In fact, it has the earmarks of a victory hymn. The congregation begins by rehearsing the theological tradition handed down to them by their ancestors (vv. 1–3). God drove the pagan nations out of the land of Canaan and gave that land to his covenant people. The Israelites did not conquer the land by their own power. No, God conquered it by his invincible power and gave it to his people because he had chosen them to be the special object of his favor. As the text puts it (v. 3b), God had caused the "light of" his "face" to shine on them. The expression "light of the face," which refers to a cheerful, smiling face (cf. Job 29:24), is a Hebrew idiom for acceptance and favor (cf. Prov. 16:15; note also Pss. 4:6; 89:15 and passages using the related verbal form—Num. 6:25; Pss. 31:16; 67:1; 80:3, 7, 19).

In response to the congregation's rehearsal of God's mighty deeds, the leader of the congregation, perhaps the king, declares one of Israel's central theological traditions: "You are my king, O God, the one who decrees victories for Jacob" (v. 4). Picking up on their leader's confidence, the people then declare their confidence in God: "By your power we push back our adversaries; in your name we stomp on those who oppose us" (v. 5). In verse 6 the leader again speaks, pointing out that he does not place his trust in human weapons, while in verses 7–8 the people join him, affirming that God alone gives victory and that he deserves the praises of his people.

But, at this point the guitar strings snap, as it were, and we hear a series of sour, discordant notes. The victory hymn suddenly changes to a bitter lament, sharply contrasting what might and should have been with what actually had occurred. It's as if the congregation is saying: "OK, we've recited the party line. We've rehearsed the tradition and repeated the theological truths we've always believed and affirmed. These are the words we expected to be singing. But, we can't go any further, Lord. Here's the way we really feel."

In this next section (vv. 9–16) the people pour out their hearts before God. In contrast to verses 1–8, which rehearse God's past victories for his people, the people now express their sense of abandonment by God. The people are confronted by a harsh reality and their dilemma illustrates a truth we must acknowledge: *There are times when our experience seems to contradict our theological creed.* Judah all but accuses God of having rejected and humiliated his people (v. 9a). He has not accompanied their armies on to the battlefield on this most recent occasion (v. 9b). No, God has seemingly fought against his people, causing them to retreat before their enemies (v. 10). Rather than fulfilling his responsibility as Israel's Shepherd, God has allowed the predator to ravage and devour the helpless flock (v. 11a). He has scattered his people among the nations (v. 11b), probably a reference to his people being taken away as prisoners of war and then being sold as slaves, which would have resulted in their being dispersed throughout the ancient Near Eastern world. In verse 12 the people even compare God to a merchant who no longer values an item and sells it for virtually nothing just to get rid of it. They feel like such a worthless item. Even worse, they must endure both national and individual humiliation as the surrounding nations hurl insults at them and mock their defeat (vv. 13–16).

At this point, based on what we know about Israel's propensity to sin, one expects the congregation to say: "Lord, we realize that we've sinned and that's why we've experienced this defeat. Please forgive us and restore us to your favor." But, surprisingly we get just the opposite.

Rather than confessing sin, the congregation claims to have been faithful to God. When this would have been true in Judah's long, sin-ridden history is unclear. However, in this case we have to take their words at face value, for we have no narrative context that would invalidate their claim. If we take the words at face value, then the people, prior to this defeat, had not forgotten God (v. 17a). They had remained faithful to his covenant (v. 17b). Their hearts, standing for their thoughts and motives, had remained true to God, and their footsteps, standing for their lifestyle and actions, had not strayed from God's prescribed path (v. 18). They had not been so foolish as to worship other gods, not even secretly, for they knew that God is all-knowing and is aware of even "the secrets of the heart/mind" (vv. 20–21).

Nevertheless, from their perspective at least, God had violently crushed them and devastated their land, making it more fit for packs of wild dogs than people (v. 19a). God had, as it were, covered the entire land with deep darkness, symbolic here of defeat and ruin (v. 19b). Though the people had remained faithful to God, they felt that their devotion had brought them only persecution and death (v. 22a). They felt like helpless, stupid sheep being led away to the slaughtering block (v. 22b). The language in verses 19 and 22 is especially ironic in light of Psalm 23:4. There God is portrayed as a shepherd who carefully guides his sheep through the valley of deep darkness. However, according to Psalm 44, he overwhelms them with deep darkness and allows them to be slaughtered like sheep. The people were confronted by another harsh reality: *There are times when tragedy overtakes innocent people.*

Having poured out their complaint before God and having protested their innocence, the congregation concludes with a cry for help (vv. 23–26). Their tenacious faith reminds us of an important spiritual principle: *Even during difficult times, when God seems distant and unfair, God's people may still seek his intervention* (23–26). The people maintain their faith in God despite their perception that he is their enemy. The words of verse 23, where the congregation suggests God is sleeping, are particularly startling, especially when one recalls the hymnic affirmation of Psalm 121:4 that "he who watches over Israel will neither slumber or sleep." But again, the people are being honest with God and rather than hurling fire down upon them, God gives their honest prayer his stamp of approval by canonizing it in Scripture. From their perspective, it seemed as if God was sleeping on the job. His face may have shined on their ancestors, but this generation felt that he had hidden his face from them and was calloused to their misery and oppression (v. 24). They felt trampled down, as if they were lying in the dust of the ground (v. 25). But with their last ounce of energy, they beg God to intervene and deliver them (v. 26). And the last phrase in the psalm is the key—"because of your unfailing love." It seemed as if God's love, which earlier generations had experienced, had indeed failed and that he had reneged on his promises. However, despite appearances, this courageous generation of faithful believers appeals to this divine attribute, the one that had to be genuine if they were to retain any hope for the future.

Psalm 44 reminds us that faith comes in different forms. Sometimes faith is robust and takes the form of confident affirmations. But sometimes, in the context of intense suffering and confusion, when God seems to have abandoned us or let us down, faith may take the form of holding on for dear life. It's as if the authors of Psalm 44 are surrounded by flames. As you peer through the flames, you hear them desperately crying out to God for help, even though they think God set the fire. We have a tendency to think that faith should always look the same, but Psalm 44 reminds us we can't be that rigid in our outlook. People suffer at different levels and they can express their faith in God in different ways.

Psalm 44 also reminds us that God doesn't fit in a box. Though the authors were not guilty of any special, heinous sins which brought God's wrath down upon them, they still suffered. Their experience reminds us that God can and sometimes does bring inexplicable trials along, just as he did to righteous Job. When that happens, when reality seems to contradict theology, confusion can occur. But this psalm also reminds us that *when unexplained tragedy challenges our creed, we can cling tenaciously to theological truths while pouring out our souls before the Lord in honest, heartfelt prayer.*

(4) The Proverbs on the Theme of Money

If I Were a Rich Man!

One of my favorite musicals is *Fiddler on the Roof,* a story about a Jewish peasant family in early-twentieth-century Russia attempting to preserve its identity and cherished traditions, while at the same time being forced to adapt to the realities of a changing and unpredictable world. The main character in the story is Tevye, a poor milkman trying to eke out a living for his wife and five daughters. Every once in a while, especially after a particularly back-breaking day, Tevye reflects upon his economic condition and dreams about what it would be like to be rich. He concludes his song "If I Were a Rich Man" by asking God: "Would it spoil some vast eternal plan if I were a wealthy man?"

Like Tevye, all of us, at some time or other, have daydreamed about what we would do, or how we would live, if money were no object. Christians respond to the subject of wealth in a variety of ways. There are some who claim that God wants to bless his children with material wealth. At the opposite end of the spectrum, others reject the quest for wealth as something inherently evil. Still others, probably the great majority, have mixed feelings. They secretly long for wealth, because they know the advantages that money carries with it. But, at the same time, they feel uncomfortable, perhaps even guilty, about such desires, because they know the Bible condemns greed and materialism.

Since the Book of Proverbs claims to give insight and direction for living in a wise and God-pleasing manner, one would expect to find something there on the subject of wealth and money. After all, economics and money are basic to life. When we open the pages of Proverbs, we see that the book does indeed have a great deal to say about the subject of material wealth and what our attitude should be toward money. Proverbs provides us with some very realistic, practical, and godly insights on this issue. It's very difficult to distill the book's teaching on this subject into a few concise statements, but I've risked the danger of oversimplification and tried to do just that. The Book of Proverbs gives us at least five principles concerning wealth and our attitude toward it.

(1) According to Proverbs, *wealth is not necessarily something negative or evil.* In fact some proverbs assume that economic wealth is desirable. Lady Wisdom, for example, promises riches to those who heed her advice (8:18, 21; cf. 24:3–4). According to Proverbs 10:22, the Lord's blessing can sometimes take the form of material wealth (cf. also 22:4).

(2) Of course, for those so blessed there are certain obligations. *Those whom God blesses with material wealth are to honor God with their riches* (3:9). One of the specific ways in which they can do this is by being generous to the poor (14:31; 19:17; 21:13; 22:2, 9; 28:22, 27).

(3) Several proverbs, in rather realistic fashion, acknowledge that *the rich seemingly have many advantages over others,* especially their opposite number, the poor. Money can provide a degree of security (10:15), popularity (19:4, 7), and power (22:7).

(4) But before you rush out and begin your pursuit of riches, consider a fourth important principle. *The obvious advantages of wealth must be kept in perspective and not overrated.* At times riches can have their disadvantages and money can never provide lasting or ultimate security (11:4, 28; 13:8; 23:4–5; see also Luke 12:13–21).

(5) *There are many things that are more important than material wealth,* including the quality of one's character and relationships. More specifically, wisdom (3:13–15), righteousness/justice (28:6), a proper attitude toward and relationship with God (15:16), relationships characterized by love (15:17; 17:1), and a good reputation (22:1) are all more important than wealth.

Recall the scene from the movie *Citizen Kane,* where billionaire Charles Kane, surrounded by his vast wealth, dies whispering "Rosebud," the name of the little sled he played with as a small child before his mother cold-heartedly shipped him off to boarding school. To the very end he was haunted by two things that were more important to him than all his riches, but which his money could never recover or buy—the innocence of his youth and his mother's love. Or consider the life of the Woolworth heiress Barbara Hutton, who squandered away her wealth on seven husbands as she searched for fulfillment in life and died a miserable recluse. The narrator of a TV documentary on her life summarized her life this way: "Her life illustrates the old platitude: 'Money does not buy happiness.'"

Perhaps when all is said and done, the view of Agur, recorded in Proverbs 30:8b–9 is the best attitude to have: "Don't give me wealth or riches; just give me the food I need for each day. Otherwise I might become complacent and self-deceived and say, "Who is the LORD?" Or I might become poor, resort to theft, and damage the reputation of my God." Agur suggests a balanced approach is best. On the one hand, one should not be overly concerned about riches, because wealth can easily produce a proud and self-sufficient attitude that has little, if any, place for God. On the other hand, there is nothing honorable about poverty either, for the pressures created by poverty can lead one into sin as well. The preferable attitude is to be content with having the necessities of life. In this way one has what one needs and remains consciously dependent on God (cf. 1 Tim. 6:6–10).

10 Why Not Give It a Try?

Some Exercises for You to Do

This chapter includes several exegetical exercises for you to do. A variety of genres are represented, including a narrative text (Gen. 2–3), a prophetic speech (Amos 5:1–17), an exhortation from a didactic text (Prov. 5:15–23), a psalm of petition (Ps. 12), and a hymn (Ps. 29). In each case we follow the method outlined and illustrated in chapter 8.

Genesis 2–3

Step 1

The first step is to mark out the narrative unit. The limits of this narrative unit are clearly marked. It is introduced by the heading אֵלֶּה תוֹלְדוֹת, "these are the generations of" (lit.), or "this is the account of what happened to" (2:4). As elsewhere in Genesis (cf. 6:9; 10:1; 11:10, 27; 25:12, 19; 36:1, 9; 37:2), this formula introduces the account that follows, whether it be a genealogical record or a narrative (as here). The unit concludes with man's expulsion from the garden. Chapter 4 begins the story of life outside the garden. The disjunctive clause at the beginning of 4:1 (וְהָאָדָם יָדַע, "now the man had sexual relations") introduces this new episode in the larger narrative.

Try to develop a tentative outline of the paragraph divisions within the narrative. In addition to shifts in thematic focus, look for formal markers, such as disjunctive clauses.

Step 2

Outline the basic structure of each paragraph by delineating the narrative framework, nonstandard constructions, and quotations/dialogues embedded within the narrative. Using the categories listed in chapter 6, analyze the function of each main clause in the narrative framework, each nonstandard construction, and the various grammatical construc- 279 tions within quotations. Make as many observations as possible on how the narrative structure contributes to the narrator's rhetorical strategy.

As you work through the narrative, the following questions will require special attention:

(1) What type of clauses predominate in 2:5–6? What is their function in the narrative?

(2) What type of clause introduces 2:10? Identify its specific function. How do verses 10–14 contribute to the narrative? (For what reason does the author include this information?)

(3) What is the precise function of the clauses introduced with *wayyiqtol* forms in 2:15?

(4) What is the precise function of the clause introduced with a *wayyiqtol* form at the beginning of 2:19? Evaluate the NIV translation, "Now the LORD God *had* formed." Is this valid here? What may have motivated the NIV translators to use the past perfect here? (Hint: Compare the sequence of creation outlined in chapter 2 with the order of creation in chapter 1.)

(5) What type of clause is introduced by וְהַנָּחָשׁ in 3:1? What is the precise function of this clause?

Steps 3–5

As you work through the narrative verse by verse, do steps 3–5 as outlined in chapter 8. This will be the most time-consuming part of your study. Be alert! Be thorough! Careful observation and diligent spadework will often unearth gold nuggets! To help you in your search, I have included several specific questions you will need to consider. (However, this list of questions hardly exhausts the subject matter!)

(1) Does 2:5 contradict chapter 1? (Chapter 1 indicates plant life preceded the creation of humankind, but chapter 2 suggests the creation of man preceded the existence of plant life.) Is verse 5 referring to the same types of plants as chapter 1? (Where else does the phrase עֵשֶׂב הַשָּׂדֶה occur in Genesis? Is שִׂיחַ used in chapter 1?)

(2) What are the implications of the statement "and there was no man cultivating the ground"? Does cultivating the "ground" (הָאֲדָמָה) characterize man's activity before or after the fall? (In this regard see 2:15 and 3:17–19, 23. Does the language of 2:15 differ from that of 2:5 in any important way? In light of the description of Eden in 2:9, how is גַּן, traditionally rendered "garden," best translated?)

(3) What is the significance of the imperfect יַעֲלֶה in 2:6? (If the perfect had been used here, what would its significance have been?)

(4) What is the case and specific case function of the noun עָפָר, "dirt, dust," in 2:7? How is the author depicting God here? (Study usage

of the verb יָצַר, "form," elsewhere, especially in the human sphere, which provides the background for the anthropomorphic imagery here.)

(5) Is "soul" the best way to translate נֶפֶשׁ in 2:7? If not, offer an alternative. (Study use of the phrase נֶפֶשׁ חַיָּה elsewhere in Genesis 1–11 and read BDB's discussion on p. 659, category 2.)

(6) What is the significance of the plural form of the noun חַיִּים, "life," in 2:9? What is the case and specific case function of the noun חַיִּים, "life," in the phrase "tree of life?" In what sense is this a "tree of life"? (See 3:22.)

(7) What is the meaning of the merism "good and evil" (2:9)? (You will need to study usage of the phrase elsewhere, especially with the verb יָדַע and the related verbal noun דַּעַת.) What is the precise meaning of "knowledge" here? (Note that this "knowledge" is possessed by God and the group with whom he speaks in 3:22. See also 3:5.) In what sense is the tree a "tree of knowledge"? (See 3:6, where the tree seems to be associated with the acquisition of "wisdom.")

(8) How should the predicative active participle יֹצֵא be translated in 2:10? How about the imperfect יִפָּרֵד and the perfect with waw-consecutive (וְהָיָה) in the same verse? (Is the author describing a pre-Flood geographical reality or a situation existing in his own time? Don't make assumptions; instead make your decision on the basis of how you understand 2:11–14. Do these verses seem to be describing a pre-Flood reality or a situation contemporary with the author? Note: The stream mentioned in verse 10 is the source of the rivers named in verses 11–14, suggesting that the whole section is describing either an earlier or contemporary [with the author] situation.)

(9) How are the infinitives construct לְעָבְדָהּ וּלְשָׁמְרָהּ (2:15) functioning in relation to the preceding main verb?

(10) How is the imperfect תֹּאכֵל functioning in 2:16? What is the significance of the infinitive absolute (אָכֹל) being placed before the verb?

(11) Does the phrase בְּיוֹם, "in the day of" (2:17, see also v. 4), when followed by an infinitive construct, have to mean "on the very same day," or can it mean "when, at the time"? (You will need to study its usage elsewhere.)

(12) Is "helper" the best translation of עֵזֶר (2:18)? If not, offer an alternative word or phrase. (Study usage of the term and its related verb elsewhere. Is the idea of a subordinate role or position inherent in the word? In this regard consider also the meaning and implications of the following phrase כְּנֶגְדּוֹ.)

(13) What is the function of 2:19–20 in the story? (Did God really think he would find an עֵזֶר among the animals?)

(14) Does the man's naming of the animals (2:19–20) establish or suggest his authority over them? (You will need to study usage of the expressions קָרָא לְ- and קָרָא שֵׁם לְ- elsewhere.)

(15) Does the statement לְזֹאת יִקָּרֵא אִשָּׁה, literally, "to this one it shall be called, 'woman'" (2:23), imply the man's authority over the woman? Or, is he simply anticipating that people will recognize the resemblance of the woman to the man and give her an appropriate name? (Study the usage of the niphal of קָרָא with the preposition לְ- elsewhere. BDB, 896, 2. d. [1] gives a list of passages.) In this regard, consider the causal/explanatory clause that follows in verse 23.

(16) What is the function of the imperfect יַעֲזָב in 2:24? In light of your classification of the imperfect, how should the forms וְדָבַק and וְהָיָה be interpreted and translated? Is the verse simply stating facts or giving an exhortation? To answer these questions you should examine other examples of עַל־כֵּן followed by the imperfect, especially in Genesis, and consider the following questions: Who is speaking in verse 24? Is this a continuation of the quotation in verse 23, or is the narrator adding an editorial comment? (In light of your findings, evaluate the popular view that this verse offers advice for marriage.)

(17) In light of Exodus 20:12 and the nature of the ancient Israelite extended family structure, should יַעֲזָב (2:24) be understood literally or hyperbolically? (Study the use of the verb elsewhere with human subjects and objects. See BDB, 737, 2. b. [1] for a list of texts. What semantic notion[s] does the verb normally carry in such contexts?)

(18) What is meant by the phrase "one flesh" (2:24)? (The phrase is not used elsewhere, so unfortunately a survey of usage is impossible. The best we can do is examine the man's statement in 2:23, "This one, this time, is bone from my bones and flesh from my flesh." Find other passages where "bone" and "flesh" are used in proximity to each other. When someone shares another's "bone and flesh," what idea is conveyed? How does that inform our understanding of the meaning of the phrase "one flesh"?)

(19) What is the significance of the couple being naked and unashamed (2:25)?

(20) What is the significance of the imperfect יִתְבֹּשָׁשׁוּ in 2:25? (If the perfect had been used here, what would its significance have been?)

(21) What is the precise meaning of עָרוּם in 3:1? Does the word have a negative connotation here?

(22) Discuss textual note "a" in 3:1 of BHS.

(23) Discuss how the serpent alters God's words (compare 3:1b, 4 with 2:16–17).

(24) Discuss how the woman alters God's words (compare 3:2–3 with 2:16–17). (In your discussion evaluate the variant readings listed in textual notes "a" and "b" in 3:2 of BHS.)

(25) What is the precise meaning of לְהַשְׂכִּיל in 3:6?

(26) What is the precise meaning of קוֹל in 3:8? (By relating יוֹם to an Akkadian cognate meaning "storm," some have suggested that רוּחַ הַיּוֹם later in the verse means "the wind of the storm," rather than "the breeze of the day."[1] How might this interpretation affect one's understanding of קוֹל? Hint: Does קוֹל ever refer to an element of a storm? If one follows this line of interpretation, how does it affect one's picture of God in this verse?)

(27) Identify and classify the case of the noun הָאִשָּׁה in 3:12. Explain the significance of this construction as it pertains to the man's self-defense.

(28) What is the precise meaning of the verb נָשָׁא (cf. הִשִּׁיאַנִי) in 3:13?

(29) Should the statement אָרוּר אַתָּה מִכָּל־הַבְּהֵמָה (3:14) be translated "you are cursed more than all the beasts of the field" (comparative use of the preposition מִן) or "you are cursed (and banished) from all the beasts of the field" (separative use of the preposition מִן and metonymic use of the verb אָרַר, "curse")? Examine the use of the construction אָרוּר מִן, "cursed from," in 4:11. In that passage is the preposition מִן comparative (cf. 3:17 in this regard) or separative (cf. 4:14 in this regard)?

(30) Is the statement עָפָר תֹּאכַל, "you will eat dirt" (3:14), ironic in light of the fact that the serpent tempted the woman to eat fruit (פְּרִי, cf. vv. 2–3, 6, 11)? (Note the Hebrew soundplay between עָפָר and פְּרִי.)

(31) Do the singular pronouns and pronominal suffixes referring to the woman's offspring necessarily mean that an individual (as opposed to posterity in general) is in view in 3:15? Can זֶרַע, "offspring," be used collectively? (See BDB.) If so, can collective זֶרַע appear with singular verbs and modifiers? (See Gen. 16:10; 22:17; 24:60.)

(32) Does the direct address to the serpent in 3:15b necessarily mean that the serpent, rather than its offspring (cf. v. 15a), will engage in hostilities with the woman's offspring? Or could the serpent be addressed as representing its offspring? (In this regard study the Hebrew text of Gen. 28:14.)

(33) Is NIV's translation of the verbs in 3:15b accurate or misleading? (Are different verbs employed in the Hebrew text?) Do the choice of verbs and the order of the statements (note that the reference to the woman's offspring's action precedes the reference to the serpent's action) suggest mutual hostility or do they imply that the woman's offspring will defeat the serpent?

(34) Should the phrase עִצְּבוֹנֵךְ וְהֵרֹנֵךְ (3:16) be understood as a hendiadys referring to one idea (labor pains, cf. NIV) or to two separate notions

---

1. See, for example, Jeffrey J. Niehaus, *God at Sinai* (Grand Rapids: Zondervan, 1995), 155–59.

(pain and conception/trembling)?[2] Note the statement that immediately follows in the text (בְּעֶצֶב תֵּלְדִי בָנִים).

(35) What does the noun תְּשׁוּקָה mean in 3:16? (Study usage of the word elsewhere, especially in 4:7.)

(36) How should the imperfect form יִמְשָׁל (3:16b) be classified and translated?

(37) Are there any verbal echoes of the couple's sin in God's words to the man in 3:17–19? (Think in terms of soundplay; in this regard note especially בְּעִצָּבוֹן תֹּאכֲלֶנָּה in v. 17 and וְאֶל־עָפָר תָּשׁוּב in v. 19.)

(38) What is the point of 3:20? (Do the man's words indicate that God has given him a reprieve of sorts? In this regard note 2:17.)

(39) Should God's clothing the man and woman with skins (3:21) be viewed positively? Or, is this a foreboding statement that anticipates their expulsion from the garden and/or highlights their alienation from God and each other? (Examine 2:25 and 3:7–11. What was the significance of their nakedness before their sin? Why were they ashamed of their nakedness after they sinned?)

(40) How is the participle הַמִּתְהַפֶּכֶת (3:24) syntactically related to the preceding noun הַחֶרֶב? How is the hithpael stem functioning here? How should the participle be translated here? (Study usage of the verb elsewhere in the hithpael stem.)

Steps 6–7

Now do steps 6–7 as outlined in chapter 8 and then develop an exposition of the passage. Don't just focus on selected verses, but try to reflect the theme of the entire narrative in its larger literary context. Here's a suggestion—think of chapter 2 as a contrastive background for chapter 3. Chapter 2 depicts what the world was like before the Fall and gives us a taste of what it should and could have been like, while chapter 3 describes what happened to the world and gives us insight into why it is plagued by conflict and death. Consider this question: Does the New Testament suggest a reversal of what we see in chapter 3 and a return to the ideal depicted in chapter 2 for those who are in Christ?

Amos 5:1–17

Step 1

In prophetic literature speech units are arranged in an anthological manner. Determining the limits of the various speech units is the interpreter's

---

2. Traditionally הֵרֹנֵךְ has been taken as meaning "your conception," but recent etymological research suggests the form is derived from a root הרר (not הרה) and means "your trembling." See David T. Tsumura, "A Note on הרנך (Gen. 3,16)," *Biblica* 75 (1994): 398–400.

first task. Several factors point to Amos 5:1–17 being a distinct unit. Verse 1 begins with שִׁמְעוּ אֶת־הַדָּבָר הַזֶּה, "hear this word," which appears to be an introductory call to attention in this section of the Amos anthology (see 3:1 and 4:1). Verse 18 begins with הוֹי, "woe," which often signals the beginning of a new speech unit. The prophet also employs the structural device of inclusio, where certain themes utilized at the beginning of the speech reappear in the conclusion, forming a bracket for the speech. Verses 2–3 contain a lament (קִינָה, v. 1), while the theme of lamentation also dominates verses 16–17. Just after the introduction (see vv. 4–6) and just before the conclusion (see vv. 14–15) the prophet exhorts the people to "seek" (דָּרַשׁ) the Lord and his righteous standards, respectively. So the speech may be outlined as follows:

A Introductory Lament (vv. 1–3)
B Exhortation ("Seek!", vv. 4–6)
C Central Core (vv. 7–13)
B' Exhortation ("Seek!", vv. 14–15)
A' Concluding Image of Lamentation (vv. 16–17)

Step 2

Working through the text in a verse-by-verse fashion and utilizing the categories discussed in chapter 6, analyze the poetic parallelism of the speech. (Note: The headings within the speech lie outside the parallelistic structure. See vv. 1, 4a, 16a, 17b.)

Steps 3–5

As you work through the text verse-by-verse, do steps 3–5 as outlined in chapter 8. As you do your exegesis here are some issues you will need to consider:

(1) How are the perfects functioning in verse 2? (Remember this is a lament or dirge. The prophet is playing the role of a future mourner who is witnessing Israel's demise.)

(2) What type of genitive is יִשְׂרָאֵל (v. 2)? To what is the prophet comparing Israel? How does this metaphor contribute rhetorically and emotionally to his speech?

(3) What does the Lord mean when he commands, "Seek me!" (v. 4). (Does the following context offer any clues as to what "seeking" the Lord means here? Note especially vv. 14–15.)

(4) How does the imperative (with prefixed waw) וִחְיוּ, "and live!" (v. 4) relate to the preceding command ("seek me!")? (Note the construction לְמַעַן תִּחְיוּ following the command to "seek" in verse 14.)

(5) In light of the preceding command ("seek me!"), do you find the prohibition, "don't seek Bethel" in verse 5 somewhat ironic? (What does the name "Bethel" mean?)

(6) Explain how soundplay contributes to the prophet's warning, "for Gilgal will surely go into exile"(v. 5).

(7) What semantic nuance does אָוֶן have in verse 5?

(8) Discuss the rhetorical impact of the comparison to fire in verse 6.

(9) How does verse 7 relate syntactically to its context? (Does it go with what precedes or follows?) How is the article on the form הַהֹפְכִים functioning? Discuss textual note "a" in BHS. (What arguments can be made in favor of the proposed emendation? against it?)

(10) What is the point of the comparison in verse 7a? (How have they made justice like "wormwood"?)

(11) In light of the parallelism, what is the precise semantic nuance of צְדָקָה in verse 7?

(12) At first verses 8–9 seem to fit rather awkwardly, but perhaps that very awkwardness highlights their content. Why does the prophet insert this lengthy description of the Lord here? What divine characteristic(s) does it highlight and how does it contribute thematically to the speech?

(13) How are the finite verb forms שָׂנְאוּ (a perfect) and יְתָעֵבוּ (an imperfect) functioning in verse 10?

(14) What is the precise semantic nuance of צַדִּיק (v. 12) in this context? (Does the term have a religious or legal connotation here?)

(15) What is the precise semantic nuance of הַמַּשְׂכִּיל in verse 13? What does יֹדֵם mean here? (Your answer to the first of these questions will impact your decision on the second.)

(16) What is meant by "good" and "evil" (v. 14) in this context?

(17) What is the significance of the divine name "Lord God of Hosts" here (vv. 14–16)?

Steps 6–7

Now do steps 6–7 as outlined in chapter 8 and develop an exposition of the passage. One might condense and summarize the message of this speech as follows:

(A) Death is around the corner (1–3)!
  (B) You need to repent (4–6)
    (C) because you stand guilty and doomed before God (7),
      (D) the all-powerful, sovereign judge (8–9).
    (C′) You stand guilty and doomed before him (10–13),
  (B′) so you need to repent (14–15).
(A′) Otherwise death is around the corner (16–17)!

Unless one wants to construct a sermon in a chiastic fashion, it is better to combine the corresponding points in the chiasmus when developing a sermonic outline. Here is a sample expositional outline of the passage:

(1) The wages of sin are death (1–3, 16–17).
(2) Repentance (i.e., radically changed behavior), not ritual, is the door to spiritual life and divine blessing (4–6, 14–15).
(3) How we treat others matters to God (7, 10–13).
(4) Sinners must reckon with God's sovereign power and authority (8–9).

Proverbs 5:15–23

Step 1

This passage is actually the conclusion to the larger exhortation that begins in 5:1. The father urges his son to follow his advice (v. 1), so he can become wise (v. 2) and avoid the pitfall of the adulteress (vv. 3–6). The father then extends his appeal to all his sons (v. 7), warning each one (he switches back to second singular forms in v. 8, after briefly employing the plural in v. 7) of the negative consequences of adultery. The appeal concludes in verses 15–23 with a third series of exhortations accompanied by motivating arguments.

Step 2

Working through the text in a verse by verse fashion and utilizing the categories discussed in chapter 6, analyze the poetic parallelism of the speech.

Steps 3–5

As you work through the text verse-by-verse, do steps 3–5 as outlined in chapter 8. As you do your exegesis here are some issues you will need to consider:

(1) In light of the preceding context, the language of verse 15 is obviously not to be taken literally. What does "drinking water" refer to? Why is it an apt comparison? To whom/what does "your own cistern" refer? (Note v. 18.)
(2) Is a בְּאֵר (v. 15b) the same as a בּוֹר, "cistern"? Is there any significance to this slight change in image?
(3) To whom/what does "your springs" refer in verse 16? (Some see this as referring to the son's sexual potency. Is this valid? Of whom

is the imagery of water used in verse 15 [note also v. 18]? Could the referent be the same here? If so, what is the significance of the switch in images? [What exactly are מַעְיְנֹת? How do they differ from a cistern and well? In this regard note "channels of water" in v. 16b] How exactly is the referent being portrayed through this image?)

(4) The NIV translates verse 16 as a rhetorical question. Is this necessary? (Are there any interrogative markers?) The NIV interprets this verse as warning about activity to avoid or prevent. But is there another interpretive option? Could the sentence simply be descriptive of the water source's capabilities? If so, how might the imperfect verb form יָפוּצוּ be understood? If the sentence is descriptive, then it is a motivating argument for obeying the exhortation of verse 15 (not a continuation of the exhortation). What would be the motivating argument here?

(5) The NIV translates verse 17 as an exhortation. Is this necessary? (Is the prefixed verb יִהְיוּ a distinct jussive form, or is it ambiguous?) Instead of taking the verse as an exhortation, is there another option? Could the sentence be taken as descriptive of the water source? If so, the statement is a motivating argument supporting the exhortation of verse 15. What would be the motivating argument here?

(6) In conjunction with #5 you will need to determine the referent of זָרִים in verse 17. (Note carefully the gender of the form. Are women in view here? In this regard examine v. 20 and note the gender of the forms זָרָה and נָכְרִיָּה used there.)

(7) The NIV also translates verse 18 as an exhortation. Is this necessary? (Is the prefixed verb יְהִי a jussive form?)

(8) To whom does "your fountain" refer? Relate this to the earlier images employed.

(9) What does it mean for a "fountain" to be "blessed" (בָּרוּךְ) (v. 18)?

(10) "Rejoice" (שְׂמַח) is metonymic here (v. 18). What is the underlying reality?

(11) How should אֲהָבִים be understood in relation to אַיֶּלֶת (v. 19)? How should חֵן be understood in relation to יַעֲלַת? (Are the underlying reality and image mixed here?) Verse 19a is not a complete sentence. Is it related syntactically to what follows or precedes? Why would the father compare the son's wife to these animals? (Is he hinting that the son is like a buck or male goat?)

(12) Discuss textual problem "b" in verse 19 of BHS. (Should we read "her love" or "her breasts"?)

(13) How are the prefixed verbal forms in verse 19b functioning?

(14) Comment on the use of the verbs רָוָה and שָׁנָה in verse 19b. Is there a comparison or image involved here?

(15) To whom do זָרָה and נָכְרִיָּה refer (v. 20)? (Is a literal "foreigner" really in view here?)

(16) Comment on the rhetorical force of the anthropomorphic phrase "eyes of the Lᴏʀᴅ" (v. 21) in this context.

(17) What type of action does the active participle מְפַלֵּס (v. 21) envision? What is the meaning of פָּלַס here? What is the underlying reality?

(18) Discuss the imagery of verse 22.

(19) What is the precise meaning of תָּמַךְ (used in the niphal) in verse 22? (Note the parallelism.)

(20) What is the precise meaning of מוּסָר in verse 23?

(21) What is the precise meaning of the verb שָׁגָה in verse 23? Is there any irony involved in its use? (Note its use as well in vv. 19–20. Does the repetition of the verb facilitate any thematic correlations between vv. 19, 20, and 23?)

(22) What nuance does the preposition -בְּ have in relation to the verb "die" (in the first line) and to "go astray" (in the second line)?

(23) How are the imperfect verbal forms in verses 22–23 functioning?

Steps 6–7

Now do steps 6–7 as outlined in chapter 8 and develop an exposition of the passage. Here is a sample expositional outline for the passage that gives some hints as to how I answer the above questions:

(1) A man should seek sexual fulfillment from his own wife (v. 15), for she is more than capable of satisfying his needs (vv. 16–19).

(2) A man should seek sexual fulfillment from his own wife (v. 20), for God is watching and guarantees that immorality will be self-destructive (vv. 21–23).

Psalm 12

Step 1

In this psalm of petition the psalmist asks God to intervene in his experience (vv. 1–4, Eng./= vv. 2–5 Heb.), receives an oracle promising deliverance (v. 5/6), and then affirms his confidence in the reliability of the divine promise (vv. 6–8/7–9).

Step 2

Working through the text in a verse by verse fashion and utilizing the categories discussed in chapter 6, analyze the poetic parallelism of the speech.

Steps 3–5

As you work through the text verse-by-verse, do steps 3–5 as outlined in chapter 8. As you do your exegesis here are some issues you will need to consider:

(1) Who are the "godly" and the "faithful" mentioned in verse 1/2? (You will need to study the usage of the terms elsewhere. Develop a character profile of this group.) Explain the use of the singular noun in the first line (note the plural in the second line).

(2) According to BDB, what is the meaning of the verb פָּסוּ (v. 1/2)? (What supporting etymological evidence do they offer?) What verb corresponds to פָּסוּ in the parallel structure of the verse? What does it mean? Discuss BHS textual note "b" and the options listed there.

(3) What is the precise nuance of שָׁוְא (v. 2/3)?

(4) Explain what the phrase שְׂפַת חֲלָקוֹת, "lip of smoothness," means (v. 2/3; see also v. 3/4, where "lips of smoothness" is used)?

(5) What does the idiomatic phrase "with a heart and a heart" mean (v. 2/3)? (For help here, consult GKC, 396, para. 123f, and W–O, 116.) For help in understanding the general concept in view here, see Psalm 28:3b.

(6) Why does the NIV translate יַכְרֵת (v. 3/4) as a prayer? (Is the form a jussive?)

(7) What does the statement לִלְשֹׁנֵנוּ נַגְבִּיר, literally, "to our tongue we will make (?) strong" (v. 4/5) mean? Evaluate BHS textual note "a."

(8) What does the statement שְׂפָתֵינוּ אִתָּנוּ, literally, "our lips (are) with us(?)" (v. 4/5) mean?

(9) In the phrase מִשֹּׁד עֲנִיִּים (v. 5/6) how is the preposition מִן functioning? (See BDB, 579–80, cat. 2.) What are the case and case function of עֲנִיִּים?

(10) Translate the phrase מֵאַנְקַת אֶבְיוֹנִים (v. 5/6). What is the precise meaning of the noun אֲנָקָה (which appears in v. 5/6 in a construct form)? What are the case and case function of אֶבְיוֹנִים?

(11) Explain how יָפִיחַ לוֹ (v. 5/6) relates syntactically to what precedes. What type of clause are the NIV and NAS understanding here? (Is this a valid proposal? Can this type of clause be structured in this way? See W–O, 338.) According to the NIV, who is the subject of יָפִיחַ and the antecedent of the pronominal suffix with לוֹ‎-? According to the NAS, who is the subject of יָפִיחַ and the antecedent of the pronominal suffix with לוֹ‎-? If one were to emend יָפִיחַ to יָפֵחַ, a newly discovered noun meaning "witness" (see K–B, 424), would the resulting reading make sense?

(12) In what sense are the Lord's words "pure" (v. 6/7)? What specific "words" are in view here?

290 (13) What is the point of the comparison in verse 6b/7b? What is the sig-

nificance of the reference to "sevenfold" purification? (Examine usage of שִׁבְעָתָיִם elsewhere in the Old Testament.)

(14) Note the person, gender, and number of the pronominal suffixes on the two verbs in verse 7/8. What/who is the antecedent of the suffixes? Also discuss textual notes "a" and "b" in BHS.

(15) Is the statement in verse 8/9 an independent clause, or should it be subordinated to the preceding statement?

Steps 6–7

Now do steps 6–7 as outlined in chapter 8 and develop an exposition of the psalm. Here is a sample expositional outline:

(1) The Lord promises to protect his oppressed people (vv. 1–5, Eng.).
(2) Since God's promises are reliable, his people can be confident of his protection, even during the worst of times (vv. 6–8).

The psalmist probably envisioned physical protection in the here-and-now. The theme needs to be qualified for New Testament believers, whom Jesus warned would undergo persecution and even death. The basic principle still applies, but the protection should be viewed in spiritual and eschatological terms (see Rom. 8:31–39).

Psalm 29

Step 1

This hymn contains a call to praise God (vv. 1–2) followed by reasons why he is deserving of praise (vv. 3–11). This structure is typical of the hymnic genre.

Step 2

Working through the text in a verse-by-verse fashion and utilizing the categories discussed in chapter 6, analyze the poetic parallelism of the speech.

Steps 3–5

As you work through the text verse-by-verse, do steps 3–5 as outlined in chapter 8. As you do your exegesis, here are some issues you will need to consider:

(1) Who are the בְּנֵי אֵלִים (v. 1)? (Study usage of the phrase elsewhere, as well as terms that appear in parallelism with it elsewhere.)
(2) What is the meaning of הַדְרַת (v. 2)?

(3) To what specifically does the phrase קוֹל יהוה (vv. 3–9) refer in this psalm? (Speech? or something else?)

(4) How is the perfect הִרְעִים (v. 3) functioning here?

(5) Should the phrase מַיִם רַבִּים (v. 3) be understood literally or figuratively? (Study the usage of the phrase elsewhere in the Old Testament, especially in poetic texts.) If the language is taken literally, what is the referent? If the language is taken figuratively, what do the waters symbolize? Is it possible to see both a literal referent on the surface and an underlying symbolic meaning?

(6) Discuss the use of the preposition -בְּ in verse 4.

(7) How is the *wayyiqtol* verbal form וַיְשַׁבֵּר functioning in verse 5. (Note the active participle in the preceding line and see GKC, 329, para. 111u.)

(8) Discuss the comparison in verse 6. What is the underlying physical reality?

(9) What does חֹצֵב (v. 7) mean here? How is the following phrase אֵשׁ לֶהָבוֹת syntactically related to חֹצֵב?

(10) How are the prefixed verbal forms functioning in verse 8?

(11) What does the verb יְחוֹלֵל (polel of חִיל/חוּל) mean in verse 9? (Evaluate the traditional view that the verb here means "causes to go into labor." Does the verb ever have this causative nuance in its other uses in this stem?) In conjunction with this question, discuss textual notes "a" and "b" in BHS. What are some arguments for and against the proposed emendations?

(12) How is the *wayyiqtol* verbal form וַיֶּחֱשֹׂף functioning in verse 9? (Note the prefixed verbal form in the preceding line and see GKC, 329, para. 111t.)

(13) What is the referent of מַבּוּל in verse 10? (To what does the word refer elsewhere? Would that referent make sense in this context, or is there a more likely referent in the immediate context? Note verse 3.) In conjunction with this question, also consider these questions: (a) What is the function of the article on the noun? (b) How are the verbal forms functioning in this verse?

(14) How are the prefixed verbal forms functioning in verse 11?

(15) What is the precise meaning of עֹז (v. 11) in this context?

(16) What does the phrase "bless . . . with peace" (v. 11) mean? What precise nuance does שָׁלוֹם have here? How does the second half of the verse relate logically to the first half?

Steps 6–7

Now do steps 6–7 as outlined in chapter 8 and develop an exposition of the psalm. A summary statement of the psalm's message might be: Our sovereign, incomparable God is praiseworthy because he exerts his awesome power on behalf of his people.

General Index

Scripture Index